MODERN HUMANITIES RESEARCH ASSO   .1 ION
CRITICAL TEXTS
VOLUME 46

EDITORS
JUSTIN D. EDWARDS and CATHERINE MAXWELL

ABRAHAM FRAUNCE
THE SHEPHERDS' LOGIC AND
OTHER DIALECTICAL WRITINGS

Abraham Fraunce
The Shepherds' Logic and Other Dialectical Writings

Edited by
Zenón Luis-Martínez

Modern Humanities Research Association
2016

Published by

The Modern Humanities Research Association
Salisbury House
Station Road
Cambridge CB1 2LA
United Kingdom

First published 2016

ISBN 978-1-78188-124-8

Copies may be ordered from www.criticaltexts.mhra.org.uk

CONTENTS

ACKNOWLEDGEMENTS

I wish to acknowledge the support provided first by the Spanish Ministry of Science and Innovation and later by the Ministry of Economy through their programme 'Promoción General del Conocimiento', Project FFI2010–19279, 'English Poetic and Rhetorical Treatises of the Tudor Period'. I also wish to thank the members of this project Lorena Laureano, Attila Kiss, Elena Domínguez Romero, Dominique Bonnet, and very especially Sonia Hernández Santano, whose edition of William Webbe's *A Discourse of English Poetry* has been produced at the same time as this, and with whom I have shared the uncertainties and pleasures of seeing each other's work in progress. The Library Services of St Louis University were kind enough to send through interlibrary loan the microfilm of Sister Mary M. McCormick's unpublished edition of Fraunce's manuscript. The institutional support for our research project allowed me to visit the British Library and Cambridge University Library, whose staff offered useful assistance in my consultation of sources and materials. It has also endorsed my participation in several conferences and seminars. Among these, the 25th Conference of the Spanish and Portuguese Society for English Renaissance Studies (SEDERI) in Oviedo in 2014 gave me the opportunity to rethink my introduction after Andrew Hadfield's questioning of a chief argument of this book, i.e., how effective Fraunce is as a reader of Spenser. I hope I have opened up ways toward answering this and other questions. The International Seminar 'Speaking Pictures: Poetry, the Arts of Discourse, and the Discourse of the Arts', held in Huelva in October 2014, was a unique occasion to share my work on Fraunce with specialists. In addition to the project members mentioned above, Sarah M. Knight, György E. Szönyi, Gavin Alexander, Michael Hetherington, Cinta Zunino, Rocío G. Sumillera, and Manuel J. Gómez Lara enriched the contents of this seminar with their contributions and provided valuable feedback on mine. The English Department at the University of Huelva has been a supportive setting for the development of my research. My colleague Jefferey M. Simons revised the manuscript and offered precious advice for its improvement in the form of annotations, conversations and emails. His generosity, his knowledge and his care for words have made this a much more readable book.

The long way to the completion of this volume has been a time of transitions. Adjusting to those in the midst of pressing circumstances has made me revisit, at times with amusement and at other times with apprehension, Fraunce's jarring description of 'the perpetual vexation of spirit and continual consumption of body incident to every scholar'. If I remain in good shape after these five years it is thanks to my daughter, Inés, who was born at the same time as this project, and to my wife, Débora, to whom this edition is dedicated.

ABBREVIATIONS

This list contains frequently quoted sources, as well as those used in the Textual Notes.

Beurhaus I	Beurhaus, Friedrich (Fridericus Beurhusius), *In P. Rami Regii professoris Clariss. Dialecticae libros duos [...] Explicationum quaestiones: quae Paedagogiae logicae de docenda discendaque dialectica. Pars Prima* (London: Henry Bynneman, 1581)
Beurhaus II	Beurhaus, Friedrich, *De P. Rami dialecticae praecipuis capitibus disputationes scholasticae, & cum iisdem variorum logicorum comparationes: quae Paedagogiae logicae pars secunda, qua artis veritas exquiritur* (London: Henry Bynneman, 1582)
Brooks-Davies	Spenser, Edmund, *Selected Shorter Poems*, ed. by Douglas Brooks-Davies (London: Longman, 1995)
CPY	*The Countesse of Pembrokes Yuychurch. Conteining the Affectionate life, and Vnfortunate Death of Phillis and Amyntas* (London: Thomas Orwin, for William Ponsonby, 1591)
LL	*The Lawiers Logike, Exemplifying the Praecepts of Logike by the Practise of the Common Lawe* (London: William How, for Thomas Gubin and Thomas Newman, 1588)
McCormick	McCormick, Sister Mary M., ed., *A Critical Edition of Abraham Fraunce's 'The Sheapheardes Logike' and 'Twooe Generall Discourses'* (Unpb. PhD Dissertation: St Louis University, 1968)
Ms	London, British Library, Add MS 34361: *The Sheapheardes Logike: Conteyning the Praecepts of that Art Put Downe by Ramus [...] Together with Twooe General Discourses, the One Touchinge the Prayse and Ryghte Vse of Logike, the Other Concernynge the Comparison of Ramus his Logike with That of Aristotle*
ODNB	*Oxford Dictionary of National Biography*, ed. by David Cannadine (2004, online edn), <http://global.oup.com/oxforddnb>
OED	*Oxford English Dictionary* (2013, 3rd online edn), <http://www.oed.com>
Piscator; Ramus/Piscator[1]	Piscator, Johannes, *In P. Rami Dialecticam Animadversiones. Exemplis Sacr. literarum passim illustrata* (London: Henry Bynneman, 1581)

---

[1] Ramus/Piscator, when Ramus's text of the *Dialectiace libri duo* is cited from Piscator's edition.

Q, Q₁, Q₂	Spenser, Edmund, *The Shepheardes Calender Conteyning Twelue Aeglogues Proportionable to the Twelue Monethes* (London: Hugh Singleton, 1579; 2nd edn London: Thomas East for John Harrison, 1581)
Rawlinson	Oxford, Bodleian Library, Rawlinson MS 345.1: Untitled, containing a Latin essay in praise of Dialectic, followed by a collection of Latin emblems
SC	*The Shepherds' Calendar* (examples in this edition)
SL	*The Shepherds' Logic* (this edition)
Tilley	Tilley, Morris Palmer, *A Dictionary of Proverbs in England in the Sixteenth and Seventeenth Centuries* (Ann Arbor: University of Michigan Press, 1950)

For Débora

INTRODUCTION

The Sheapheardes Logike, Conteyning the Praecepts of that Art Put Downe by Ramus is the most important of the three works on the art of logic by Abraham Fraunce (1559?–93?) preserved in the British Library Add MS 34361. The manuscript is completed by 'twooe general discourses, the one touchinge the prayse and ryghte vse of Logike, the other concernynge the comparison of Ramus his Logike with that of Aristotle'.[1] *The Shepherds' Logic* is an adaptation of Petrus Ramus's *Dialecticae libri duo* (Paris, 1556) with scholarly commentaries collected from continental sources. We know from the author that the composition of the two shorter essays and at least an early drafting of *The Shepherds' Logic* took place during his last years in Cambridge, between 1581 and 1583, a crucial moment for the Ramist reform of the arts of discourse in England.[2] Fraunce embraces the essential tenets of Ramus's thought. He defends the priority of logic over the other arts and favours its theoretical separation from rhetoric. He also endorses a single rule for scientific discussion (*method*) that proceeds from general definitions to particular precepts. Fraunce's Ramism is likewise manifest in his observance of one of its most remarkable accidentals, namely the illustration of the principles of logic with poetic examples.[3]

But this portrait of Fraunce as an orthodox Ramist needs some qualifications. First, Fraunce's preference of English over Latin removes his treatise from the front line of international philosophical discussion and aligns with non-academic renderings of Ramus's work, like Roland MacIlmaine's *The Logike of the Moste Excellent Philosopher P. Ramus Martyr* (1574, 2nd edn 1581) or Dudley Fenner's *The Artes of Logike and Rethorike* (1584). Second, his use of Johannes Piscator's *In P. Rami Dialecticam animadversiones* (London, 1581) as his main source for Ramus's text and the commentaries reveals some discrepancies with Ramist ideas. Third, Fraunce replaces Ramus's poetic examples (mainly Virgil, Ovid and Horace) with over 130 instances from Edmund Spenser's *The Shepheardes Calender* (1579). This audacious choice, conspicuous from the work's title, allots to the pastoral *opera prima* of a thriving vernacular voice the place that Ramus had given to a first-rate Latin poetic anthology. The result is a redefinition of the illustrative role that the poetic example played in Ramist manuals. In casting Spenser's shepherds as genuine models of natural reasoning, Fraunce concedes to the pastoral mode logical priority over the other poetic genres. His examination of the discursive edifice of Spenser's verse also

---

[1] London, British Library, Add MS 34361, fol. 2ʳ. Unless otherwise stated, further quotations of *The Shepherds' Logic* (spelling modernized) and its companion essays are from the present edition. Book, chapter, line numbers in the present edition, and folio signatures in brackets are provided for each citation. *The Shepherds' Logic* is abbreviated as SL.

[2] Abraham Fraunce, *The Lawiers Logike, Exemplifying the Praecepts of Logike by the Practise of the Common Lawe* (London: William How, 1588), ¶1ʳ (Appendix I.1, 1–2). Further citations of this work use the abbreviation LL.

[3] These and other aspects of Ramus's thought are treated in subsequent sections of this Introduction. The best comprehensive account of Ramist logic continues to be Walter J. Ong, *Ramus, Method, and the Decay of Dialogue: From the Art of Discourse to the Art of Reason*, 2nd edn, intro. by Adrian Johns (Chicago: The University of Chicago Press, 2004, 1st edn 1958). The most updated intellectual biography of Ramus is James Veazie Skalnik, *Ramus and Reform: University and Church at the End of the Renaissance* (Kirksville, MT: Truman State University Press, 2002).

claims a logical rationale for the practice of literary criticism. Moreover, Fraunce betrays his aspirations regarding the two intellectual circles connected by Spenser's book, namely those of Philip Sidney and Gabriel Harvey.[4]

The unpublished and presumably unfinished nature of the extant text of *The Shepherds' Logic* adds further interpretative difficulties. In 1588 Fraunce published *The Lawiers Logike, Exemplifying the Praecepts of Logike by the Practise of the Common Lawe*. In its Preface he accounts for the long process of revision that transformed the design and gave a new title to an earlier project of a logical treatise. This assertion identifies *The Shepherds' Logic* as the matrix from which the new book springs. Fraunce certainly incorporated the text of *The Shepherds' Logic* in different degrees of revision into the new work. *The Lawyers' Logic* also reduced the number of examples from Spenser and downplayed poetry's centrality by juxtaposing to each quotation of *The Shepherds' Calendar* one specimen from jurisprudential literature.[5] These differences grant *The Shepherds' Logic* the status of an independent and almost unique work for its distinct and exclusive focus on the relations between logic and poetry.[6]

Structurally, *The Shepherds' Logic* observes the expository method of the Ramist manual, starting with a general definition of the art, and proceeding to divisions, subdivisions, examples and explanatory annotations of keywords and concepts.[7] Fraunce devotes his first book to the invention of logical arguments, and the second to the disposition of arguments into axioms, axioms into syllogisms, and syllogistic argumentations into organized or methodical discourse. The almost exclusive place assigned to Spenser's *Calendar* in the examples contrasts with the variety of references in the annotations: Aristotle, Porphyry and Cicero among the classics; Peter of Spain and Duns Scotus among the scholastics; Philipp Melanchton, Johann Sturm, and Jacques Charpentier among the contemporary traditionalists; and Ramus, Omer Talon, Johann Piscator and Friedrich Beurhaus among the contemporary reformers.[8] Fraunce's frequent attacks on 'monkish men', 'dunses', and 'Sorbonnists' reveal a position that is more anti-scholastic and

[4] The few studies addressing the relations between Abraham Fraunce's logical works and *The Shepherds' Calendar* usually focus on *The Lawyers' Logic* and not on *The Shepherds' Logic*. See Ralph S. Pomeroy, 'The Ramist as Fallacy-Hunter: Abraham Fraunce and the *Lawiers Logike*', *Renaissance Quarterly*, 40.2 (1987), 224–46; Tamara E. Goeglein, 'Reading English Ramist Logic Books as Early Modern Emblem Books: The Case of Abraham Fraunce', *Spenser Studies*, 20 (2005), 225–52; E. Armstrong, *A Ciceronian Sunburn: A Tudor Dialogue on Humanistic Rhetoric and Civic Poetics* (Columbia, SC: University of South Carolina Press, 2006), pp. 115–26; and Peter Mack, 'Spenser and Rhetoric', in *The Oxford Handbook of Edmund Spenser*, ed. by Richard A. McCabe (Oxford: Oxford University Press, 2010), pp. 420–36 (pp. 430–31). On the literary relations between Fraunce, Spenser and Sidney, see Kathrine Koller, 'Fraunce and Edmund Spenser', *ELH*, 7.2 (1940) 108–20, and Steven W. May, 'Marlowe, Spenser, Sidney and — Abraham Fraunce?', *The Review of English Studies, New Series*, 62 (2010), 30–63.
[5] LL, ¶1ʳ⁻ᵛ (Appendix I.1, 18–21).
[6] The only text coetaneous with *The Shepherds' Logic* that addresses this issue is William Temple's *Analysis tractationis de Poesi contextae a nobilissimo viro Philippe Sidneio equite aurato* (1585–86?). Further citations of this work are from the only modern edition and translation of its extant manuscript: *William Temple's 'Analysis' of Sir Philip Sidney's 'Apology for Poetry'*, ed. and trans. by John Webster (Binghamton, NY: Center for Medieval and Early Renaissance Studies, 1984).
[7] See Ong, *Ramus, Method*, pp. 245–47.
[8] These readings reveal Fraunce's acquaintance with the Cambridge logical curriculum and with the newest developments in Ramist logic. On the former question, see Lisa Jardine, 'The Place of Dialectic Teaching in Sixteenth-Century Cambridge', *Studies in the Renaissance*, 21 (1974), 31–62; William T. Costello, *The Scholastic Curriculum at Seventeenth-Century Cambridge* (Cambridge, MA: Harvard University Press, 1958), esp. pp. 45–55; and Peter Mack, *Elizabethan Rhetoric: Theory and Practice* (Cambridge: Cambridge University Press, 2002), Chapter 2. On the latter, see William Hotson, *Commonplace Learning: Ramism and its German Ramifications, 1543–1630* (Oxford: Oxford University Press, 2007), esp. Chapter 3 (pp. 101–26).

anti-Catholic than anti-Aristotelian.[9] With the exception of Laurence Chaderton, the work mentions no other English Ramists.[10]

The two companion essays are theoretical supplements to the handbook-like exposition in *The Shepherds' Logic*. In the Preface to *The Lawyers' Logic*, Fraunce calls these two pieces 'small and trifling beginnings', and hints at 1581 as the date of their conception — the year he claims to have met their dedicatee Philip Sidney.[11] The first, 'Of the Nature and Use of Logic', is a one-fifth English abridgement of his only Latin work on the subject, a sixteen-leave-long untitled treatise also preserved in manuscript form.[12] Far from being the triviality that Fraunce advertises, the English version addresses two major theoretical concerns of Ramism: the relations between natural and artificial logic, and the art's practical dimensions of composition and textual analysis. The title of the second is self-explanatory: 'A Brief and General Comparison of Ramus his Logic with That of Aristotle'. In it Fraunce presents to Philip Sidney's judgement a dispute held in Cambridge between 'an obstinate Aristotelian' and 'a methodical Ramist'.[13] This survey of general views and reciprocated complaints echoes the Cambridge controversy about method held in 1580 and 1581 between the Aristotelian lecturer Everard Digby and his Ramist adversary William Temple.

This volume presents Fraunce's three early dialectical works, as well as an Appendix with significant excerpts from *The Lawyers' Logic*. Its only predecessor, Sister Mary M. McCormick's unpublished doctoral thesis of 1968, is an old-spelling transcription of the manuscript with an introduction, explanatory notes, a collation of Spenser quotes and a glossary.[14] McCormick's important contribution is at its strongest in the accurate transcription of the text and the illuminating account of its Ramist context, but is less precise in identifying sources and in assessing the work's import to Renaissance literary theory and practice. This edition presents the texts in modernized spelling, tracks down their sources, and newly examines their context in the attempt to draw out the literary and philosophical implications of Fraunce's work. As a whole, it claims that Fraunce's logic for shepherds is chiefly a book for poets and about poetry, a first-hand document showing how scholarly training in the arts of discourse could enlighten the composition and interpretation of poetic texts.[15]

---

[9] Originally a Catholic, Ramus converted to Protestantism around 1561 and died during the events ensuing the St Bartholomew's Day Massacre of the Huguenots in August 1572, a fact that fostered a cult of Ramus as a Protestant martyr. On Ramus's death, see Nicolas de Nancel's *Petri Rami Vita* (1599), in Peter Sharratt, 'Nicolaus Nancelius, *Petri Rami Vita*. Edited with an Introduction', *Humanistica Lovaniensia: Journal of Neo-Latin Studies*, 24 (1975), 161–277 (pp. 267–73). See also the attempt to attribute responsibility in the murder to Ramus's scholarly rival Jacques Charpentier, in Charles Waddington, *Ramus: sa vie, ses écrits et ses opinions* (Paris: Ch. Meyrueys, 1855), pp. 267–75. See also Skalnik, *Ramus and Reform*, p. 27; and Ong, *Ramus, Method*, pp. 27–29. On perceptions of Ramus as a Protestant martyr in England, see Sarah M. Knight, 'Flat Dichotomists and Learned Men: Ramism in Elizabethan Drama and Satire', in *Ramus, Pedagogy and the Liberal Arts: Ramism in Britain and the Wider World*, ed. by Steven J. Reid and Emma Annette Wilson (Farnham: Ashgate, 2013), pp. 47–67 (pp. 50–55).
[10] More detailed discussion of Fraunce's use of Chaderton and further speculation on conspicuous absences, notably William Temple's, are offered in due course in the present Introduction.
[11] LL, ¶1ʳ (Appendix I.1, 6).
[12] Oxford, Bodleian Library, MS Rawlinson 345.1.
[13] 'A Brief and General Comparison', 13 (fol. 32ʳ).
[14] Sister Mary Martin McCormick, *A Critical Edition of Abraham Fraunce's 'The Shepheardes Logike' and 'Twooe Generall Discourses'* (Unpb. PhD Dissertation: St Louis University, 1968).
[15] As John Webster has argued about William Temple's analysis of Sidney's *Defence of Poetry*, 'though the English Renaissance is rich in theoretical statements about what educated readers were to expect from literature, it is poor in examples that show what such readers actually did with the texts they read', perhaps because 'the written form of such analyses seemed quite ordinary to those who wrote them', 'Introduction', in *William Temple's 'Analysis'*, p. 11.

The Ramist Context for *The Shepherds' Logic*

The significance of *The Shepherds' Logic* is upheld by its indebtedness to Ramism. Critical consensus about the influence of Pierre de la Ramée, or Petrus Ramus (1515–72), does not always entail a positive appreciation of his work. Ramus earned both steadfast devotees and severe detractors in his own time and in later ages. He was frequently reviled on grounds of his simplification of his classical precedents and his affront to the scholarly rigour of his humanist contemporaries. Stupido's remark that 'Mr Peter maketh all things verie plaine and easie' in the anonymous comedy *The Pilgrimage to Parnassus* (1598), Thomas Nashe's complaints about Ramus's 'raylyng' against 'the subtiltie of Logique', or Francis Bacon's rating of him 'below the sophists' are proof of a stereotyped late Elizabethan attitude after a quarter of a century of scholarly engagement with Ramus's ideas since his death in 1572.[16]

The earliest evidence of Ramus's impact in Britain, found in the Latin correspondence of Roger Ascham (1515–68), is symptomatic of the ambivalent reactions that his scholarship provoked. Ascham's first letter to his fellow humanist Johannes Sturm (1507–89) protested against the attacks on Aristotle and Cicero perpetrated by a blustering 'Cephas Chlononius' — a humorous Greek translation playing on the meaning of Petrus, a stone, and Ramus, a branch (4 April 1550).[17] But in a later letter to Sturm, Ascham moderated his views (29 June 1552): Ramus, he says now, has reasonably attacked the scholastics rather than Aristotle himself, and his critique of the Greek philosopher is a pose of self-defence before his fellow scholars.[18] Ascham's changing

---

[16] *The Pilgrimage to Parnassus*, 3.236–27, in *The Pilgrimage to Parnassus, with the Two Parts of The Return from Parnassus*, ed. by William Dunn Macray (Oxford: Clarendon Press, 1896); Thomas Nashe, *The Anatomie of Absurditie* (London: J. Charlewood, 1589), E2ʳ; Francis Bacon, *Temporis Partus Masculus* (1605), in Benjamin Farrington, *The Philosophy of Francis Bacon* (Chicago: The University of Chicago Press, 1966), pp. 57–72 (p. 63). On Bacon's views of Ramus, see Craig Walton, 'Ramus and Bacon on Method', *Journal of the History of Philosophy*, 9.3 (1971), 289–302. On late sixteenth-century parodies of Ramus, see Knight, 'Flat Dichotomists and Learned Men', pp. 61–66. Twentieth-century criticism has continued to rely on Bacon's negative characterization of Ramus as 'a begetter of handy manuals' (Farrington, p. 63). See, for instance, Norman E. Nelson, 'Peter Ramus and the Confusion of Logic, Rhetoric and Poetry', *The University of Michigan Contributions in Modern Philology*, 2 (1947), 1–22. Hardin Craig labelled Ramus 'the greatest master of the short-cut the world has ever known', *The Enchanted Glass: The Elizabethan Mind in Literature* (New York: Oxford University Press, 1936), p. 143. See Ong's derogatory definition of Ramus as '*usuarius*, the usufructuary, the man living off the increment of intellectual capital belonging to others', *Ramus, Method*, p. 7. See also E. Jennifer Ashworth, *Language and Logic in the Post-Medieval Period* (Dordrecht: D. Reidel, 1974), pp. 15–17, for a characterization of Ramus's manual as a 'messy little book', 'lacking in breadth and perception' (pp. 16, 15). For recent reassessments attempting to rescue the figure of Ramus from these characterizations, see the papers in the following three important collections: Kees Meerhoff and Jean Claude Moissan, eds, *Autour de Ramus: Texte, théorie, commentaire* (Cap-Saint-Ignace, Quebec: Nuit Blanche, 1997); Mordechai Feingold, Joseph S. Freedman and Wolfgang Rother, *The Influence of Petrus Ramus: Studies in Sixteenth and Seventeenth Century Philosophy and Sciences* (Basel: Schwabe, 2001), and Steven J. Reid and Emma Annette Wilson, eds, *Ramus, Pedagogy and the Liberal Arts*. Particularly, see in this third collection Peter Mack, 'Ramus and Ramism: Rhetoric and Dialectic', pp. 7–23 (pp. 7–9) for a survey of attacks and misinterpretations of Ramus. A new important volume is announced: *The Brill Companion to Ramism*, ed. by Emma Annette Wilson and Sarah M. Knight (Leiden: Brill, 2015).

[17] Roger Ascham, *Disertissimi viri Rogeri Aschami, Angli, Regiae maiestati non ita pridem a Latinis epistolis, familiarium epistolarum libri tres* (London: Francis Coldock, 1576), B6ᵛ. See *Letters of Roger Ascham*, ed. by Alvin Vos, trans. by Maurice Hatch and Alvin Vos (New York: Peter Lang, 1989), p. 161.

[18] 'Sed ego Rami consilium intelligo μιμητής esse non vult, ne videretur sequi Aristotelem', *Disertissimi viri Rogeri Aschami*, D8ʳ ('But I understand Ramus's strategy: he does not want to be an imitator, lest he appear to follow Aristotle', *Letters of Roger Ascham*, p. 199). On Ascham's opinions of Ramus in the letters and in *The Schoolemaster* (1570), see Laurence V. Ryan, *Roger Ascham* (Stanford: Stanford University Press, 1963), pp. 147–49. Also Mordechai Feingold, 'English Ramism: A Reinterpretation', in *The Influence of Petrus Ramus*, pp. 126–76 (pp. 159–60).

opinions on Ramus's quarrels with tradition reveal a growing respect for the academic prestige of the Paris Regius Professor of Rhetoric in the early 1550s. His anti-Aristotelian reputation is alleged to have started with his MA thesis, defended in 1536, whose title his pupil and earliest biographer Johann Thomas Freige (1543–83) reports to have been 'Quaecumque ab Aristotele dicta sunt, commentitia esse' (Whatever things were said *by/after* Aristotle are fictions).[19] Whether Ramus actually said this or defended such a thesis remains conjectural. But he continued debunking the authority of Aristotle's *Organon* and its scholastic developments. His *Aristotelicae animadversiones* (1543) was printed nineteen times in the sixteenth century.[20]

The core of Ramus's attack concerned the faulty arrangement of Aristotle's dialectical works. Ramus complained about the redundancies of many Aristotelian principles. In particular, he condemned Aristotle's threefold division of logic into apodictic, dialectic and sophistic. For Ramus, there was not one art of logic for scientific argumentation, another for opinion and a third for fallacious reasoning. While the latter should be entirely removed from logic, the first two should fall under a single logical system, valid both for universal truths and human judgements. This involved a pruning and reordering of the *Organon*. The *Categories* and the first seven books of the *Topics*, as well as Porphyry's *Isagoge*, should constitute the basis for a new treatment of dialectical invention. *On Interpretation*, and the *Prior* and *Posterior Analytics*, should be reformulated under the banner of disposition or judgement. And the last book of the *Topics* and the *Sophistical Refutations* affected the use and not the doctrine of logic. Ramus's earlier critique took final shape in his French and Latin manuals, the *Dialectique* (1555) and the *Dialecticae libri duo* (1556). The latter's reduction of the *Organon* to one-tenth of its original length is at the heart of the accusations of banality launched against its author.[21]

But there is much in Aristotle that Ramus found worthy of acknowledgement. The most significant instance is his adaptation of three rules that he found in the *Posterior Analytics*. The first of them, the *lex veritatis* (Fraunce's 'rule of truth'), prescribed that all precepts of an art or discipline be universal and necessary affirmations — those in which the predicate is always true of the subject. The second, the *lex iustitiae* (Fraunce's 'rule of righteousness'), helped Ramus discriminate axioms belonging to one art from those belonging to others: each art should therefore deal only with what is proper to it. The third, the *lex sapientiae* (Fraunce's 'rule of wisdom'), recommended the arrangement of axioms from general to less general, so that the explication of an art became a set of principles ranging from the most universal rules to its particulars.[22]

---

[19] Johannes Freige, *Petri Rami Vita per Ioannem Thoman Freigium*, in Petrus Ramus, *Collectaneae, praefationes, epistolae, orationes Petri Rami Professoris Regii* (Maburg: Paul Egenolff, 1599), pp. 580–625 (p. 585), quoted in Skalnik, *Ramus and Reform*, p. 34. On the senses of the word *commentitia*, see Ong, *Ramus, Method*, pp. 45–47; and Philip W. Cummings, 'A Note on the Transmission of the Title of Ramus's Master's Thesis', *Journal of the History of Ideas*, 39.3 (1978), 481.

[20] Walter J. Ong, *Ramus and Talon Inventory: A Short-Title Inventory of the Published Works of Peter Ramus (1515–1572) and of Omer Talon (m. 1510–1562) in their Original and Variously Altered Forms* (Cambridge, MA: Harvard University Press, 1958), pp. 56–66. *Aristotelicae animadversiones* was finally expanded into the 'Scholae Dialecticae', a section of *Scholae in liberales artes* (1569). See also Skalnik, *Ramus and Reform*, p. 42.

[21] See Craig, *The Enchanted Glass*, p. 144. A summary of the attacks on Ramus by Paris Aristotelians can be consulted in Ong, *Ramus, Method*, pp. 214–24. See also Feingold, 'English Ramism', pp. 160–64, for an account of the complaints against English Ramists for their reliance on epitomes.

[22] Ramus transformed into laws the three terms that define the truth of a logical premise in Aristotle's *Posterior Analytics*, I.4, 73a, Loeb II: p. 43: κατὰ παντός, or 'predicated of all' (*lex veritatis*), καθ'αὐτο, or '*per se*' (*lex iustitiae*) and καθόλου, or universal (*lex sapientiae*). Ramus first formulated these laws as 'du tout', 'par soy', and 'vniuersel premierement' in his *Dialectique* (Paris: André Wechel, 1555), L2ᵛ–L3ʳ. See more detailed discussions in Ong, *Ramus, Method*, pp. 258–62; Wilbur Samuel Howell, *Logic and Rhetoric in England: 1500–1700* (New York: Russell & Russell, 1961), pp. 149–53; Skalnik, *Ramus and Reform*, pp. 44–45; and the 'Glossary' in Webster, ed., *William Temple's 'Analysis'*, pp. 46–47.

These laws, but very especially the latter, laid the basis for Ramus's theory of method. Ramus believed in the foundational status of logic, and thus in its practical role in the explanation of all the other arts. Accordingly, the principles of logic should be first discussed by recourse to the rules of logical method, and the same should apply later to other disciplines like rhetoric and grammar. Ramus started with definition: logic, or its synonymous term dialectic, is *ars bene disserendi*, the art of appropriate reasoning. It is primarily a pedagogical art of communication, but one that needs to be differentiated from rhetoric. In assigning the procedures of invention and disposition to logic, and in reserving elocution and delivery for rhetoric, Ramus treaded on well-known ground established by Rudolph Agricola's *De inventione dialectica* (1479). Like Cicero before him, Agricola's system prioritized invention over disposition. His work is pioneering in what Lisa Jardine has described as 'extracting from Aristotelian logic the bare minimum of formal apparatus and building on this a largely descriptive study of language usage'.[23] But Ramus went further than Agricola in his reduction of the contents of logic, in part dictated by the reallocation of some of its earlier contents to grammar and rhetoric on grounds of the *lex iustitiae*. The first book of the *Dialecticae libri duo*, 'De Inventione', is devoted to the study of arguments or proofs, that is, the separate compartments of reasoning that enable a complete enquiry into the nature of an object. The first division of arguments differentiates artificial from inartificial. Artificial or internal arguments have the power of arguing by themselves, whereas inartificial arguments depend on external testimony. Artificial arguments can be primary or derivative (*argumenta prima* or *a primis orta*). The first kind involves six essential categories: cause, effect, subject, adjunct, opposites and comparatives. The second distinguishes three: reasoning from name, from distribution and from definition. These categories allow further subdivisions, but, as Wilbur Howell has argued, the nine terms plus one general group of inartificial arguments would conform ten basic items, in imitation of the ten Aristotelian predicaments — substance, quantity, quality, relation, place, time, posture, habit, action and affection.[24]

For Ramists, though not for all logicians, judgement followed invention.[25] Judgement involves the disposition of the separate parts of reasoning into larger units of discourse. The Latin manual's second book, 'De Iudicio', begins with a theoretical discussion of its terms, definitions and main concerns. It then proceeds to the most elementary form of disposition, namely the arrangement of two arguments into an axiom with the aid of a copula. The formulation of an axiom like 'Man is an animal' may be sufficient for judging its truth. Only when this certainty is not possible, when an axiom is 'doubtful' or 'not plain', as Fraunce puts it, it will need to be 'sent' to the more complex form of syllogistic reasoning.[26] Syllogism demands the invention of a third term that will act as an arbitrator between the two arguments of an uncertain axiom. A Spenserian instance from Fraunce's *The Lawyers' Logic* exemplifies the procedure. The axiom 'Paris is no good

[23] Jardine, 'The Place of Dialectic', p. 52. On Agricola's revival of Ciceronian topical dialectics and his impact on Ramus, see primarily Peter Mack, *Renaissance Argument: Valla and Agricola in the Traditions of Rhetoric and Dialectic* (Leiden: Brill, 1993), especially chapters 6, 7, 8 and 17. See also the summary in E. Jennifer Ashworth, 'Developments in the Fifteenth and Sixteenth Centuries', in *Handbook of the History of Logic*, II: *Medieval and Renaissance Logic*, ed. by Dov M. Gabbay and John Woods (Amsterdam: Elsevier, 2008), pp. 609–44 (pp. 631–37).
[24] Howell, *Logic and Rhetoric in England*, pp. 156–57.
[25] Agricola was the first important humanist dialectician to put invention before judgement, so Ramus's decision reveals Agricola's influence. Philipp Melanchton prioritized judgement, to which he devoted the first three books of his *Erotemata Dialectices* (1549), while invention was relegated to the fourth and last book. See Mack, *Renaissance Argument*, pp. 286–89, and 298–302. More generally on Agricola's influence on Ramus, see Peter Mack, 'Agricola and the Early Versions of Ramus's Dialectic', in *Autour de Ramus*, pp. 17–35.
[26] SL, II.9, 32 (fols 22ᵛ–23ʳ).

shepherd' cannot be judged true from the start. But the invention of a third term, 'to leave his flock to fetch a lass', mediates between the other two and finally secures its confirmation through syllogistic disposition:

> *He that leaveth his flock to fetch a lass is no good shepherd;*
> *But Paris did leave his flock to fetch a lass;*
> *Therefore Paris is no good shepherd.*[27]

In Ramus's system, the syllogism encompassed the six procedures of reasoning admitted by Aristotelians: 1) the syllogism proper; 2) the enthymeme, or abridged syllogism; 3) induction, or conclusion not directly derived from the premises; 4) example; 5) sorites, or concatenated progression of enthymemes, and 6) dilemma. Ramus also pruned the modes and figures of syllogistic reasoning propounded by Aristotle and the scholastics, and paid particular attention to compound syllogisms.[28]

The manual closes with a discussion of method, arguably Ramus's most important contribution to the study of logic. Method comes last because it must play its role only once a subject has been properly apprehended in its different parts. But it is of primary importance, as it prescribes the whole mode of discussion of any object in science. Ramus differentiates between two kinds of method, natural and prudential. Natural method (*methodus naturae*) is the logical procedure for the explication of all sciences, and establishes the pedagogical essence of Ramism. Any scientific discussion should begin with a definition of an object by specifying its genus and differences, and then proceed to division into its particulars by means of dichotomy. Method should be one and single, and should aim at clarity of explanation without relinquishing the aspiration to formal elegance. Scholars frequently emphasize the Platonism inherent to Ramus's conception of method — a quality that becomes conspicuous in the *Dialectique*:

> And briefly this artificial method seems to me like a long chain of gold, as it seemed to Homer, whose links are the degrees depending one upon the other, and all linked so precisely together that nothing can be taken away without breaking the order and continuation of the whole.[29]

Ramus also envisaged an exceptional procedure for those cases where convenience advised acting otherwise. In his view, orators, philosophers, historians and especially poets sometimes needed to find alternative arrangements of discourse, not so much in accordance with the rules of art, but with the character of their readers and audiences. The *methodus prudentiae* and *crypticus methodus* are of special interest for the poet, as they contemplate the classical four-part rhetorical oration, as well as necessary omissions, amplifications and rearrangements in fictional discourse. Their admission to the doctrine of logic testifies to one of the few theoretical incursions into the field of rhetoric that Ramus allowed in his dialectical manuals.[30]

Ramist logic is hence a simplified system, stripped of the niceties of scholasticism and designed for purposes of scholarly discussion. The ultimate goal of logic is the communication of knowledge. It involves praxis, and its use is acknowledged to be universal. All human beings are

---

[27] LL, C2^v–C3^r (Appendix I.2).

[28] On the evolution and changes of Ramus's discussions of syllogism, or first judgement, see Ong, *Ramus, Method*, pp. 183–86; and Mack, 'Agricola and the Early Versions', p. 28.

[29] 'E bref ceste methode artificielle me semble quelque longue chaine d'or, telle que seint Homere, de laquelle les anneletz soyent ces degrez ainsi dépendants l'n de l'autre, & tous enchainez si iustement ensemble, que rien ne s'en puisse oster sans rompre l'ordre & continuation du tout', *Dialectique*, Q1^v. See also Webster's 'Introduction', in *William Temple's 'Analysis'*, p. 24. On Ramus's Platonism, especially his ideas about third judgement or ascent to divine knowledge, see Ong, *Ramus, Method*, pp. 189–90.

[30] See Peter Mack, 'Ramus and Ramism: Rhetoric and Dialectic', in *Ramus, Pedagogy and the Liberal Arts*, pp. 7–23 (pp. 13–14).

naturally endowed with logical skills, and artificial logic should imitate those abilities. Parallel to other arts of imitation, the mimetic power of logic must serve to polish or improve the natural imperfections of human reason. This step from nature to doctrine must be completed by the use of art. At this practical level, Ramus conceived of two essential operations for the logician: *genesis*, on the one hand, aims at the composition of discourse, either by imitation or by original creation; *analysis*, on the other hand, involves decomposing a given discourse in order to explain its parts. Seen as a whole, the Ramist edifice is founded on the conceptual triad *natura, doctrina, exercitatio* (or *usus*): this triad grants the art of logic a primordial and universal value, its theoretical sustenance, as well as its first place in the production of scientific and non-scientific discourse. The illustrative materials, frequently taken from classical literature, supply the link between these three terms: they must function as repositories of natural reasoning, as examples of technical principles, and also as models for the production of new discourse.[31]

The impact of Ramism in England marks the developments of logic in the last quarter of the sixteenth century, and to a lesser extent in the first half of the seventeenth.[32] Until then the university curriculum had remained primarily Aristotelian. That was the case at Oxford during the entire sixteenth century. Oxford kept its faith to Aristotle and to the scholastic, terminist tradition of Peter of Spain (*c.* 1215–77) and John Buridan (f. 1358), which scholars like Walter Burley (1275–1344) and Robert Holkot (1290–1349) helped consolidate.[33] The situation was different at Cambridge. As Lisa Jardine has argued, the interest in humanists like Agricola, Melanchton and Sturm fostered a place-orientated study of logic which, despite its strong Aristotelian base, tended towards simplification and an emphasis on the art's practical aspects.[34] The impact of Agricola and Melanchton was evident in John Seton's *Dialectica* (1545, and reprinted more than ten times before 1640). Following Melanchton, Seton reversed the Agricolan priority of invention over judgement, devoting his first three books to *iudicium* and only the last one to the study of the topics.[35] The example of Seton's manual was followed by several vernacular works, the two most important being Thomas Wilson's *The Rule of Reason, Conteyining the Arte of Logique* (1551) and Ralph Lever's *The Arte of Reason, Rightly Termed Witcraft* (1573). The first, reprinted several times before the advent of Ramism, was the reference English manual in the mid-sixteenth century. Wilson followed Seton in discussing *iudicium* before *inventio*, and is remarkable for his attention to the notion of natural logic.[36] The second is unfairly remembered more for its idiomatic eccentricities than for its content. Written in the midst of the inkhorn controversy, Lever sought to create purely vernacular terms for all logical concepts. 'Witcraft'

[31] Ramus's clearest exposition of logic in this light is his early *Dialecticae institutiones* (1543). On these three terms in relation to Ramus's use of poetic illustrations, see Kees Meerhoff, '"Beauty and the Beast": Nature, Logic and Literature in Ramus', in *The Influence of Petrus Ramus*, pp. 200–14.

[32] On the influence of Ramus's logic in England, see Howell, *Logic and Rhetoric in England*, pp. 146–246; 'Introduction', in *The Logike of the Most Excellent Philosopher P. Ramus Martyr, Translated by Roland MacIlmaine (1574)*, ed. by Catherine Dunn (Northridge, CA: San Fernando Valley State College, 1969), pp. xix–xxii; Feingold, 'English Ramism', in *The Influence of Petrus Ramus*, pp. 126–76; Marco Sgarbi, *The Aristotelian Tradition and the Rise of British Empiricism: Logic and Epistemology in the British Isles (1570–1689)* (Dordrecht: Springer, 2013), pp. 23–27.

[33] Sgarbi, *The Aristotelian Tradition*, p. 13; James McConica, 'Humanism and Aristotle in Tudor Oxford', *The English Historical Review*, 94 (1979), pp. 291–317. McConica's analysis of John Case's critique of Ramus in his *Summa veterum interpretum in universam dialecticam Aristotelis* (Frankfurt 1580, London 1584) aids his conclusion that the reception of Ramus at Oxford was, unlike at Cambridge, far from sympathetic (pp. 299–302).

[34] Jardine, 'The Place of Dialectic'.

[35] Howell, *Logic and Rhetoric in England*, pp. 49–56; Sgarbi, *The Aristotelian Tradition*, p. 21.

[36] Howell, *Logic and Rhetoric in England*, pp. 12–31; 'Introduction', in Webster, ed., *William Temple's 'Analysis'*, pp. 14–15; Sgarbi, *The Aristotelian Tradition*, pp. 21–22.

(logic), 'speechcraft' (rhetoric), 'saywhat' (definition), 'foreset' (subject) or 'backset' (predicate) are words whose fleeting existence in the English language are due to Lever's linguistic efforts.[37]

The first enthusiast of Ramist logic at Cambridge was Laurence Chaderton (1536–1640). In his long life and career as a lecturer he counted among his pupils Gabriel Harvey, Edmund Spenser, William Temple and Abraham Fraunce. Chaderton's lectures on logic are not extant, and Fraunce's quotations in *The Shepherds' Logic* are the only witnesses of his writings in this field.[38] But the consolidation of Ramism in England took place right after Ramus's murder during the events ensuing the St Bartholomew's Day Massacre in August 1572. Undoubtedly aided by the growing reputation of Ramus as a Protestant martyr, the new Cambridge intelligentsia around Gabriel Harvey explored and embraced Ramist ideas.[39] Harvey became a fellow of Pembroke Hall in 1570, and in 1574 he became University Praelector in Rhetoric. Originally a staunch defender of the Ciceronian florid style, Harvey's discovery of Ramus's *Ciceronianus* meant, in his own account, a turning point in his career.[40] His own *Ciceronianus*, printed in 1577 and containing the inaugural lecture for the 1576 Cambridge course on Rhetoric, propounds a guide to Ramist tenets beyond the mere technicalities of doctrine. In this sense, his preferment of the Ramist version of Ciceronianism entailed an ideal of excellence 'in conformity with the most careful usage of speech and thought'.[41] Harvey advocated an imitation not just of Cicero's 'Latinity but his resources of wisdom and factual knowledge', not just his 'letters, speeches, lectures, and treatises, but much rather the teachers, the course of studies, the labors of memory, and the vigils of thought by which so great an orator was made'.[42] Harvey insisted on praxis and action. Even his defence in *Rhetor* (1577) of the theoretical separation of logic from rhetoric results in the joining of the two arts for the practical purposes of genesis and analysis.[43] As Adams

[37] Howell, *Logic and Rhetoric in England*, pp. 57–63; Sgarbi, *The Aristotelian Tradition*, pp. 22–23; Joseph S. Subbiondo, 'Ralph Lever's *Witctaft*: 16th-Century Rhetoric and 17th-Century Philosophical Language', in *Historical Linguistics 1993: Papers from the Sixth International Conference on the History of the Language Sciences*, ed. by Kurt R. Jankowsky (Amsterdam: John Benjamins, 1993), pp. 179–86.
[38] Chaderton is mentioned in SL, title page (fol. 2r), I.3, 89 (fol. 8v), I.19, 14–27 (fol. 16v), and II.2, 11–16 (fol. 20r), though not in LL. On Chaderton's life, see Evelyn Shirley Schuckburg, *Laurence Chaderton, First Master of Emmanuel; Richard Farmer, Master of Emmanuel, An Essay* (Cambridge: Macmillan and Bowes, 1884).
[39] On Harvey's Ramism, see 'Introduction' in *Gabriel Harvey's 'Ciceronianus'*, ed. by Harold S. Wilson, trans. by Clarence A. Forbes (Lincoln, NE: University of Nebraska Studies, 1945), pp. 16–32; Howell, *Logic and Rhetoric in England*, pp. 250–54; Warren B. Austin, 'Gabriel Harvey's "Lost" Ode on Ramus', *Modern Language Notes*, 61.4 (1946), 242–47; John C. Adams, 'Ramus, Illustrations and the Puritan Movement', *Journal of Medieval and Renaissance Studies*, 17 (1987), 195–210, and 'Gabriel Harvey's *Ciceronianus* and the Place of Peter Ramus' *Dialecticae libri duo* in the Curriculum', *Renaissance Quarterly*, 43.3 (1990), 551–69.
[40] 'Tu, tu primus, acutissime Rame effecisti, ut, qui soli antea probarentur Itali [...] nunc nimis in quibusdam iudicarem curiosos: in quibusdam non satis perspicaces' ('You, you first, most acute Ramus, effected such a change of heart in me that the Italian humanists who formerly had enjoyed my exclusive esteem [...] now appeared to me partly hyperfinical and partly not quite so perspicacious'), *Gabriel Harvey's 'Ciceronianus'*, pp. 72–73. Wilson's 'Introduction' to this edition dates Harvey's 'conversion' to Ramist ideas in 1569 (p. 18).
[41] 'Ciceronianum, id est [...] egregium, atque accuratissimae loquendi, sentiendique consuetudini consentaneum', *Gabriel Harvey's 'Ciceronianus'*, pp. 70–71.
[42] 'Sic in Cicerone imitando, non latinitatem solam, sed ornatum, prudentiam, cognitionem rerum, vitae in primis, morumque virtutem: neque solum Ciceronis epistolas, orationes, scholas & disputationes, sed multo magis pedagogus, processus artium, labores ediscendi, & vigilias meditationum, quibus orator tantus instructus est', *Gabriel Harvey's 'Ciceronianus'*, pp. 72–73. Harvey quotes here Ramus's introductory remarks in his own *Ciceronianus*. See Petrus Ramus, *Petri Rami Regii Eloquantiae Professoris Ciceronianus* (Basel: Pernam, 1573), B2v.
[43] In the *Rhetor*, Harvey follows Ramus in his discussion of the art in light of the triad *natura*, *doctrina* and *exercitatio*. Accordingly, he tends to separate rhetoric from logic when the two arts are approached from a theoretical perspective: 'Tribuamus, o mi Cicero, suum cuique: & quod erit Rhetoricam, Rhetoricae; quod Dialecticum, Dialecticae, quod ab aliis sororibus, affinibusque mutuatum, id illis ipsis, a quibus mutuati sumus,

has argued, ethical orientation and practical training for civic life are inherent to Harvey's Ramist pedagogy, whose reliance on literary illustration 'show[s] the connection between dialectic and practical action and demonstrate[s] the existence of reason and knowledge in a wide spectrum of humane pursuits'.[44] In the hands of Chaderton and especially of Harvey, Ramism took a most appealing shape for those men like Fraunce whose interest in the humane dimension of the arts went far beyond pure philosophical speculation.[45]

In contrast to the more pragmatic orientation in the 1570s, the next decade saw a tendency toward specialized philosophical discussion of Ramus's works. In 1581, a series of Latin commentaries of the *Dialecticae libri duo* by continental scholars began to be published in London. Friedrich Beurhaus's *In P. Rami Dialecticae libros duos Explicationum quaestiones* (1581) was followed by two new instalments in 1582 and 1583. Johann Piscator's *In P. Rami Dialecticam Animadversiones* enjoyed a second London edition in 1581 after its Frankfurt publication a year earlier. In close engagement with these volumes, a number of philosophical commentaries were issued from Cambridge. The pedagogical practice and philosophical works of Everard Digby (*c.* 1550–92) are evidence that Ramism was not accepted at Cambridge without opposition and controversy. In 1580, Digby published a short treatise in which he criticized Ramus's single method. Digby's main point was a distinction between a method for the discovery of knowledge, based on a Platonic ascent from particulars to universals, and a method for teaching, based on descent from general precepts. This text initiated a polemic with his younger colleague William Temple (*c.* 1555–1627), who denounced the Aristotelian confusions of his rival. This controversy was not isolated. Temple, an orthodox Ramist, engaged in philosophical debate with Piscator after the publication of the *Animadversiones*, and a long epistle to the German logician was appended to his 1584 edition and commentary of Ramus's *Dialectica*.[46] With these works, Temple emerged as the most competent philosophical Ramist in England. His work had continuations in Nathaniel Baxter's *Quaestiones et responsiones in Petri Rami dialecticam* (London 1585, 2nd edn Frankfurt 1588). Baxter, a former tutor of Philip Sidney, remarkably included a partition of logic into *praecepta* and *usus* before the traditional division of the art into invention and disposition, thus emphasizing logic's practical dimension.[47]

---

acceptum referamus', Gabriel Harvey, *Rhetor* (London: Henry Bynneman, 1577), G1ᵛ. ('Let us grant, my Cicero, to each his own, to Rhetoric what is Rhetoric's, and to Dialectic what is Dialectic's, and when we borrow from my other sisters and relations, let us acknowledge our debt to them', *Gabriel Harvey's 'Rhetor'*, trans. by Mark Reynolds, 2001, <http://comp.uark.edu/~mreynold/rhetengn.html>). On the other hand, his recommendations about praxis endorse the combined application ('duplicem Analysin') of both arts (*Gabriel Harvey's 'Ciceronianus'*, pp. 84–85). On the Ramist conjunction of the arts in use, see Peter Mack, 'Ramus Reading: The Commentaries on Cicero's *Consular Orations* and Virgil's *Eclogues* and *Georgics*', *Journal of the Warburg and Courtland Institutes*, 61 (1998), 111–41; Mack, 'Ramus and Ramism', pp. 20–22; Meerhoff, 'Beauty and the Beast', pp. 212–14.

[44] Adams, 'Gabriel Harvey's *Ciceronianus*', p. 559. See also Hugh F. Kearney, *Scholars and Gentlemen: Universities and Society in Pre-Industrial Britain* (London: Faber & Faber, 1970), p. 52.

[45] See Andrew Hadfield, *Edmund Spenser: A Life* (Oxford: Oxford University Press, 2012), pp. 59–63 on Cambridge Ramism, its primarily Protestant context and Harvey's influence on his students.

[46] The best summary of this controversy is Lisa Jardine, *Francis Bacon: Discovery and the Art of Discourse* (Cambridge: Cambridge University Press, 1974), pp. 59–65. As Jardine observes, the Digby/Temple polemic is representative of the traditionalists' sense of the shortcomings of Ramism in accounting for processes of discovery of knowledge, as well as the Ramists' 'aim to establish the unique efficacy of a simplified and rationalised version of Ramus's divisive method as a teaching method' (pp. 64–65). See also Elizabeth Boran, 'Temple, Sir William (1554/5–1627)', *ODNB* (2004) <http://www.oxforddnb.com/view/article/27121>, accessed 19 August 2013.

[47] See Nathaniel Baxter, *Quaestiones et responsiones in Petri Rami dialecticam* (Frankfurt: Johann Wechel, 1588), A1. See also Andrew Hadfield, 'Baxter, Nathaniel (*fl.* 1569–1611)', *ODNB* (2004): <http://www.oxforddnb.com/view/article/1733>, accessed 19 August 2013.

Temple and Baxter had continuations in late sixteenth- and seventeenth-century Ramist epitomes and manuals, culminating in John Milton's *Artis logicae plenior institutio ad Petri Rami methodum concinnata*, published a hundred years after Ramus's death.[48]

A third and equally important dimension of British Ramism is translation and adaptation into English. The Scottish scholar Roland McIlmaine produced the first English rendering of Ramus's manual: *The Logike of the Most Excellent Philosopher P. Ramus Martyr* (1574, 2nd edn 1581) is a simplified translation, deleting some of the examples from classical poetry and adding other from Scripture. MacIlmaine, who had also published Latin scholarly editions of the *Dialecticae libri duo*, exhibited his Protestant allegiances in the very title of his work. Its prologue made clear the author's religious concerns by declaring that logic should be a useful art for theologians. McIlmaine's manual is proof that Ramist educators and popularizers 'were concerned with teaching substance as well as technical procedures through the imitation of illustrations'.[49] And this substance was in accordance with the religious dimension that Ramus's figure had acquired after his conversion to Protestantism in 1561 and his later death at the hands of the Catholic supporters of the Duke of Guise in 1572.[50] McIlmaine's theological standpoint was adopted by Dudley Fenner's *The Artes of Logike and Rhetorike* (Middleburg 1584). Fenner, later a protégé of the theologian Thomas Cartwright (1535–1603), was a Calvinist preacher who had studied at Peterhouse College, Cambridge, in 1575, although he left the University without a degree. His Biblical examples and doctrinal syllogisms, testifying to the marriage of Ramism and reformed theology more than a decade after Ramus's death, had continuations in seventeenth-century works, of which Thomas Granger's *Syntagma Logicum, or The Divine Logike* (1620) and Anthony Wotton's *Dialectic* (1620) are representative instances.[51]

Cambridge pedagogical practice, philosophical commentary and controversy, and vernacular popularizations are the aspects of Ramist influence that helped shape Fraunce's early logical writings. If viewed as a synthesis of these three trends, *The Shepherds' Logic* stands out as a remarkable achievement. Fraunce coincides with MacIlmaine and Fenner in the choice of English, in his persistent anti-Catholic rhetoric and in the conviction that 'Logic is necessary for a divine'.[52] Unlike MacIlmaine and Fenner, Fraunce preferred lay over Biblical matter in his choice of examples, although this did not deter him from advancing the Protestant stance that informed other vernacular versions of Ramist logic. If Fraunce did not meet Spenser in Cambridge, then his acquaintance with the *Calendar* and his determination to use it so extensively may have been encouraged by Harvey or more probably by Sidney. The Protestant content and contexts of *The Shepherds' Calendar* serve Fraunce's particular interests with respect to the intellectual circles to which the work was addressed.[53] The copious selections from the

---

[48] Sgarbi, *The Aristotelian Tradition*, pp. 25–27; Howell, *Logic and Rhetoric in England*, pp. 229–38.

[49] Adams, 'Gabriel Harvey's *Ciceronianus*', p. 560.

[50] MacIlmaine's 'Epistle to the Reader' insists that the 'utilitie and profitte' of offering Ramus's book in English translation is not only a matter of acquainting the reader with the art, but also of teaching the reader 'to make thy matter playne and manifest with familiar examples & authorities out of the worde of God: to sett before the auditor (as euery head shall geue the occasion) the horrible and sharpe punyshing of disobedience, and the ioyfull promises appartayning to the obedient and godlie', Roland MacIlmaine, *The Logike of the Moste Excellent Philosopher P. Ramus Martyr* (1574), ed. by Catherine M. Dunn (Northridge, CA: San Fernando Valley State College, 1969), pp. 3, 7.

[51] Patrick Collinson, 'Fenner, Dudley (*c.* 1558–1587)', *ODNB* (2008): <http://www.oxforddnb.com/view/article/9287>, accessed 5 Aug 2013. See also Hadfield, *Edmund Spenser*, pp. 61–62, for a reading of Fenner's divine syllogisms as examples of his Calvinist theology. On later works, see Howell, *Logic and Rhetoric in England*, pp. 229–33.

[52] SL, I.4, 101–02 (fol. 4ᵛ).

[53] A summary of the Protestant partisan stance of Spenser's book, its publication and its dedication to Sidney can be consulted in the 'General Headnote' to the work in Edmund Spenser, *Selected Shorter Poems*, ed. by

Calendar usually foreground a particular substance supplementing the treatise's formal training in logical precepts: this substance is the reformed humanism that Harvey promoted in his teachings and that Sidney endorsed through his works and patronage. A clear instance of this convergence comes up in Fraunce's account of a subclass of the argument of distribution dealing with the partition of a subject into its adjuncts. Fraunce picks three quotes from the *Calendar*, each from one of the so-called theological eclogues. First, 'Thomalin, in "July", divideth the countryman into goatherds and shepherds — they, keeping hills; these, loving valleys'. Second, Diggon Davy, in 'September', classes bad shepherds as idle, covetous or false. And third, Fraunce recalls Piers's similar division in 'May' of evil shepherds into 'hirelings and idle bellies'.[54] Even if Fraunce is not overtly concerned with Spenser's religious allegory and satire, his choice of examples reveals his intention not only to teach logical procedures of division, but to do so by focusing on Spenser's differentiation between Protestant and Catholic clerics.[55] In embracing the confluence of technique and matter recommended by Harvey, Fraunce also endorses the Protestant substance of an emerging national literature.

But Fraunce's allegiance to vernacular interests does not entirely distance his work from academic aims. More conspicuously than previous translators, he retains the structure and method of discussion of the Ramist manual, and displays knowledge of current scholarly debates. Thus, his adherence to Piscator allows him to balance praise of Ramus's achievement with the inclusion of voices less sympathetic to Ramus like Melanchton, Ascham or Sturm.[56] His attentiveness to contemporary polemics is also clear in his satirical account of the Digby/Temple controversy in 'A Brief and General Comparison'. And his acquaintance with the intellectual basis of Ramus's logic beyond the handbook's insistence upon technical precept surfaces in 'Of the Nature and Use of Logic'. *The Shepherds' Logic* and its accompanying essays thus offer a compendium of late sixteenth-century English attitudes to Ramist logic, as well as a most suggestive unfolding of innovative ideas about the pertinence of logic to poetic theory and practice. Fraunce's logical writings disclose the author's comprehensive approach to the discipline, his command of classical and modern sources, as well as his sensitivity to major intelectual developments and the literary achievements of his time. Beyond this scholarly sufficiency, his logical works hint at other sorts of personal ambition that his biography may help enlighten.

Douglas Brooks-Davies (London: Longman, 1995), pp. 7–8. For other views relating Spenser's *Calendar* to reformist Protestantism, see Anthea Hume, *Edmund Spenser: Protestant Poet* (Cambridge: Cambridge University Press, 1984), pp. 15–28; John N. King, *Spenser's Poetry and the Reformation Tradition* (Princeton: Princeton University Press, 1990), pp. 35–42, and 'Spenser's Religion', in *The Cambridge Companion to Spenser*, ed. by Andrew Hadfield (Cambridge: Cambridge University Press, 2001), pp. 200–16; also Jeffrey Knapp, 'Spenser the Priest', *Representations*, 81.1 (2003), 61–78, who argues that '[f]or Spenser, the Elizabethan *via media* in religion had authorized a newly expansive vision of the poet' endorsed in *The Shepherds' Calendar* (p. 64).

[54] SL, I.23, 2–19 (fol. 18ᵛ). It is not casual that 'July' (25 examples), 'May' (22) and 'September' (16) are the three eclogues most used by Fraunce. See Appendix II.

[55] On the ecclesiastical eclogues' allegorical readings, see the headnotes to 'May', 'July' and 'September' in Edmund Spenser, *Selected Shorter Poems*, ed. by Douglas Brooks-Davies, pp. 80, 112–13, 141. Alternatively, other critics have emphasized a lack of resolution in Spenser's religious dichotomies in these eclogues. See James Kearney, 'Reformed Ventriloquism: *The Shepeardes Calender* and the Craft of Commentary', *Spenser Studies*, 26 (2011), 111–51; and Evan Gurney, 'Spenser's "May" Eclogue and Puritan Admonition', *Spenser Studies*, 27 (2012), 193–219.

[56] On the differences between Melanchton and Ramus, see Joseph S. Freedman, 'Melanchton's Opinion of Ramus and the Utilization of Their Writings in Central Europe', in *The Influence of Petrus Ramus*, pp. 68–91. On Ascham and Sturm's discrepancies with Ramus, see this Introduction, 17n and 18n.

Abraham Fraunce (1559?–93?): Life, Works and Literary Significance

In the introductory remarks to his recent biography of Spenser, Andrew Hadfield reminds us 'how little we know about so many important figures, making the gaps in the biographical records of Shakespeare and Spenser seem typical rather than unusual and therefore in need of explanation'. Among other examples, he cites the case of our author: 'Almost nothing is known about the life of Abraham Fraunce (1559?–1592/3?), a key figure within the Sidney circle, who was among the first to appreciate the importance of Spenser's work'.[57] It is precisely the little we do know that allows us to connect Fraunce to Sidney, but also that prevents us from determining how important his role within Sidney's circle was, how close he was to his patron, and how much closer he would have liked to be. What follows examines known facts and evidence, and advances explanations or speculations on some significant gaps concerning Fraunce's literary relations and ambitions.

The English scholar, poet and lawyer Abraham Fraunce was born in Shropshire, in the heart of the Welsh Marches, probably in Shrewsbury.[58] Young Fraunce attended Shrewsbury School, as attested by his re-inscription in the School Register in January 1571. Philip Sidney had entered the school earlier, and must have left after Fraunce was enrolled, a possibility that suggests his early noticing of the younger schoolboy as the origin of Sidney's patronage. Moore Smith has carefully examined the school's ordinances and confirmed its high standards for classical languages and literature, as well as its special interest in the theatre, fostered by its first master Edward Ashton.[59] This must have encouraged the young Fraunce's literary curiosity. Fraunce left Shrewsbury for Cambridge, and matriculated as a pensioner of St John's in May 1576, most likely under the Sidneys' patronage. He became a Lady Margaret scholar in November 1578, then obtained his BA and became a Fellow of St John's in 1580. His MA commencement took place in 1583, and that same year he moved to London and began his training as a lawyer at Gray's Inn.

Fraunce's earliest connections with literary circles belong to his Cambridge period. He appears on the actors' list of the Emmanuel College play *Ricardus Tertius*, by Thomas Legge, and in the comedy *Hymenaeus*.[60] His earliest extant works must be assigned to these Cambridge years. A first manuscript containing an untitled treatise on the use of dialectic, the precedent for one of the essays in this volume, and a collection of 'Emblemata varia', the basis for a later published treatise on emblems, has been dated by Katherine Duncan-Jones as early as 1578 or 1579, when

[57] Hadfield, *Edmund Spenser*, p. 4. The most recent full biographical account of Fraunce is William Barker, 'Fraunce, Abraham (1559?–1592/3?)', *ODNB* (2010): <http://www.oxforddnb.com/view/article/10133>, accessed 5 August 2013. Edmond Malone's biographical note and assessment of Fraunce's literary value is still of interest. See *The Plays and Poems of William Shakespeare Comprehending a Life of the Poet and an Enlarged History of the Stage* (London, 1821), II: pp. 239–45.

[58] Henry Moore Smith, whose biographical account continues to be authoritative after more than a century, speaks of the connections of the Fraunce surname with the Shrewsbury Company of Glovers, and speculates on the possibility of one Thomas Fraunce, Churchwarden of the Abbey Church, being Abraham's father. See 'Introduction', in *Victoria, A Latin Comedy by Abraham Fraunce*, ed. by Henry Moore Smith (Louvain: A. Uystpruyst, 1906), pp. xiv–xl (p. xv).

[59] Moore Smith, 'Introduction', in *Victoria*, pp. xv–xviii.

[60] The name of Abraham Fraunce appears as the actor playing a Citizen of London in one of the surviving manuscripts of Legge's tragedy (Emmanuel College, Cambridge Ms 71, fols 35ʳ–56ʳ). The play was performed at St John's College at the Bachelor's Commencement Feast in March 1579. See Martin Wiggins and Catherine Richardson, *British Drama 1533–1642: A Catalogue*. II: *1567–1589* (Oxford: Oxford University Press, 2012), pp. 227, 231. The second play, catalogued by Wiggins and Richardson as *Comedy of Julia and Europhilus*, was also performed at St John's in 1578–79, and had Fraunce in the role of Ferdinand. See *British Drama*, II: p. 240, and Moore Smith, 'Introduction', in *Victoria*, p. xix.

Fraunce was still a BA candidate. Duncan-Jones's reasons are based on the coloured cover illustration of the volume in relation to its elaborate Latin dedication to Sidney. The illustration shows a scene from Book III of Virgil's *Aeneid* representing Achaemenides, the castaway left by Ulysses on Polyphemus's isle, as he begs Aeneas and his men to take him with them in their ship before the menacing presence of the Cyclops' cave. The initials 'A.F.' can be read under Achaemenides. In Duncan-Jones's interpretation, 'Fraunce was bidding Sidney farewell as he went off on some expedition which he himself would have liked to join'. The dedication, she argues, would then follow right after a letter addressed by Sidney to the Earl of Leicester on 16 December 1577 in which he begged leave of absence from court, possibly in relation to a military involvement in the wars of the Netherlands that Sidney projected but did not carry out at that time.[61] The Virgilian motto 'Tollite me Teucri' ('Take me with you, Trojans') presides over the scene, an injunction that, in line with Duncan-Jones's hypothesis, should be read allegorically as a request for consent to join Sidney's proposed undertaking. But it could also be a more general petition of patronage, employment, or even access to Sidney's family or to a literary coterie ('Teucri') gathered around Philip (Aeneas) since the late 1570s, in which other Cambridge intellectuals like Gabriel Harvey and Edmund Spenser had some participation, and of which the young author was aware. Moreover, Fraunce's apologies for his delayed completion of the work seem to accord less with the theory of a particular occasion than with a request for protection or favour: 'However, neither the more troublesome burden of poverty nor the surge of occupations allowed me to bring to an end what I had begun recently'.[62] This interpretation would allow for a slightly later date, perhaps around 1580, a time when, if we attend to the author's later account in the Preface to *The Lawyers' Logic* (1588), Fraunce and Sidney had not yet met personally.[63] In that case, the dedication of this first manuscript could have encouraged their first personal encounter in 1581.

The dedication of a second manuscript, Fraunce's Latin comedy *Victoria*, to Master Philip Sidney reveals its composition to be earlier than January 1583, the date when Sidney was knighted.[64] The third manuscript contains *The Shepherds' Logic* and its companion essays, which are the subject of the present volume. As argued below in this Introduction, the extant copy is certainly of a later date, although its works were begun or in some cases finished in this period. Fraunce's extensive use of *The Shepherds' Calendar* does not seem to point to a personal acquaintance with Spenser during his Cambridge years, as Spenser must have definitively left earlier than or around the time Fraunce entered Cambridge.[65] Gabriel Harvey might have been

---

[61] Katherine Duncan-Jones, *Sir Philip Sidney: Courtier Poet* (London: Hamish Hamilton, 1991), p. 155. Moore Smith also believed this manuscript to be Fraunce's farewell gift to Sidney, though on a later occasion: 'The date must have been either Feb. 1582 when Philip Sidney was sent to escort Anjou to Antwerp and stayed abroad till the autumn, or Nov. 1585 when he went out with Leicester to the war in the Low Countries. As Sidney is not described as a knight, the earlier date is the probable one', 'Introduction', in *Victoria*, p. xxvii.

[62] 'Sed neque paupertatis onus aetna grauius, neque negociorum fluctus permiserunt, vt quod nuper inchoaueram, ad exitum perducerem', Rawlinson, fol. 1ʳ, transcribed in Moore Smith, 'Introduction', in *Victoria*, p. xxviii.

[63] LL, ¶1ʳ (Appendix I.1, 1–7). See Virgil, *Aeneid*, III.599–602, Loeb I: pp. 388–89: 'per sidera testor, per superos atque hoc caeli spirabile lumen, / tollite me, Teucri ; quascumque abducite terras; / hoc sat erit' ('By the stars I beseech you, by the gods above and this lightsome air we breathe, take me, O Trojans, carry me away to any lands whatever; that will be enough'). A later date would also allow for reading the dedication in the context of the alleged sympathies professed by Sidney and Dyer to Harvey, and particularly to Spenser. See this Introduction, 183n.

[64] The manuscript of *Victoria* (Kent Archives Office Ms, U1475/Z15) is Fraunce's holograph presentation copy to Sidney. Moore Smith concludes that the composition and fair copy belongs to the last part of the author's stay in Cambridge ('Introduction', in *Victoria*, p. xx).

[65] Spenser's definitive departure from Cambridge is hesitantly dated between his BA graduation in 1573 and his MA graduation in July 1576. Hadfield ventures an early date, either 1573 or January 1574. See *Edmund Spenser*, p. 82.

in part responsible for Fraunce's interest in Spenser, but their close acquaintance between 1575 and 1583 cannot be certified. Fraunce's involvement in the quantitative reformation of English verse and his devotion to Ramist logic may have been first encouraged by Harvey personally, by Harvey's lectures, or by Fraunce's reading of the published correspondence with Spenser. Harvey's presence in *The Shepherds' Logic* is at best indirect through Fraunce's quotations of Hobbinol's speeches, and the evidence suggests a later date for personal associations between the two men.[66] A sounder possibility for the origin of the project is Fraunce's alleged first personal encounter with Sidney in 1581. Sidney, whose sympathetic views of Ramism are well-known, could also have asked Fraunce to employ a book dedicated to him and whose content and quality suggested a promising marriage between logic and poetry.[67] If Fraunce embarked on this project as a response to Sidney's suggestion, a dedication to him would have been the expected result. However, he dedicated the extant version of the work to Edward Dyer, a circumstance that has not been considered particularly remarkable for a manuscript that was most probably produced before Sidney's death. Dyer was a lifelong friend and part of Sidney's most intimate circle, a fact that would make this dedication appear as an extension of Fraunce's prestige within his main patron's literary coterie. But, even if fostered by Sidney himself, the turn to Dyer may be due to unfulfilled ambitions on Fraunce's part. The appointment of another Cambridge Ramist, William Temple, as Sidney's personal secretary in 1585, after Temple's dedication to Sidney of his own logic, may be a reason behind Fraunce's turn to Dyer, or even behind Fraunce's abandoning the publication prospects of *The Shepherds' Logic* after reaching its last stages of revision at Gray's Inn. Later sections of this introduction make a more detailed case for this hypothesis.

Fraunce's presence in Sir Philip's funeral procession in the train of his servants on 16 February 1587 attests to his continued attachment to the Sidneys in his most fruitful period as a writer.[68] He is not, however, included in Alexander Neville's compilation *Academiae Cantabrigiensis Lachrymae* (1587), one of the four collections of Latin funeral elegies dedicated to Sidney's memory, in which we find contributions by Cambridge scholars like William Temple and Gabriel Harvey.[69] *The Lamentations of Amintas for the Death of Phillis* (1587), Fraunce's translation in English hexameters of Thomas Watson's Latin collection of pastoral elegies *Amyntas* (1585),

---

[66] E.K. plays with the identification of Harvey as Hobbinol until the gloss to 'September', 176: 'now I think no man doubteth but by Colin is meant the author self, whose special good friend Hobbinol saith he is, or, more rightly, Master Gabriel Harvey, of whose special commendation, as well in poetry as rhetoric and other choice learning, we have lately had sufficient trial in diverse his works', Brooks-Davies, p. 156. 'Fraunce's acquaintance with Harvey during their Cambridge years is entirely conjectural, yet Fraunce had both opportunity and motive to become friends with Gabriel and his younger brothers, Richard and John', Steven W. May, 'Marlowe, Spenser, Sidney and — Abraham Fraunce?', p. 45. May later argues for Fraunce's active participation in the promotion in 1587 of *The Faerie Queene* for publication (pp. 47–50).

[67] On Sidney's sympathies and possible objections to Ramist logic, see George H. Hallam, 'Sidney's Supposed Ramism', *Renaissance Papers* (1963), 11–20.

[68] 'Mr Fraunce' appears among the names mentioned in Richard Lea's account, although he is not mentioned by Thomas Lant in the most famous rendering of the funeral. See Sander Bos, Marianne Lange-Meyers, and Jeanine Six, 'Sidney's Funeral Portrayed', in *Sir Philip Sidney: 1586 and the Creation of a Legend*, ed. by Jan Adrianus van Dorsten, Dominic Baker-Smith and Arthur F. Kinney (Leiden: Brill, 1986), pp. 38–61 (p. 56).

[69] See *Academiae Cantabrigiensis Lachrymae tumulo nobilissimi equitis* (London: John Windet, 1587), L4^v–M1^v (Temple), A1^r–A2^r, A3^v–A4^r (Harvey). On this, the other two collections from Oxford and the one from Leiden, see Dominic Baker Smith, 'Great Expectation: Sidney's Death and the Poets', in *Sir Philip Sidney: 1586 and the Creation of the Legend*, pp. 83–102; John Buxton, 'The Mourning for Sidney', *Renaissance Studies*, 3 (1989), 46–56; and Gavin Alexander, *Writing After Sidney: The Literary Response to Sir Philip Sidney 1586–1640* (Oxford: Oxford University Press, 2006), pp. 56–75.

contains a dedication to Mary Herbert, Countess of Pembroke, and a mention of the author's sorrowful condition — which may be in part a veiled reference to her brother's death.[70] Thomas Nashe's Prologue to Robert Greene's *Menaphon* (1589) praised 'sweete Master France by his excellent translation of Master Thomas Watsons sugred Amintas'.[71] And Thomas Lodge, in the Induction to the Countess of Shrewsbury of his *Phillis* (1593), spoke of a close association of Watson and Fraunce that seems to have continued until their adjacent deaths:

> And tho the fore-bred brothers they haue had,
> (Who in theyr Swan-like songes Amintas wept)
> For all their sweet-thought sighes had fortune bad,
> And twice obscur'd in Cinthias circle slept:
> Yet these (I hope) vnder your kind aspect,
> (Most worthy Lady) shall escape neglect.[72]

This translation was Fraunce's first published specimen in English hexameters. The cause of quantitative verse found in Fraunce a most staunch defender after Harvey and Spenser, its earlier Cambridge supporters, had abandoned all practical interest in it.[73]

Fraunce was called to the bar on 8 February 1588, and he returned to Shropshire, where he obtained an office as attorney at the Court of the Marches, located in his native Shrewsbury. Henry Herbert, Lord Pembroke, then President of the Council of Wales, must have supported his promotion at this point. This same year saw the publication of three of Fraunce's works in London. The first was the Latin treatise *Insignium, Armorum, Emblematum, Hieroglyphicorum, et Symbolorum*, dedicated to Robert Sidney, containing a three-part theoretical explication and commentary of emblems and impresas after Paolo Giovio's example.[74] The second and third, *The Lawiers Logike, exemplifying the precepts of Logike by the practise of the Common Lawe* and *The Arcadian Rhetorike, or the Praecepts of Rhetorihe made plaine by examples Greeke, Latin, English, Italian, French, Spanish*, constitute his definitive statements in the Ramist elucidation of the arts of logic and rhetoric.

In August 1590, Lord Pembroke wrote to Burghley, Lord Treasurer of England, recommending Fraunce for a vacancy as Queen's Solicitor at the Council of the Marches. A second letter in September and an audience with Elizabeth on 18 April 1591 were not enough for Pembroke to obtain his protégé's promotion to the post. It remains to be decided whether the Sidneys offered all their support on this occasion, or whether a possible implication of Fraunce in the unauthorized first edition of Sidney's *Astrophil and Stella* (1591) could have

---

[70] 'Mine afflicted mind and crased bodie, together with other externall calamities haue wrought such sorowfull and lamentable effects in me, that for this whole yeare I haue wholy giuen ouer my selfe to mournfull meditations', *The Lamentations of Amyntas for the Death of Phillis, Paraphrastically Translated out of Latine into English Hexameters by Abraham Fraunce* (London: John Wolfe, 1587), ¶2ʳ.

[71] Robert Greene, *Menaphon* (London: T[homas] O[rwin], 1587), A1ʳ.

[72] Thomas Lodge, *Phillis: Honoured with Pastorall Sonnets, Elegies, and Amorous Delights* (London: John Busbie, 1593), A4ʳ. Moore Smith eschews any possible reference to Fraunce's death in this text, as he endorses the theory that he lived until 1633 ('Introduction', in *Victoria*, p. xxi). Thomas Watson died in 1592. For the conjecture of a less amicable relation between Watson and Fraunce after the latter's 'unacknowledged translation' of his *Amyntas*, see Roger Kuin, *Chamber Music: Elizabethan Sonnet Sequences and the Pleasures of Criticism* (Toronto: University of Toronto Press, 1988), p. 179.

[73] May, 'Marlowe, Spenser, Sidney and — Abraham Fraunce?', p. 34. On Fraunce's influence on a circle of St John's students writing quantitative verse, see pp. 32–40.

[74] *Insignium, Armorum, Emblematum Hieroglyphicorum, et Symbolorum, quae ab Italis Imprese Nominantur, Explicatio: Quae Symbolicae Philosophiae Postrema Pars Est* (London: Thomas Orwin, 1588). Part III of this work also exists in a shorter version in a holograph manuscript, also dedicated to Robert Sidney. Fraunce also incorporated here parts of his earlier manuscript work 'Emblemata varia', dedicated to Philip (Moore Smith, 'Introduction', in *Victoria* pp. xxiii–iv).

changed their minds about his deserts at the last minute.[75] In any case, 1591 saw the beginning of a series of poetry books in English hexameters dedicated to Mary Sidney. *The Countesse of Pembrokes Emanuel, Conteining the Nativity, Passion, Buriall, and Resurrection of Christ*, was followed that same year by the pastoral volume *The Countesse of Pembrokes Yvychurch*. The first part of the latter volume was a modified translation of Torquato Tasso's play *Aminta* (1573), the second a corrected and expanded version of his 1587 translation of Watson's elegies. Fraunce's changes were made in order to accommodate Mary Sidney as the character of 'peareles Pembrokiana'.[76] To this volume were appended Fraunce's revision of his former translation of Virgil's Second Eclogue, originally printed with a logical analysis in *The Lawyers' Logic*, and a translation of the first lines of Heliodorus's *Aethiopian History*. This was succeeded by *The Third Part of the Countesse of Pembrokes Yvychurch, Entituled Amintas Dale* (1592).[77] Fraunce's most original work of fiction is also his last book, a series of mythological narratives in hexameters after Ovid's *Metamorphoses* followed by prose explications. Besides featuring the Countess again, the book is also remarkable for finishing with an allegorical tale of three astrologer brothers in which a satire of the Harveys has been detected.[78]

The end of Fraunce's literary career in 1592 makes the prolongation of his life until 1633 highly unlikely. Two versions of Fraunce's death have rivalled in critical and biographical accounts. The earliest, and most probably wrong, account has Fraunce as an attorney in the Marches until 1633, the year when he allegedly wrote a letter celebrating in verse the nuptials of Lady Margaret Egerton, daughter of John Egerton, first Earl of Bridgewater, and President of the Council of Wales since 1631. The attribution of that letter to Fraunce, made by the antiquary Joseph Hunter, was proved mistaken by Skretkowitz, who concluded that Hunter had conflated Abraham Fraunce with Abraham Darcie.[79] If Lodge's reference to the 'Swan-like songes' for Amyntas is taken for the deaths of Watson and Fraunce, then 1592 or 1593 makes a more plausible date to account for the abrupt ending of Fraunce's re-launched literary career.[80] The continuous references in his work to his 'crazed' body since his Cambridge years may be commonplace, or perhaps a clue revealing a frail constitution leading to an early death.[81] Steven May has recently

---

[75] The case for the Herberts' unstinted support of Fraunce in this cause is made by Steven W. May, 'Marlowe, Spenser, Sidney and — Abraham Fraunce?', p. 56. May quotes two manuscript letters of 25 August 1580 and 18 April 1591 to argue that Fraunce saw his favour with the Earl of Pembroke and his wife Mary Sidney increased. Roger Kuin considers Fraunce responsible for the theft of the manuscript that served as copy-text for the unauthorized edition of *Astrophil and Stella* (1591). See *Chamber Music*, pp. 176–89. In accordance with this hypothesis, Fraunce's thwarted appointment was 'a severe slap on the wrist from the inner Circle' of the Sidneys (p. 186).

[76] *The Countesse of Pembrokes Yvychurch, Conteining the Affectionate Life, and Unfortunate Death of Phillis and Amyntas: That in a Pastorall; This in a Funerall* (London: Thomas Orwin, 1591), B2ᵛ.

[77] The Latin dedicatory verse contains Fraunce's only extant reference to Sidney's death, in the form of a compliment to the Countess, who is called 'the likeness of dead Philip' ['morientis imago Philippi'], *The Third Part of the Countesse of Pembrokes Yvychurch — Wherein Are the most Conceited Tales of the Pagan Gods in English Hexameters* (London: Thomas Woodcocke, 1592), A2ʳ.

[78] *The Third Part of the Countesse of Pembrokes Yvychurch*, P1ʳ–Q1ᵛ.

[79] Viktor Skretkowitcz, 'Abraham Fraunce and Abraham Darcie', *Library*, 5.31 (1976), 239–42. Harvey's mention of Fraunce in a marginal note to his copy of *The Workes of our Ancient and Learned English Poet, Geffrey Chaucer* (London: John Islip, 1598), fol. 394ᵛ, may also mislead its readers into believing Fraunce to be alive at that time. See Gabriel Harvey, *Marginalia*, ed. by Henry Moore Smith (Stratford-upon-Avon: Shakespeare Head Press, 1913), p. 233.

[80] Michael G. Brennan, 'The Date of the Death of Abraham Fraunce', *Library*, 6.5 (1983), 391–92.

[81] 'A Brief and General Comparison', 278 (fol. 36ʳ); *The Lamentations of Amyntas*, ¶2ʳ (see this Introduction, 70n); See also LL, ¶2v (Appendix I.1, 61–63), where Fraunce complains that the pains derived from too much study 'did yet so rack my ranging head and bring low my crazed body, that I felt at last when it was too late the perpetual vexation of spirit and continual consumption of body incident to every scholar'.

identified a Shrewsbury burial register on 14 May 1593 of a certain Abraham Fraunce that may very well belong to our author.[82]

Fraunce's critical neglect after his death makes him a literary figure in need of reassessment.[83] His status is that of a second-rate poet, the champion of a cause for the quantitative renovation of English metre that was born dead. Ben Jonson's remark that 'Abram Francis in his English hexameters was a Fool' seems to have doomed his posthumous reputation.[84] Only recently his role as an innovative poet has been assessed in connection with his work as a translator and compiler using multilingual sources.[85] As a scholar, he is valued as an epitomizer 're-presenting the work of classical or continental writers to an English audience'.[86] And yet Fraunce enjoyed a considerable notoriety during his lifetime.[87] William Webbe's oblique reference in his *A Discourse of English Poetrie* (1586) attests to the high esteem which his then little known works had among a circle of illustrious acquaintances — most probably Harvey, Spenser, Sidney and Dyer. Speaking of Abraham Fleming (1552?–1607), Webbe adds:

> To whom I would heere adioyne one of hys name, whom I know to haue excelled, as well in all kinde of learning as in Poetry most especially, and would appeare so, if the dainty morselles, and fine poeticall inuentions of hys, were as common abroad as I knowe they be among some of hys fréendes.[88]

In the third of his *Foure Letters* (1592), Harvey placed Fraunce beside Edmund Spenser, Richard Stanihurst, Thomas Watson, Samuel Daniel and Thomas Nashe for his 'studious endeuours, commendably employed in enriching, and polishing [his] natiue tongue, neuer so furnished, or embellished as of late'.[89] Harvey also equated Astrophil and Amyntas as 'none of the idlest pastimes of sum fine humanists'.[90] Meres ranged Fraunce with Sidney and Spenser among the best English poets for pastoral.[91] To Peele, he excelled as 'a peerelesse sweet Translator of our time'.[92] Spenser's 'Corydon though meanly waged, / Yet hablest wit of most I know this day' is traditionally recognized as a praise of Fraunce while a lowly-salaried lawyer in the Marches in 1591 — or perhaps, too, as a man of high merits who was never duly recompensed with higher

---

[82] 'Marlowe, Spenser, Sidney and — Abraham Fraunce?', p. 62.

[83] Edmond Malone's comprehensive judgement is typical of this neglect: 'Neither his English hexameters, nor this odd and motley mixture of law, logick, and poetry, will, I fear, much raise Abraham Fraunce in the opinion of the present day. But he must be estimated by the notions which prevailed in his own time, and by the judgement of his contemporaries; among whom the praise of Spenser cannot but cast some degree of splendour around his name', *The Poems and Plays of William Shakespeare*, II: p. 243.

[84] Ben Jonson, 'Conversations with William Drummond', in *The Complete Poems*, ed. by George Parfitt (Harmondsworth: Penguin, 1984), p. 462.

[85] See Carla Marengo Vaglio, 'Words for the English Nation: Toquarto Tasso in Abraham France's *The Arcadian Rhetorike* (1588)', *Revue de Littérature Comparée*, 62.4 (1988), 529–32; Alessandra Petrina, 'Polyglottia and the Vindication of English Poetry: Abraham Fraunce's *Arcadian Rhetorike*', *Neophilologus*, 83 (1999), 317–29; María de la Cinta Zunino Garrido, 'Boscán and Garcilaso as Rhetorical Models in the English Renaissance: The Case of Abraham Fraunce's *The Arcadian Rhetorike*', *Atlantis*, 27.2 (2005), 119–34; Anna-Maria Hartmann, 'Abraham Fraunce's Use of Giovanni Andrea dell'Anguillara's *Metamorfosi*', *Translation and Literature*, 22 (2013), 103–10.

[86] Barker, 'Fraunce, Abraham', *ODNB*.

[87] The best summary of Fraunce's reputation among his contemporaries is found in Koller, 'Fraunce and Edmund Spenser', pp. 108–10.

[88] William Webbe, *A Discourse of English Poetrie* (London: John Charlewood, 1586); C4[r].

[89] *Foure Letters, and Certaine Sonnets*, in *The Works of Gabriel Harvey*, ed. by Alexander B. Grosart (Printed for Private Circulation, 1884), pp. 218–19.

[90] *Marginalia*, p. 232.

[91] Francis Meres, *Palladis Tamia* (London: P. Short, 1598), Oo4[r].

[92] George Peele, *The Honour of the Garter Displayed in a Poeme Gratulatorie* (London: Charlewood, 1593), A4[r].

offices by his patrons.[93] And Thomas Nashe's praise of Fraunce's translations in hexameters provides an alternative view countervailing Jonson's.[94]

Fraunce's access to manuscripts of Sidney's *Arcadia* and *Astrophil and Stella* and of Spenser's *The Faerie Queene* is documented through his use of sources in *The Arcadian Rhetoric*. This proves his excellent literary relations at a mature period in his literary career.[95] However, *The Shepherds' Logic* belongs to an earlier moment in which his pedigree within the Sidney circle was still in the process of consolidation. In any case, and despite his lifelong attachment to the Sidneys, the extant evidence about Fraunce might suggest that his personal expectations from the Sidney family were higher than his rewards. We may wonder whether the frustration of his appointment as Queen's Solicitor may be a second chapter to his earlier failure to obtain from Sidney that position of privilege gained by another Cambridge logician, William Temple. The unpublished and unfinished nature of *The Shepherds' Logic* may be proof that his early desire that the Teucrians admit him in their ship was never entirely fulfilled.

From *The Shepherds' Logic* to *The Lawyers' Logic*: Texts and Dates

The bibliographic file in the British Library Catalogue indicates that the text of *The Shepherds' Logic* contained in the undated Add Ms 34361 'probably represents an earlier stage' of *The Lawyers' Logic*. It also asserts that 'the matter (including the Spenser quotations) is partially the same [...] but the differences are very considerable', the main reason for these discrepancies being that 'none of the quotations from law-books are here included'.[96] A short, unsigned prefatory note to the 1969 facsimile reproduction of the manuscript states the matter somewhat differently:

> *The Sheapheardes Logike*, although apparently never printed, formed the basis of Fraunce's *Lawiers Logike*, 1588. As stated on the title-page the work takes many of its illustrations of the Ramist principles of logic from Spenser's *Shepheardes Calender*, 1579. *The Lawiers Logike* is an expansion of this text with the addition of more illustrations of interest to lawyers.

Here *The Shepherds' Logic* is acknowledged to be both a 'work' and a 'text' forming a 'basis' whose 'expansion' results in the definitive published version of 1588. It also adds a conjectural, though unsubstantiated, date of 1585 to the work's title.[97]

These two accounts reveal the difficulty of establishing the nature of the three texts in the manuscript, their dates of composition, or the date of the copy. Any attempt to elucidate this problem must be made with a view to *The Lawyers' Logic*. In the Preface 'To the Learned Lawyers of England, Especially the Gentlemen of Gray's Inn', Fraunce informs us of a seven-year span between his earlier pieces, 'a general discourse concerning the right use of Logic, and a contracted comparison between this of Ramus and that of Aristotle', and his published work of 1588. 1581 was then the year of 'these trifling beginnings', which, by the encouragement of his new acquaintance Philip Sidney, led to 'a further travailing in the easy explication of Ramus his Logic'. This latter phrase describes Fraunce's idea of *The Shepherds' Logic* as seen in 1588,

---

[93] Edmund Spenser, *Colin Clouts Come Home Againe*, in *The Works of Edmund Spenser: A Variorum Edition*, ed. by Edwin Greenlaw and others, 11 vols (Baltimore, MD: The Johns Hopkins University Press, 1932–49), VII: *The Minor Poems, Part One*, ed. by Charles Grosvenor Osgood and Henry Gibbons Lopsteich (1943), 382–83 (p. 158). See also the editor's notes (pp. 465–66).

[94] See this Introduction, 71n.

[95] See May, 'Marlowe, Spenser, Sidney and — Abraham Fraunce?'

[96] See entry for *The Sheapheardes Logike* at <http://searcharchives.bl.uk>, last accessed 29 January 2015.

[97] Abraham Fraunce, *The Shepherd's Logic [ca. 1585?]* (Menston: The Scholar Press, 1969), 'Note' (unnumbered page).

a project conceived not long after 1581 and subjected to numerous layers of rewriting and transformation:

> Six times in these seven years have I perused the whole, and by a more diligent overseeing corrected some oversights — thrice at St John's College, in Cambridge; thrice at Gray's Inn, since I came to London. This last alteration hath changed the name of the book, and this new name of the book proceeded from the change of my profession.[98]

However, his picture of the meticulous process that leads from the earlier plan to the published work contrasts with the poor results that he describes at the end of *The Lawyers' Logic*: 'Thus have I at last made an end of a confused meditation, patched up, I fear me, rather in great haste than with good speed'.[99] McCormick believed Fraunce's judgement of *The Lawyers' Logic* to contain 'less hyperbole than he intended'. She pertinently argued that '[t]he awkward assembly of parts, achieved mainly by unintegrated juxtaposition, does reflect a "patched up" quality, not in keeping with the seven years spent in its composition'.[100] The structural disarray of the final work's outcome is probably more the result of hasty addition than of long, painful labour. We should notice that Fraunce's account of a seven-year course of composition concerns the whole journey from *The Shepherds' Logic* to *The Lawyers' Logic* and not the composition of the latter only. Moreover, it is not entirely clear whether the 'last alteration' changing the book's title and including all the forensic materials refers to the last three revisions, allegedly carried out at Gray's Inn, or simply to the sixth and very last. *The Lawyers' Logic* is about five times the length of the text of *The Shepherds' Logic* in the extant manuscript. This fact should make us wonder how many of the three last revisions and how much of the five-year period between his arrival in London in 1583 and the publication of *The Lawyers' Logic* he consumed in shoving the 75,000 words absent from *The Shepherds' Logic* into the faulty edifice of his new treatise. Before new internal evidence can be adduced here, it is necessary to assess previous attempts to date the manuscript and to clarify the nature of the text.

After close examination of all Fraunce manuscripts more than one century ago, Moore Smith concluded about Add Ms 34361 that

> the whole book [...] seems prepared for the press. It perhaps took this form after Sidney's death on 17 Oct. 1586, otherwise one would have expected it to be dedicated to him rather than to Dyer. But in this case, one is surprised [*sic.*] to see no reference to Sidney's loss.[101]

Moore Smith arguably grants *The Shepherds' Logic* the status of a finished work and not of a mere draft. His reasons are the presence of Fraunce's own hand in the first two pages, the first of them containing the full title of the main work and of the two appended essays, the second including a signed dedicatory poem to Edward Dyer. These would authorize a text prepared by a scribe. Moore Smith also preferred a late date, although his arguments made it hard for him to opt for an earlier or later moment in relation to Sidney's death. His arguments are in any case the opposite of Walter Ong's careless entry 731 in his *Ramus and Talon Inventory*: 'It is very likely an exercise by Fraunce done while studying or possibly tutoring, and hence would date probably somewhere around 1580'.[102] Ong's suggestive idea of a study exercise, very possibly the origin

---

[98] LL, ¶1ʳ (Appendix I.1, 4–7, 8–11).
[99] LL, Kk1ʳ. See also McCormick, pp. 26–27. Ironically, these words that Fraunce uses as a conclusion to *The Lawyers' Logic* are borrowed from the opening paragraphs of his earlier essay 'Of the Nature and Use of Logic', and thus are themselves an instance of his 'patch-up' technique: 'and so an end of a confused meditation, patched up, I fear me, in more haste than good speed', 27–28 (fol. 29ʳ).
[100] McCormick, 27.
[101] Moore Smith, 'Introduction', in *Victoria*, p. xxiii.
[102] Ong, *Ramus and Talon Inventory*, pp. 462–63.

of the project, has against its early dating the author's own remarks in *The Lawyers' Logic*, as well as the proximity of the publication of the first edition of Spenser's *Calendar* in 1579. Ong's pupil and former editor of the text, Sister Mary M. McCormick, conjectures either a *terminus ante quem* of June 1583 — the time when Fraunce left Cambridge — or a late *terminus a quo* after 17 October 1586. But none of her evidence, as she recognizes, can be considered conclusive.[103] It seems fair to have expected a reference to Sidney's loss in the case of a late date, especially if we recall that Fraunce was a participant in Sidney's funeral procession.[104] Despite the disadvantage of leaving *The Shepherds' Logic* as the only work by Fraunce not dedicated to him or to a member of his family, a date before Sidney's death seems more feasible.

Yet decisions as to how much earlier the work is continue to be problematic. McCormick's *terminus ante quem* of June 1583 would have the advantage of considering Fraunce's own landmark for a third revision in Cambridge the completion of the work, or at least the incomplete termination of the project. Ralph Pomeroy, who in his 1983 article was not aware of McCormick's edition, seemed to consider this latter option of Fraunce's abandoning an incomplete work after June 1583. In his account, the manuscript is an early, incomplete draft of a projected work that included the two earlier pieces: '[t]hough Fraunce attempted to rewrite these manuscripts (three times, by his account) before he left St John's College in 1583, the results dissatisfied him. By the time he took up the rewriting task again at Gray's Inn, he had given up the original project in favor of a new one'. And after three new rewritings he completed *The Lawyers' Logic*.[105]

Pomeroy's interpretation has the benefit of conceiving *The Shepherds' Logic* and *The Lawyers' Logic* as two independent projects and two independent works, regardless of the degree of completion of the former or the degree of success of the latter. The idea of *The Shepherds' Logic* as a mere 'unpublished precursor' of the 'composite' work is thus dispelled.[106] And yet the endorsement of an early date is unsustainable by a closer examination of the manuscript's text in light of some of its direct sources. Fraunce's acknowledged debts throughout his treatise would allow McCormick's *terminus ante quem* as a sound possibility. If, as the present edition contends, Fraunce translated Ramus from Piscator's own text of the *Dialecticae libri duo* in his *Animadversiones*, he must have used the London edition of 1581 (the second came out in 1583). And of the three London volumes of Beurhaus's Ramist commentaries and comparisons (1581, 1582 and 1583) he only quotes the first and second. But at least one of his unacknowledged sources point in a different direction. No scholar has detected the far from fortuitous parallels between Dudley Fenner's *The Artes of Logike and Rethorike* (1584) and *The Shepherds' Logic*. The present edition records in its footnotes several obvious matches, but two cases are offered here for comparison. Translating Ramus on the formal cause, Fenner writes:

> But the naturall forme of things, though they may be conceyued by reason, yet they can not well be vttered by speache. The artificiall forme of things is much more easie to bee conceyued in reason, and vttered in wordes: and therefore of such speaches there be many.

Fraunce's translation reads:

> But the natural forms of things, though they may be conceived by reason, yet they cannot well be uttered by speech. The artificial form of things is much more easy both to be conceived in reason and expressed by word. And therefore of such forms there be very many.[107]

[103] McCormick, pp. 32–34.
[104] See this Introduction, 68n.
[105] Pomeroy, 'The Ramist as Fallacy-Hunter', p. 234.
[106] The term 'unpublished precursor' is Tamara E. Goeglein's. See her 'Reading English Ramist Logic Books', p. 250, 14n. The term 'composite' is used in this sense by Koller, 'Fraunce and Edmund Spenser', p. 110.
[107] Fenner, *The Artes*, B2^r; SL, I.2, 20–23 (fol. 9^v).

In the book on Disposition or Judgement, Fenner translates Ramus's comment on connexive syllogisms thus:

> Here oftentimes the former parte of the proposition maketh not the assumption, but that which is greater or of more force to conclude then it is.

Fraunce writes:

> Here oftentimes the former part of the proposition maketh not the assumption, but that which is greater and of more force to conclude than it is.[108]

Two translations undertaking such different approaches to Ramus's text and employing such different logical terminology as Fenner's and Fraunce's can only yield these parallel texts by direct transmission, and it remains to be determined who plundered whom. The published status of Fenner's text and Fraunce's plagiarizing habits in *The Shepherds' Logic* give a higher chance to the latter. Moreover, Fenner's stay in Cambridge, which he left without graduating perhaps in the late 1570s, more than probably prevents his having known Fraunce's later logical manuscripts.[109] A new *terminus ad quem* for the manuscript version of *The Shepherds' Logic* should be established after the publication of Fenner's treatise in 1584, a fact that compels us to reinterpret Fraunce's narrative of the six-stage revision process. As early as 1584, and probably after (in 1585 or 1586), we must place Fraunce at Gray's Inn, during his fourth or fifth revision of *The Shepherds' Logic*, incorporating corrections that include borrowings from Fenner. The manuscript copy was produced after this revision, in all likelihood no earlier than 1585, and then the story can continue after Moore Smith and McCormick or after Pomeroy: either 1) Fraunce considered the text finished and ready for a publication prevented for unknown reasons, or 2) he changed his mind about his project and proceeded to write *The Lawyers' Logic* out of his former materials. Yet it is not to be doubted that, while Fraunce was at work on *The Shepherds' Logic*, he considered it an entirely different book from his later achievement. Moreover, *The Lawyers' Logic* was a more hasty enterprise, probably entailing 'the last alteration' out of the six that Fraunce carried out. The great amount of material that he added in such a short period explains its cumulative arrangement and more chaotic design, as well as its author's disaffection with the results.[110]

The work's dedication 'To the Right Worshipful Master Edward Dyer' poses new difficulties. Dyer's closeness to Sidney seems to attenuate the conspicuous problem of *The Shepherds' Logic* as the only work by Fraunce not dedicated to Sidney or to a member of his family. The two shorter essays, written before *The Shepherds' Logic*, were dedicated to Sidney and must be dated before he was knighted on 13 January 1583, as the uncorrected dedication of 'A Brief a General Comparison' titles him 'Master'. Dyer was the dedicatee of other manuscripts at the time.[111] But the dedication of *The Shepherds' Logic* raises the question as to whether Dyer was the natural move to make after Sidney's death, or whether Fraunce had reasons to dedicate it to Dyer, or better, not to dedicate it to Sidney while the latter was still alive.

---

[108] Fenner, *The Artes*, C4ᵛ; SL, II.14, 17–18 (fol. 25ʳ).

[109] Fenner must have left the University soon after his matriculation. He is reported to have spent some time in Cranbrook as a preacher, and then left England for Antwerp sometime in the mid 1570s and stayed there until 1583. See Collinson, 'Fenner, Dudley', *ONDB*, and Charles Henry Cooper and Thomson Cooper, *Athenae Cantabrigienses*, II: *1589–1609* (Cambridge: Deighton, Bell, and Co., 1861), pp. 72–74.

[110] And hence Malone's description of the book as an 'odd and motley mixture of law, logick, and poetry', as well as McCormick's general assessment of the work (see this Introduction, 83n and 100n).

[111] Ralph M. Sargent, *At the Court of Queen Elizabeth: The Life and Lyrics of Sir Edward Dyer* (Oxford: Oxford University Press, 1935), p. 64.

In the absence of biographical evidence, conjecture remains the only path towards an answer, and the figure of Sir Philip Sidney's personal secretary, William Temple, may provide a plausible argument. Five years older than Fraunce, Temple received his Cambridge MA in 1581, a year after Fraunce received his BA, two years before Fraunce received his MA, and in the same year as Fraunce claimed to have met Sidney and started writing about logic in English. At that time, Temple was already the most talented Cambridge Ramist. In 1580 he had maintained a bitter polemic with the Cambridge Aristotelian lecturer Everard Digby. Digby, five years Temple's elder, had published a pamphlet attacking Ramus's notion of a single method, which met Temple's reply a few months later that same year with a pseudonym, Franciscus Mildapettus. This pamphlet, *Admonitio de unica P. Rami methodo reiectus caeteris retinenda*, also contained a critique of Digby's earlier *Theoria Analytica* (1579), a work mixing Aristotelian logic with esoteric lore of Neoplatonist and Cabbalistic influence. Digby replied at the end of the year with a new pamphlet entitled *Everardi Digbei Cantabigensis admonitioni Francisci Mildapetti responsio* (1580). Temple's final reply came under his own name in 1581. Digby's first pamphlet, *De Duplici methodo libri duo, unicam P. Rami Methodo refutantes*, was written in the form of a dispute between two characters named 'Aristotelicus' and 'Ramista'. This seems to have inspired Fraunce's caricature of Digby and Temple as the two 'wrangling sophisters', the 'obstinate Aristotelian' and the 'methodical Ramist' of 'A Brief and General Comparison'. In the tradition of the fictional debate, Fraunce refrains from judging the contenders and appoints Sidney as a neutral arbiter of the dispute. This is as much Temple as there is in all of Fraunce's logical works. Temple was later known for his polemic with Johann Piscator, which was published in 1582 in London in the form of a letter exchange. Temple's critique of Piscator addressed some of the latter's major disagreements with Ramus, and must be viewed as the work of an orthodox Ramist responding to those who tried to find an equidistant position between Ramus and more traditional viewpoints like Melanchton's.[112] Started after this response, Fraunce's *The Shepherds' Logic* is one of those works that qualifies his admiration to Ramus from a Piscatorian *via media*. Fraunce's alleged satire and his own philosophical position in *The Shepherds' Logic* may underpin his personal and academic distance from Temple.

Temple's edition and commentary of Ramus's *Dialecticae libri duo* was published in Cambridge in 1584 with a new response to Piscator in 29 chapters. The work was dedicated to Sidney with a letter dated 4 February. By this time, Fraunce must have finished his Cambridge revisions of *The Shepherds' Logic*. Sidney's reply to Temple in a letter of 23 May 1584 enthusiastically confirmed receipt of the book and the epistle, and encouraged Temple to visit him at court in his next trip to London.[113] Temple, then schoolmaster at Lincoln Grammar School, was appointed Sidney's personal secretary in November 1585, and remained by Sidney's side until his master's death on 17 October 1586. Fraunce had dedicated his earlier logical works to Sidney, and thus they remained in the extant manuscript, produced after Temple's book and letter to Sidney. And yet, the main work in this manuscript turned to Sidney's friend Edward Dyer and, in spite of its appearance as a finished manuscript, never reached the press. Whether Fraunce was disappointed by Sidney's promotion of Temple for a position he desired for himself, whether Sidney suggested to Fraunce that he seek his fortunes elsewhere, or whether the withdrawal of *The Shepherds' Logic* relates to its containing a former essay satirizing the man that was now an intimate collaborator of his patron, are circumstances that cannot be affirmed

---

[112] See Hotson, *Commonplace Learning*, p. 104.
[113] See *P. Rami Dialecticae libri duo, scholiis G. Tempelli Cantabrigiensis illustrati* (Cambridge: Thomas Thomas, 1584), ¶2ʳ–¶4ᵛ, for Temple's dedication. For Sidney's reply, see *The Defence of Poesie, Political Discourses, Correspondence, Translations*, ed. by Albert Feuillerat (Cambridge: Cambridge University Press, 1923), p. 145.

beyond surmise.[114] But these may be reasons behind Fraunce's abandonment of his project after 1584, or for dating the manuscript in the period while Temple was in office as Sidney's secretary — a possibility that would make the extant version coetaneous with the other important English Ramist work on logic and poetry, Temple's *Analysis tractationis de Poesi contextae a nobilissimo viro Philippe Sidneio equite aurato*. Only after this moment did the discarded texts acquire the status of drafts to be used in a later project.

The ways in which the three works included in the manuscript supplied material for *The Lawyers' Logic* have been accurately described by previous scholars.[115] These techniques account for Fraunce's acknowledged fondness for patch-up. Thus the last two pages of his Preface 'To the Learned Lawyers of England' are adapted almost verbatim from the Aristotelian's words and the Ramist's reply in 'A Brief and General Comparison'.[116] A section of Fraunce's conclusion, which he pastes to his commentaries on the last chapter on method in Book II, is in fact a patchwork of sentences and paragraphs culled in a disorderly way from 'Of the Nature and Use of Logic'.[117] Fraunce also incorporated a large section of his untitled Latin logic as a practical appendix to Book I of *The Lawyers' Logic*. This contains an instance of genesis or composition for rehearsal of the topics of invention taken from Sturm's *Nobilitas Literata* (1549) and an instance of analysis from Cicero's *De Amicitia*. Both are mentioned, although not included in full, in the shorter essay 'Of the Nature and Use of Logic'.[118] And of course most of *The Shepherds' Logic* is incorporated into *The Lawyers' Logic* in varying degrees of revision or with no revision at all.

A revealing instance of this incorporation is supplied by the poetic examples from *The Shepherds' Calendar*, a full comparative table of which is offered as Appendix II of the present edition. The table testifies to the suppression of some 40 examples from the manuscript and the addition of some 10 examples that are not in the manuscript version. This procedure may be proof of Spenser's loss of prominence in a work that is no longer a philosophical or a poetic logic, and in which the poetic examples are acknowledged to be an aesthetic remnant of a former project. But it can also testify to the contrary, namely to Fraunce's having had further thoughts and having added sections to *The Shepherds' Logic*, a fact that would not grant to the manuscript the status of a finished work. Another example that speaks in the same direction is the inclusion of a translation and analysis of Virgil's Second Eclogue, an appendix that would be arguably more significant to *The Shepherds' Logic* than to *The Lawyers' Logic*. In addition to these, several passages and commentaries in the new work would have made good sense in a finished version of *The Shepherds' Logic*. The clearest example is Fraunce's replacement of the Ciceronian example of 'Rullus' in I.2 as part of his annotations on invention with the above-quoted Paris instance from Spenser's 'July'.[119] While the theoretical explanation remains unchanged, this particular

[114] McCormick analyses Ethel Seaton's two arguments in relation to the scarcity of Spenser quotes in *The Arcadian Rhetoric* as possible impediments for the publication of *The Shepherds' Logic* ('Introduction', in *A Critical Edition*, pp. 35–36). The first is that Fraunce must have tried to guard Sidney's poetic reputation by not giving too much publicity to Spenser. The other concerns the publication of William Webbe's *Discourse of English Poetrie* (1586), a work that also contains several quotations from *The Shepherds' Calendar* — although many fewer than *The Shepherds' Logic* — and that could have spoiled Fraunce's market. See 'Introduction', in Abraham Fraunce, *The Arcadian Rhetorike*, ed. by Ethel Seaton (Oxford: Basil Blackwell, 1950), p. xl. Neither of these arguments goes beyond speculation.

[115] Moore Smith, *Victoria*, pp. xxiv–xxxv; McCormick, pp. 26–31; Pomeroy, 'The Ramist as Fallacy-Hunter', pp. 227–34.

[116] 'A Brief and General Comparison', 20–32, 141–64 (fols 32ʳ, 34ʳ); LL, ¶¶2ᵛ–¶¶3ʳ.

[117] 'Of the Nature and Use of Logic', 27–28, 159–66 (fols 29ʳ, 31ʳ); LL, Kk1ʳ.

[118] Rawlinson, fols 9ʳ–12ᵛ; LL, Y1ᵛ–Aa1ᵛ; 'Of the Nature and Use of Logic', 152–58 (fol. 31ʳ).

[119] Compare SL, I.2, 54–73 (fols 5ᵛ–6ʳ), with LL, C2ᵛ–C3ʳ (Appendix I.2).

usage of Spenser adds consistence to the design of an ideal, finished version of *The Shepherds' Logic* that Fraunce never accomplished or has not reached us.

The present edition includes, at times in the form of bracketed additions to the main text, at others as footnotes or appendixes, those passages from *The Lawyers' Logic* that seem of interest to the former work.

From *The Shepherds' Logic* to *The Lawyers' Logic*: Sources and the Evolution of Fraunce's Logical Thought

Fraunce planned and drafted the earlier versions of *The Shepherds' Logic* at St John's College while pursuing his MA degree. His sources testify to his acquaintance with those works that were of current use in the Cambridge arts curriculum, as well as with the continental innovations in Ramist dialectic.[120] Among the former, Aristotle's seven books of the *Organon*, Porphyry's *Isagoge*, and Cicero's *Topica*, *De inventione* and *De oratore* are among his favourite references. Although he does not mention Agricola's *De Inventione dialectica* (1479), he must have been familiar with it. Fraunce refers to Melanchton twice, so he was most probably directly acquainted with the *Erotemata dialectices* (1549). However, his use of Melanchton may be derivative of Piscator's *Animardversiones in P. Rami dialecticam* (1st edn 1580). This may also apply to Peter of Spain's definition of logic as 'ars artium', which he must have taken from Beurhaus or Piscator. Fraunce also acknowledged the influence of Laurence Chaderton's Cambridge dialectic lessons. And he also shows direct familiarity with some of Ramus's detractors, such as Jacques Charpentier, or 'Carpentar', whose *Animadversiones in libros tres Dialecticarum institutionum Petri Rami* (1554) he cites.

Friedrich Beurhaus's commentaries and comparisons are, as McCormick has argued, 'a supplementary resource to which Fraunce may refer the reader'.[121] And yet, McCormick's assumption that the four-time invoked 'second part of Beurhuisius' was 'the question and answer section which follows each chapter' is mistaken, as she cites Beurhaus through the 1587 Cologne edition of the *Dialectica P. Rami*.[122] Despite her awareness of the earlier London editions of his commentaries, these seem not to have been available to her. Beurhaus's Ramist works were published in London in three parts in 1581, 1582 and 1583. Of these, Fraunce cites the first and especially the second, a fact that justifies that reference. From this second volume, Fraunce found particularly useful Beurhaus's catalogue of maxims, 'thirty-four out of invention, forty-eight out of judgement', summarizing Ramus's logic.[123]

But Fraunce's major sources are Ramus's works, especially the *Dialecticae libri duo*, of which *The Shepherds' Logic* is partly a translation, and Piscator's *Animardversiones in P. Rami dialecticam*, whose first London edition of 1581 Fraunce most probably used. In fact, internal evidence suggests that Fraunce also employed Piscator's book as a direct source for the text of Ramus's manual. Walter Ong has echoed the printer André Wechel's complaint that Ramus's works 'all came into the world like bear cubs [...] and that the author kept licking them into new

---

[120] See this Introduction, 8n.
[121] McCormick, p. 42.
[122] McCormick, p. 75, 18n.
[123] SL, I.2, 113–14 (fols 6^{r-v}). Friedrich Beurhaus, *In P. Rami Regii professoris Clariss. Dialecticae libros duos [...] Explicationum quaestiones: quae Paedagogiae logicae de docenda discendaque dialectica. Pars Prima* (London: Henry Bynneman 1581), *De P. Rami dialecticae praecipuis capitibus disputationes scholasticae, et cum iisdem variorum logicorum comparationes: quae Paedagogiae logicae pars secunda, qua artis veritas exquiritur* (London: Henry Bynneman, 1582) are subsequently referred to as Beurhaus I and II. The catalogue of Ramist maxims can be consulted in Beurhaus II, O4^{r}–O6^{r}.

shapes indefinitely'.[124] In the case of the *Dialecticae libri duo*, its reshaping was not only due to authorial revision but also to the work's multiple commentators after Ramus's associate Omer Talon. These revisions concerned alterations of the text as well as the rearrangement of certain chapters. Fraunce's first two chapters in Book I are helpful in this sense. The division of their materials and the name of the chapters, 'What Logic Is' and 'Of the Parts of Logic and Diverse Kinds of Arguments', follow Ramus's 'Quid dialectica' and 'De partibus dialecticae, deque argumenti generibus'. These titles and this division cannot be found in editions of Ramus before Piscator's 1580 Frankfurt edition, and are customary after him.[125] Other sources of evidence are Fraunce's translation or adaptation of sentences that he could have read in some editions of the *Dialecticae libri duo*, but not in others. Speaking about relative arguments, Fraunce argues that these are contraries insofar as one denies the other, but not insofar as they are related by natural proximity and reciprocation, as a father to a son or vice versa. I provide Fraunce's text and its Latin source:

> But, according to this affection, they are not contraries, but rather natural agreeable causes. Then only they are contraries when they are applied to one and the selfsame thing, in the same time, and in the same respect.

> Atqui argumentum talis relationis contrarium nihil habet, imo arguit mutuas causas: tu es igitur meus filius: at cum dico, sum tuus pater, non igitur sum tuus filius, tum contraria vere sunt.[126]

Fraunce adapts the first sentence, and replaces the Latin example with a general statement in his second sentence. He cannot have found this Latin text in editions of the *Dialecticae libri duo* previous to McIlmaine's (1579) or Piscator's.[127] But he cannot have taken the previous chapter division from McIlmaine. These instances, and the systematic use of Piscator as a basis for his commentaries, make the use of one single volume including his two main sources a convenient working method for him and a plausible explanation of his handling of primary materials.

Fraunce's faithfulness to the *Dialecticae libri duo* is not exclusive or unqualified. Departures from its text must be accounted for in a threefold way. First, Fraunce made some changes in *The Shepherds' Logic* that point to relatively minor divergences from Ramus's ideas. Second, there are aspects of Ramus's thought absent in the *Dialecticae libri duo* that Fraunce found important for his project. Third, Fraunce's reliance on Piscator is the source of conceptual discrepancies with Ramus.

Fraunce's changes of his source concern the reduction of the number of chapters, sometimes grouping in one what in Ramus falls into two or more chapters. Thus, he groups Ramus's two-chapter discussion of testimony into one (I.32–33 become I.26), or the four-chapter discussion of method into one single and shorter chapter (II.17–20 become II.18). Significantly, Ramus's discussion of two kinds of 'arguments made of the first', conjugates and notation, are suppressed after Laurence Chaderton's judgement.[128] Fraunce also adds an appendix to his chapter on

---

[124] Ong, *Ramus, Method*, p. 172. But Ong provides a wrong citation for Wechel's observation. This is actually found in his Preface to the Reader of Omer Talon, *Rhetorica, e P. Rami regii professoris praelectionibus observata* (Frankfurt: Andreas Wéchel, 1577), A4r.

[125] See Johann Piscator, *In P. Rami Dialecticam Animadversiones* (Frankfurt; Andreas Wéchel, 1580), A6r, A7r, and its later London edition (London: Henry Bynneman, 1581), A6r, A7r. The latter is subsequently abbreviated either as Ramus/Piscator (when quoting Ramus's text) or as Piscator (when quoting the commentary). See also Petrus Ramus, *Dialecticae libri duo* (Frankfurt: Andreas Wéchel, 1586), A5v, A6r.

[126] SL, I.10, 7–9 (fol. 13v); Ramus/Piscator, I.14, C5v.

[127] See Petrus Ramus/Roland McIlmaine, *Dialecticae libri duo. Exemplis omnium artium et scientiarum illustrati, non solum divinis, sed etiam mysticis, mathematicis, physicis, medicis, juridicis, poëticis et oratoriis, per Rolandun Makilmenaeum Scotum* (Frankfurt: Andreas Wéchel, 1579), D4r.

[128] SL, I.19, 14–27 (fol. 16v).

method, called 'Of the Elenchs', which the present edition has made into Chapter 19 of Book II. This addition is revealing, as fallacies were discarded by Ramists from the doctrine of logic.[129] Fraunce might have derived his discussion of the elenchs directly from Aristotle's *On Sophistical Refutations*, from Sturm's *Partitionum Dialecticarum Libri IIII*, or from Freige's *Rhetorica, Poëtica, Logica* (1580). The latter, like Fraunce, appended the discussion of the elenchs to that of method.[130] Fraunce's perception of 'some use' in the elenchs again witnesses to his indebtedness to other trends in logical doctrine previous to Ramism.[131]

Fraunce's commitment to Ramism is proved by his acquaintance with other works by Ramus, which he employed actively both in *The Shepherds' Logic* and in *The Lawyers' Logic*. Howell has amply documented the latter's indebtedness to the French version of Ramus's logic manual, the *Dialectique* (1555). Few of these borrowings are present in the earlier work, so the larger number of instances in *The Lawyers' Logic* is evidence of the fact that Fraunce continued to use the French version after he abandoned the first project.[132] The usefulness of the French version is unquestionable, since this work contained more theoretical discussion in the form of annotations than the more precept-orientated Latin manual. The same applies to the earlier works of Ramus like the *Partitiones dialecticae* (1543), the *Dialecticae institutiones* (1543) or the *Animadversiones aristotelicae* (1543), which, in their original form or in any of their subsequent enlargements, served Fraunce for his annotations of *The Shepherds' Logic* and more amply for the two shorter essays. The attacks on Aristotelianism in 'A Brief and General Comparison' and the discussion of natural logic are the most significant instances of Fraunce's reliance on these works.[133]

Fraunce's use of Piscator's annotations deserves more ample treatment. The text of *The Shepherds' Logic* mentions Piscator twelve times in order to record coincidences, disagreements or borrowings from his commentaries. Especially significant are those detailed discussions and classifications which Fraunce transforms into Ramist explanatory diagrams in those chapters of Book I devoted to the arguments from cause. And yet, these acknowledged citations and borrowings constitute an insignificant part of Fraunce's systematic use of Piscator's annotations. Even in those rare cases where Fraunce claims originality for his arguments there is a source behind him. And that source is frequently Piscator. To mention one instance, Fraunce's veiled critique of Charpentier's reprehension of the Stoic division of logic into invention and judgement claims to be carried out 'in my fancy', while in fact he is translating a commentary of Piscator's literally.[134]

The scope of Fraunce's indebtedness to Piscator is registered in detail in the footnotes of the present edition. But its implications, philosophical and other, must be accounted for here. The *Animadversiones in P. Rami dialecticam* were first published in 1580 by André Wechel in Frankfurt. Its impact in England is explained by the two editions it enjoyed in 1581 and 1583. Johannes Piscator was by then an influential pedagogue, later responsible for preparing the

---

[129] See *Aristotelicae animadversiones*, K4[r] on the uselessness of the fallacies, and Ong, *Ramus, Method*, p. 174, for a summary of Ramus's arguments.

[130] See Johann Sturm, *Partitionum Dialecticarum Libri IIII* (Strasbourg, Rihel, 1566), Book IV; and Johann Thomas Freige, *Rhetorica, Pöetica, Logica, ad Vsum Rudiorum in Epitomen Redacta* (Nuremberg, 1580), M1[r]–M4[r].

[131] SL, I.18, 53 (fol. 27[r]).

[132] Howell, *Logic and Rhetoric in England*, p. 227. Two examples in Howell's list are already present in *The Shepherds' Logic*: the critique of the two logics of Aristotle's making (SL, I.2, 35–37 [fol. 5[v]]; Ramus, *Dialectique*, A2[r–v]), and the idea of the syllogism as an arithmetical deduction (SL, II.9, 35–36 [fol. 23[r]]; Ramus, *Dialectique*, M1[r]).

[133] On Ramus's progressive streamlining of theoretical discussion in his Latin manual see Mack, *Renaissance Argument*, pp. 343–44.

[134] SL, I.2, 18 (fol. 5[r]).

philosophical curriculum of the Herborn Academy at its foundation in 1584. As Howard Hotson
has argued, the philosophical importance of Piscator's *Animadversiones* is the basis of his
pedagogical work at an institution whose arts curriculum was designed in order later to prepare
its students in the higher faculties of law, medicine or theology. German Ramism had served the
lower training in the *gymnasia*, but the higher aspirations of the provincial academies demanded
an upgrading of Ramist tenets. Piscator's solution was not to turn to Aristotle's *Organon*, but to
the work of the former *praeceptor Germaniae* and associate of Luther Philipp Melanchton, who,
like Ramus, found inspiration for his reforms of dialectic in Agricola's *De inventione dialectica*.
Melanchton's dialectic was more theoretically dense than Ramus's in its closeness to Aristotle's,
and Piscator embarked on a project towards finding a compromise between Melanchton and
Ramus which Hotson has termed semi-Ramism, or more precisely Philippo-Ramism.[135]
Piscator's involvement in at least two polemics with the orthodox Aristotelian Digby and the
staunch Ramist Temple is explained by his *via media*.[136] Fraunce's adoption of a Piscatorian
perspective must be then interpreted as new in his context, as it takes issue with the extreme
positions embraced by his Cambridge contemporaries.

An interesting case of Piscator's influence and of Fraunce's discrepancies with Ramus is found
by a comparison of the treatment of the arguments from cause in *The Shepherds' Logic* and in
The Lawyers' Logic. The first devotes the third chapter of Book I to the final and the efficient, and
the fourth to the material and the formal causes. Posthumous editions of Ramus's *Dialecticae
libri duo* customarily started with the different sorts of efficient cause, then proceeded to matter,
then form, and ended with the final cause. Fraunce's rearrangement not only altered the number
of chapters (two against six in Ramus), but most significantly the order of the discussion and the
grouping of the four arguments around a different theory of causality. In Fraunce's own
argument, '[a] cause is either without the thing caused and made, or in it'.[137] The external causes
concern the finality and making of the thing, while the internal causes (matter and form) are
those that explain its essence. As Fraunce informs us in his annotations, 'Piscator admitteth this
distribution of causes as more convenient than that of Ramus, but Beurhusius and some others
like better that of Ramus'.[138] Piscator had criticized Ramus's unnamed categorization ('genere
anonymo') of cause, while Talon had justified his associate's classification on grounds of
anteriority (efficient and material) and posteriority to the thing (formal and final).[139] Fraunce's
acceptance of Piscator is not without justification: 'For my part, seeing Logic is an art of
reasoning, and in reason the end is always first considered, although in use and practice last put
down, I see good reason why I should give it the first place'.[140] But he later changed his mind
and accepted Ramus's opinion: accordingly, in *The Lawyers' Logic* he devoted his third chapter
to the efficient and material, or 'before the thing caused', and the fourth to the formal and final,
or 'in and with the thing caused'.[141] In Fraunce's explanation, this change is justified by a more
thorough analysis of both Aristotle's and Ramus's views, as well as by a self-defensive position
against his critics. Thus, he still holds the validity of his former endorsement of Piscator when
he affirms in his commentaries that '[t]he formal and material cause be essential parts of the

---

[135] Hotson, *Commonplace Learning*, pp. 101–05. As Hotson argues, Piscator 'began introducing Ramist
emendations into his lectures on Melanchton's dialectic and ended up inserting Philippist corrections into his
reading of Ramus' (p. 103).

[136] See *Commonplace Learning*, p. 105. Hotson mentions Piscator's response to staunch Aristotelians, Everard
Digby among others. As to Ramists, his polemic with Temple is well-known.

[137] SL, I.3, 2 (fol. 7v).

[138] SL, I.3, 70–71 (fol. 8v).

[139] See SL, I.3, 6n.

[140] SL, I.3, 71–73 (fol. 8v).

[141] LL, D3r–I1r.

thing caused; the end and the efficient are not so'.[142] And yet, other reasons hold priority in his decision to rearrange his arguments:

> Ramus in his French Logic placeth the end first, according to Aristotle in the second of his *Physics*, the end is first in conceit and consideration, though last in execution. But in the last edition of his Latin Logic he setteth it in the last place, respecting rather *finem rei* than *efficientis scopum et intentionem*, which last revolution of his I follow at this present, yet not so resolutely, but that I can be content to hear their advice, who bid us take heed that we confound not the final cause with the thing caused.[143]

Indeed, Ramus's *Dialectique* had discussed the final cause first, then proceeded to the formal and efficient, and closed with the material cause. This order had been kept in the first and second editions of his Latin manual (1556 and 1560). Ramus's reasons are Aristotle's argument in the *Physics* that the best way to explain natural generation is by reference to what is at the end of the process, regardless of the temporal priority of the initiating or efficient cause.[144] But the 1566 edition of the *Dialecticae libri duo* gave priority to the temporal over the explanatory argument.[145] Though reluctantly and weighing other reasons, Fraunce admits this to be a more convenient explanation at the end of his own process of revision. His change of mind might account for Piscator's loss of prominence in the later work. But it primarily shows Fraunce as a prudent and active thinker evolving into more carefully pondered positions after the examination of a larger number of sources and opinions. Like Ramus's cubs licked into new shapes, Fraunce's two logics also speak to the importance of process over result.

Despite all these alterations, *The Shepherds' Logic* observes in essence the principles and structure of Ramus's manual, especially if compared with *The Lawyer's Logic*. In the latter, Fraunce carried out drastic changes affecting the organization of Book I. This consists of the discussion of 'secondary' arguments (what in *The Shepherds' Logic* are called 'made of the first') before the 'compared' arguments. The consequence of this is that 'simple' and 'compared' cease to be a division of primary arguments in order to affect all places of invention. The present edition includes an Appendix with a comparative table of contents of *The Shepherds' Logic*, Piscator's edition of Ramus's *Dialecticae libri duo*, and *The Lawyers' Logic*. McCormick's tabulation of the contents of *The Shepherds' Logic* and Fraunce's own table for *The Lawyers' Logic* can be also consulted.[146]

A Ramist Dichotomy: From *The Shepherds' Logic* to *The Arcadian Rhetoric*

In *The Rule of Reason* (1551), the logician Thomas Wilson described the complementary nature and functions of dialectic and rhetoric by invoking the well-known analogy attributed to the Stoic philosopher Zeno of Citium by authors like Cicero and Quintilian:

---

[142] LL, G3^v.

[143] LL, H1^r.

[144] On the explanatory priority of the final cause for Aristotle, see Andrea Falcon, "Aristotle on Causality", *The Stanford Encyclopedia of Philosophy*, ed. by Edward N. Zalta (2014), <http://plato.stanford.edu/archives/spr2014/entries/aristotle-causality>, last accessed 12 July 2014: 'Aristotle argues that there is no other way to explain natural generation than by reference to what lies at the end of the process. This has explanatory priority over the principle that is responsible for initiating the process of generation'.

[145] Compare Ramus, *Dialectique*, A3^v–C2^v, and *Dialecticae libri duo, praelectionibus illustrati* (Paris: André Wechel, 1556), C1^r–C4^v, with *Dialecticae libri duo, Audomari Talei praelectionibus illustrata* (Paris: André Wechel, 1566), B8^v–D1^r.

[146] See McCormick, pp. 214–15, and LL, Ll3^{r-v}.

Bothe these Artes are much like sauing that Logique is occupied aboute all matters, and doeth playnly and nakedly set furthe with apt wordes the summe of thinges by the way of Argumentacion. Againe of the other side Rethorique vseth gay painted Sentences, and setteth furth those matters with fresh colours and goodly ornamentes, and that at large. Insomuche, that *Zeno* beyng asked the difference betwene Logique and Rethorique, made answere by Demonstration of his Hande, declaring that when his hande was closed, it resembled Logique, when it was open and stretched out, it was like Rethorique.[147]

As Howell has written, this simile gave 'both arts the same flesh and blood, the same defensive and offensive function, and the same skeletal structure'. The differences between the tight fist and the open hand, emblematizing plain argumentation versus indulgence in ornament, did not so much estrange logic from rhetoric as they endorsed the notion that a complete theory of communication was in need of their complementary powers.[148] Roman rhetoricians treated *inventio* and *dispositio* as overlapping concerns of both arts, while *elocutio*, *pronuntiatio* and *memoria* were additionally attributed to rhetoric. It was the task of humanist logicians, particularly under the influential guide of Rudolph Agricola's *De inventione dialectica*, to detect methodological confusions in this distribution and suggest ways toward their clarification.

Ramus followed Agricola's lead.[149] He perceived that the confusions of logic and rhetoric were less Aristotle's fault than Cicero's, Quintilian's, and Aristotle's medieval followers'. And he invoked the *lex iustitiae* to delineate clear boundaries between the theoretical concerns of logic and rhetoric. In consonance with Agricola's ideas, *inventio* and *dispositio* should be allocated to logic only, while rhetoric should remain the exclusive realm of *elocutio* and *pronuntiatio*. His proposal was criticized for promoting the divorce of the *ars bene disserendi* from the *ars bene dicendi*, *logos* from *lexis*, *ratio* from *oratio*. But it was also attacked for the opposite reason, namely for regarding as true logic what was essentially a rhetoricized form of dialectic.[150] Ramus's poetic citations in his exemplifications of logical *inventio* were regarded as rhetorical strategies justifying truth by appeal to authority and not by philosophical demonstration. Moreover, his admission of a poetic method, which made possible dispositions of discourse that differed from the natural or scientific method, was rendered suspect of conflating the legitimate aims of logic with mere rhetorical persuasion.[151]

However, the picture of logic and rhetoric as either unconnected or merged disciplines does little justice to Ramus's thought, which, as scholars like Duhamel, Meerhoff and Mack have proved, is in this respect more sophisticated than usually recognized.[152] Mack has argued that the simplification of Ramus often stems from scholarly attention to the Latin textbooks on logic and rhetoric as disjoined from his more theoretical and analytical writings. Omer Talon's *Rhetorica* (1548) and the *Dialecticae libri duo* are streamlined accounts, exclusively concerned with definitions, divisions and self-explanatory examples, and containing little in the form of theoretical speculation. This is particularly true of the logic textbook, whose subsequent editions after 1556 abridged the discussion and reduced the number of examples, leaving room almost exclusively for precept. And yet, Ramus's writings before 1550 were richer in philosophical

---

[147] Thomas Wilson, *The Rule of Reason, Conteinyng the Arte of Logique* (London: Richard Grafton, 1551), B3r–v. See Cicero, *Orator*, 32.113, Loeb V: pp. 388–91; and Quintilian, *Institutio oratoria*, 2.20.7, Loeb I: pp. 352–53.
[148] Howell, *Logic and Rhetoric in England*, p. 4.
[149] On Ramus's reliance on Agricola in the different phases of his work, see Mack, 'Agricola and the Early Versions of Ramus's Dialectic'.
[150] Ong, *Ramus, Method*, p. 49. The harshest attack in contemporary criticism is Nelson, 'Peter Ramus and the Confusion of Logic, Rhetoric and Poetry', pp. 13–14.
[151] Goeglein, 'Reading Ramist Logic Books', p. 226.
[152] Pierre Albert Duhamel, 'The Logic and Rhetoric of Peter Ramus', *Modern Philology*, 46.3 (1949), 163–71; Meerhoff, 'Beauty and the Beast'; Mack, 'Ramus and Ramism'.

discussion of important notions like natural logic or the practical uses of the art. As these materials disappeared from the textbooks, they were incorporated in Ramus's own commentaries of classical literary texts, as well as in his lessons on the liberal arts.[153] In these works, Ramus reiterates that the clear-cut distinction which should prevail at the level of *doctrina* does not necessarily rule man's natural abilities of reasoning and communication, and therefore should not be observed in practical use. Logic should be given primacy both at the level of analysis and composition of texts, rhetoric being a supplementary verbal clothing of the primary act of reason. The metaphor of the heart and the mouth provided Ramus with a powerful image of the necessary union of the arts:

> As much truly as reason to logic, let speech be proper to rhetoric. Neither let the seat of the heart be placed in the mouth, nor the seat of the mouth in the heart. And yet, as nature married in a most faithful society the duties of the heart and the tongue, so use and practice must unite the gifts of rhetoric and logic.[154]

Ramus's tenet is clear: nature and use counsel union precisely where doctrinal convenience fosters separation. Ramus's pedagogical aim is crucial here. As Kees Meerhoff has amply documented, his early Paris lectures established a plan for the *trivium* consisting of a three-year theoretical syllabus of Latin and Greek grammar, a fourth year exclusively devoted to rhetoric and a final year of dedication to dialectic. But this curricular design was accompanied by a practical programme of composition and analysis in which the new skills acquired through learning the latest discipline were exercised in combination with previously attained knowledge. Practice worked cumulatively through the combination of skills acquired separately in the theoretical approach to each art.[155] As Ramus explains in *Pro Philosophica Parisiensis Academiae disciplina oratio* (1551), one of his inaugural Paris lessons, the study of dialectic in the fifth year leads to the combined exercise of the three arts:

> and we unite the use of the three common arts to practise and explain all matters, whose different precepts we taught earlier in different years, so that we can practise and explain the same question elegantly with grammatical expression, with rhetorical diction and ornaments distinctly, and with dialectical reason, that is, with stable argument, with true enunciation, with consistent syllogism, with definite method illustriously. The fifth year is in this way devoted to the dialectical arts, in dialectical exercises by us: the use of the three arts, Grammar, Rhetoric and Dialectic, is practised in joined study.[156]

Ramus's frequent use of the word *coniunctio* and its derivatives has not passed unnoticed. As Meerhoff insists, Ramus is 'the man of the *coniunctio*, of the integration of discursive competences'.[157] Ramus promulgates the union of philosophy and eloquence ('cum philosophia

---

[153] Mack, *Renaissance Argument*, pp. 343–48. See also Mack, 'Agricola and the Early Versions'.

[154] 'Quamvis enim dialecticae ratio, rhetoricae oratio propria sit: nec cordis in ore, nec oris in corde sedes posita sit, tamen ut cordis, et linguae officia fidelissima societate natura coniunxit: sic rhetoricae et dialecticae munera usus et exercitatio copulare debebit', Petrus Ramus, *Animadversiones Aristotelicae* (Paris: Jacques Bogard, 1543), L4^r.

[155] Meerhoff, 'Beauty and the Beast', pp. 212–13.

[156] 'Triumque communium ad res omnes tratandas et explicandas artium usum coninungimus, quarum distincta praecepta distinctis temporibus antea docuimus, ut eadem quaestionem locutione Grammatica & eleganti, dictione Rhetorica & ornamentis insigni, ratione Dialectica, id est, argumento stabili, enunciatione certa, syllogismo constanti, methodo distincta & illustri tractemus & exponamus. Quintus annus in Dialecticis artibus, in Dialecticis exercitationibus hoc modo nobis instituitur: trium artium, Grammaticae, Rhetoricae, Dialecticae usus, coniuncto studio tractatur', Ramus, *Pro Philosophica Parisiensis Academiae disciplina oratio* (Paris: André Wéchel, 1557), C1^v.

[157] Meerhoff, 'Beauty and the Beast', p. 214.

eloquentiam coniungamus') in order to train competent practitioners rather than mere theorists ('artium exercitatiores quam doctores malimus'), thus endorsing the practical dimension inherent to humanist pedagogy.[158]

Like their master, early Cambridge Ramists exercised their activity primarily in the lecture theatre. *The Shepherds' Logic* pays a poignant tribute to Fraunce's teacher Laurence Chaderton's 'life and learning'.[159] Gabriel Harvey's praise of Chaderton's efficient teaching of dialectic testifies to the synergies between the Praelectorships in Logic and Rhetoric at the time of Fraunce's arrival in Cambridge.[160] Harvey's own lessons evince the dissemination of the Ramist ideal of the *coniunctio artium*. In the *Rhetor* he could praise Agricola for 'having unravelled so difficult and tangled a knot' tying the doctrines of dialectic and rhetoric by giving each art what exclusively belongs to it.[161] But Harvey, like Ramus a Professor of Rhetoric, did not envisage the teaching of his subject without the aid of the art of arts. Accordingly, he defended Ramus's version of ideal Ciceronianism, a writing practice that conforms to a most careful usage of speech and reason ('accuratissimae loquendi, sentiendique consuetudini consentaneum') rather than to a mere concern with style.[162] Harvey counselled the reading of Erasmus, Ramus, and Freige's commentaries of Cicero in order to achieve an idea that is ultimately Ramist: 'Consider not merely the flowering verdure of style, but much rather the ripe fruitage of reason and thought [...] Unite dialectic and knowledge with rhetoric, thought with language'.[163] For the practical purposes of explaining Cicero's works ('explicandi Ciceronis exercitationem'), he recommended the double analysis ('duplicem Analysin') characteristic of Ramist practice: 'Let us make rhetoric the expositor of the oratorical embellishments and the arts which belong to its school, and dialectic the expositor of invention and arrangement. Both these methods of analysis will be very pleasant for me to teach and, believe me, they will be very useful for you to learn'.[164]

If, as Harold F. Wilson has conjectured, Fraunce sat among the freshman hearers of the *Ciceronianus* in the Easter term of 1576, it would not be adventurous to see the direct influence of Harvey behind Fraunce's remarks on rhetoric in *The Shepherds' Logic*.[165] From the start, Fraunce wants to state clearly that his idea of λόγος gives reason pre-eminence over speech.[166] While he endorses the leading role of logic as the 'art of arts', he can also affirm the separation of the two arts in doctrine and their alliance in use: 'To talk of Logic when you put down Rhetoric is nothing to the purpose, and to cast in Rhetoric among precepts of Logic is absurd. But he that

[158] Ramus, *Pro Philosophica Parisiensis Academiae disciplina oratio* (Paris: André Wéchel, 1557), B4^r–v. I derive this point from Meerhoff, 'Beauty and the Beast', p. 212.
[159] SL, I.19, 15–19 (fol. 16^v).
[160] *Rhetor*, B2^r–v. Harvey's practice proclaims the need to combine the 'threefold instrument of Nature, Art and Practice, without which no one can join the ranks of the outstanding orators' ('huic triplici est opus instrument, Naturae, Artis, Exercitationis: sine quo nemo potest in praestantium Oratorum numerum aggregari'), *Rhetor*, B2^v, trans. by Mark Reynolds.
[161] *Rhetor*, H2^r, trans. by Mark Reynolds.
[162] *Ciceronianus*, ed. by Wilson, p. 70–71.
[163] 'non solum floridam istam verborum viriditatem, sed multo magis sententiarum, rationumque fructuosam maturitatem respicite [...] Dialecticam, scientiamque cum Rhetorica, mentem cum lingua consociate', *Ciceronianus*, ed. by Wilson, pp. 82–83.
[164] 'illam (Rhetoricam) oratoriarum exornationum, eiusque quod proprium est huius scholae, artificij; hanc (Dialecticam) inuentionis, collocationisque explicatricem: vtramque cum mihi ad aperiendum iucundissimam, tum vobis ad discendum, mihi credite, peropportunam', *Ciceronianus*, ed. by Wilson, pp. 85–87. As Peter Mack argues, 'we can find examples of people who admired and taught Ramus' works because the brevity of his textbooks of rhetoric and dialectic allowed for more time to be spent on the analysis of literary texts. The most obvious example of this is Gabriel Harvey', 'Ramus and Ramism', p. 21.
[165] Wilson, 'Introduction', in *Ciceronianus*, p. 10.
[166] SL, I.1, 2 (fol. 3^r).

hath learned the one may yet the other, and join the use of the two, whose precepts are both distinct'.[167] He can similarly recommend the replacement of the 'rigorous rules of some dunses prescribed' for syllogistic reasoning with a more natural and practical approach based on the imitation of classical literary texts: 'it shall be sufficient for a political man to follow a more easy and elegant kind of disputation, joining Rhetoric with Logic as Plato in Greek, and Cicero in Latin used to do'.[168] And he can also advance a notion of logic that cuts across the requirements of the high, middle or low style, but in disregard of mere rhetorical ornament:

> With lovers, she [Logic] loveth to speak like a wanton; with kings, she counselleth in a prince's palace; with men of the country, she sits in the sheepcotes; with senators, she gravely decideth controversies; in school, she directeth subtle philosophers; at home, she admitteth the simple artificer. As high as the highest, as low as the lowest, and mean with those of middle meaning. A preacher commeth to persuade the people, to exhort the congregation: but who can away with his persuasion, or who careth for his exhortation, unless he bring a sermon rather fraught and furnished with store of arguments than flowing and flourishing with show of ornaments — the one being the effort of Logic of all men commended, the other but a trick of Rhetoric, of many condemned?[169]

The Ramist intertwining of logic and rhetoric takes place at the levels of content and method. A. J. Smith long ago observed that '[t]he Rhetorics of Talaeus and Fraunce, shorn by Ramus's decree of Invention and Disposition, treat only the schemes and tropes, and their authors proceed in the same stark fashion as the logicians, merely giving the figure with the briefest of descriptions and illustrations'.[170] More recently, Peter Mack has affirmed of Ramus's manuals (and Fraunce's are primarily translations of Ramus's and Talon's) that they propose a 'highly selective approach to the syllabi of rhetoric and dialectic [that] can be seen as a strongly dialectical approach to a syllabus which is primarily rhetorical'.[171] *The Shepherds' Logic* and *The Arcadian Rhetoric* are parallel and complementary Ramist manuals. As Tamara Goeglein has argued, these look like logically inspired rhetorical handbooks or poetry anthologies, since the methodology is logical, while the language of the illustration is poetic. This duality facilitates a bimedial, emblematic *modus legendi* whereby the poetic example supplies an ekphrastic *pictura* facilitating the comprehension of the theoretical precept.[172] Thus, when Fraunce explains in *The Shepherds' Logic* that 'the matter is the cause of the which a thing is made', the Spenserian example of 'the honey bee / Working her formal rooms in wexen frame' is adduced in order to produce a Sidneian speaking picture, an eloquent painting of the truth behind the abstract formulation.[173] *The Arcadian Rhetoric* supplies the complementary argument by explaining the rhetorical mechanisms that express the material cause: 'The *Metonymia* of the materiall cause is, when the matter is put for the thing thereof made'. This definition is exemplified by Sidney's line 'Who euermore will loue Apolloes quill?'[174]

Yet at other times the collaboration of logic and rhetoric takes place in the opposite direction to that suggested by Goeglein. In these cases, it is logical analysis that helps disentangle the intricacy of poetic language. When Fraunce explains the 'distinct' or 'severed similitude' (Ramus's

---

[167] SL, I.1, 119–21 (fols 4ᵛ–5ʳ).
[168] 'Of the Nature and Use of Logic', 163–65 (fol. 31ʳ).
[169] 'Of the Nature and Use of Logic', 95–104 (fol. 30ʳ).
[170] A. J. Smith, 'An Examination of Some Claims for Ramism', *The Review of English Studies, New Series*, 28 (1956), 348–59 (p. 350). See also George Watson, 'Ramus, Miss Tuve, and the New Petromachia', *Modern Philology*, 55.4 (1958), 259–62
[171] Mack, 'Ramus and Ramism', p. 23.
[172] Goeglein, 'Reading English Ramist Logic Books', pp. 226–27, 232.
[173] SL, I.4, 2–3, 7–10 (fol. 9ʳ); SC, 'December', 67–68.
[174] Abraham Fraunce, *The Arcadian Rhetorike*, ed. by Ethel Seaton, pp. 5–6.

'disiuncta simlitudo'), an argument from comparison using four terms, his Spenserian example relies on the reader's analytical ability to reduce a complex rhetorical formulation to its bare logical skeleton:

> Thou barren ground, whom winter's wrath hath wasted,
> Art made a mirror to behold my plight:
> Whilom thy fresh spring flowered, and after hasted
> Thy summer proud, with daffadillies dight;
> And now is come the winter's stormy state,
> Thy mantle marred wherein thou masked'st late.
>
> Such rage as winter's reigneth in my heart,
> My life-blood freezing with unkindly cold,
> Such stormy stours do breed my baleful smart
> As if my year were waste, and woxen old.
> And yet, alas, but now my spring begun,
> And yet, alas, it is already done.[175]

Fraunce produces the example with no further explanation, so unfolding the four basic terms of the comparison remains the reader's task: namely, as the 'barren ground' (1) is exposed to the effects of the changing seasons (2), so 'my heart' (3) is exposed to its changing passions (4).

Seen in this light, Fraunce's endeavours constitute one more chapter in Walter Ong's account of Ramism as 'largely the story of unresolved tensions between the logical and the rhetorical traditions'.[176] In accordance with the Ramist *lex iustitiae*, Fraunce's two manuals keep logic and rhetoric separate in the process of doctrinal instruction. Yet the poetic example supplies a common *modus legendi* for the two arts by making explicit the Ramist contention that poets are endowed with a privileged ability for imitating natural reasoning. Conversely, the manuals also endorse a combined logico-rhetorical *modus faciendi* for poetry: mastery of the arts of discourse, Fraunce implicitly tells us, will enable new poets to emulate the models of excellence offered by the literary tradition. This principle not only endowed poetry with a primarily communicative purpose — a point that modern Jakobsonian theories of the poetic function would put to question.[177] It also, as Wilbur Howell has written, granted the specificity of poetry with respect to logic and rhetoric:

> So far as critics of that time postulated a difference between poetry, on the one hand, and logical and rhetorical discourse, on the other, their thinking might be described by saying that the two latter kinds of discourse were respectively considered to be closed and open, according to Zeno's analogy, whereas the former was regarded as having both characteristics at once. That is, poetry was thought to be a form of communication which [...] spoke two simultaneous languages.[178]

Fraunce's diptych of *The Shepherds' Logic* and *The Arcadian Rhetoric* must be regarded as a two-step manual of instruction for readers and poets, proposing excellent models for analysis and imitation. In the hands of its users, their poetic examples should act as reminders of the

---

[175] SL, I.17, 53–64 (fols 15ᵛ–16ʳ); 'January', 19–30.
[176] Ong, *Ramus, Method*, p. 49.
[177] 'Poetic employs, but subordinates, the arts of logic and rhetoric and of course grammar as necessary to the intelligibility of any art of communication', Sister Miriam Joseph, *Shakespeare's Use of the Arts of Language* (New York: Columbia University Press, 1947), p. 18. 'Englishmen of these two centuries did not waste their time in the vain effort to deny to poetry a primarily communicative function. Nor had the science of aesthetics yet been invented to insulate poetry from any contact with logic and rhetoric', Howell, *Logic and Rhetoric in England*, p. 5.
[178] Howell, *Logic and Rhetoric in England*, p. 5.

inseparable nature of the two arts. As Meerhoff has written, in their role as 'superior users of that natural light instilled in everyone', poets 'are presented as models to be imitated and, if possible, surpassed'.[179] By making possible the union of logic and rhetoric, Fraunce's endorsement of the Ramist idea of poetry also seeks the definitive *coniunctio* of nature with art.

Logic, Poetry and Poetics: From *The Shepherds' Calendar* to *The Shepherds' Logic*

Edmund Spenser's *The Shepheardes Calender Conteyning twelue Æglogues proportionable to the twelue monethes* was published anonymously in 1579. The book's dedication to Sidney appears to be Spenser's last-minute decision. The uncorrected prefatory lyric 'To His Book', signed by 'Immeritô' (i.e., Undeserving), still bears signs of the author's original intention to dedicate the volume to his employer and Sidney's uncle, Robert Dudley, Earl of Leicester.[180] The Sidney-Leicester connection and the printing of the volume at the presses of Hugh Singleton reinforce its Protestant allegiance, traceable in the anti-Catholic satire of some of its eclogues and in its allegorical engagement in the opposition to the proposed marriage of Queen Elizabeth with the Duke of Alençon, a cause endorsed by the courtly faction of Spenser's patrons.[181] The book combined emblematic presentation with the learned glosses by 'E.K.', whose prefatory letter to Gabriel Harvey praised the virtuosity of the new poet and explained its choice of the pastoral genre.[182] This complex presentation aligned the project's format with scholarly editions of well-known continental and classical poets, thus making of *The Shepherds' Calendar* the most ambitious debut by a young English poet. If Spenser was actually welcomed into the circle of Sidney and Dyer, as he confirms to his friend Gabriel Harvey in one of his letters, his admission must have been encouraged by Sidney's positive appreciation of the book.[183]

All these features of the *Calendar* must have been attractive to Fraunce, especially if Sidney originated or at least encouraged the project of *The Shepherds' Logic*. Sidney's sympathies for Ramism were nurtured by his Huguenot friend Hubert Languet (1518–1581), who in 1572 introduced him to Ramus in Paris shortly before the latter's murder. If the 1581 encounter with Sidney is the genesis of *The Shepherds' Logic*, Fraunce's engagement with Spenser's text was a sustained effort of about seven years, a timespan that saw two new editions of the *Calendar* (1581 and 1586). Fraunce's replacement of classical with vernacular verse had a precedent in Ramus, whose *Dialectique* (1555) put beside Virgil and Ovid poetic examples by, among others, Clément Marot (1496–1544) and the Pléiade poets Pierre Ronsard (1524–85), Joachim du Bellay (1522–60) and Étienne Pasquier (1529–1615). But the focus on a single poet and work and the foregrounding of that work's title in the manual's own name are exclusive features of *The*

[179] Meerhoff, 'Beauty and the Beast', p. 214.
[180] See H. R. Woudhuysen, 'Leicester, Robert Dudley, Earl of', in *The Spenser Encyclopedia*, ed. by A. C. Hamilton (Toronto: University of Toronto Press, 1990), p. 432. Woudhuysen rightly argues that 'him that is the president / Of noblesse and of chivalry' and 'his Honour' would be inappropriate in reference to Sidney (SC, 'To His Book', 3–4, 11, in Brooks-Davies, p. 16).
[181] See Brooks-Davies, pp. 7–8; Wayne Erickson, 'Spenser's Patrons and Publishers', in Richard A. McCabe, *The Oxford Handbook of Edmund Spenser*, pp. 106–24 (pp. 111, 117).
[182] For a summary of the debates of E.K.'s identity and for the case of E.K. as Spenser, aided and inspired by Harvey, see Louise C. Schleiner, 'Spenser's "E.K." as Edmund Kent (Kenned/of Kent): Kyth (Couth), Kissed, and Kunning-Conning', *English Literary Renaissance*, 20 (1990), 374–407, and D. Allen Carroll, 'The Meaning of E.K.', *Spenser Studies*, 20 (2005), 169–81.
[183] In his letter to Harvey of October 1579, the time of the publication of the *Calendar*, Spenser proclaims that 'the twoo worthy gentlemen, Master Sidney and Master Dyer [...] haue me, I thanke them in some vse of familiarity', *The Works of Edmund Spenser: A Variorum Edition*, x: *The Prose Works*, ed. by Rudolf Gottfried (1949), p. 6.

Shepherds' Logic that make Fraunce's attention to poetry in a logic manual unique. Unlike its coetaneous treatises on poetics, namely Sidney's *Defence of Poesy* or William Webbe's *A Discourse of English Poetry* (1586), Fraunce showed no explicit interest in assessing the literary quality of the *Calendar*, in commenting its poetic features or in discussing its authorship. However, by making Spenser's shepherds his titular characters and his sole authorities of logical wisdom, Fraunce placed the relations between poetry and logic at the centre of his project.

The later absorption of the text of *The Shepherds' Logic* into *The Lawyers' Logic* had as a result the demotion of the *Calendar* to an ancillary role. Fraunce cut down the number of instances from Spenser significantly, and attached to each of the poetic examples another from jurisprudence in Law French. He also felt the need to justify before a new readership of jurists the eccentricity of the juxtaposition of poetry and law. In his 'Preface to the Lawyers of England', his earlier logical works are dismissed as 'small and trifling beginnings', and *The Shepherds' Logic* is passingly referred to as an 'easy explication of Ramus his Logic'. Even if the literary training of most of his Inns of Court colleagues would be without question, Fraunce adopted an apologetic tone to justify his Cambridge education and his former commitment to writing a poetic logic. The preservation of the examples from *The Shepherds' Calendar* is therefore presented as a vestige of his former dedication: 'because many love Logic that never learn Law, I have retained those old examples of the new *Shepherds' Calendar* which I first gathered, and thereunto added these also out of our Law books, which I lately collected'.[184] Fraunce's phrasing is remarkable in its substitution of philosophy for poetry as the term that vindicates the presence of Spenser's lines. Moreover, the quotations from the 'new' work are considered an 'old' remnant of his former interests. *The Lawyers' Logic* thus serves a double purpose. On the one hand, it makes up for Fraunce's abandoned idea of a scholarly/poetic logic. On the other, it puts forward a new treatise for lawyers, a project that, in spite of a former tradition ranging from Cicero's *Topica* to contemporary Ramist handbooks like Freige's *Partitiones Iuris* (Basel, 1571) or *Logica Iureconsultorum Libri Duo* (Basel, 1582), he considered odd enough to require justification.[185] His preface's invention of a 'great tenurist' who questions 'that a good scholar should ever prove a good lawyer' reveals his rhetorical strategy: by first putting lawyer and logician at odds, the work is presented as an attempt to undo the apparent paradox of his own trajectory.[186]

Fraunce saw no such oxymoron in a shepherds' logic. The reasons seem clear, as lawyer and shepherd do not bear the same logical relation to their subject. Fraunce's lawyers act as both sources and recipients of logical instruction. As the author affirms in the dedicatory verses, 'I sought for Logic in our Law, and found it as I thought', or, in the Preface, 'our Law is most fit to express the precepts of Logic'.[187] The law provides a corpus of logical examples, and reciprocally logic becomes an aid to law professionals. By contrast, Fraunce's shepherds are allegorical rather than real presences. The dwellers of Spenser's poetic universe and their feigned discourses are transplanted to a new logical environment. *The Shepherds' Logic* is a poetic logic not only because it is a logical treatise with poetic examples, but mainly because it designs a poetic setting, a sort of primordial Arcadian scenario where logic finds, to use a Shakespearean phrase, its own local habitation. Signalling the pastoral mode as the origin of natural reason is Fraunce's most original conception in the early book, and one that is dismissed in *The Lawyers' Logic*.

---

[184] LL, ¶1ᵛ (Appendix I.1, 19–21).
[185] On Ramist logic and law, see Guido Oldrini, 'The influence of Ramus' Method on Historiography and Jurisprudence', in *The Influence of Petrus Ramus*, pp. 215–27.
[186] LL, ¶2ʳ (Appendix I.1, 39–40)
[187] LL, ¶1ᵛ (Appendix I.1, 18).

The dedicatory verses to Edward Dyer anticipate Ramist theory in the form of poetic allegory. Fraunce proceeds by setting the contrast between logic and the other six liberal arts: whereas these are defined (in logical terms) by their relation to one single 'subject', logic's 'stream' has no restrictions to 'flow' along the different forms of knowledge. Logic is therefore the art of arts that Fraunce consistently claims throughout his treatise. From its seat in heaven, Logic supplies a primordial discursive matrix for the rest of the disciplines of knowledge. Logic's 'light' crosses all spaces of human mental activity, '[f]rom King's abode to Palinode, from sheepcote unto star'. Within this range of possibilities, Fraunce's discovery of the 'sheepcote' supplies the ideal space of reasoning that justifies Logic's 'love to simple countryman' — the index to Fraunce's endorsement of the Ramist theory of natural reason.[188] Even before becoming *ars*, logic is a natural ability found universally in the human mind. Consequently, in the first chapter of *The Shepherds' Logic* Fraunce draws on Ramus's early works to advocate a primordial division of logic into *natura* and *ars*, and a further division of the latter into *doctrina* and *usus* (or *exercitatio*), as the two necessary dichotomies previous to the discussion of doctrine's concern with *inventio* and *dispositio*.[189] This conceptual mapping involves the acceptance of natural logic as a prior condition to artificial logic, which remains an art of imitation. In this context, 'the monuments and disputations of excellent authors' are invoked as authoritative illustrations of the principles of doctrine.[190] Literature supplies distinguished repositories of natural reasoning, thus grounding its *auctoritas* on Aristotelian ἀρετή, or excellence. Authority becomes the best antidote against the useless technicalities of scholastic logic. Ramus's classical exemplars were mainly, though not exclusively, poetic. Fraunce takes a step forward in limiting his scope to poetry, to one particular genre and to one particular work. His choice of the 'sheepcote' instils pastoral simplicity to poetic excellence, thus authorizing pastoral poetry as the catalyst for the Ramist conjoining of *natura*, *doctrina* and *usus*.

The theoretical dimension of Fraunce's assemblage of poetry, pastoral and logic needs to be reassessed in the light of modern scholarly approaches to them. Ramist logic employed poetry to illustrate doctrine in use, but was not particularly concerned with poetics. This theoretical gap was addressed by mid twentieth-century scholars. In her encyclopaedic *Shakespeare's Use of the Arts of Language* (1947), Sister Miriam Joseph examined theories of composition (*genesis*) and reading (*analysis*) in sixteenth-century England, and concluded that traditionalist and Ramist theories of discourse showed more fundamental likenesses than differences. Joseph's underlying premise was that the Ramist emphasis on *inventio* and *dispositio* as exclusive operations of logic could be neutralized by considering the figures of speech a derivation of dialectical arguments and procedures of reasoning.[191] For its part, Rosemond Tuve's ground-breaking *Elizabethan and Metaphysical Imagery* (1947) underscored an essentially Ramist character in the sixteenth- and early seventeenth-century mechanics of poetic composition and imagery. In her view, 'Ramist writings do not leave to mere inference and suggestion this conception of the unity of all writing and thinking, grounded as these are in logic. They state the notion boldly and insistently'.[192] Accordingly, poetry's usefulness in proving a rational basis for all discourse justifies the

---

[188] SL, p. 56 (fol. 2ᵛ).

[189] This is in fact the arrangement of Ramus's *Dialecticae institutiones*. See Meerhoff, 'Beauty and the Beast', p. 205.

[190] SL, I.1, 26 (fol. 3ʳ).

[191] Joseph, *Shakespeare's Use of the Arts of Language*, esp. pp. 3–40. As Fraunce did with Spenser, Joseph makes Shakespeare her privileged exemplar for use of the doctrine in order to vindicate both his representative and exceptional character as first and best poet of his age.

[192] Rosemond Tuve, *Elizabethan and Metaphysical Imagery: Renaissance Poetic and Twentieth-Century Critics* (Chicago: The University of Chicago Press, 1947), p. 337.

exemplary role attributed to it by Ramists. Tuve's interest in poetic imagery explains her attention to *inventio* rather than to *dispositio*. The Ramist concept of argument, for its emphasis on the endless '*relatableness*', or to use Fraunce's word, the 'affections' between words and things, favours the search for functional rather than for decorative imagery. This argumentative basis of poetic imagery also justifies a tendency to stylistic balance.[193]

Fraunce's employment of Spenser can be adduced as a valid instance of Tuve's major conclusions. First, the traditional alignment of the pastoral with the middle or low style favours his choice of *The Shepherds' Calendar* as a model of plainness and accuracy of expression, far from rhetorical excesses.[194] Second, his logical analysis of poetry foregrounds arguments that at first sight seem ordinary and commonplace. Thus Hobbinol's complaint about Rosalind:

> Ah faithless Rosalind, and void of grace,
> That art the root of all this ruthful woe.

For Fraunce, this is plainly 'an argument of cause only for explication' — namely, Rosalind's unfaithfulness as the source of the lover's woe.[195] But his manual aspires to more subtle entanglements between poetic expression and accuracy in argument. When Fraunce explains the formal cause, he reminds us that 'the natural forms of things, though they may be conceived by reason, yet they cannot well be uttered by speech'. Yet Spenser's shepherd Cuddy manages to supply 'the accidental and external form together, with some effects of his bullock':

> Seest how brag yond bullock bears,
> So smirk, so smooth, his pricked ears?
> His horns bene as broad as rainbow bent;
> His dewlap as lithe as lass of Kent.
> See how he venteth into the wind:
> Weenest of love is not his mind?[196]

Simple and compared arguments of invention, Fraunce implies, are combined here to depict the bullock's complexion as the formal cause of his love. For its part, poetic language makes the utterance possible by providing the suitable words that make the argument intelligible.

Tuve's theories are seminal to any logical approach to early modern poetry.[197] More recent work on Fraunce's use of Spenser has proposed refinements of her arguments from the

---

[193] Speaking of Renaissance poetic images, Tuve argues that '[t]he nature of their terms might range from the most subtle of abstractions to the most ordinary of daily objects, for their logical function outweighed the old considerations which dictated the terms of 'amplifying imagery', while emphasis upon relations to dialectic impelled poetry toward the middle style and relaxed certain kinds of decorum conventionally observed in the two extreme styles', *Elizabethan and Metaphysical Imagery*, p. 353.

[194] The ascription of pastoral poetry to the middle or low style is an ambiguous issue in classical and Renaissance genre theory. A symptomatic case of this ambivalence is William Scott's treatment of the subject in *The Model of Poesy*. Whereas he first affirms that the pastoral presents 'mean matter in mean style', he later rectifies this by affirming that its 'phrase and style must be the lowest and basest', even if he concedes that 'sometimes Virgil will raise his quill to a higher note', perhaps with the *Georgics* rather than the *Bucolics* in mind (pp. 18, 80). In English, the ambivalence comes partly from the sense of the term 'mean', glossed as 'low', but also as 'middle'. For a discussion that favours the identification of the *Calendar* with the low style and *Colin Clouts Come Home Againe* with the middle style, see Patrick Cheney, 'Spenser's Pastorals: *The Shepheardes Calender* and *Colin Clouts Come Home Againe*', in *The Cambridge Companion to Spenser*, pp. 79–105. Sir Philip Sidney favours that opinion about the *Calendar* when he comments on the 'framing of his style to an old rustic language' (Alexander ed., *'Sidney's Defence of Poesy'*, p. 44). For a conception of the Spenserian middle style as florid, especially in *The Faerie Queene*, see David Scott Wilson-Okanamura, *Spenser's International Style* (Cambridge: Cambridge University Press, 2013).

[195] SL, I.2, 188–90 (fol. 7ᵛ); 'June', 115–16.

[196] SL, I.4, 20–21, 40–47 (fol. 9ᵛ); 'February', 71–76.

[197] A major contestation of Tuve's theories is found in A. J. Smith, 'An Examination of Some Claims for

perspective of recent literary theory. Tamara Goeglein has drawn on semiotics in order to find a semantic resemblance between the discourses of logic and poetry, not in the works of Renaissance poets, but '*within* Ramist dialectic manuals'.[198] For Goeglein, this resemblance is explained by the mimetic quality of the literal language of logic and the figurative language of poetry. Poetry and logic are thus interchangeable discourses.[199] Although Ramism regards poetic language as rhetorical, its ultimate interest in poetry lies in its capacity to exemplify rational precepts. Ramus reduces poetry to a 'linguistic trace of our immaterial mental processes', a Platonic 'ur-text of mental discourse'.[200] Accordingly, Fraunce's Spenserian insertions in *The Lawyers' Logic* function as logical emblems illustrating in a more accessible way the abstract, sometimes abstruse, principles of logical doctrine. Goeglein considers poetry a sort of syllogistic middle term arbitrating the relations between logical doctrine and natural reason.[201] For its part, Edward Armstrong's critique of Goeglein's semiotic approach is grounded on the conviction that Ramist logic 'marks a significant reconfiguration of learning and poetry, the matter that constitutes them, the ends toward which they are directed, and the relationship of each to each'. Armstrong points to the contradictions inherent in *The Shepherds' Calendar* between a humanist poetic voice, conceiving poetry in terms of moral action, and its Ramist commentator, E.K., who undermines the moral dimension of poetry by emphasizing formal issues. This is also the case of Fraunce's use of Spenser in *The Lawyers' Logic*: 'even if the "sparkling" examples of natural reason can be culled from poetry, they will need to be generalized and methodically disposed in order to be understood properly', because logic and not poetry has the ability to unravel and teach poetic truth. For Armstrong, Fraunce supplies the practical side of William Temple's refutation of Sidney's defence of the superiority of poetry: although poetry can exemplify natural reason, the capacities of shaping poetic fictions and of enlightening the meanings of poetic discourse remain the sole prerogative of logic.[202]

Goeglein and Armstrong have stressed the need to clarify Fraunce's somehow cryptic use of Spenser. The interchangeability of poetry with logic, poetry's emblematic easing of the abstruseness of logical precepts, or logic's refutation of poetry's creative and explanatory potentials are suggestive interpretations of Fraunce's conceptual aims. Yet these conclusions are in part the effect of an approach that prioritizes the *The Lawyers' Logic* over *The Shepherds' Logic*. Rather than exploring relations of conflation, substitution or exclusion, *The Shepherds' Logic* sails in the direction of a collaborative enterprise between the arts in which each maintains its own identity. Moreover, and as John C. Adams has argued, English Ramism is an attempt to unite pedagogical innovation with the more traditional ideals of humanist education rather than a

Ramism'. Smith argues that 'Ramists had little to say about verse', mainly because their aim was not 'to establish an especially close relationship between verse and dialectic, but merely to illustrate in the most persuasive manner the dictum that Logic is a general Art' (pp. 353–54).

[198] Tamara A. Goeglein, '"Wherein hath Ramus been so offensious?": Poetic Examples in the English Ramist Logic Manuals', *Rhetorica*, 14 (1996), 73–101 (p. 80).

[199] Goeglein, 'Wherein hath Ramus', p. 87.

[200] Goeglein, 'Wherein hath Ramus', pp. 100–01.

[201] These ideas are later developed in Goeglein, 'Reading English Ramist Books'.

[202] Armstrong, *A Ciceronian Sunburn*, pp. 116, 126, 138. Armstrong's conclusions lead to equating Fraunce's ideas with those of Temple in the commentary to Sidney: 'At fingere Causas, effecta, subjecta, adjuncta, caeteraque argumenta, nihil aliud est quam invenire causas, effecta, subjecta, adjuncta. Quamobrem fictio erit idem quod rei, quae nondum extiterir, inventio. id si ita est, ars fictionis non ad poesin sed ad dialecticam inventionem pertinebit: qua non solum res verae sed etiam fictitiae cogitantur' ('But feigning causes, effects, subjects, adjuncts and all the other arguments, is nothing other than inventing causes, effects, subjects, adjuncts. Therefore, fiction-making will be the same as the invention of something that does not yet exist. But if this is so, then the art of fiction-making will pertain not to poetry, but to dialectical invention, through which are conceived not only true things, but fictions as well'), *William Temple's 'Analysis'*, ed. by Webster, pp. 80–81.

project aiming at the separation of technique from content.[203] In this sense, when Fraunce brings *The Shepherds' Calendar* to the centre of *The Shepherds' Logic*, one should not forget that Spenser's excerpts continue to work as vessels of poetic content. Recently, scholars like Peter Mack or Kees Meerhoff have contended that Ramism made formidable efforts leading to the union of philosophy and eloquence, of reason and discourse.[204] As Meerhoff argues, by putting poetry at the centre of the triad *natura*, *doctrina*, and *usus*, Ramus endowed ancient poetic texts with a triple function. In terms of nature, poetry supplies the universal matrix of logical reasoning. In terms of doctrine, it helps illustrate theoretical principles. In terms of use, it becomes an object for analytical praxis and a model for the composition of new texts.[205]

Use or praxis is crucial to Ramist logical theory in general and to the relations between poetry and logic in particular. Ramism pays special attention to textual analysis — the operation known as *retexere*. This process conveys first a reduction of a passage or of a whole literary text to an argumentative, axiomatic and syllogistic deep structure in order later to delineate its logical *consecutio*, or sequential arrangement in terms of method.[206] Conversely, this transformation of texts into logical arguments, axioms and syllogisms constitutes a source of *inventio* for the genesis of new texts. Analysis and genesis lay the foundation for the practice of literary criticism and literary composition. Fraunce's own ideas about the practical use of logic find their clearest exposition in the tables included in *The Lawyers' Logic*. There Fraunce divided logical exercise into its two 'special' operations of genesis and analysis. For both, he recommended detailed observance of logical procedures leading from invention to disposition, from arguments to method. Specifically for genesis, 'or framing of anything by our own industry', Fraunce recommended translation and imitation of the best authors and subjects in order later to proceed to original composition.[207]

The conscientious mining for arguments, axioms, syllogisms and instances of method finds its neatest illustration in Hobbinol's report of Colin's praise of Elisa in 'April'. Fraunce quotes six excerpts distributed in thirteen examples from these lines in *The Shepherds' Logic*. Thus, he proves that the poetic efficacy of Elisa's praise is sustained by arguments from subject, adjuncts, cause and effects, distribution of general into specials, syllogistic proof of the truth of her perfection, and methodical arrangement of the proofs:

> For our *Calendar*, although shepherds are not wont to bind themselves to any over-strict method in speaking, yet that song of Colin Clout rehearsed by Hobbinol, in 'April', may be a pretty president of others to follow, where he, after a poetical invocation and general proposition of that which he hath in hand, I mean the praises of Elisa, commeth nearer the matter and first putteth down the causes, then the subject and adjuncts of Elisa orderly.[208]

Fraunce's analysis of 'April' not only exemplifies the step-by-step procedures of logical reasoning. It also recommends the *Calendar* as a model for the composition of poetic praises. 'April'

---

[203] See Adams, 'Gabriel Harvey's *Ciceronianus*', p. 552, particularly his critique of the contention that Ramist pedagogical innovations constitute an abandonment of the moral idealism of traditional humanism and its conception of the arts. This last argument is defended in Anthony Grafton and Lisa Jardine, *From Humanism to the Humanities: Education and the Liberal Arts in Fifteenth- and Sixteenth-Century Europe* (Cambridge, MA: Harvard University Press, 1986).

[204] Meerhoff, 'Beauty and the Beast', and 'Précepte et usage: Un Commentaire Ramiste de la 4ᵉ Philippique', in *Autour de Ramus*, pp. 305–70; Mack, 'Ramus and Ramism', and 'Ramus Reading'.

[205] In Meerhoff's own words, '[t]he elegance of Ramist logic proves this in a repetitive manner: all the riches of the literary text, all the devices of oratorical invention celebrate the miracle of human creation', 'Beauty and the Beast', p. 211.

[206] Meerfoff, 'Beauty and the Beast', p. 210.

[207] LL, Ee4ʳ (Appendix I.3, p. 167).

[208] SL, II.18, 40–45 (fol. 26ᵛ). On Fraunce's uses of Spenser's 'April', see Appendix II.

becomes 'a pretty president of others to follow' in its observance of natural forms of reasoning. Moreover, by stressing Spenser's straightforwardness, Fraunce pinpoints the sobriety and decorum of the pastoral style as the hinge joining logic and poetry.

Fraunce's engagement with the pastoral genre was consistent throughout his career. His use of *The Shepherds' Calendar* had a continuation in the quantitative-verse translation and logical analysis of Virgil's Second Eclogue in *The Lawyers' Logic* (1588), and in the quotations from Sidney's *Arcadia* and the eclogues of Garcilaso de la Vega (1501?–36) in *The Arcadian Rhetoric* (1588). Fraunce's other contributions include his translation of Thomas Watson's eleven Latin pastoral elegies *The Lamentations of Amintas* (1587), and the first two parts of *The Countesse of Pembrokes Yuychurch* (1591), which contains a pastoral play, a funeral elegy and a revision of his translation of Virgil. Fraunce expounded his ideas about poetry in another work connected with the pastoral genre, *The Third Part of the Countesse of Pembrokes Yvychurch* (1592). The prose commentary following the first eclogue blends Plato, Aristotle and Sidney to commend 'poetry, a speaking picture, and paynting, a dumbe poetry', as sister mimetic arts representing 'vnder an amyable figure and delightsome veyle' various stages of truth in a sort of Platonic ladder:

> He that is but of a meane conceit, hath a pleasant and plausible narration, concerning the famous exploites of renowmed Heroes, set forth in most sweete and delightsome verse, to feede his rurall humor. They, whose capacitie is such, as that they can reach somewhat further then the external discourse and history, shall finde a morall sence included therein, extolling vertue, condemning vice, euery way profitable for the institution of a practicall and common wealth man. The rest, that are better borne and of a more noble spirit, shall meete with hidden mysteries of naturall, astrologicall, or diuine and metaphysicall philosophie, to entertaine their heauenly speculation.[209]

At their most earthly level, the 'meane conceit' and the 'rurall humor' suggest the shepherd's rustic intellect, content to relish a 'plausible narration' — a phrase that stresses the logical aspiration to reason and truth that Fraunce had attributed to the 'fained' discourses of Spenser's characters in *The Shepherds' Logic*. The ascent to highest levels of interpretation does not take truth away from this primary level of reading.

This poetic ideal is not distant from other conceptions of pastoral poetry formulated in England not long after. Puttenham's refutation in *The Art of English Poesy* (1589) of Scaliger's placing of pastoral as the first of the genres in historical-chronological terms is of relevance to Fraunce's imagination of a logical Arcadia. Puttenham's denial of the first place to the eclogue is argued in terms of the difference between nature and 'artificial poesy'. 'The poet', Puttenham claims, 'devised the eclogue long after the other dramatic poems, not of purpose to counterfeit or represent the rustical manner of loves and communication, but under the veil of homely persons and in rude speeches to insinuate and glance at greater matters'. And yet, eclogues

> should be the first of any other, and before the satire, comedy, or tragedy, because, say they, the shepherds' and haywards' assemblies and meetings, when they kept their cattle and herds in the common fields and forests, was the first familiar conversation, and their babble and talk under bushes and shady trees, the first disputation and contentious reasoning.[210]

---

[209] Fraunce, *The Third Part of the Countesse of Pembrokes Yvychurch*, B1ᵛ–B2ʳ.

[210] George Puttenham, *The Art of English Poesy*, ed. by Frank Whigham and Wayne E. Rebholz (Ithaca: Cornell University Press, 2007) pp. 127–28. See Julius Caesar Scaliger, *Poetices libri septem* (Geneva: Jean Crespin, 1561), I.4, B1ᵛ. An English translation of Scaliger's relevant passages can be consulted in Frederick Morgan Padelford, *Select Translations from Scaliger's Poetics* (New York. Henry Holt, 1905), p. 21.

Pastoral discourse claims primacy by way of nature and not by way of art.[211] Spenser's pastoral *mimesis* will admit further levels of reading, as William Scott acknowledged in the recently discovered *The Model of Poesy* (1599): 'When [...] by discourse and dialogue reduced to shepherdish and rustical imitation either natural, moral, or historical knowledge is delivered, or divine (as I take it is plain in Master Spenser's *Shepheardes Calender* to be meant), it maketh the *pastoral*'.[212] But Fraunce's avoidance of allegorical readings of Spenser circumscribes his focus on pastoral 'discourse and dialogue' to the illustration of 'natural knowledge'. Fraunce must have applauded E.K.'s understanding of Spenser's poetry as a compound of logical and rhetorical virtues in the prefatory epistle to Harvey:[213]

> Not less, I think, deserveth *his wittiness in devising, his pithiness in uttering*, his complaints of love so lovely, his discourses of pleasure so pleasantly, his pastoral rudeness, his moral wiseness, his due observing of decorum everywhere: in personages, in seasons, in matters, in speech, and generally *in all seemly simplicity of handling his matter and framing his words*.[214]

E.K.'s praise signals the four operations that Ramist doctrine recast in the arts of logic and rhetoric:

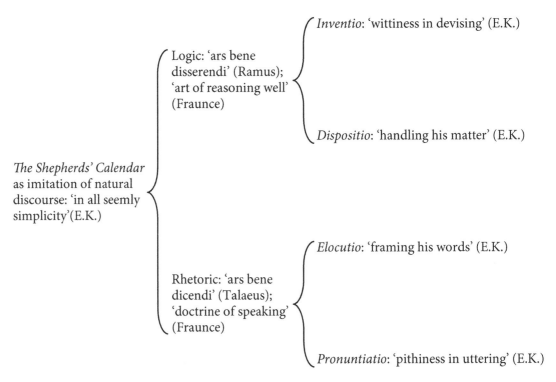

The Shepherds' Logic singles out Spenser's pastoral discourse as a model of the first art, that is, the logical 'devising' of arguments and 'handling' of matter in the 'seemly simplicity' of the shepherds' poetic imitations of the simple man's modes of reasoning, leaving any concern with the operations of rhetoric for a different manual. With the aid of 'the monuments and

---

[211] For Renaissance theories of the pastoral and Spenser's handling of them, see Colin Burrow, 'Spenser's Genres', in *The Oxford Handbook of Edmund Spenser*, ed. by Richard McCabe, pp. 403–19 (pp. 406–09).

[212] William Scott, *The Model of Poesy*, ed. by Gavin Alexander (Cambridge: Cambridge University Press, 2013), p. 21.

[213] On E.K. as a Ramist commentator, see the recent convincing case made by E. Armstrong, *A Ciceronian Sunburn*, especially pp. 42–53.

[214] SC, 'Dedicatory Epistle', in Brooks-Davies, ed., *Edmund Spenser: Selected Shorter Poems*, pp. 18–19, emphasis added.

disputations of excellent authors' — and Spenser's eclogues are elevated to such a category by Fraunce — artificial logic imitates natural reasoning in order to teach it ways toward its improvement:

> [A]rt, which first was but that scholar of nature, is now become the mistress of the same, as it were a table or glass wherein she, seeing and viewing herself, may wash out those spots and blemishes of natural imperfection. For there is no nature so constant and absolute but, by looking and perusing her own force, it may be bettered; no nature so weak and imperfect which by the help of art is not confirmed.[215]

Spenser's pastoral universe is then consonant with Ramist logic in its endorsement of an ideal of natural reasoning as the foundation of all human discourse. As Fraunce made clear in his reflections on poetic method, Spenser's 'April' 'may make us believe that even shepherds, by the light of nature, did, as much as in them lay, express this method in their speeches'.[216] Tuve has argued that Fraunce's Ramist tenet here is 'not that poetry is logically complicated but that logic is natural to poets — as to all other reasoning men'.[217] But Fraunce's meaning is more complex: by being able to shape the discourse of shepherds poetically, Spenser's art helps the reader understand that logical discourse has its origin in that 'light of nature' before and beyond the formalizations of the art of logic. Poetry enables logic in its attempt to explain the unity of all forms of thought and discourse.

The move from *The Shepherds' Calendar* to *The Shepherds' Logic* explains Fraunce's transformation of a pastoral into a logical Arcadia in which the shepherds' discourses are stripped to their barebones. In Fraunce's hands, Spenser's poetic landscape becomes a dialectical theatre made of the arguments of topical logic. This does not make Fraunce a limited reader of Spenser. It simply explains his Ramist programme as a necessary foundation for later and more sophisticated interpretations. In this, Fraunce is hardly the academic logician who, like Temple, proclaimed the absolute priority of logic over poetry in the analysis and refutation of Sidney's *Defence*. An important difference between them should be brought forth here. Temple's reduction of fiction to a prerogative of the logician led him to deny the validity of poetic genres:

> Furthermore, to distinguish kinds of poets through differences in their subjects is no more to be allowed than to create different species of logicians through differences in what they are to explain […] And if anyone were to distribute the logician in this way, he should say that one kind is heroic or tragic, treating matters that are weighty and worthy in their outcome; another is comic, dealing, that is, with lighter personages; another is satiric, inveighing, obviously, against men's vices; another bucolic, holding forth about fields and cattle; another elegiac, weaving amorous things […] But if on the other hand such a distribution of the logician is wrong, your distribution of the poet will still not be good enough. For just as those matters above all are dealt with through the same faculty of the logician […] similarly […] they are all treated together through the same faculty of the poet.[218]

---

[215] SL, I.1, 28–32 (fol. 3ʳ⁻ᵛ).

[216] LL, K3ʳ. This sentence comes in the form of an addition to the above-quoted passage on method in SL, II.18, 41–45 (fol. 26ᵛ). See this Introduction, 208n.

[217] Tuve, *Elizabethan and Metaphysical Imagery*, p. 338.

[218] 'Deinde e subiecti varietate genera poetarum distinguere non magis licet quam e rei explicandae dissimilitudine differentes species dialecticorum efficere […] Equid si quis ita dialecticum distribuat ut dicat alium heroicum esse tragicumve tractantem scilicet res gravissimas & eventu admirabiles: alium Comicum, disserentem nempe de levioribus personis: alium Satyricum, invehentem nimirum in hominum vitia: alium Bucolicum, disputantem videlicet de agro & bove; alium elegiacum, texentem amatoria […] si dialectici ejusmodi distributio vitiosa sit, non erit poetae distributio satis accurata. Nam ut eadem dialectici facultate res illae tractantur […] sic […] eadem tamen poetae facultate tractantur universae', *William Temple's 'Analysis'*, ed. by Webster, pp. 86–87.

For Fraunce, however, the generic differences between those subjects are pertinent to the point of making pastoral poetry the centre of his conception of natural logic and the only source of his examples. In writing a shepherds' logic, Fraunce violates the Ramist *lex iustitiae* and 'puts poetry, as it were, in the house of logical invention, mixing these two disciplines', despite William Temple's advice to the contrary. Fraunce not only acknowledges 'some gift peculiar to poetry' ['aliquo proprio munere poeseos'] that Temple only grants to the dialectician.[219] He goes further by signalling the pastoral as the catalyst of the collaborative enterprise of logic and poetry. The immediate effect is putting logic in the house of literary criticism: Fraunce's dialectical analysis grants Spenser the status of a classic and promotes him as a vernacular model for later pastoral literature in England. Canonizing Spenser's poetic abilities on logical grounds is a substantial achievement of Fraunce, who also claims for himself the status of a literary connoisseur in the eyes of Sidney and Dyer. Others would come later to add to his logical readings more complex moral, historical, or spiritual allegories of the *Calendar*.

Theory and Use: 'Of the Nature and Use of Logic' and 'A Brief and General Comparison between Ramus his Logic and That of Aristotle'

The two shorter essays in the manuscript are theoretical companions to *The Shepherds' Logic*. Although the order of composition of the three pieces may not respond to any intentional plan on Fraunce's part, the sequence beginning with 'Of the Nature and Use of Logic', continuing with 'A Brief and General Comparison of Ramus his Logic with That of Aristotle', and closing with *The Shepherds' Logic* mirrors in content the evolution of Ramus's own work from the earlier *Partitiones dialecticae*, *Dialecticae institutiones* and *Aristotelicae animadversiones* to the French *Dialectique* and the Latin *Dialecticae libri duo*. While the emphasis of the earlier works falls on the discussion of logic as an *ars imitativa*, the importance of exercise, and the need to prune and order the scholastic dialectical programme derived from Aristotle's *Organon*, the later manual draws on these theoretical premises in order to establish the precepts and canons of the reformed doctrine.[220] Fraunce's self-fashioning trajectory as a Ramist thinker is better explained through his two earlier efforts to clarify, however tentatively, the philosophical grounds of his project. As Fraunce completed them while still a student in pursuit of his MA Degree, the two essays offer valuable insights not only into the shaping of his own thought, but also into the scholarly debates about the meaning and the teaching of logic in late sixteenth-century Cambridge.

The title of the first essay, 'Of the Nature and Use of Logic', maps its conceptual scope. Even if doctrine stands centre stage in the teaching of logic, the art itself acquires full meaning through its mimetic relation to natural reasoning and through the purpose of practical use. In terms of Fraunce's own theory of cause, natural reasoning would supply the matter and the natural form, doctrine the artificial form, and use the final cause of logic. Ramus had stated in the *Dialecticae institutiones* that, of the three fields of logic, nature and use were intrinsic to man ('insitae'), while doctrine remained extrinsic and thus to be acquired through teaching ('sola extrinsecus a magistris assumenda est').[221] In accordance with this division, the essay proceeds to the examination of its first part, of which nature supplies the necessary first step. Fraunce's argumentation proceeds, in strictly Ramist terms, by depicting the origin of logic as God's natural imprint upon man's mind. Fraunce defends experience, observation and induction as the procedures that enlighten man's natural reasoning. These are made manifest in the

---

[219] '[Aristoteles] collocat poesin velut in domicilia logicae inventiones violata lege καθ'αὐτο', *William Temple's 'Analysis'*, ed. by Webster, pp. 82–83.

[220] This is the sort of distribution of Ramus's dialectical contents pointed out by Mack. See *Renaissance Argument*, pp. 343–44.

[221] Ramus, *Dialecticae institutiones*, A6ʳ.

authoritative exemplars of the classics. In contrast with these, the scholastic derivations of dialectic are unnecessary corruptions of the art. Fraunce accuses the scholastics of having hoarded the art of logic in order to keep it for their own consumption, thus making it odious and inaccessible for everyday use or for practical application in other disciplines. The comparison between the Aristotelians and two proverbial gluttons constitutes one of the few humorous moments in Fraunce's works. Against such 'monkish devices', Fraunce propounds that we seek the examples of true logic in a scale that ranges from the unscholarly, intuitive reasoning of countrymen when dealing with their harvest to the discoursing of excellent men like Xenophon's Cyrus, Homer's Ulysses and Nestor, Plato's Socrates, or Livy's Menenius Agrippa. Fraunce's ladder of excellence not only has the advantage of keeping for logic the role of an art of arts, cutting across all disciplines of human knowledge. It also reserves for those on the highest step of the Platonic ladder the exemplary role in the exposition of doctrine. In orthodox Ramist fashion, Fraunce defends the authority of classical literature as the mediating discourse between artificial precept and natural reasoning. And thus he paves the way for the promotion of Spenser's pastoral poetry to its exclusive exemplary role in *The Shepherds' Logic*: its combination of simplicity and excellence would later situate the pastoral mode at both ends of the ladder.

Example also supplies the link between the two concerns of this first essay, justifying the move from nature to use. Fraunce briefly sketches genesis and analysis as the two sides of logic's 'double practice'. Doing and undoing, composition of one's own work and examination of previous models, must guide the student's practical exercises in all aspects of the art, from invention's arguments to disposition's axioms, syllogisms and method. Fraunce's advice replicates his former opposition between natural reasoning and abstruse scholasticism. Following nature's counsel, *usus* must privilege truth, sobriety and elegance over the 'straight forms and rigorous rules' of scholastic technicalities, especially in what concerns syllogistic reasoning. The Ramist theory of use is conceived as the antidote against a long history of the abuse of logic.

Although 'Of the Nature and Use of Logic' does not contain an overt dedication, Sidney is undoubtedly that person who 'desireth to hear' and 'deserveth to have', as the Preface to *The Lawyers' Logic* and the short Latin treatise that is the basis of this essay make clear. The latter contains a lavish epistle in which the young student offers Sidney not only his present work, but the upcoming fruits of his literary labour.[222] Fraunce, whose Ramist investigations had been encouraged by an enthusiastic Sidney, declares his allegiance to the Ramist cause with the tact of the humble scholar seeking his patron's protection and recognition. He thus avoids too categorical statements that might importune his reader's opinions or tastes. Fraunce translates from his earlier Latin essay a restrained pronouncement of Ramism over which litotes presides:

> I love Plato, I like Aristotle, and Ramus always I cannot reprehend. If there be anything either good in Plato, or profitable in Aristotle, I take it by their leave. I thank them for that I take. But if Ramus and the rest amend that which they began, I am not either so unthankful toward these as not to accept their pains well employed, or so injurious to nature as to think her so beneficial or rather prodigal in over-liberally lashing out her gift upon Aristotle only, as that she should leave nothing to bestow upon others.[223]

---

[222] Fraunce's veiled mention of his patron in the abridged English version contrasts with the lavish dedication in the Latin essay: 'Juveni ornatissimo / Maecenati optimo, Curiali absolute / Philippo Sidneio / revera Φιλίππῳ / A.F. S.P.D. [Salutem plurimam dicit]', Rawlinson, fol. 1ʳ. I quote from Moore Smith's partial transcriptions of the manuscript in his 'Introduction', in *Victoria*, p. xxviii.

[223] 'Of the Nature and Use of Logic', 16–21 (fol. 29ʳ). 'Platonem admiror, amo Aristotelem, Ramum vbique non reprehendo: si quid vel verum habeat Plato, vel probatum Aristoteles, assumo: gratias habeo Platoni maximas, Aristoteli non minores. Quod si Ramus meliora protulerit, non sum ita vel Ramo ingratus vt illius beneficia non agnoscam, vel naturae iniquus eam vt existimem omnes sapientiae suae thesauros in vnicum Aristotelem ita coniecisse, nihil vt reliquerit, quod alijs largiatur', Rawlinson, fol. 4ʳ, transcribed in Moore Smith, 'Introduction', in *Victoria*, p. xxxi.

If Ramism is to be a vehicle of access to Sidney, the efficacy of such an instrument still has to be confirmed.

The relation between the Latin treatise and the English abridgement would deserve a more detailed explanation than can be offered here. Suffice it to say that Fraunce at times proceeds by translation or paraphrase, at others by abridgement of an argument, and at others by referring the reader to those sections of the original that he has decided to omit. This latter method is particularly significant in Fraunce's treatment of practical examples of the use of logic. Hence his exercise of genesis in invention out of Sturm's *Nobilitas literata* and of analysis in invention through Cicero's *De amicitia*, which, in spite of their omission from the English essay, were reused in *The Lawyers' Logic* as appendixes to Book I.[224]

The second piece, 'A Brief and General Comparison of Ramus his Logic with That of Aristotle', contains in its full title an overt dedication 'to the Right Worshipful his very good Master and Patron, Master Philip Sidney'. The term 'Master' in the dedication reveals the original composition to be before January 1583, the date when Sidney was knighted. A correction of Sidney's title from 'Master' to 'Sir' would have been expected in the manuscript, but this circumstance seems to have passed unnoticed to the author or the scribe. Fraunce's complaint in the closing paragraph about its hasty composition during a country stay, away from his Cambridge books, led Moore Smith to surmise that the essay had been written during a vacation in his native Shrewsbury.[225]

The academic context of this essay has been discussed in earlier sections of this introduction. Fraunce's more than likely caricature of the diatribe between the 'obstinate Aristotelian' Everard Digby and the 'methodical Ramist' William Temple allows him to appear before Sir Philip Sidney not so much as a 'determiner' but as 'a plain interpreter', leaving the arbitrating role to his patron. As in the previous essay, Fraunce's Ramist allegiances are toned down under a veil of neutrality: 'as I never name Ramus without some reverence, so I always speak of Aristotle with admiration'.[226] And yet, Fraunce's attack would have been clear to his readers. Fraunce fashions a bitter dialogue between his two protagonists, and does not spare a harsh introductory remark: 'the rudeness of these wailing and wrangling sophisters' exempts the author from all responsibility for the tone of the dialogue, claiming for himself an equidistance and temperance whose aim is Sidney's favour. It is ironic that three years later the orthodoxy of the Ramist sophister, if we can identify William Temple behind this caricature, would promote him to the position of personal secretary of Fraunce's lifelong protector.

The dialogue registers the divided opinions in late sixteenth-century Cambridge about Ramism and its pertinence to the study of the arts. The Aristotelian condemns Ramus's reduction of the *Organon* and the consequent impoverishment of the arts curriculum. His complaint is also launched at the Ramists' disrespect for the medieval and modern scholastics, and his brief but thorough survey of Aristotle's *Organon* is meant as a plea for the traditional approach to the study of dialectic.[227] The Aristotelian's main theoretical standpoint is the distinction of three different modes of reasoning: apodictic or necessary, used for science; topical, dialectical or probable, concerned with opinion; and sophistic, or fallacious. This division justifies the arrangement of the *Organon* into six books, one of the main reasons for Ramist attacks and a point in need of tenacious defence:

[224] LL, Y1ᵛ–Aa1ᵛ; Rawlinson, fols 8ᵛ–12ʳ.
[225] 'A Brief and General Comparison', 278 (fol. 36ʳ). See Moore Smith, 'Introduction', in *Victoria*, p. xxxii. This would make the summer of 1582 a probable date of composition.
[226] 'A Brief and General Comparison', 9–10 (fol. 32ʳ).
[227] On the prevalence of Aristotle and the changes in the sixteenth-century approach to dialectic at the English universities, see Mack, *Elizabethan Rhetoric*, pp. 55–57. Useful comparative tables of the Aristotelian and Ramist curricula are found in Mack, 'Ramus and Ramism', pp. 10–12.

What is order, if this be not method? Or what is method, if this be out of order? This hath Aristotle observed in his *Organon*, and this have his scholars observed by imitation, beginning at the least and so by little and little ascending to the greatest.[228]

The case for Aristotelian order is controversial, as it involves the defence of an inductive method, from the particular to the general, in opposition to Ramus's defence of a mode of exposition that proceeds from the general to the particular.

The Ramist's reply is a point-by-point refutation of the Aristotelian's speech, first in diminishing the philosophical authority of those invoked by his antagonist, and then in dismantling the tenets of Aristotelianism. Ramus's *Aristotelicae animadversiones*, in its 1543 version or in a later rewriting, is behind the content and aggressive tone of a speech which might also bear the trace of Temple's own writings against Digby.[229] The Ramist's speech becomes an endorsement of Ramist logic, insofar as it exposes the disarray and excesses in Aristotle and his followers. Thus, he first questions the priority of syllogistic reasoning when applied to the threefold division into apodictic, dialectical and sophistic. Instead, a single art of logic proceeding from invention to disposition needs to be advanced. This new art will involve a pruning and redistribution of Aristotelian terms, predicables, antepredicaments, predicaments and postpredicaments into a reasonable number of places or arguments of invention. As to disposition, the elimination of conversion, reduction and equipollence in the new system must result in more simplified modes and figures for syllogisms. Finally, the elenchs, or fallacies, should be removed from logic, as the new art is concerned with truth only, leaving no place for sophistical reasoning. In sum, Ramism advocates a streamlined model not on grounds of philosophical banality, but in light of a *lex iustitiae* that will keep within logic what exclusively belongs to it, and will devolve to the other arts what is legitimately theirs.

If the logic curriculum is certainly one axis around which 'A Brief and General Comparison' revolves, the other is the figure of Ramus himself. Ramus had been dead for a decade when Fraunce wrote a piece that perfectly registers the two sides of his legacy. For the Aristotelian, Ramus is the perpetrator of a doctrine that is 'six leaves long, and eight days' labour', an art that allows cobblers and carters to pass for reputable philosophers. If Ramus began his *Aristotelicae animadversiones* by praising Prometheus as the discoverer of a philosophical fire that Aristotle and his followers had extinguished, Fraunce's Aristotelian retorts by equating Ramus's scholarly endeavours with the follies of Icarus and Phaeton.[230] Conversely, the Ramist presents his master as the true follower of Aristotle, the one who, by pruning his books and eradicating the excesses of his alleged followers, has 'perfited' his work and restored order to the rather chaotic arrangement of the *Organon*, thus reinstating a dignity which Aristotle's alleged defenders had damaged.[231] A few years later, Christopher Marlowe's memorable staging of the murder of Ramus in *The Massacre at Paris* (1593) would put in verse these same arguments in favour and against the St Bartholomew martyr:

RAMUS   O good my lord,
Wherein hath Ramus been so offensious?
GUISE   Marry, sir, in having but a smack in all,
And yet didst never sound anything to the depth.
Was it not thou that scoff'dst the *Organon*,
And said it was a heap of vanities?

---

[228] 'A Brief and General Comparison', 59–62 (fol. 32ᵛ).
[229] See 'A Brief and General Comparison', 33n.
[230] 'A Brief and General Comparison', 38–40 (fol. 32ᵛ). For Ramus's use of the Prometheus myth see *Aristotelicae animadversiones*, A2ʳ–B1ᵛ. A commentary of this passage can be found in Ong, *Ramus, Method*, pp. 172–73.
[231] 'A Brief and General Comparison', 158–61 (fol. 34ʳ).

He that will be a flat dichotomist,
And seen in nothing but epitomies,
Is in your judgement thought a learned man [...]
RAMUS   [...] I knew the *Organon* to be confus'd,
And I reduc'd it to a better form:
And this for Aristotle will I say,
That he that despiseth him can ne'er
Be good in logic or philosophy;
And that's because the blockish Sorbonnists
Attribute as much unto their works,
As to the service of the eternal God.[232]

Also in dialogic form, Fraunce's essay is the precedent for a longer list of later portraits in popular literature of one of the most controversial figures of Renaissance learning.[233]

The Text and the Present Edition

The text of *The Shepherds' Logic* and its two accompanying essays is preserved in MS Add 34361 at the British Library. The manuscript has 36 leaves in folio size. Moore Smith's description of the manuscript in 1906 stated that 'it is a vellum cover, the pages are ruled round the margin, and unnumbered', while McCormick, who did not inspect the original, pointed out in 1969 that the folios were numbered on the upper right margin of the recto sides.[234] The leaves are actually numbered by pencil, so numbers must have been added after Moore Smith's examination. The first leaf is blank, and the second (2ʳ⁻ᵛ) contains the title page on the recto side, and a 14-line dedicatory poem in iambic pentameters, distributed in seven couplets on the verso side, and dedicated to Edward Dyer. These two pages are presumably in Fraunce's own hand, as inferred by Henry Moore Smith after comparison of their calligraphy with Fraunce's holograph in Rawlinson MS 345.1. The rest of the leaves are distributed as follows:

3ʳ–28ᵛ: *The Shepherds' Logic*.
29ʳ–31ᵛ: 'Of the Nature and Use of Logic'.
32ʳ–36ʳ: 'A Brief and General Comparison of Ramus his Logic with that of Aristotle, to the Right Worshipful his very Good Master and Patron, Master Philip Sidney'.

These leaves are copied in a different handwriting, a court hand that is neater in the earlier than in the last pages. The disposition of the text of the *The Shepherds' Logic* observes the arrangement into chapters of a Ramist manual. Each of them generally contains a first expository section in which precepts are defined and concepts classified. This section, generally but not always, uses larger margin indentations. This is followed by the Spenser quotations, also marked by a different indentation. A section of commentaries of key concepts usually ensues: these concepts are marked as entries by closing round parentheses.

---

[232] Christopher Marlowe, *The Massacre at Paris*, in *The Complete Plays*, ed. by Mark Thornton Burnett (London: J. M. Dent, 1999), 9.24–53. For useful commentaries of this scene in relation to Ramism, see Emma Annette Wilson, 'Method in Marlowe's *Massacre at Paris*', *Renaissance Papers 2011*, ed. by Andrew Shifflett and Edward Gieskes (Rochester, NY: Camden House, 2012), pp. 41–52, and Knight, 'Flat Dichotomists and Learned Men', pp. 47–49, 55–60.
[233] On these representations of Ramus, see Feingold, 'English Ramism', pp. 162–68, and Knight, 'Flat Dichotomists and Learned Men', pp. 61–66.
[234] 'Introduction', in Moore-Smith, ed., *Victoria*, p. xvi; McCormick, p. 1.

This edition of *The Shepherds' Logic* and its two companion essays takes MS Add 34361 as its copy text. However, and this applies especially to *The Shepherds' Logic*, I have not provided merely an edited transcription of the original manuscript, which has been collated with relevant passages of *The Lawyers' Logic*, as well as with McCormick's unpublished, old-spelling edition. The result is a text that emends some errors in the manuscript on grounds of a better reading in *The Lawyers' Logic* or in McCormick. The comparison of Fraunce's text with its Latin sources when a reading is doubtful has likewise resulted in some emendations of a manuscript reading. I have also incorporated several passages from *The Lawyers' Logic* to the text of *The Shepherd's Logic* in the form of bracketed additions. These additions speculate on the possibility that Fraunce could have incorporated them into a final or ideal version of *The Shepherds' Logic*. The most important additions are examples from *The Shepherds' Calendar* used in the latter published work, but not in the manuscript. When additions seem too intrusive or disruptive, but still relevant to Fraunce's idea of *The Shepherds' Logic*, I have included them in footnotes and, exceptionally, in Appendix I.2 (the Paris example). Other texts in Appendix I provide relevant information about the composition of *The Shepherds' Logic* (I.1), Ramist tabulations clarifying important concepts (I.3), and Fraunce's notable translation of Virgil's Second Eclogue and his Ramist analysis.

This edition presents the text in modernized spelling and punctuation. I have newly transcribed the text using the manuscript and the facsimile edition, and compared the results with McCormick's text. The draft of my own (unpublished) semidiplomatic transcription has been the basis for the modernization. An old-spelling transcription/edition can be consulted in McCormick. The decision to modernize the spelling is in consonance with other recent editions of early modern treatises of rhetoric and poetics. More specifically, Frank Whigham and Wayne E. Rebholz's edition of Puttenham's *The Art of English Poesy* (2007), and Gavin Alexander's edition of the manuscript of William Scott's *The Model of Poesy* (2013), have guided my reasons to proceed as I have done with Fraunce's spelling and punctuation. Whigham and Rebholz's idea of an intended reader that can range from the specialist to the beginning graduate student presides over the editorial decisions adopted here.[235]

Punctuation is mostly editorial, and variants are not recorded in the Textual Notes. The difficulties of adapting early modern rhetorical and non-standarized punctuation to present-day syntactic punctuation are great, and I hope to have produced satisfactory solutions for a readable and reliable text. Paragraphing is frequently editorial, although I have respected the manuscript's frequent use of short paragraphs, especially when these provide definitions, classifications and principles at the beginning of each chapter, following Ramus's technique. McCormick's choices in punctuation and paragraphing, although frequently different from mine, have been extremely useful. I have also regularized book and chapter headings and titles.

Fraunce's spelling has been consistently modernized. In the process of editing the text, the publication of Gavin Alexander's edition of *The Model of Poesy* made me aware of similar problems and similar solutions in his text, so his editorial policy has been inspiring in many cases. In modernizing the spelling of words I have followed the *Oxford English Dictionary*. When the manuscript has two similar forms for the same word, as *diverse* and *divers*, I have chosen the most ususal (*diverse*). When the manuscript uses two spelling forms for one word, such as *definition/difinition*, *description/discription*, these have been regularized to the modern standard, in accordance with *OED* (the first of the pair, in these two cases). If *OED* has a separate entry for an archaic form, the manuscript form has been kept, if identical to *OED*, or regularized to that *OED* form: this is the case of *appliable, excellency, fallation* (Ms 'fallacian' and 'fallacion'),

---

incontinency, *insolency*, *unorderly*, or *satisfised* (Ms 'satisfacied'). Where a form is reported in *OED* as a historical spelling, but that form embodies a different understanding of the word's etymology or sound, then that form is preserved: such is the case of *connexion*, *flower delice*, *mervail*, or *perfit* (and its derivates), among others. Capitalized words in Ms have been silently regularized to modern use, with the exception of 'Logic' (Ms 'Logike') and other nouns designating arts or sciences ('Grammar', 'Rhetoric', 'Arithmetic', etc.).

I have regularized the spelling and italicized words which the manuscript gives in Latin or Greek. For Latin, I have followed the *Oxford Latin Dictionary* (1698 edn). For Greek, I have used Liddell and Scott's *A Greek-English Lexicon* (1883). Only exceptionally does the manuscript transliterate Greek words, and only in those cases I have given a word in transliterated form.

Modernization also affects all the texts from *The Lawyers' Logic* added to the main text, or in the form of footnotes, appendixes and quotations. I have used the digitalized EEBO copy listed in the Short Title Catalogue as STC 11344 as my copy text, although I have consulted other copies. The rest of early modern texts quoted from pre-1660 editions are given in their original spelling.

In addition to the difficult decision of presenting a manuscript in modern spelling, the most problematic point in this respect has been in regard to Spenser's texts. Due to its deliberately archaic linguistic usages and its etymologies in flux, Spenser's poetry is almost always excluded from present-day editorial preferences for editing Renaissance poetry in modern spelling. The very idea of spelling the title *The Shepherds' Calendar* instead of the original *The Shepheardes Calender* is extremely odd for the early modern scholar. But, for the sake of consistency, the treatment of Spenser's text should be the same as Fraunce's. My reading of the work's title as *The Shepherds' Calendar*, not *The Shepherd's Calendar*, determines my understanding of Fraunce's titles as *The Shepherds' Logic*, not *The Shepherd's Logic*, and consistently *The Lawyers' Logic*.[236] The only modern-spelling critical edition of *The Shepherds' Calendar*, Douglas Brooks-Davies's, has been very engaging and useful. I subscribe point by point to the brief section 'Why modernise Spenser' in his introduction, especially the claim that 'it is actually with an unmodernised text that we miss the force of the archaisms and dialect words [...] Whereas, if an editor modernises while leaving these forms as presented in the original, old spelling text [...], they stand out as the signals Spenser intended them to be'.[237] While this is the procedure adopted here, I have not followed Brooks-Davies's text for two reasons: first, some of his choices in modernizing certain words, especially in his use of hyphens, are not adopted here; second, and most important, while Brooks-Davies's copy text is obviously Q_1, mine must be necessarily the manuscript of *The Shepherds' Logic*, and occasionally *The Lawyers' Logic*. Fraunce's texts sometimes alter the readings of Spenser's quartos, often for purposes of emendation, even of modernization of an archaism. A revealing case is the manuscript's 'glitter and' instead of Spenser's present participle 'glitterand'. In those cases, unless specified in the footnotes, I have always reverted Fraunce's readings to those in the quartos. I have also regularized shepherds' names when spelled in more than one form. In the Textual Notes I have offered a collation of the Spenser passages in *The Shepherds' Logic* with the first two quartos of *The Shepherds' Calendar* (Q_1 and Q_2, or simply Q when the readings of the two quartos are identical), as well as with *The Lawyers' Logic*, McCormick's unpublished edition of *The Shepherds' Logic*, and Brooks-Davies's modern-spelling

---

[236] In reading Spenser's title thus, I follow Brooks-Davies, and differ from other scholars like Claire McEachern, who consistently spells *The Shepherd's Calendar*. See 'Spenser and Religion', in *The Oxford Handbook of Edmund Spenser*, ed. by Richard A. McCabe, pp. 30–47. The facsimile edition of Fraunce's work has *The Shepherd's Logic* as its title.

[237] 'Introduction', in Brooks-Davies, ed., *The Shorter Poems of Edmund Spenser*, p. 2.

edition of *The Shepherds' Calendar*. I quote directly from Brooks-Davies in those cases where I provide a text of the *Calendar* that is not given in the manuscript or in *The Lawyers' Logic*.

All of Fraunce's quotations of, and references to, *The Shepherds' Calendar* are catalogued in Appendix II. These include the passages in *The Shepherds' Logic* and/or *The Lawyers' Logic*. Catalogue numbering follows the order of occurrence of these quotes in *The Shepherds' Calendar*, from the preliminary poem 'To His Book' to 'December'. Fraunce often uses a quote or refers to the same passage more than once: in those cases, either of repetition of a quote or of partial coincidence of lines, the repeated passages are given the same number in the catalogue and are differentiated by subscript letters (i.e., lines 17–18 of 'May' are quoted twice, so these two occurrences are listed as 34_a and 34_b). The catalogue also contains the locations of these quotes by referring to book, chapter and folio number of *The Shepherds' Logic* (SL), and book, chapter and signature of *The Lawyers' Logic* (LL). Differences between Fraunce's uses of Spenser in his two treatises can be checked in the catalogue. Italicized references in the catalogue indicate my insertion in the text of this edition of a quotation that is not in the original manuscript. I have also added in my text parenthetical citations of eclogue, line number and catalogue number.

Fraunce's treatment of his Renaissance Latin sources involves literal translation, abridgement or paraphrase, whether acknowledging or not his debts. I have recorded all the sources that I have been able to track down in the footnotes. In these, references to Ramus's *Dialecticae libri duo* seldom include the text in Ramus/Piscator, unless it is necessary to prove some point. When I quote from the commentaries of Ramus (Piscator, Beurhaus and others), I usually include the Latin text from which Fraunce translates. If Fraunce gives a distant paraphrase of these texts, then I provide both Latin text and my own literal translation. Editorial treatment of these Latin texts has been minimal: I have regularized *v/u* and *i/j* to modern standards, and expanded the ampersand to 'et'. Sixteenth-century Latin texts quoted from other present-day editions have been obviously left unaltered. For classical texts, and their translations, I have used, unless otherwise noted, the editions in the Loeb Classical Library. To the usual standards for citing classical texts, I have added page numbers in the Loeb volumes.

Appendix III presents a comparative Table of Contents of *The Shepherds' Logic, The Lawyers' Logic* and Ramus's *Dialecticae libri duo* as edited by Piscator in 1580–81. This table guides the reader to a better understanding of Fraunce's revisions and evolving logical thought, some aspects of which have been dealt with in this Introduction.

Finally, the Glossary accounts for unusual and archaic words both in Fraunce's text and Spenser's examples. The final Bibliography includes a complete list of works cited throughout this edition.

THE SHEPHERDS' LOGIC

The Shepherds' Logic,

Containing the precepts of that art put down by Ramus. Examples fet° out of *The Shepherds' Calendar*. Notes and expositions collected out of Beurhusius, Piscator, Master Chaderton and diverse others.[1] Together with two general discourses, the one touching the praise and right use of Logic, the other concerning the comparison of Ramus his Logic with that of Aristotle.

To the Right Worshipful Master Edward Dyer.[2]

---

[1] **Ramus**] On the life and career of Pierre de la Ramée, or Petrus Ramus (1515–72), see Introduction, pp. 4–8. **Beurhusius**] Friedrich Beurhaus, or Fridericus Beurhusius (1536–1609), was a German theologian and logician. His defence of Ramist logic was published in England in three parts between 1581 and 1583. **Piscator**] Johannes Fischer, Lat. Piscator (1546–1625), was a reformed theologian and pedagogue. His *In P. Rami Dialecticam Animadversiones* (London, 1581) records his agreements and disagreements with Ramus, and is the principal source of *The Shepherds' Logic*. On his identity, see Walter J. Ong, 'Johannes Piscator: One Man or a Ramist Dichotomy?', *Harvard Library Bulletin*, 8 (1954), 151–62. **Master Chaderton**] Laurence Chaderton (1536–1640) lectured on classical languages and Ramist logic at Christ's College, Cambridge (1568–84), and was later the first Master of Emmanuel College (1584–1622). He took part in the translation of the King James Bible (1611).
[2] **Master Edward Dyer**] Edward Dyer (1543–1607), English poet and courtier, closely allied with the Sidneys since the 1570s. On the work's dedication, see Introduction, pp. 15, 22–25.

[2ᵛ]   Some arts we bind to some one kind of subject severally,°
As this to count, and that to mount above the crystal sky,
To measure land with skilful hand, to frame or file the tongue,
Or to delight the weary sprite with sweet and pleasant song.[1]
But Logic's light doth shine outright: her streams do flow so far
From Kings' abode° to Palinode,° from sheepcote° unto star,
No reason then why monkish men[2] should keep her from abroad
Of idle fools, oppressed in schools, and always overtrod.
By this we preach, by this we teach; she in the heaven sits,
10 Yet shepherd's swain° doth not disdain, but meekly him admits.
That this is true, lo here: a new and fresh logician,
Who minds to prove what is her love to simple countryman
By those that keep in field their sheep, a *Shepherds' Logic* framed;
So be it aught,° or be it naught,° the less cause to be blamed.

     Your Worship's, most humbly to be commanded,
                       Abraham Fraunce.[3]

---

[1] **Some arts […] pleasant song**] The other six liberal arts besides logic — arithmetic, astronomy, geometry, grammar, rhetoric and music.
[2] **monkish men**] scholastic philosophers.
[3] **Abraham Fraunce**] These couplets in rhymed fourteeners and the title-page are in Fraunce's hand in Ms (Moore Smith, 'Introduction' in *Victoria*, p. xxiii). See also Introduction, p. 27, on the content of this poem.

BOOK I: OF INVENTION

CHAPTER 1

∽

What Logic Is

Logic is an art of reasoning well.¹

Λόγος in Greek signifieth reason. Of *Λόγος* is derived this word *λόγικη*, which, albeit it is an adjective and must have some such like word as 'art', 'science' or 'faculty' to be adjoined unto it as his substantive, yet it is substantively taken and used in Latin, as also in our English tongue, the substantive for briefness being omitted, as Piscator noteth.² Sturmius and some others derive this word 'Logic' from *Λόγος*, and *Λόγος* betokeneth° 'speech' or 'talk',³ whose opinion, although the other name of this art (which is *διαλεκτική, ἀπό τοῦ διαλέγεσθαι*,⁴ 'to speak' or 'talk') do in some respect° seem to confirm, yet for that the chief or rather whole force° and virtue of Logic consisteth in reasoning, not in talking, and because reasoning may be without talking, as in meditation and consultation with a man's self. As also for that this derivation is most appliable°
10 and convenient to our English word 'reasoning', I hold it as most significant.

So an art] An art, as Lucian doth define it, is nothing else but a collection, or, as it were, a body of certain precepts which are practised and used for some profitable end and purpose in man's life.⁵ Which definition of his excludeth all idle inventions of some monkish brains, which have either defaced the right use of liberal arts, as in Logic quiddities,° formalities,° modals,° suppositions,° and such like, or perverted good manners, as arts of loving, magic, quaffing,°⁶ with the rest of that heathenish rabble.°

---

¹ **Logic [...] well]** 'Dialectica est ars bene disserendi', Ramus/Piscator, I.1, A6^r.

² **this word *λόγικη* [...] noteth]** 'Vocabula haec, *διαλεκτική* et *λόγικη*, sua natura adiectiva sunt: sed usurpantur substantiva: eo quod brevitatis studio substantivum omittitur: quod est *δύναμις* [faculty], vel *ἐπιστήμη* [science], vel *τέχνη* [art]', Piscator, I.1, A6^r.

³ **Sturmius [...] 'talk']** 'Est autem ita nominata, quod artificiosae et subtilis orationis viam demonstret ac patefaciat' ('Moreover, it is thus named because it can show and disclose the manner of an artful and subtle speech'), Sturm, *Partitionum*, B1^v. Johannes Sturm, or Sturmius (1507–89), is a crucial figure of pre-Ramist dialectic. On his thought and influence see Ong, *Ramus, Method*, pp. 232–36.

⁴ **διαλεκτική, ἀπό τοῦ διαλέγεσθαι]** literally, 'dialectic, from "to speak"'. See Piscator, I.1, A6^r: 'Caeterum *διαλεκτική* dicta est *περί τὸ διαλέγεσθαι*, id est a colloquendo'.

⁵ *So an art* **[...] man's life]** '*Est ars*] Dialecticam esse artem, probant vulgo ex artis definitione quam tradit Lucianus his verbis [...]: Ars est veluti corpus doctrinae, constans praeceptionibus exerceri solitis ad utilem aliquem in vita finem', Piscator, I.1, A6^v. See Lucian 'The Parasite', 4, Loeb III: pp. 246–47. **Lucian]** The Assyrian-born Greek writer Lucian of Samosata (*c.* 120–200 AD) was the author of about eighty satiric dialogues and treatises on issues as varied as religion, ethics and politics. His work was highly influential in Renaissance England.

⁶ **arts of loving, magic, quaffing]** Literary considerations of love as an art refer back to the Ovidian tradition of the *ars amatoria*. Fraunce's complaint about the Renaissance revival of the occult sciences or *artes magicae* as

It is said here that Logic is an art, to distinguish artificial Logic from natural Logic. Artificial Logic is gathered out of diverse examples of natural Logic, which is that engraven gift and faculty of wit and reason shining in the particular discoursing of several° men, whereby they both invent and orderly dispose, thereby to judge of that they have invented. This, as it is to no man given in full perfection, so diverse have it in sundry measure. And because the true note and token resembling nature must be esteemed by the best and most excellent natures, therefore the precepts of artificial Logic both first were collected, and always must be conformable to these sparks of natural reason, not lurking in the obscure headpieces° of one or two loitering friars, but manifestly appearing in the monuments° and disputations of excellent authors.[7] And then is this of art most certain than that of nature, because of many particulars in nature a general and infallible constitution of Logic in art is put down. So that art, which first was but that scholar of nature, is now become the mistress of the same, as it were a table or glass wherein she, seeing and viewing herself, may wash out those spots and blemishes | of natural imperfection. For there is no nature so constant and absolute but, by looking and perusing her own force,° it may be bettered; no nature so weak and imperfect which by the help of art is not confirmed.[8]

Of reasoning] This our English word of reasoning is more proper and fit to express the nature of Logic than either that other word of disputing, derived from *disputare*, or the like, as *disserere* and *docere*,[9] used of Cicero,[10] Ramus, and Melanchton[11]— although I know that Beurhusius standeth in defence of those words used of Ramus,[12] and I am not much to mislike them in respect of any other Latin words, yet not altogether to compare them with this our English word. For the word 'disputing', which cometh of *disputare*, it is metaphorical, as Varro reporteth, and so is *disserere*, the one being borrowed of the vine master, the other fet° from the sower. For as the first cutteth off superfluous branches in his vines, which is properly *disputare*, so the other disperseth the seed in diverse places, and not confusedly throweth all in one heap, which is the natural signification of this word *disserere*.[13] Now, because the Logician cutteth off all idle and

[3ᵛ]

---

inimical to reason and the *artes liberales* is also patent. In relation to 'quaffing', or drinking, a veiled reference to Vincentius Opsopoeus's *De arte bibendi libri tres* (Nuremberg, 1536) has been noted by McCormick, p. 59.

[7] **It is said […] excellent authors**] The invective against monasticism and scholasticism excepted, Fraunce's views of natural and artificial logic adapt Ramus, *Dialecticae institutiones*, A2ʳ–A3ᵛ.

[8] **And then […] not confirmed**] Fraunce partly adapts and partly translates Ramus's discussion of the art of logic as a picture of natural reasoning, and therefore as an imitation of nature: 'Quamobrem summa diligentia, ut Apelles Alexandrum picturus, omnes ei partes, partiumque proprietates intueretur: ita monitiones illas humanis ingeniis insitas, atque ingenitas observabit, easque animadversas, et notatas in naturae simillimam tabulam, imaginemque; concludet, et differentibus ad imitando proponet: ut hoc artificioso quasi speculo natura formae suae dignitatem perspicere, et si qua macula sit aspersa, delere, atque eluere possit. Atque ita ars (quae discipula naturae prius fuerat) ei magistra quodammodo fiet. Nulla enim natura est tan firma, constansque, quin sui cognitione et virium suarum descriptione firmior atque constantior: nulla tam languida et abiecta est quin adiumento artis acrior et alacrior effici possit', *Dialecticae institutiones*, A7ᵛ. This claim of the priority of logic over the other arts contrasts with Sidney's claim that it is the 'speaking picture' of poetry that makes things 'better than nature', Alexander, ed., *Defence of Poesy*, p. 8.

[9] **This […] docere**] Compare with Roland MacIlmaine's translation: 'Dialecticke otherwise called Logicke, is an arte which *teachethe to dispute* well', *The Logike of P. Ramus*, B1ʳ, emphasis added.

[10] **used of Cicero**] Cicero calls dialectic 'ratio diligens disserendi' ('the careful rule of reasoning'), *Topica*, 2.6, Loeb II: pp. 386–87.

[11] **Melanchton**] Philipp Melanchton (1497–1560) was a German Lutheran theologian and philosopher. His *Erotemata dialectices* (Leipzig, 1549) influenced Ramus's defence of logic as an art of teaching, and of method as a pathway to knowledge. See Ong, *Ramus, Method*, pp. 158–60, 236–40.

[12] **Beurhusius […] Ramus**] For this defence of Ramist terms, see Beurhaus I, B5ᵛ–B6ᵛ.

[13] **For the word […] disserere**] Fraunce paraphrases Piscator, I.1, A6ᵛ–A7ʳ: 'Disserendi autem verbum hoc loco […] per metaphoram usurpatum, idem valet quod Docere. Sumpta metaphora ab olitoribus, ut Varro admonet. Quemadmodum enim olitor diversa semina in diversas areas serit […] Disputare enim (si Varroni credimus)

unnecessary curiosities whereof there is no use in reasoning, and handleth diverse questions in diverse places distinctly, not everything in every place disorderedly, therefore have the logicians friendly presumed upon the good nature of those two countrymen in using their words to express a more elegant thing, although at the first not properly, yet by continuance of time so significantly that the usurped *usucapio*° is now more known than the natural possession. Yet, for that both these rehearsed properties of Logic be rather particular functions of method than general operations of the whole art, it is plain that this word 'disputing', with his original *disputare*, and 50 that *disserere*, if you respect the natural signification thereof, are not sufficient to express the whole nature of Logic — although I am not ignorant, and I said before that Beurhusius applieth those words to the general use of the art, not restraining them to those two several° functions belonging to method.[14] Whose judgement, as use alloweth, so I do not reject, but yet, by his leave, leave his Latin words behind our English.

Melanchton useth this word *docere*: *docere* is to teach, and Logic is an art of teaching.[15] But then mark what I mean by teaching: for you must not only restrain the signification of it in such sort as though there were no teaching but only in schools among philosophers or in pulpit among preachers, but generally he teacheth whosoever maketh another man know that whereof before he was ignorant, whether he do it by exploration and illustration, or proof and conclusion.[16] And 60 thus, if we take this word, it is somewhat more general than *disputare*, or *disserere*, used of Ramus and Cicero, yet not so ample as the nature of this art, whose force° is seen not only in teaching [4ʳ] others, but also in learning thyself, in discoursing, thinking, | meditating, and framing of thine own, as also in discussing, perusing, searching, and examining what others have either delivered by speech or put down in writing. The first is called γένεσις, the second ἀνάλυσις:[17] wherein consisteth the whole use of Logic, as in the particular discourse thereof I will now largely put down hereafter.[18]

As far then as man's reason can reach, so far the use and virtue extendeth itself of this art of reasoning, which is therefore called λογική, of the internal form, essence, and nature consisting in reason, but διαλεκτική, of the external manner and order of working, which is commonly 70 done by speech and talk, as that word importeth.[19] And this I think to be the most convenient

---

proprie significat, diligenter vites putare. Quare Disputare pro Docere, metaphora a vinitore est. Quemadmodum enim vinitor vites putat, id est, superflua sarmenta ferro amputat, ita qui docet, is superflua, id est aliena et quae ad rem non pertinent, amputare atque omittere debet'. See also Varro, *On the Latin Language*, 6.63–64, Loeb I: pp. 230–33.

[14] **Berhusius [...] method]** Beurhaus I, B6ʳ lists the functions of logical reasoning: 'Disserere [...] significat indicare, exhibere, adhibere, afferre argumenta, arguere, considerare, meditari, intelligere, ostendere, invenire, disponere, iudicare, meminisse, docere, disputare, ratiocinari, disceptare, et omnino [...] ratione uti' (*Disserere* means to indicate, to present, to extend, to bring forth arguments, to argue, to consider, to ponder, to discern, to show, to invent, to dispose, to judge, to remember, to teach, to dispute, to ratiocinate, to discuss, and altogether to use reason); **those two several functions]** *disputare* and *disserere* in their original senses.

[15] **Melanchton [...] teaching]** 'Dialectica est ars seu via, recte, ordine, et perspicue docendi', Melanchton, *Erotemata*, B1ʳ. Piscator prefers Melanchton's definition to Ramus's: 'melior Philippi definitio videtur', I.1, A7ʳ.

[16] **But then [...] conclusion]** 'Dilligenter tamen hic cavendum, ne docendi verbum quod hic proprium est, arctius restringamus quam natura eius postulat: hoc est, ne concionatores tantum in templis, ne professores, atque praeceptoris in scholis docere putemus. Non ita est: sed docet quicumque alterum in cognitionem rei incognitae ducit: sive is naturam rei declaret, sive demonstret sententiae veritatem', Piscator, I.1, A7ʳ.

[17] **whose force [...] ἀνάλυσις]** Fraunce adapts Piscator, I.1, A7ʳ: 'Quo loco [...] ἀνάλυσις authorum'.

[18] **particular discourse [...] hereafter]** 'Of the Nature and Use of Logic', in this volume.

[19] **As far [...] importeth]** Fraunce adapts Piscator, I.1, A7ʳ: 'Quare haec ars non solum tam late patet, quam late patet hominum sermo: sed etiam quam late patet usus humanae rationis. Unde non solum διαλεκτική apellata est, a sermone: verum etiam λογική, a ratione. Sermonis, docere est; rationis, discere. Quare Dialectica et docendi et discendi ars est' (Therefore this art not only extends so broadly as human speech does, but also as does the use of human reason. And thus it is not only called dialectic, by dint of speech, but truly also logic,

distinction of these two names, λογική and διαλεκτική, although Ramus useth them both as one.²⁰ The thing included in these two names is known already by that which hath been said, whose most ample and almost infinite use and power hath never had in any tongue a more general and proper name than this of reasoning, as we use it nowadays. We reason in schools as philosophers, in pulpit as preachers, in Westminster as lawyers and judges, in court as princes and lords, in country, at cart, at plow,° at home, abroad. Yea, not so much as the milkmaid without reasoning selleth her milk, the physician with reason persuadeth his patient, the schoolmaster teacheth his boys with reasoning, the captain ruleth with reasoning. And what shall I say more? Whatsoever it be, nay, whatsoever thou canst imagine to be, although it be not,²¹ yet by reasoning it is
80 invented, taught, ordered, confirmed.

And therefore Logic hath been for a long time untolerably° abused of those miserable Sorbonnists²² and dunsical° quidditaries,° who thought there was no Logic out of their soft brains, no reasoning out of their intricate quodlibets,° no disputing without *arguitur quod sit*,° no teaching without *probatur quod non*,° no part of this science without *ergo*° and *igitur*,° whereas indeed the true use of Logic is as well apparent in simple, plain, and easy explication as in subtle, strict, and concised probation. Read Homer, read Virgil, read Demosthenes, read Tully, marry, read Sir John Cheke, read Master Ascham,²³ and see the true use of natural Logic the ground of artificial, far different from this rude and barbarous kind of outworn sophistry, which, if it had any use at all, yet this was all to feed the vain humours of some curious heads in obscure schools,
90 whereas the art of reasoning hath somewhat to do in everything, and nothing is anything without this one thing.²⁴

Other arts are tied to certain subjects, as Arithmetic to numbers, Astronomy to the motion of the stars, and so of others. But Logic is an art of arts, a science of sciences, the hand of Philosophy,
[4ᵛ] the instrument | of all learning.²⁵ It teacheth orderly, it proveth strongly, it sheweth plainly, it persuadeth forcibly° any art, any cause, any question, any man whatsoever. What then (will some man say), need we any other arts, if Logic alone can suffice for all? I answer: Logic alone is sufficient to help all, yet Logic sufficeth not for all. Logic telleth how to reason, dispute, examine, prove or disprove anything; but the thing to be reasoned, disputed, examined, proved or

by dint of reason. Teaching belongs to speech; learning, to reason. Therefore Dialectic is the art of teaching and learning).

²⁰ **Ramus useth them both as one**] 'Dialectica est ars bene disserendi: eodemque sensu Logica dicta est', Ramus/Piscator, I.1, A6ʳ.

²¹ **whatsoever […] be not**] Fraunce's admission of fiction within the realm of logic accords with his use of poetic examples throughout his treatise.

²² **Sorbonnists**] doctors at the Sorbonne, trained in scholastic logic and opponents of Ramus. On Paris logicians like Antonio de Gouveia (1505–66) or Jaques Charpentier (d. 1574), see Ong, *Ramus, Method*, pp. 215–23.

²³ **Read […] artificial**] Compare with LL, B3ʳ: 'Read Homer, read Demosthenes, read Virgil, read Cicero, read Bartas, read Torquato Tasso, read that most worthy ornament of our English tongue *The Countess of Pembroke's Arcadia*, and therein see the true effects of natural Logic'. The works of Guillaume Du Bartas (1544–90) and Torquato Tasso (1544–96), as well as Sidney's then unpublished *Arcadia*, are among Fraunce's main literary sources in *The Arcadian Rhetoric* (1588). **Sir John Cheke**] (1514–70) English humanist, theologian and courtier. He was Regius Professor of Greek at St John's, Cambridge. **Master Ascham**] Roger Ascham (1515–68), one of the most notable Tudor humanists. Educated at St John's, he is author of the pedagogical manual *The Schoolmaster* (1570).

²⁴ **nothing […] thing**] no art can claim to be so without the aid of Logic.

²⁵ **But Logic […] learning**] 'Dialectica est ars artium et scientia scientiarum ad omnium methodorum principia viam habens' [Dialectic is an art of arts and a science of sciences, having the way to the principles of all methods], *Peter of Spain: Summulae logicales*, ed. by I. M: Bochenski (Marietti: Torino, 1947), p. 1. Fraunce's source must be Melanchton, *Erotemata*, B2ᵛ, or Beurhaus II, F5ᵛ, both of which cite this definition. Fraunce's omission of Peter of Spain (c. 1215–77), who became Pope John XXI, helps explain his anti-Catholic and anti-scholastic bias; **the hand of Philosophy**] See 'A Brief and General Comparison', 12n.

100 disproved, that Logic cannot afford, and therefore it is to be sought of such arts as profess such things. So that Logic is profitable unto all, and yet not one of them all unprofitable, but even as they without this be mangled and confused, so this without them is bare and naked. Logic is necessary for a divine, yet Logic yieldeth no divinity. But when a preacher hath by continual perusing of the Sacred Scriptures furnished himself with store of matter, then Logic will teach him how to teach others, and not only that, but also how to learn himself, yea, how and in what order to read the Scriptures, to defend, to confute, to instruct, to reprehend. For, as Arithmetic teacheth to count money, not to find money, and Astronomy to mark the motion of the stars, not to make the nature of the stars, and Geometry how to measure ground, not how to purchase ground, so Logic can tell you how to reason of things, and yet reserveth the peculiar doctrine of the same things to the several° professors thereof. I do not deny but the one and the same man

110 may purchase ground, measure ground, and also reason of the nature of the same ground. But he purchaseth it by one art, measureth it by another, and reasoneth of it by a third. He purchaseth it as a farmer, measureth it as a geometer, reasoneth of it as a logician. And although one man may be furnished with all these three properties, yet every art must have his own by the law of justice.° Confusion must be avoided, and the precepts of every art distinctly put down, although the use of the same precepts may be common and concur altogether in one man, if one man be skilful in all arts. For, as virtues are so knit together that he which is indued° with the perfect habit of one is in a good readiness to all the rest, so is all good and liberal learning so friendly enclosed in the eternal band° of Encyclopaedia that, if you join them, they are most mighty, if you sever them, they can scarce stand.[26] To talk of Logic when you put down Rhetoric is nothing

120 to the purpose, and to cast in Rhetoric among precepts of Logic is absurd. But he that hath learned the one may yet the other, and join the use of the two, | whose precepts are both distinct.[27]

[5ʳ]

Of reasoning well] This word, 'well', doth sever the perfection of art from the weakness of nature, and therefore whereas Piscator reprehendeth Ramus for putting in this addition, 'well',[28] his reprehension were as well left out as put in. And yet indeed the very name of an art includeth this word 'well', every art being an habit of doing that well whereof it is an art.[29]

[26] **eternal band [...] scarce stand**] the circle comprising the seven liberal arts. See Thomas Elyot: 'the circle of doctrine | whiche is in one worde of greeke Encyclopedia', *The Boke Named the Gouernour* (London: Thomas Berthelet, 1531), F8ᵛ. Ralph Lever argues that 'artes art knit together in such a bande of knowledge, that no man can be cunning in anye one, but he must haue some knowledge in manye', *The Arte of Reason, Rightly Termed Witcraft* (London: Henry Bynneman, 1573), F5ᵛ.
[27] **Rhetoric [...] Logic**] Fraunce draws on Melanchton's question 'Quid disserunt Dialectica et Rhetorica?', *Erotemata*, B2ᵛ–B3ᵛ. See Introduction, pp. 29–35, on the separation of logic from rhetoric, as well as on their joining in practice.
[28] **Piscator [...] 'well'**] Piscator (I.1, A6ᵛ) finds the adverb redundant.
[29] **And yet [...] an art**] Fraunce paraphrases Piscator, I.1, A6ᵛ: 'Ars enim omnis, bene seu recte faciendi agendive habitus est'. LL's addition insists on the separation of Logic from Rhetoric: 'Howsoever it be, it appeareth that to reason well and artificially is the duty and end of Logic. For it is not essential unto Logic always to persuade, no more than to a physician always to heal', B4ʳ.

~

CHAPTER 2

Of the Parts of Logic and
Diverse Kinds of Arguments[1]

There be two parts of Logic: invention and judgement, which is also called disposition.

Invention is a part of Logic concerning inventing of arguments.

An argument is that which is affected to argue something, of which sort be all such things as are alone and by themselves conceived or understood by reason.

An argument is either artificial or inartificial.

Artificial is that which argueth by itself.

Artificial is either the first, or that which is made of the first.

The first, which hath his being of itself.

The first is either simple or compared.

Simple is that which is simply considered.

Simple is either agreeable or disagreeable.

Agreeable is that which agreeth with the thing which it doth argue.

The agreeable is either absolutely agreeable or after a certain manner.

The absolutely agreeable is either the cause or the thing caused.[2]

This Stoical division of Logic into invention and judgement as into his essential parts is reprehended of some, who think that judgement is not any particular part of Logic, but rather an adjunct generally dispersed throughout the whole art, because, say they, there is use of judgement even in invention, to wit, in choice of arguments.[3] But, in my fancy, they might better have found some fault with these words, 'judgement' and 'invention', than reprehended the partition, which is most true if they consider what the Stoics did understand by these words. For by *iudicium*, or judgement, is meant nothing else but a disposition, ordering, or collocation of the arguments already invented, to the end that a man may judge the better of them. So that here,

---

[1] **Title**] Fraunce translates the title 'De partibus Dialecticae, deque argumentis generibus', Ramus/Piscator, I.2, A7ʳ, not found in editions of Ramus's *Dialectica* before 1580. See Introduction, p. 26.

[2] **There be [...] thing caused**] This section, indented in the manuscript, translates Ramus/Piscator I.2, A7ʳ⁻ᵛ; **compared**] McCormick's emendation 'compared' can be defended on the grounds of Ramus's naming this kind of argument 'comparatum'. See Ramus/Piscator, I.2, A7ᵛ.

[3] **This Stoical division [...] choice of arguments**] 'Partitio haec Stoicorum fuit, authore Cicerone in *Topicis* [...] Sed hanc partitionem nonnulli hodie reprehendunt: existimantes, iudicium non esse peculiarem Dialectices partem, sed commune totius artis adiunctum, per totam partem fusum; quippe quod et in inventione iudicio opus sit, nimirum in delectu argumentorum', Piscator, I.2, A7ᵛ. See Cicero, *Topica*, 2.6, Loeb II: p. 386, who criticizes the Stoics' negelect of one part — 'ars inveniendi', or τοπική — in favour of the other — 'via iudicandi', or διαλεκτική; **reprehended of some**] For instance, Jaques Charpentier, referred to as 'Carpentar' below. See 17n to this chapter.

by *metonymia*,° judgement is taken for disposition, the effect for the cause, for judgement ariseth of the ordering and disposing of arguments.[4] And therefore I have put down both these words together. So likewise the inventing and the excogitation° of arguments is not here meant to be the first part of Logic, but the art of inventing, by the same figure, *metonymia*,° as Piscator noteth, the inventing being the first of that part of Logic which teacheth to invent.[5] They might therefore have changed the words, but left the thing, which yet they have not done, but brought in a new division of Logic, sometimes into three parts, as apodictical, topical, elenchical, sometimes into

30 two, by name apodictical and dialectical.

[5ᵛ]   Topical they | will have to be a several kind of art of reasoning by probable arguments. Apodictical, that which disputeth by necessary conclusions, as though there were not one and the same art, science, and order of reasoning both by probable and necessary arguments, and the selfsame places of arguments both in the one and the other, as causes, effects, adjuncts, etc., both contingent and necessary. The occasion of this their new division was offered them out of Aristotle, who, because he divideth a proposition into topical and apodictical, they by and by will needs have a double Logic.[6] They might better have inferred here upon a double syllogism, topical and apodictical, but yet double only in respect° of the matter, not in respect° of the form, which nevertheless causeth all distinction. For example sake, because a goldsmith maketh a cup

40 sometimes of silver, sometimes of gold, shall I think therefore he hath two arts of making cups? So a logician, because he sometimes inventeth and disposeth probable arguments, sometimes necessary, shall I therefore say he hath two arts of inventing and disposing?[7] For, as for that kind of Logic which they call elenchical, seeing it is no Logic at all, but rather the abuse and perversion of Logic, I see no cause why it should be taught in Logic. Yet if any man think that the true precepts of Logic, once known, will not be sufficient to descry the falseness of sophistical argumentations, he may to his contentation seek for a full discourse thereof out of some commentary,[8] and not overcharge the art itself with unnecessary institutions.° I grant there is

---

[4] **in my fancy […] arguments**] Fraunce's claim of originality conceals a new borrowing through translation: 'Verum illi (quod pace eorum dixerim) non attendunt, quid Stoici vocabulo Iudicii intellexisse videantur: nempe argumentorum inventorum dispositionem seu collocationem ad bene iudicandum. Itaque iudicium pro dispositio dixerunt per metonymiam effecti. Iudicium enim, id est, intelligentia explicationis, ex argumentorum dispositione nascitur', Piscator, I.2, A7ᵛ.

[5] **So likewise […] to invent**] Fraunce simplifies Piscator, who explains the logical sense of *inventio* as a result of metaphor and metonymy: '*inventio*] Invenire, proprie est in rem quam quaesieris, venire id quod corporis est, rerumque corporearum: corporis enim motu, oculorumque aspectu, et quaerimus et invenimus. Est igitur hic metaphora a corpore ad animum: nam inventio hic est argumentorum, id est, earum rerum quae ad docendum requiruntur excogitatio. quanquam hic inventionis nomine non ipsa illa excogitatio, sed eius ars per metonymiam effecti intelligitur' (*Invention*: To invent is properly, in the thing which you will enquire, to approach that which pertains to the body and to bodily matters: thus we search and discover by attending to the motion of the body and the look of the eyes. It is then a metaphor from the body to the soul: and thus this invention is of the arguments, that is, a contriving of those things that require to be taught. Yet the very act of inventing is not referred here by the name of invention, but its teaching, by metonymy of the effect), Piscator, I.2, A8ʳ.

[6] **a double Logic**] On Ramus's critique of Aristotle's preference for a double system of logic, one for science and the other for opinion, see Howell, *Logic and Rhetoric*, p. 154. Quoting from Ramus's *Dialectique*, A2ʳ⁻ᵛ, Howell sees in the defence of one single art dealing with the necessary (science) and the contingent (opinion) the key to the Ramist reform.

[7] **Topical […] disposing?**] 'Topicam igitur faciunt artem argumentandi ex contingentibus seu probabilibus: Apodictica vero, ex necessariis […] Duplex quidem hinc oritur syllogismus, Topicus et Apodicticus: sed ratione tantum materiae duplex, non autem ratione formae. […] Declaremus rem simili. Auribaster poculum nunc ex auro facit, nunc ex argento, num igitur quia materia poculi duplex est, ars etiam faciendi poculum erit duplex? […] Sic etiam disputator argumenta seu probabilia seu necessaria pari ratione invenit ac disponit', Piscator, I.2, A7ᵛ–A8ʳ.

[8] **out of some commentary**] See SL, II.19, 1n for instances of those commentaries.

something profitable in the elenchs, as also in the predicaments,° and some other tractates° of the same kind.⁹ But, if we shall put down all in Logic for true Logic which hath any help to Logic,
50   we shall never make an end of Logic.

Invention] Invention and Judgement are not two several° arts of Logic, as though we should have one Logic to find arguments and another to judge of the same, but they be two essential parts of the whole which, joined, make one true Logic.

Invention is]¹⁰ For invention, remember these three notes. First, the doctrine of invention is general, and not restrained only to the finding out of a *medium*,° which they commonly take for the only argument, but absolutely and universally appliable° to the inventing of anything either true or fained° whatsoever.¹¹ Secondly, the arguments in invention must be considered severally, singularly, and alone; thenafter to be disposed and ordered by certain precepts, thereby to judge of the truth or falsehood of the same, as for example:

60   *Rullus*¹²   *a popular man.*

These, barely put down as two arguments, to wit, the subject and the adjunct, are afterwards disposed in an axiom to judge the truth thereof thus:

      Rullus is no popular man.

But, because this is contingent and doubtful, it is confirmed by another argument, that is to say, by an effect and working of Rullus: I mean *opprimere populum*, 'to injury° and oppress the people'. So then here be three bare arguments, or two joined in the axiom before and the third alone, which they call the third argument, or *medium*,° thus:

      1) *Rullus is no*   2) *popular man*
[6ʳ]   3) *to oppress the people.*

70   Whereof it is concluded in this wise syllogistically:

      No oppressor of the people is popular;
      But Rullus oppresseth the people;
      Therefore Rullus is not popular.

In this order:

First, of single arguments we make axioms, which axioms, if of themselves they be perceived and granted, they be straightways° judged as true or false. And this is the first part of judgement in axioms, called *axiomaticum*, determining only truth and falseness in propositions. Now, if these axioms be doubtful, then thereof be made questions, which are to be proved by third arguments fet° from the affections° of the other two which were joined in the axiom. And lastly
80   are to be concluded by syllogism, the only judge of all consequence or inconsequence, as finally method hath only to deal with the ordering and settling of many axioms, thereby to give sentence

---

⁹ **I grant […] same kind**] For Fraunce's general assessment of Aristotle see 'A Brief and General Comparison', in this volume; **elenchs**] See I.19.

¹⁰ **Invention is**] See Appendix I.2 for Fraunce's rewriting of this annotation in LL by replacing the Rullus example with Spenser's 'July', 145–48, SC 66_d.

¹¹ **the inventing of anything either true or fained whatsoever**] See also LL, Q3ᵛ, for Fraunce's assertion that logic applies to both fact and fiction: 'All Logic is general, and appliable as well to things imagined as things that be extant in truth; and therefore to words also, as words have causes, effects, subjects, adjuncts and other arguments to be considered'.

¹² **Rullus**] Publius Servilius Rullus was a Roman tribune who in 63 BC proposed the agricultural laws against which Cicero wrote three of his extant orations, *De lege agraria contra Rullum*. Fraunce derived his syllogism from I.8.23–26, Loeb VI: pp. 362–66. See also G. V. Sumner, 'Cicero, Pompeius and Rullus', *Transactions and Proceedings of the American Philological Association*, 97 (1966), 569–82.

of methodical proceeding or unorderly confusion. And therefore I see no reason why I should, with the common logicians, chop in canons, maximae and rules of consequence, as they call them, applying them to every argument in invention, seeing that syllogisms, and only syllogisms, are the true and only rules of consequence and inconsequence, as I said before.[13]

The occasion, as I think, of this their error hereof arose because, if an enthymeme be denied, we commonly confirm it by some axiom, which indeed is nothing else but the supplying of the part wanting, as either the *maior*, or *minor*, or else some prosyllogism. And this rule, canon or maxima being so supplied, a plain syllogism proceedeth, the only determiner of coherence. And
90   as all the force of consequence is in syllogisms, so all the power of arguing is of the several° affection° of every argument to the thing argued, which affection° is truly and artificially put down in invention in such sort that from every definition and precept in invention such rules, maximae, canons, axioms, consectaries,° corollaries,° or howsoever you term them, may easily be deduced, and, when necessity requireth, shall be of us put down distinctly in their several° places. For, as for most of those outworn maximae huddled up in schools, they be either unnecessary, and may easily be perceived by the definitions and explanations of the arguments, or else not generally true, but in part, and therefore in no wise to be put down in art, but rather to be reserved for commentaries, as that: *qualis causa, talis effectus*, 'such as the cause is, such must the effect be', which cannot stand but by a number of frivolous and sophistical
100   distinctions.[14]

He that listeth to see the true canons of Ramus's Logic compared at large with these lame rules, let him read the second part of Beurhusius.[15] I have kept me only to such maximae, both in invention and judgement, as are put down orderly by Ramus and are essentially belonging to this art, of which sort be those which Beurhusius hath collected in comparison-wise out of Ramus,
[6ᵛ] | thirty-four out of invention, forty-eight out of judgement.[16] The maximae or canons of invention, therefore, are nothing else but certain rules containing the several° force° and affection° of arguments. The canons of axioms, such precepts as declare the use and force of axioms. And so, in a word, the canons of syllogisms and method are precepts touching the consequence and inconsequence of the one, and the perspicuity or confusion of the other. Neither are there any
110   rules of consequence at all either in invention or judgement, but only those of syllogisms.

But here may a doubt arise: for, seeing that every axiom and rule of invention is a part of judgement (because it is an axiom, and every axiom is of judgement), it may seem that invention and judgement be not distinct parts, but rather, as was objected before out of Carpentar, confounded the one with the other.[17] I answer: the rules and precepts of invention be indeed axioms, and therefore, consequently, parts of judgement. But so, that you must take them to be

---

[13] **And therefore […] before**] Fraunce draws on one of Beurhaus's questions, 'An Maximae sint pars seu doctrina Iudicii logici?', in whose answer these maxims of judgement or rules of consequence ('maximae iudicariae seu regulae consequentiarum') are discussed and dismissed. See Beurhaus II, N6ʳ–O2ʳ.

[14] **The occasion […] sophistical distictions**] Fraunce's defence of the use of syllogisms as the valid procedure for determining coherence is based on Beurhaus II, N7ʳ; ***qualis causa, talis effectus***] 'possita enim caussa, ponitur effectus', Beurhaus II, N7ʳ.

[15] **the second part of Beurhusius**] Beurhaus II contains several *comparationes* between Ramus and former logicians. Throughout that book the scholastic rules of consequence applying to every argument are scrutinized, and their validity frequently refuted.

[16] **thirty-four out of invention, forty-eight out of judgement**] Beurhaus's Ramist maxims, or 'Ramea Firmamenta', are extracted from Ramus's text, so Fraunce reflects them only when he follows Ramus literally or closely. For the whole list of maxims, see Beurhaus II, O4ʳ–O6ʳ. Fraunce's indebtedness to this list is annotated throughout by referring the maxims by kind (*Inv* and *Jud*) and subscript number.

[17] **objected before out of Carpentar**] 'Dispositionem definis, rerum inventarum aptam ad iudicandum collocationem: inventionem autem, argumenti excogitationem. Cum igitur rei inventae dispositio sit, solius argumenti logica erit collocatio. Quibus si adiecero, argumenti collocationem argumentationem esse […] an

the fruits of judgement already showed in ordering the axioms and rules of invention, or examples of judgement teaching the part of invention, not as though those precepts were put down in invention to teach a man how to judge either axiomatically, syllogistically, or methodically, for that belongeth to the second part of Logic. For, if you so take them, then every
120   axiom is not straightway a part of judgement, but only such rules and precepts that teach to make, order and frame axioms. For otherwise every precept of every art, because it is an axiom, should be taken for a part of judgement in Logic, whereas indeed they be but the fruits and examples of that logical judgement appearing in the constitution of every art. And so in invention every rule is an axiom, every rule doth judge; but every rule teacheth not how to frame an axiom, every rule showeth not how to judge, which only is the peculiar duty of logical judgement.

The third and last thing that I said was worthy the observation in this logical invention is this: that the art and doctrine of every argument is distinct, firm, constant, and immutable. Yet the affection° of the argument may be altered, changed, and diversely considered either in the same things diversely compared among themselves, or in one thing referred to diverse, as:[18]

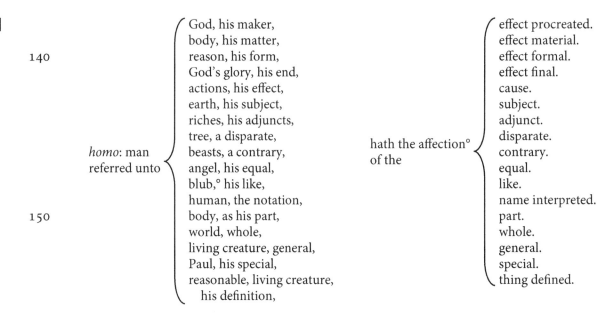

130   God { created man. / preserveth man. / is not man. / is not like man.   So the affection° is of the { cause procreant with the effect. / cause conservant with the effect. / disparates among themselves. / unlikes.

In like manner, if one thing be referred to many, and drawn as it were through the places of arguments, as:

140

homo: man referred unto {
God, his maker,
body, his matter,
reason, his form,
God's glory, his end,
actions, his effect,
earth, his subject,
riches, his adjuncts,
tree, a disparate,
beasts, a contrary,
angel, his equal,
blub,° his like,
human, the notation,
body, as his part,
world, whole,
living creature, general,
Paul, his special,
reasonable, living creature, his definition,
}

150

hath the affection° of the {
effect procreated.
effect material.
effect formal.
effect final.
cause.
subject.
adjunct.
disparate.
contrary.
equal.
like.
name interpreted.
part.
whole.
general.
special.
thing defined.
}

non efficietur, logicam collocationem universam argumentatione contineri?' (You define disposition as the apt collocation for the judgement of things invented; invention, on the other hand, as the contriving of arguments. While disposition is then of a thing invented, logic will be the collocation of the argument only. If I add out of these that argumentation is the collocation of an argument, is it not rather shown that the whole logical collocation is contained in the argumentation?), Jacques Charpentier, *Animadversiones in Libros tres dialecticarum Institutionum Petri Rami* (Paris: Thomas Richard, 1554), E1ʳ. For Charpentier's critique of Ramus, see Neal W. Gilbert, *Renaissance Concepts of Method* (New York: Columbia University Press, 1960), p. 236, and Ong, *Ramus, Method*, pp. 220–23.
[18] **as**] The ensuing two tables translate those in Beurhaus I, C3ᵛ–C4ʳ. Although Fraunce does not cite his source here, he does in LL, C4ʳ⁻ᵛ.

Yet the art is certain and immutable, for that which is a cause can never be an effect in the same respect,° unless the affection° be changed, and that is in the argument, not in the art.

An argument] Every thing hath his several° name according to his natural property or imposition of man. But Logic, respecting a second use in the several° things, hath given them an
160 artificial and secondary name. As fire hath his name usually known, but because it is considered of logicians as a cause of heat, therefore hath it his second note and name, and is called a cause, one of the arguments, for that it argueth heat, and so in others.

In that which is affected] By this affection° we learn whether an argument agree or disagree with another, and how it agreeth: whether as cause, subject, and so forth.

To argue] To argue is general, either in inventing only one argument by the affection° of the other, as when by the notion of the cause we seek the effect; or else, in placing them axiomatically or dianoetically,° we argue some other thing, either by explication or confirmation. The first consideration is of arguments severally° conceived and alone by themselves. The second, as they be placed by judgement. And therefore Piscator's animadversion in this place is to small purpose.[19]

170 *All such things as are alone*] Except those words which do but bind and knit together the parts of speech, as conjunctions, which signify nothing; except, again, copious and rhetorical phrases, whose many words express but one thing, as a man of an excellent and heavenly wit, where the words be many, the arguments but two, the subject and adjunct; lastly, except full comparisons, omissions, definitions, and descriptions where the argument is put down in a whole proposition. This noteth Beurhusius, although not very necessarily.[20] For Ramus saith not all such words as are alone, but all such reasons or things that are alone and by themselves conceived, as no doubt these arguments be which he here excepteth. For although there be many words, yet they all express but one conceit of reason, and that is the single and sole argument that we here talk of.

But to let that pass: he that taketh this word 'argument' only for a proof or confirmation shall
180 never attain to the meaning of this art. Indeed it properly signifieth that thing only which doth prove and confirm, but here it hath catachrestically° a more general signification for want of a more convenient word, and betokeneth° not only demonstrations, but also declarations without any syllogism or form of concluding.[21]

---

[19] **Piscator's animadversion [...] small purpose**] '*Per se considerata*] Hoc minus recte dictum videtur. Argumenta enim per se et absolute considerari non possunt: quum argumentum non possit esse aut intelligi sine eo quod arguitur, id est, argumento demonstratur vel etiam declaratur: ut causa non potest sine effectu, subiectum sine adiuncto, etc.'; (*By themselves considered*: This expression seems less right. For arguments cannot be considered by themselves and absolutely, since an argument cannot be and understood without that which argues, that is, demonstrated or declared by the argument: as the cause cannot be without the effect, the subject without the adjunct, etc.), Piscator, I.2, B1ʳ. LL is more specific in its critique of Piscator: 'and therefore Piscator's animadversion in this place is to small purpose, whereas he reprehendeth Ramus for saying that every several thing considered alone is an argument. For he in so saying meant not that an argument should be so alone, as though it had no affection or relation to any other thing, but so severally considered, as that in Invention we should not intermeddle with axiomatical, syllogistical, or methodical conjoining and setting together of the same several arguments, for that doth wholly and only belong to disposition', LL, D1ᵛ.

[20] **This noteth Beurhusius**] '*An igitur singulae voces in oratione sunt argumenta? Non; quemadmodum nec singulae significant res; sed quaedam ad vinciendam sententiam adhibentur. Itaque quae voces singulae significant singulae notiones, essentiales scilicet sententiae partes, eae etiam sunt argumenta: ut, Homo, Animal, vivit, edit, bibit et infinita alia vocabula quae singula argumenta comprehendunt*' (Is every word in a sentence then an argument? No; certainly not all of them signify things, but are employed in order to bind a sentence. Therefore those single words which mean single notions, namely essential parts of speech, are arguments: like man, animal, lives, eats, drinks and many other endless terms which comprehend single arguments), Beurhaus 1, C2ᵛ; **although not very necessarily**] because it concerns grammar, not logic.

[21] **without any form of concluding**] LL adds: 'and so doth *arguere* in Latin signify *declarare, ostendere, perspicuum manifestumque facere, vt in Virgilio:* "*Degeneres animos timor arguit*" [*Aeneid*, 4.13, Loeb I: p. 396], *id est, ostendit*', LL, D1ᵛ.

[7ᵛ]   The like error is that of them which | think there is no judgement but only in framing a
syllogism, whereas the first, if not the chief judgement, is in axioms, then in syllogisms, and lastly
in method. Yet nevertheless the same kind of argument may commonly serve both to declare
and confirm (although some there be which only declare). So in the end of the Sixth Eglogue²²
of *The Shepherds' Calendar*, Hobbinol useth an argument of cause only for explication:

> Ah faithless Rosalind, and void of grace,
190   That art the root of all this ruthful woe. ('June', 115–16; SC 55)

In the Ninth Eglogue, Diggon Davy useth the same kind of argument to the same purpose.
The words be these:

> Their ill haviour gars men missay
> Both of their doctrine and of their fay.° ('September', 106–07; SC 85)

And yet here the cause argueth his effect, although there be no syllogistical probation intended,
for that the proposition by itself seemed to Diggon true enough.²³ Now, for the other part: no
man doubteth but that an argument of the cause may be well used for confirmation, whereof
examples be everywhere apparent. Let no man therefore think there is no Logic where there is
no conclusion because every argument serveth not everywhere only for confirmation.²⁴
200   *All such things as are alone*] That is, not placed in axioms or syllogisms, yet having a relation
to that they prove.
         Artificial] I see no reason, saith Piscator, why testimonies should be called inartificial
arguments, seeing that there is as good art showed in applying them as in finding other
arguments. And if in art there ought to be nothing without art, either invention wanteth art or
testimonies be not inartificial.²⁵ I answer in a word: they be not called inartificial for that they
want art, but because they argue not of themselves, but by the help of some artificial.²⁶ As for
that other distribution of arguments into internal and external,²⁷ Ramus indeed sometimes used
the like, but afterwards, perceiving that a testimony was oftentimes as well adjoined and inherent
in the thing, as many internal arguments were (as all *consentanea*, except *forma*, *materia*,
210   *adiuncta*, *totium*, *partes*, *definitio*, and all *dissentanea*),²⁸ he changed those former names, and
brought in place thereof this distribution simple, which hath a simple relation, which relation
maketh it not compound, as might seem, sith° it is no comparison, but an affection° of one to
another, as not only in simple arguments appeareth, but also in compounds. The difference only
is this, that in simple arguments the relation is simple, in compounds compared, either in
quantity or in quality.

---

²² **Eglogue**] Fraunce prefers 'eglogue' to 'eclogue', thus silently subscribing to Spenser's false etymology as
explained in in SC, 'General Argument', Brooks-Davies, pp. 26–27.

²³ **And yet […] true enough**] Fraunce avers that the truth of both arguments of cause in these poetic examples
— woman's faithlessness as a cause of a lover's woe and the priests' bad behaviour as the cause of men's critique
of (Catholic) doctrine — makes syllogistic proof unnecessary.

²⁴ **let no man […] confirmation**] The fact that syllogistic confirmation is not necessary in these examples does
not make them illogical.

²⁵ **I see […] not artificial**] This passage follows Piscator, who regards the division into artificial and inartificial
arguments as faulty ('vitiosa'): 'Testimonium enim, quod inartificialis argumenti nomine intelligitur, nos minus
artificiale est, quam caeterorum argumentum quodlibet', Piscator, I.2, B1ʳ.

²⁶ **inartificial […] artificial**] In accordance with this argument, Dudley Fenner had preferred to translate
'artificiall' and 'lesse artificiall', *The Artes*, B3ᵛ.

²⁷ **that other […] internal and external**] Fraunce refers to the division of arguments into 'insita' and 'assumpta'.
See Piscator, I.2, B1ʳ.

²⁸ *consentanea*, *dissentanea*] 'agreeable' and 'disagreeable' arguments, whose different kinds are explained in
subsequent chapters.

Agreeable] So that, the one being affirmed, the other must be affirmed; one denied, the other denied, either necessarily or contingently. For this agreement signifieth nothing else but this same consecution.°29

---

[29] *Agreeable* […] **consecution**] '*Quod consentit cum re quam arguit*] Ita scilicet, ut altero affirmato, etiam alterum affirmandum sit: itemque utro negato, alterum quoque negandum: sive necessario, sive probabiliter. Hac enim consequutio per istam consensionem inteligenda est', Piscator, I.2, B1ᵛ. Fraunce later acknowledged this borrowing in LL, D2ᵛ.

CHAPTER 3

~

Of the Final and the Efficient Cause[1]

A cause is that by whose power and force° a thing is.[2]
　　A cause is either without the thing caused and made, or in it.
　　The cause without the thing is either the end or the efficient.
　　The end is a cause for the which, or for whose sake, the thing is.
　　Palinode, in the Fifth Eglogue:

> Good is no good but if it be spend:
> God giveth good for none other end. ('May', 71–72; SC 39)

[8ʳ]　　Thenot, in the Second Eglogue:

> It chanced after upon a day
> 10　　The husbandman° self to come that way
> Of custom for to surview° his ground
> And his trees of state in compass round. ('February', 143–46; SC 19)

The end of good is to be spent; the end of the husbandman's° going abroad was to view his ground.
　　The efficient is a cause from the which a thing is. Colin, in the First Eglogue:

> A thousand sithes° I curse that careful° hour
> Wherein I longed the neighbour town to see,
> And eke ten thousand sithes° I bless the stour°
> Wherein I saw so fair a light as she.
> 20　　Yet all for nought: such sight hath bred my bane.
> Ah God, that love should breed both joy and pain! ('January', 49–54; SC 7ₐ)

Again, in the Second Eglogue the Briar useth the efficient and the final cause:

> Ah, my sovereign Lord of creatures all,
> Thou placer of plants both humble and tall,
> Was not I planted of thine own hand
> To be the primrose of all thy land,
> With flowering blossoms to furnish the prime
> And scarlet berries in summer time? ('February', 163–68; SC 20)

---

[1] **Title**] On Fraunce's departures from Ramus in this and next chapter, see Introduction, pp. 28–29, and the notes in this chapter.

[2] **A cause […] a thing is**] 'Caussa, est cuius vi res est', Ramus/Piscator, I.3, B1ᵛ.

In 'April', Hobbinol declareth the procreant causes of Elisa in that his song:

30   Pan may be proud that ever he begot
             Such a bellibone.°
         And Syrinx rejoice that ever was her lot
             To bear such an one. (91–94; SC 31ₐ)

In 'May', Piers useth conservant causes:

         But tract of time and long prosperity
         (That, nurse of vice; this, of insolency)
         Lulled the shepherds in such security
         [That, not content with loyal obeisance,
         Some gan° to gape for greedy governance
40   And match themself with mighty potentates,
         Lovers of lordship, and troublers of states.]³ (117–23; SC 41ₐ)

In 'June', Hobbinol reciteth a number of particular efficients of delight and pleasure, describing thereby the place where he was, thus:

         Lo, Colin, here the place, whose pleasant site
         From other shades hath weaned° my wandering mind.
         Tell me, what wants me here to work delight?
         The simple air, the gentle warbling wind
         So calm, so cool, as nowhere else I find;
         The grassy ground with dainty daisies dight;
50   The bramble bush, where birds of every kind
         To the waters' fall their tunes attemper° right. (1–8; SC 50)

In 'July', Thomalin, describing the time of the years poetically, in the end bringeth in the Dog Star as cause of death:

         And now the Sun hath reared up
             his fiery-footed team,°
         Making his way between the Cup
             and golden Diadem;
         The rampant Lion hunts he fast
             with Dog of noisome breath,
60   Whose baleful barking brings in haste
             pine,° plagues, and dreary death.⁴ (17–24; SC 58)

[8ᵛ]   *A cause*] The Grecians have significant words: ἅιτιον, ἀιτίατον. The Latinists, nothing so proper, unless you take those dunsical° words *causa, causatum*, which we imitate in English to very good purpose, as 'the cause' and 'the thing caused'. Whereas the word 'cause' comprehendeth end, efficient, matter, and form, so 'the thing caused', answering ἀιτίατον in Greek, and *causatum* in Latin, containeth the several° effect of every particular cause. As proportionably we may say 'the end' and 'the thing ended', 'the maker' and 'the thing made', or 'the matter' and 'the thing material', 'the form' and 'the thing formed'. For otherwise, although in Latin this word 'effect' doth stand for all four, yet it only betokeneth° that which is made of the efficient.

---

³ **That […] of states**] These lines are added in this edition, cueing on Ms's 'etc.'.
⁴ **Cup, Diadem, Lion, Dog**] The astrological realities and metaphors behind these references are noted by E.K. See Brooks-Davies, p. 123. As J. C. Eade summarizes, 'The cup is Crater, standing on the back of Hydra; the diadem is Corona Borealis (Ariadne's Crown); the lion is Leo, and the dog is Canis Major, which rises with the sun in high summer. In Spenser's time, the Dog Star was associated with the plague, and the poet depicts the panting hound as spreading infection, as E.K. notes', 'Constellations', in *The Spenser Encyclopedia*, ed. by A. C. Hamilton (Toronto: University of Toronto Press, 1990), p. 190.

70   *Without the thing*] Piscator admitteth this distribution of causes as more convenient than that
of Ramus, but Beurhusius and some others like better that of Ramus.[5] For my part, seeing Logic
is an art of reasoning, and in reason the end is always first considered, although in use and
practice last put down, I see good reason why I should give it the first place. The end may be thus
more fully distinguished out of Piscator,[6] but yet it is not any absolute division:

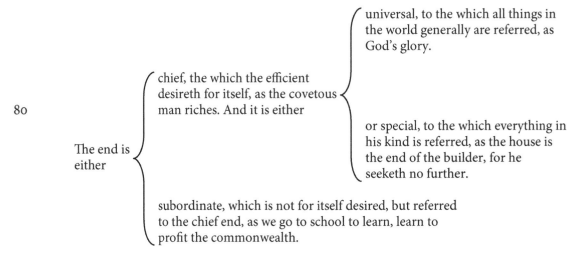

80

The end is either

universal, to the which all things in
the world generally are referred, as
God's glory.

chief, the which the efficient
desireth for itself, as the covetous
man riches. And it is either

or special, to the which everything in
his kind is referred, as the house is
the end of the builder, for he
seeketh no further.

subordinate, which is not for itself desired, but referred
to the chief end, as we go to school to learn, learn to
profit the commonwealth.

The efficient] The efficient, as Master Chaderton very well noteth, and Ramus himself granteth,[7]
90   cannot be divided into any parts which are opposite and contrary one to another. For, although
it be distinguished by diverse sorts of making a thing, as by procreation and conservation, alone
and by the help of others, by itself or accidentally, which Ramus putteth down,[8] yet these be but
only several° considerations in reason, whereby rather the manner of doing than the cause itself
is distinguished. Yet for easiness and perspicuity it may be thus parted out of Piscator:[9]

---

[5] **Piscator admitteth [...] that of Ramus**] Piscator criticizes Ramus's unnamed categorization ('genere anonymo') of causes into efficient and material, on the one hand, and formal and final, on the other, and proposes the division accepted by Fraunce: 'Causa est aut externa, aut interna. Externa, quae extra effectum manet: ut efficiens et finis. Interna, quae effectum ingreditur: ut materia et forma' (The cause is either internal or external. External is that which remains outside the effect, as the efficient and final. Internal is that which enters the effect, as matter and form), Piscator, I.3, B2^r. Talon explains that, among Aristotle's various divisions, Ramus prefers that into prior and posterior: 'quatuor genera, efficientem, materiam, formam, finem praecipue probantur, et eadem P. Ramus est amplexatus, naturaque; priora praeposuit, postposuit posteriora. Nam si efficiens sit et materia, non protinus erit forma et finis: sed contra si forma sit et finis, caeteras causas necesse est antecessisse' (Four kinds — the efficient, matter, form, and the end — are chieflfy approved, and Ramus embraced these and naturally put the anterior first and the posterior after. Because, if the efficient and the matter take place, will the form and the end not come immediately after? Contrarily, if the form and the end are given, it is necessary that the other causes precede them), Ramus, *Dialectica, Audomari Talaei praelectionibus illustrata* (Cologne: Theodor Gras, 1573), I.3, B6^r. Fraunce later changed his mind and accepted Ramus's classification into efficient and material, or 'before the thing caused', and formal and final, or 'in and with the thing caused' (LL, D3^r–I1^r). This division is presented in tabular form in Beurhaus I, C6^v. This issue is treated more amply in the Introduction, pp. 28–29.

[6] **out of Piscator**] Fraunce's tables summarize the discussion in Piscator, D7^{r-v}.

[7] **Master Chaderton [...] Ramus himself granteth**] Chaderton's lessons on logic are not extant. Ramus does not make this point in any version of the *Dialectica* consulted here.

[8] **diverse sorts [...] putteth down**] See 'De efficiente procreante aut conservante' (Ramus/Piscator, I.3, B1^v–B2^r), 'De efficiente sola aut cum aliis' (I.4, B2^v–B3^r), and 'De efficiente per se aut per accidens' (I.5, B4^r). These divisions are treated more amply in Ramus, *Dialectique*, B1^r–B3^r.

[9] **parted out of Piscator**] The partitions of the first table adapt the long discussion in Piscator, B2^r (only first and last sentence quoted here): 'Efficiens, est aut generans aut corrompens. [...] Sic morbus labefactat vitam animalis', The second table also draws on Piscator, B3^r (only first and last sentence are given): 'Efficiens, est aut solitaria aut socia. [...] Adiuvans seu ministra est, quae ita principali movetur, ut etiam seipsam moveat'.

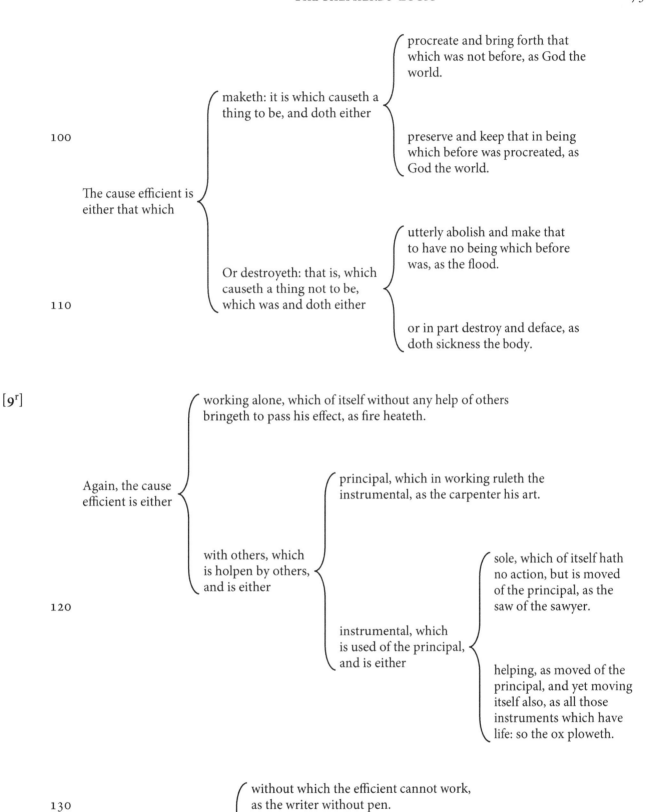

100

The cause efficient is either that which

maketh: it is which causeth a thing to be, and doth either

procreate and bring forth that which was not before, as God the world.

preserve and keep that in being which before was procreated, as God the world.

110

Or destroyeth: that is, which causeth a thing not to be, which was and doth either

utterly abolish and make that to have no being which before was, as the flood.

or in part destroy and deface, as doth sickness the body.

[9ʳ]

Again, the cause efficient is either

working alone, which of itself without any help of others bringeth to pass his effect, as fire heateth.

with others, which is holpen by others, and is either

principal, which in working ruleth the instrumental, as the carpenter his art.

instrumental, which is used of the principal, and is either

sole, which of itself hath no action, but is moved of the principal, as the saw of the sawyer.

helping, as moved of the principal, and yet moving itself also, as all those instruments which have life: so the ox ploweth.

120

130

The cause instrumental is either such

without which the efficient cannot work, as the writer without pen.

without the which the principal could work if he would.

CHAPTER 4

～

Of the Matter and the Form

The cause without the thing caused is as we have put down. Now followeth the cause in the thing made, which is either the matter or the form. The matter is the cause of the which a thing is made.[1] So, in 'August', Willy showeth what matter his cup was made of, thus:

> Then lo, Perigot, the pledge which I plight:
> A mazer° ywrought° of the maple warre.° (25–26; SC 72ₐ)

In 'December', Colin in his complaint declareth what was the matter of the bees' frame:

> Where I was wont° to seek the honey bee
> Working her formal rooms in wexen° frame.
> The grisly toadstool grown there mought° I see
> And loathed paddocks lording° on the same. (67–70; SC 105)

And, in the same complaint, the matter of his cottages:

> And learned of lighter timber cotes to frame
> Such as might save my sheep and me fro shame. ('December', 77–78; SC 106)

Again, in the same song:

> To make fine cages for the nightingale,
> And baskets of bulrushes was my wont.° ('December', 79–80; SC 107)

The form is a cause by the which a thing is that which it is, and therefore by the form things be distinguished.[2]

The form is ever inherent or, as it were, engraven in the thing, as the reasonable soul in man.

But the natural forms of things, though they may be conceived by reason, yet they cannot well be uttered by speech.

The artificial form of things is much more easy both to be conceived in reason and expressed by word. And therefore of such forms there be very many.[3]

So, in 'August', Willy describeth the form of his cup that he laid against Perigot's spotted lamb:

---

[1] **The matter […] made]** Ramus/Piscator, I.6, B4ᵛ. The translation is taken almost verbatim from Fenner: 'The matter is a cause of the which the thing caused is made', *The Artes*, B2ʳ.

[2] **The form […] distinguished]** Ramus/Piscator, I.7, B5ᵛ. Compare with Fenner: 'The forme is a cause, by the which a thing is that which it is: and so differeth from all other things', *The Artes*, B2ʳ.

[3] **The form […] many]** 'But the naturall forme of thinges, though they may be conceyued by reason, yet they can not well be vttered by speache. The artificiall forme of thinges is much more easie to bee conceyued in reason, and vttered in wordes: and therefore of such speaches there be many', Fenner, *The Artes*, B2ʳ. On borrowings from Fenner and the dating of the manuscript, see Introduction, pp. 21–22.

Then lo, Perigot, the pledge which I plight:
A mazer° ywrought° of the maple warre°
Wherein is enchased° many a fair sight
Of bears and tigers that maken fierce war.
And over them spread a goodly wild vine
30   Entrailed° with a wanton ivy twine.

Thereby is a lamb in the wolf's jaws.
But see how fast renneth° the shepherd's swain°
To save the innocent from the beast's paws.
And here with his sheephook hath him slain.
Tell me: such a cup hast thou ever seen?
Well mought° it beseem° any harvest queen.[4] (25–36; SC 72ᵦ)

In 'February', Cuddy describeth the girdle he gave Phyllis by the form:

I won her with a girdle of gelt°
Embossed° with bugle° about the belt. (65–66; SC 14)

40   And in the same eglogue he layeth down the accidental and external form together, with some
effects of his bullock:

Seest how brag° yond° bullock bears,
So smirk,° so smooth, his pricked ears?
His horns bene as broad as rainbow bent;
His dewlap as lithe° as lass of Kent.
See how he venteth° into the wind:
Weenest° of love is not his mind? ('February', 71–76; SC 16)

---

[4] **Then lo […] queen**] For a detailed commentary of Fraunce's use of this instance in LL, G3ʳ, see Goeglein,
'Reading English Ramist Logic Books', pp. 229–33.

CHAPTER 5

Of the Thing Caused

The thing caused is that which is made of the causes, which usually, though not so properly, is called the effect. Therefore, howsoever anything be moved, altered, or changed, the motion and the thing moved belong to this place, and are called effects or things caused.[1]

Praises and dispraises commonly are fet° from this place.[2] So, in 'February', Thenot telleth how the Briar made a pitiful complaint to the husbandman° dispraising and exclaiming against the Oak, by reason of his injurious dealing, which he at large putteth down the rather to incense the husbandman° against the Oak:[3]

> How falls it then that this faded Oak —
> Whose body is sere,° whose branches broke,
> Whose naked arms stretch unto the fire —
> Unto such tyranny doth aspire,
> Hindering with his shade my lovely light
> And robbing me of the sweet sun's sight?
> [10^{r}] So beat his old boughs my tender side
> That oft the blood springeth from wounds wide,
> Untimely my flowers forced to fall
> That bene the honour of your coronal.°
> And oft he lets his cankerworms light
> Upon my branches to work me more spite;
> And oft his hoary° locks down doth cast,
> Wherewith my fresh flowerets bene defaced.
> For this and many more such outrage,
> Craving your goodlihead° to assuage
> The rancorous rigour of his might,
> Nought ask I but only to hold my right. (169–86; SC 21)

---

[1] **Therefore [...] caused]** 'Effectum est quod e causis existit. Sive igitur gignatur, sive corrumpatur, sive modo quodlibet moveatur quidlibet, hic motus et res facta Effectum dicitur', Ramus/Piscator, I.9, D7^{v}. See Beurhaus II, *Inv*$_{3}$. LL adds: 'as also, sayings and writings, thoughts and all cogitations, although neither uttered nor accomplished' (I1^{r}).

[2] **Praises [...] this place]** Beurhaus II, *Inv*$_{4}$.

[3] **Briar, Oak]** Although not capitalized in Ms, Spenser's practice is observed here, as both are personified in Thenot's fable.

In 'May', Piers proveth the shepherds to be evil by their effects thus:

> Those faitours° little regarden their charge
> While they, letting their sheep run at large
> Passen their time, that should be sparely spent
> ₃₀ In lustihead and wanton merriment.
> Thilk° same bene shepherds for the devil's stead
> That playen while their flock be unfed. (39–44; SC 35ₐ)

In the same eglogue, Palinode setteth for the effects of youth agreeable to the pleasantness of the time:

> Yougthes folk° now flocken in everywhere
> To gather May buskets and smelling briar
> And home they hasten the posts to dight°
> And all the kirk pillars ere daylight,
> With hawthorn buds and sweet eglantine,
> ₄₀ And girlonds° of roses and sops-in-wine.° ('May', 9–14; SC 33ᵦ)

In 'July', Thomalin praiseth Christ, the Great Shepherd, by his effect:

> O blessed sheep, O shepherd great,
>   that bought his flock so dear,
> And them did save with bloody sweat
>   from wolves that would them tear! (53–56; SC 59ₐ)

In the Tenth Eglogue, Piers rehearseth the effects of love in these words:

> Ah fon,° for Love does teach him climb so high,
> And lifts him up out of the loathsome mire:
> Such immortal mirror as he doth admire
> ₅₀ Would raise one's mind above the starry sky
> And cause a caitiff° courage to aspire,
> For lofty love doth loathe a lowly eye. ('October', 91–96; SC 94)

Colin, in 'December', repeateth the pastimes and effects of his youth in these verses:

> Whilom° in youth, when flowered my joyful spring,
> Like swallow swift I wandered here and there,
> For heat of heedless lust me so did sting
> That I of doubted danger had no fear,
>   I went the wasteful woods and forest wide
>   Withouten dread of wolves to bene espied.

> [10ᵛ] ₆₀ I wont° to range among the mazy thicket
> And gather nuts to make me Christmas game,
> And joyed oft to chase the trembling pricket,
> Or hunt the heartless hare till she were tame.
>   What wreaked° I of wintry ages waste?
>   Tho° deemed I my spring would ever last.

> How often have I scaled the craggy° oak,
> All to dislodge the raven off her nest!
> How have I wearied with many a stroke
> The stately walnut tree, the while the rest
> ₇₀   Under the tree fell all for nuts at strife —
>   For ylike° to me was liberty and life! ('December', 19–36; SC 103ₐ)

And so after, in the same pitiful lamentation, the effects of his summer and winter be set down.[4]
But in 'March', Thomalin's long tale of Cupid hath almost nothing else but a rehearsal of his own
doing and Cupid's. The narration is this:

> It was upon a holiday,
> When shepherds' grooms han° leave to play,
>   I cast to go a-shooting.
> Long wandering up and down the land
> With bow and bolts in either hand
> 80   For birds in bushes tooting,°
> At length within an ivy-tod° —
> There shrouded was the little god —
>   I heard a busy bustling.
> I bent my bolt against the bush,
> List'ning if anything did rush,
>   But then heard no more rustling.
> Tho,° peeping close into the thick,
> Might see the moving of some quick
>   Whose shape appeared not.
> 90 But, were it fairy, fiend, or snake,
> My courage earned° it to awake
>   And manfully thereat shot.
> With that sprong° forth a naked swain
> With spotted wings like peacock's train,
>   And laughing lope° to a tree:
> His gilden quiver at his back,
> And silver bow, which was but slack,
>   Which lightly he bent at me.
> That seeing, I levelled again
> 100 And shot at him with might and main,
>   As thick as it had hailed:
> So long I shot that all was spent,
> Tho° pumy stones I hastely hent°
>   And threw, but nought availed.
> He was so wimble° and so wight,°
> From bough to bough he leaped light,
>   And oft the pumies[5] latched.
> Therewith, afraid, I ran away
> But he that erst seemed but to play
> [11ʳ]   110   A shaft in earnest snatched,
> And hit me, running, in the heel.
> Forthen° I little smart did feel,
>   But soon it sore increased,
> And now it rankleth more and more,
> And inwardly it fest'reth sore,
>   Ne wote° I how to cease it. (61–102; SC 24)

---

[4] **summer and winter be set down**] For the effects of Colin's summer, or maturity, see 'December', 55–90. For
those of winter, or old age, see 103–50.
[5] **pumy, pumies**] Present-day 'pumice' is usually a mass noun (*OED*). However, Spenser's forms are preserved
in order to differentiate a mass from a plural form.

All these effects from the beginning almost to the end be brought in for declaration sake. Only those effects of Cupid in the latter part of the narration are to prove that which Thomalin spake before, which was this:

120   Willy, I ween° thou be assot,°
        For lusty Love still sleepeth not,
            But is abroad at his game. ('March', 25–27; SC 23)

This argument of things caused is very large, containing not only deeds and words, but thoughts and words, and all motions whatsoever, as is said before. For, seeing the natural form is the cause of all motions, actions, operations, generations, corruptions, and augmentations whatsoever, why should not these things be called things caused, whenas° they come from a cause?

CHAPTER 6

~

Of the Subject

Thus much of the argument that is absolutely agreeable. Now followeth the argument after a certain manner agreeable, as be the subject and the adjunct. The subject is that whereunto something is adjoined. For, as the qualities of the body and mind are in the body and mind as subject, so a man may be described by the manner of his apparel and diet, so every place is the subject of the thing which is in it.[1]

Thenot, in 'February', saith thus:

> You thinken to be Lords of the Year
> But eft,° when ye count you freed from fear,
> Comes the breme° winter with chamfered° brows,
10 > Full of wrinkles and frosty furrows. (41–44; SC 13)

Where the brows be the subject of wrinkles and furrows. In 'April', Hobbinol beginneth his song in praise of Elisa with the subject of the place:

> Ye dainty nymphs that in this blessed brook
>   Do bathe your breast,
> Forsake your watery bowers, and hither look
>   At my request;
> And eke you virgins that on Parnass dwell,
> Whence floweth Helicon, the learned well,[2]
>   Help me to blaze
20 >   Her worthy praise.
> Which in her sex doth all excel. (37–45; SC 27)

Where the brook is the subject to their body, and Parnass mount to the well Helicon. So a little after:

> See where she sits upon the grassy green,
>   (O seemly sight!)
> Yclad° in scarlet, like a maiden queen,
>   And ermines white.
> Upon her head a cremosin° coronet,
> With damask roses and daffadillies set.
30 >   Bay leaves between
[11ᵛ] >   And primroses green
> Embellish the sweet violet. ('April', 55–63; SC 29ₐ)

---

[1] **Thus much [...] in it**] Loosely adapted from Ramus/Piscator, I.10, B8ᵛ. Fraunce provides a more literal translation in LL, L2ʳ.

[2] **Parnass [...] Helicon, the learned well**] Mount Helicon is in the same range as Mount Parnassus, so they were often confused. Hippocrene, the Muses' fountain, sprang from a stroke of Pegasus's hoof on Mount Helicon. See E.K.'s gloss on 'Helicon', Brooks-Davies, p. 74.

Where Elisa is the subject to the particulars.

In 'November', Colin beginneth his funeral song with invocation of Melpomene,[3] whom he maketh to be conversant in mourning:

> Up then, Melpomene, thou mournfull'st Muse of nine. (53; SC 95)

But, far more manifestly in the same song afterwards, he putteth down the subject wherein Dido her senses and internal faculties were occupied:

> Dido is gone afore: whose turn shall be the next?
> There lives she with the blessed gods in bliss,
> There drinks she nectar with ambrosia mixed,
> And joys enjoys that mortal men do miss. ('November', 193–96; SC 102)

And again for the place, in the same song:

> I see thee, blessed soul, I see,
> Walk in Elysian fields so free. ('November', 178–79; SC 100)

A subject] Not only οὐσία, or ὑπότασις, an essence or substance, but also whatsoever can be imagined or fained° to have anything adjunct unto it, in it, or about it. So one quality may be the subject to another, as 'virtue is commendable'. Subjects be diverse and may, for the more easy explication of them, be distinguished as Piscator putteth down, although not artificially:[4]

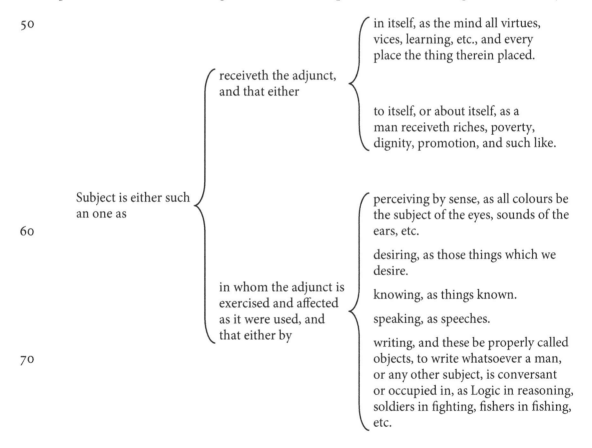

Subject is either such an one as

- receiveth the adjunct, and that either
  - in itself, as the mind all virtues, vices, learning, etc., and every place the thing therein placed.
  - to itself, or about itself, as a man receiveth riches, poverty, dignity, promotion, and such like.
- in whom the adjunct is exercised and affected as it were used, and that either by
  - perceiving by sense, as all colours be the subject of the eyes, sounds of the ears, etc.
  - desiring, as those things which we desire.
  - knowing, as things known.
  - speaking, as speeches.
  - writing, and these be properly called objects, to write whatsoever a man, or any other subject, is conversant or occupied in, as Logic in reasoning, soldiers in fighting, fishers in fishing, etc.

---

[3] **Melpomene […] mourning**] Daughter of Zeus and Mnemosyne, Melpomene was the muse of tragic poetry.
[4] **as Piscator putteth down**] 'Itaque ut ista distinguantur, notanda est subiecti divisio. Sujectum igitur aut recipit rem adjunctam, aut eam occupat et afficit. Quae docendi gratia appellentur subiectum recipiens aut occupans. Subiectum recipiens, rursum duplex est: recipit enim rem adjunctam vel in se, vel ad se. Subiectum occupans est, in quo res adjuncta (videlicet homo aut aliud animal) occupatur atque exercetur sentiendo, appetendo, cognoscendo, loquendo, scribendo; atque hoc proprie in scholis vocatur Objectum', Piscator, I.10, C1ʳ⁻ᵛ; **although not artificially**] unlike Fraunce's translation, not arranged in tabular form.

CHAPTER 7

≈

Of the Adjunct

The adjunct is that whereunto something is subjected. And as every place is the subject of the thing placed, so time, that is to say, the continuance of every thing, is the adjunct of those things which do continue in time. So also all qualities which either be proper or common are truly called adjuncts. Finally, every thing which agreeth unto another, being neither the cause nor the effect thereof, is an adjunct of the thing whereunto | it doth agree.

By proper qualities I mean such as do agree to one common subject, and every special part thereof only and always, as the faculty of laughing agreeth to man as the proper subject, and also to every special and singular man contained generally under man, and also agreeth unto man only and at all times.

10 By common qualities I mean such as do not agree after this manner.[1]

This argument, as it is not so forceable° as the subject, so it is much more copious and plentiful.[2]

Examples be excellent and infinite in the *Calendar*, but a few among many shall now suffice. And first in this speech 'To His Book':

> But if that any ask thy name,
> Say thou wert base begot with blame,
> For-thy° thereof thou takest shame. (13–15; SC 1)

Then, in 'January', Colin Clout saith:

> All as the sheep, such was the shepherd's look,
> 20 For pale and wan he was — alas the while.
> May seem he loved, or else some care he took. ('January', 7–9; SC 2_b)

Thenot, in 'February', of himself:

> Self have I worn out thrice threttie° years,
> Some in much joy, many in many tears. ('February', 17–18; SC 11_a)

Where the thrice thirty years be an adjunct.
In 'May', Piers reasoneth:

> For younkers,° Palinode, such follies fit;
> But we tway° bene men of elder wit. (17–18; SC 34_a)

---

[1] **The adjunct [...] manner**] Ramus/Piscator, I.11, C2ᵛ.
[2] **This argument [...] plentiful**] Beurhaus II, *Inv*₅.

In 'March', Thomalin argueth the spring to be at hand by these adjuncts:

30 The grass now gins° to be refreshed,
    The swallow peeps out of her nest,
      And cloudy welkin cleareth. (10–12; SC 22)

In 'July', Thomalin describeth Abel by his adjuncts compared in quality:

  As meek he was as meek mought° be,
      simple as simple sheep;
  Humble, and like in each degree
      the flock which he did keep. (129–32; SC 65)

And, in the same discourse, displaying the demeanour of our shepherds, [and their pomp and gorgeous attire,]³ he saith:

40 But now (thanked be god therefore)
      the world is well amend;
  Their weeds bene not so nighly wore,
      such simplesse mought° them shend;°
  They bene yclad° in purple and pall,°
      so hath their god them blissed°
  They reign and rulen over all
      and lord it, as they list —
  Ygirt° with belt of glitterand° gold, etc. ('July', 169–77; SC 68ₐ)

In 'April', Hobbinol doth excellently paint out Elisa in her adjunct colours, whereof I put down
50 some in the examples of subjects; the rest are there to be seen (55–63, SC 29_b; 136–44, SC 32_b).
So in 'August', Perigot his bouncing bellibone:°

[12ᵛ] *Perigot.* I saw the bouncing bellibone,°
  Willy.   (hey ho bonnibel°)
  Perigot. Tripping over the dale alone
  Willy.   (she can trip it very well)
  Perigot. Well decked in a frock of grey,
  Willy.   (hey ho grey is greet)
  Perigot. And in a kirtle° of green say,°
  Willy.   (the green is for maidens meet).
60 *Perigot.* A chaplet° on her head she wore
  Willy.   (hey ho chaplet°),
  Perigot. Of sweet violets therein was store
  Willy.   (she sweeter than the violet). (61–72; SC 74ₐ)

In 'November', Colin useth this argument very oft in declaration manner where he bewaileth Dido's death, as 'coloured chaplets'° (115), 'knotted rush rings' (116), 'gilt rosemary' (116), 'mantled meadows' (128; SC 98), etc.
Thomalin, in 'July':

  The hills, where dwelled holy saints
      I reverence and adore —
70 Not for themself, but for the saint
      which han be dead of yore. (113–16; SC 64)

---

³ **and their pomp and gorgeous attire**] Added in LL, M1ᵛ.

So much of agreeable arguments: in consideration whereof, things that differ one from another are called one, the same, or agreeable. So before, Colin, in 'January', was said to have the same look that his sheep had:

> All as the sheep, such was the shepherd's look
> For pale and wan he was (alas the while), etc. (7–8; SC 2_a)

Meaning one in adjunct, not in essence: so in like manner of the rest of the agreeable arguments we may say.

Adjunct] The same almost which the Grecians call περιουσία[4] and περιστάσις, 'circumstances'. If you take that word largely, whatsoever is added to a thing after it is once framed and made of his essential causes. Adjuncts must be proportionably distinguished, as subjects were before:[5]

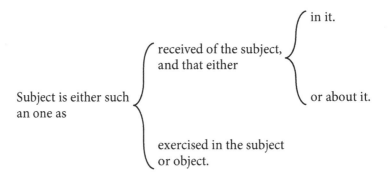

One and the same] Here is logically put down that which the dunses° perversely teach in their diverse sorts of identity and diversity, as *numero, specie, genere*, etc.[6] Some there be that give a proper and peculiar place to signs and conjectural tokens but frivolously. For they belong all other to this of adjuncts, or that other of effects, or else they | be testimonies and witnesses.[7]

[13ʳ]

80

90

---

[4] περιουσία] literally, belongings.

[5] **Table**] Fraunce silently tabulates the division in Piscator, II.11, C3ᵛ: 'Est autem hic notanda adiunctorum divisio. Adiunctum igitur aut receptum est aut occupatum. Receptum, quod subjecto vel inhaeret vel adhaeret. Occupatum, quod in subjecto seu obiecto occupatur'.

[6] **the dunses […] etc.**] Fraunce refers generally to theories of identity and individuation as first proposed by Duns Scotus (1266–1308). For a useful summary, see Richard Cross, 'Medieval Theories of Haecceity', *The Stanford Encyclopedia of Philosophy*, ed. by Edward N. Zalta (2014), <http://plato.stanford.edu/archives/ sum2014/entries/medieval-haecceity>, last accessed 10 December 2014. **dunses**] This derogatory term was replaced with the more neutral 'others' in LL, M3ʳ; ***numero, specie, genere***] literally, 'in number, in species, in kind', referring to different modes of identity and difference.

[7] **Some […] witnesses**] This commentary echoes Beurhaus II, Ee5ʳ⁻ᵛ, which bases his rejection of signs as a proper argument on Agricola and Melanchton. See Rudolph Agricola, *De inventione dialectica libri tres* (Cologne: Hero Fuchs, 1527), I.23, O3ʳ, and Melanchton, *Erotemata*, Y3ᵛ–Y4ʳ.

CHAPTER 8

Of Diverse Arguments

The agreeable arguments being finished, now followeth the disagreeable.

The disagreeable is that which disagreeth from the thing which it doth argue.

Disagreeable arguments are in respect° of themselves known alike, or one as well as another, and also do equally argue on another, albeit by their disagreement they do now plainly appear and are more easily known.

Disagreeable arguments be either diverse or opposite.

Diverse are disagreeable arguments which differ only in respect.° They are often in authors, and many be expressed by these notes: 'not this, but that', 'although', or 'albeit', 'nevertheless', or 'notwithstanding'.[1]

10   Hobbinol, in 'April':

> Nor this nor that so much doth make me mourn,
> But for the lad whom long I loved so dear
> Now loves a lass that all his love doth scorn. (9–11; SC 26)

And Thomalin, in 'July', replying on Morrell:

> Siker° thou speaks like a lewd lorel°
>   of heaven to deemen so:
> Howbe° I am but rude and borrel,°
>   yet nearer ways I know. (93–96; SC 61)

Known alike] This is properly pertaining to disagreeable arguments, as that which severeth
20   them from agreeable arguments. For the cause is better known than the effect, the subject than the adjunct. Also the cause doth more effectually argue than the effect, and the subject than the adjunct.

Disagreeable] A disagreeable argument is first, is *primum argumentum*, not *a primis ortum*,[2] for it dependeth not of the other, yet the other may be sometimes disagreeable, as causes from causes, effects from effects, etc. But this inferreth nothing else but a double confirmation of diverse affections° in the first arguments, and maketh nothing at all to prove these not to be first. For, if they were not first, but made of the first, they should have the same affections° as had their first, which now they have not, but a proper one to themselves, which consisteth in a certain opposition clean contrary to the other which were agreeable.

---

[1] **The agreeable** […] **'notwithstanding'**] Translated from Ramus/Piscator, I.12, C4^r. Fraunce inserts another example from Spenser in LL, N2^r: 'Colin, in "January": Colin loved not Hobbinol, but Rosalind' (55–60, SC 8).
[2] *primum argumentum*, not *a primis ortum*] 'a first argument, not made of the first'.

30   *Only in respect°*] Not indeed and naturally in respect° of the things themselves, which may
concur in one, but in respect° of his meaning that so put them down. Therefore, the chief use of
diverse arguments is in declaration, to wit, in distinguishing those things by reason and several°
consideration which otherwise might seem to the rude and simple to be but one and the same,
and not in concluding syllogistically.[3]

---

[3] **Only [...] syllogistically**] Fraunce draws on Piscator, although he omits the examples: '*Sola ratione*] Non
etiam re, ut opposita. Usus diversorum praecipue videtur positus in declarando, ut scilicet inter se distinguantur
quae ab imperitis propter cognationem confunduntur. Non victoriam, sed insignia victoriae reportarunt. Non
scelus fuit, sed error. Non liberalis, sed progigus est' (*Only in respect*] Not also in the sense, as the opposites.
The use of diverse arguments chiefly seems to be ordained for declaring, so that those things can be
distinguished without any doubt which can be mistaken by the ignorant on account of their affinity. They
did not bring victory, but only the badges of victory. It was not crime, but error. Not liberal, but prodigal),
II.12, C4ʳ.

CHAPTER 9

~

Of the Opposite

[13ᵛ]   Opposites are disagreeable arguments which disagree both in respect° | and in matter, or thing itself, and therefore cannot agree unto the same thing, according to the same part, respect,° or time, as the same man cannot be hot and cold in the same part of his body at the same time. So Socrates cannot be father and son to the same man, sick and whole in the same time, so that, if one of those be affirmed, the other must be denied.

Opposites are either disparates or contraries.

Disparates are opposites whereof one is equally and alike opposed unto many, as liberality and covetousness, which are disparates to themselves and their extremes.[1]

Hobbinol, in 'April', in his song of Elisa:

10   Bring hither the pink and purple columbine,
          With gillyflowers;
      Bring coronations, and sops-in-wine
          Worn of paramours.
      Strew me the ground with daffadowndillies,°
      And cowslips, and kingcups, and loved lilies.
          The pretty paunce°
          And the chevisaunce°
      Shall match with the fair flower delice.° (136–44; SC 32ₐ)

All which herbs be equally differing one from another, and are therefore disparates.

---

[1] **Opposites […] extremes**] These paragraphs abridge Ramus/Piscator I.13, C4ᵛ. See also Beurhaus II, *Inv₉*.

CHAPTER 10

Of Contraries

Contraries are opposites whereof one only is opposed to one. Contraries are expressed either affirmatively or negatively. Affirmatively, which are uttered in speech by affirmative words, and are either relatives or repugnant arguments.

Relatives are contrary affirmatives, whereof one hath his natural affection° and being of the other, whereupon they are called relatives, as a father that hath a son, a son that hath a father, by reason of the which natural relation and reciprocation they are said to be *simul*, together by nature, so that he that knoweth the one perforcely must know the other.¹ But, according to this affection,° they are not contraries, but rather natural agreeable causes. Then only they are contraries when they are applied to one and the selfsame thing, in the same time, and in the same
10   respect.°² So, in 'April', Hobbinol reasoneth: Elisa is Syrinx's daughter, sprung of heavenly race, therefore not of any mortal seed:

> [For she is Syrinx' daughter, without spot,
> Which Pan, the shepherds' god, of her begot:
>> So sprung her grace
>> Of heavenly race;
> No mortal blemish may her blot. (50–54; SC 28)].³

In 'May', Palinode useth relative words of mother and son in his tale of the Fox and the Kid:

> So schooled the Gate° her wanton son,
> That answered his mother all should be done. (227–28; SC 47)

20   *One only*] That is, when the one is so contrary to the other as there cannot be the like contrariety unto any other thing whatsoever.

Affirmatives] In affirmatives there be two words of two things which naturally repugn the one to the other, but in negatives there be two words, yet but one thing; which one thing repugneth not any other contrary thing or nature, but the bare word denying the same nature.

---

¹ **Contraries [...] the other**] Translated from Ramus/Piscator, I.14, C5ʳ; **by reason [...] the other**] Beurhaus II, *Inv*₁₀.
² **Then only [...] in the respect**] 'Atqui argumentum talis relationis contrarium nihil habet, imo arguit mutuas causas [...] tum contraria vere sunt' (Ramus/Piscator, I.14, C5ᵛ). On the absence of this text from previous editions of the *Dialecticae libri duo*, see Introduction, p. 26.
³ **For she [...] her blot**] Although these lines are not quoted in Ms, they are inserted here in order to provide the example, in accordance with Fraunce's procedure throughout the work.

CHAPTER 11

~

Of Repugning° Arguments¹

Contrary repugnant° arguments are those which directly repugn° the one to the other, as liberality to illiberality.

Piers, in 'May':

Shepherd, I list none accordance make
With shepherd that does the right way forsake,
And of the twain, if choice were to me,
Had lever° my foe than my friend he be. (164–67; SC 42)

Colin, in 'December':

Love they him called that gave me checkmate,
But better mought they have behote° him Hate. (53–54; SC 104)

[Perigot, in 'August':

Ah Willy, when the heart is ill assayed°
How can bagpipe or joints be well apaid?° (5–6; SC 71)]²

Directly] By this I mean such a kind of contrariety as cannot be between any other arguments. Therefore it is the most vehement contrariety of all the rest. Whereas Piscator, out of Aristotelians, divideth those repugnant° arguments into those that be mediate and those that be immediate, he doth nothing artificially.³ True it is that between some repugnant° arguments there be other things put, but they be disparates, and therefore not here to be mentioned. Seeing then that those things in the middle be not repugnant,° why do we divide repugnants° into mediate and immediate? For it doth not belong to Logic to show what contrary repugnant° arguments have things between, what have not, but to other arts⁴ to whom the same things appertain.°

---

¹ **Of Repugning Arguments**] This chapter adapts Ramus/Piscator, I.15, C6ʳ⁻ᵛ.
² **Perigot [...] apaid**] Added in LL, N4ʳ.
³ **Piscator [...] artificially**] 'Notanda hic est adversorum divisio: alia enim sunt mediata, alia immediata. Mediata, quae aliquid in medio habent: ut album et nigrum multos colores intermedios habent: calidum et frigidum in medio habent tepidum. Immediata adversa sunt quae nihil in medio habent: ut virtus et vitium: sanitas et aegrotatio: fides et incredulitas. Hanc divisionem tradit Aristoteles in *Categoriis* capite περί τῶν αντικείμενῶν' (Here it is to be noted the division of adverse arguments: some are certainly mediate, the other unmediated. Mediate, which have something between them, as white and black have many intermediate colours, and hot and cold have lukewarm in between. Unmediated adverse arguments are those which have nothing between them, as virtue and vice, health and illness, faith and incredulity. Aristotle teaches this division under the heading 'Of the Opposites'), Piscator, I.15, C6ᵛ. See Aristotle, *Categories*, X, 11b.15–13a.2, Loeb I: pp. 82–91; **nothing artificially**] not in accordance with the principles of the art of logic (see *OED, artificial, adj.* †8).
⁴ **other arts**] for instance, grammar, which deals with semantic notions.

CHAPTER 12

Of Contradictories

Negatives are contraries whereof one affirmeth, the other denieth the same thing that was affirmed.

Negatives are either contradictories or privatives.

Contradictories are negative contraries whereof one denieth every other thing, that only excepted which was affirmed.[1]

Diggon, in 'September':

> Her° was her,° while it was daylight,
> But now her° is a most wretched wight.° (3–4; SC 79)

Her and not her. Colin, in 'November', in his song of Dido her death:

10
> Dido my dear, alas, is dead,
> Dead, and lieth wrapped in lead:
>   O heavy hearse!
> Let streaming tears be poured out in store:
>   O carfeul verse! (58–62; SC 96ᵦ)

Thenafter followeth the contradiction:

> Why then weeps Lobbin so without remorse?
> O Lobb, thy loss no longer lament:
> Dido nis° dead, but into heaven hent° —
>   Of happy hearse!
20
> Cease now, my Muse, now cease thy sorrow's source —
>   O joyful verse. ('November', 167–72; SC 99ₐ)

Dead and not dead be contradictories.

Denieth every other thing] In every subject whatsoever, not only in that wherein the thing affirmed by nature should be, as it is in privatives.[2]

[14ᵛ]   Contradiction is generally considered in invention, either in word or sentence, because an affirmation but argueth a negation. But, as it is by certain rules and laws framed in a sentence, so causing judgement, it only belongeth to the tractate° of axioms, and is there in judgement put down.[3]

---

[1] **Negatives [...] affirmed**] Translated from Ramus/Piscator, I.16, C6ᵛ.

[2] *Denieth* [...] **privatives**] '*Ubique*] id est, in subiecto quodlibet, non autem in eo tantum in quo affirmatum suapte natura inest, ut sit in privantibus', Piscator, I.16, C7ʳ.

[3] **in judgement put down**] For the treatment of contradiction in judgement, see II.4 below.

CHAPTER 13

Of Privatives

Privatives are those whereof one denieth only in that subject whereunto the affirmative agreeth by nature. And here the affirmative is called the habit, the negative the privation.[1] So blindness is the privation of the sight in that creature only whereunto sight naturally belongeth and, therefore, deprived of sight is said to be blind.

Colin, in 'December':

> Delight is laid abed and pleasure past;
> No sun now shines, clouds have all overcast. (137–38; SC 109)

Light and darkness, or cloudiness. But more plainly Piers, in 'May':

> For what concord han° light and dark sam?°
> Or what peace has the lion with the lamb? (168–69; SC 43)

And thus much of disagreeable arguments, by which one thing is said to be different from another.

So blindness] A stone, therefore, cannot be called blind, for that it was never framed of nature to have sight.[2]

---

[1] **Privatives [...] privation**] Ramus/Piscator, I.17, C7ᵛ. The second sentence reproduces Beurhaus, *Inv*₁₁.
[2] *So blindness* [...] **sight**]: '*In eo tantum subiecto*] Ut lapis etsi facultate videndi praeditus non est, tamen non dicitur caecus; quia lapis non est subiectum naturale visus, sed animal oculatum: quod si visu careat, proprie caecum dicitur' (*Only in that subject*] Although a stone is not endowed with the faculty of sight, yet it cannot be said to be blind, because a stone is not the subject of sight by nature; only an animal has eyes, which, if it were lacking in sight, then it could be properly called blind'), Piscator, I.17, C8ʳ.

CHAPTER 14

~

Of Comparison

Thus much of the simple arguments, both agreeable and disagreeable. Now follow the compared.

Compared arguments are such as are compared one with another. They are sometime briefly expressed by plain and evident signs, and sometimes largely distinguished by two parts, whereof the first is called the proposition, the second the reddition.°

Fained° compared arguments do also prove, but by the force of the comparison, not of the things compared.

Comparison is either in quantity or in quality.

Quantity is that whereby things compared are said to be of this or that quantity. Quantity is either equal or unequal.

10 Equal are those whose quantity is equal, and therefore it is an argument from the equal when one equal is argued or declared by another.

The equal hath certain proper signs whereby it is often expressed in authors, and may, if they want, always be added for the plainer declaration thereof, as 'equal', 'alike', 'the same that', 'as well as', 'so much', 'how much', 'so many', 'how many', 'no less', 'no greater', and such like.[1] Yet equals are sometimes expressed without any note at all.

Thomalin, in 'July', useth notes:

> Alsoon° may shepherd climb to sky
> that leads in lowly dales
> As goatherd proud that, sitting high,
> upon the mountain sails. (101–04; SC 63$_a$)

20

[15^r] Willy, in 'August', speaking of the sheep that gazed on the bellibone° as they were wood:°

> *Perigot.* My sheep did leave their wonted° food
> *Willy.* (hey hoe seely° sheep),
> *Perigot.* And gazed on her as they were wood,°
> *Willy.* (wood° as he that did them keep!). (73–76; SC 75)

And afterward:

> Never dempt° more right of beauty, I ween,°
> The shepherd of Ida, that judged beauty's queen[2]. ('August', 137–38; SC 77)

---

[1] **Thus much [...] such like**] Ramus/Piscator, I.18, C8^{r-v}; **and therefore [...] by another**] Beurhaus II, *Inv*$_{14}$.
[2] **the shepherd [...] queen**] Paris, while a shepherd on Mount Ida, declared Aphrodite the fairest among Olympian goddesses, before Hera and Athena.

And, speaking of her eye, he saith:

30   As clear as the crystal glass. ('August', 80; SC 76$_b$)

'Thomalin', in July:

To kirk the narre, from god more farre[3] ('July', 97; SC 62$_a$)

In 'February', Thenot puts down equals without any notes at all:

For Youngth° is a bubble blown up with breath,
Whose wit is weakeness, whose wage is death,
Whose way is wilderness, whose inn Penance.
And stoop-gallant° Age the host of Grievance. (87–90; SC 17)

---

[3] *To kirk [...] farre*] the nearer to the church the farther from God. On this proverb see Tilley, C$_{380}$.

CHAPTER 15

Of the More

Unequals are those which have not the same quantity.

Unequal is either more or less.

The more is that whose quantity is the greater. The signs thereof are these: 'not only but also', 'rather this than that'; also a grammatical comparison.[1]

Palinode, in 'May':

> I, as I am, had rather be envied —
> All were it of my foe — than fonly° pitied. (57–58; SC 38)

Hobbinol, in 'June':

> Colin, to hear thy rhymes and roundelays
> (Which thou wert wont° on wasteful hills to sing)
> I more delight than lark in summer days. (49–51; SC 53)

[Diggon, in 'September':

> For liker bene they to pluck away more
> Than aught of the gotten good to restore. (128–29; SC 87)

And after:

> Yet better leave off with a little loss
> Than by much wrestling to leese° the gross.° ('September', 134–35; SC 89)][2]

---

[1] **Unequals [...] comparison**] Adapted from Ramus/Piscator, I.19, D3ᵛ.
[2] **Diggon [...] gross**] Added in LL, X1ᵛ.

CHAPTER 16

Of the Less

The less is that whose quantity is lesser. The signs hereof are these: 'not this only', 'but not that'; also a denial of the equal, or equality, and by a grammatical comparison.[1]
[In 'August', Perigot and Willy.

>*Perigot.* A chaplet° on her head she wore
>*Willy.*   (hey ho chaplet),°
>*Perigot.* Of sweet violets therein was store
>*Willy.*   (she sweeter than the violet). (69–72; SC 74ᵦ)][2]

Thenot, in 'November':

>She, while she was (that was a woeful word to sayen),
>For beauty's praise and pleasance had no peer. (93–94; SC 97)

Sometimes without notes.

10

---

[1] **The less [...] comparison**] Abridged from Ramus/Piscator, I.20, D5ᵛ–D6ʳ.
[2] **In 'August' [...] violet**] Added in LL, X4r.

CHAPTER 17

❧

Of the Like

Hitherto of the comparison in quantity. Now followeth the comparison in quality, whereby things compared are called either like or unlike.

Like are those which have the selfsame quality. The likeness is called proportion; and the things the | like, proportionable.

[15ᵛ]

The signs be these: 'like as', 'even as', 'and so'; also a denial of the unlike.[1]

Diggon, in 'September':

> They looken big as bulls that bene bait,
> And bearen the crag° so stiff and so state,
> As cock on his dunghill crowing crank.° (44–46; SC 80)

10   And again:

> Wellaway° the while I was so fond
> To leave the good that I had in hand
> In hope of better that was uncouth:°
> So lost the dog the flesh in his mouth. ('September', 58–61; SC 81)

And below:

> Thus chatten the people in their steads,
> Ylike° as a monster of many heads.[2] ('September', 120–21; SC 86)

And this:

> For they bene like foul wagmires° overgrassed,
20 > That, if thy galage° once sticketh fast,
> The more to wind it out thou dost swink,°
> Thou mought° aye° deeper and deeper sink. ('September', 130–33; SC 88)

Perigot and Willy, in 'August':

> *Perigot.* As the bonny lass passed by
> *Willy.*   (hey ho bonny lass)
> *Perigot.* She roved at me with glancing eye,
> *Willy.*   (as clear as the crystal glass)
> *Perigot.* All as the sunny beam so bright
> *Willy.*   (hey ho the sunbeam)

---

[1] **Now [...] unlike**] Translated from Ramus/Piscator I.21, D8ᵛ–E1ʳ.
[2] **monster of many heads**] the Hydra, but also a proverbial pejorative political reference to the people. See *OED*, *many-headed*, adj.; also Tilley, H₂₇₈.

30   *Perigot.* Glanceth from Phoebus' face forthright;
        Willy.   (so love into my heart did stream).
        Perigot. Or as the thunder cleaves the clouds
        Willy.   (hey ho the thunder)
        Perigot. Wherin the lightsome levin° shrouds
        Willy.   (so cleaves my soul asunder).
        Perigot. Or as dame Cynthia's silver ray,
        Willy.   (hey ho the moonlight)
        Perigot. Upon the glittering wave doth play,
        Willy.   (such play is a piteous plight),
40   *Perigot.* The glance into my heart did glide, etc. (77–93; SC 76ₐ)

The parts of a similitude are sometimes distinguished by three terms or parts, and sometime
by four. The first is called a continued similitude; the second, a distinct and severed similitude.[3]
For the first, Cuddy, in 'February', hath this:

        The keen cold blows through my beaten hide
        All as I were through the body gride;
        My ragged runts° all shiver and shake
        As doen high towers in an earthquake. (3–6; SC 10)

Where one part must be twice repeated to couple and continue the similitude thus: as towers
shake with an earthquake, so my runts° shake. So after, in the same place:

50   And as the louring° weather looks down,
        So seemst thou like Good Friday to frown. ('February', 29–30; SC 12)

Colin, in 'January', useth a distinct similitude with four terms:

        Thou barren ground, whom winter's wrath hath wasted,
[16ʳ]   Art made a mirror to behold my plight:
        Whilom° thy fresh spring flowered, and after hasted
        Thy summer proud, with daffadillies° dight;°
        And now is come the winter's stormy state,
        Thy mantle marred wherein thou mask'd'st late.

        Such rage as winter's reigneth in my heart,
60   My life-blood freezing with unkindly cold,
        Such stormy stours° do breed my baleful smart
        As if my year were waste, and woxen° old.
        And yet, alas, but now my spring begun,
        And yet, alas, it is already done. (19–30; SC 5)

And again:

        You naked trees, whose shady leaves are lost,
        Wherein the birds were wont° to build their bower,
        And now are clothed with moss and hoary° frost
        Instead of blossoms, wherewith your buds did flower.
70   I see your tears that from your boughs do rain,
        Whose drops in dreary icicles remain.

        All so my lustful leaf is dry and sere,°
        My timely buds with wailing all are wasted:
        Thy blossom which my branch of youth did bear

_____

[3] **The parts** […] **severed similitude**] Fraunce translates Ramus's definitions of 'similitudo continua'
(Ramus/Piscator, I.21, E1ʳ) and 'similitudo disiuncta' (I.21, E1ᵛ).

With breathed sighs is blown away and blasted,
And from mine eyes the drizzling tears descend
As, on your boughs, the icicles depend.° ('January', 31–42; SC 6ₐ)

Lastly, Piers, in 'May', compareth the apish love of her young ones with the pampering° of prelates towards their children:[4]

80   Sike° men's folly I cannot compare
        Better than to the apes' foolish care,
        That is so enamoured of her young one
        (And yet, God wote,°[5] such cause hath she none)
        That with her hard hold and strait embracing
        She stoppeth the breath of her youngling:
        So, oftentimes, whenas° good is meant,
        Evil ensueth of wrong intent. (95–102; SC 40)

Fained° similitudes have like force with others. And here, in these similitudes so explicated, Aesopical fables have very good grace.[6]

---

[4] **apish love […] their children**] On the proverbial fatality of the ape's kindness to her children see Tilley, A₂₆₄. For its emblematic use see Whitney's 'Caecus amor prolis', in *A Choice of Emblemes* (London: Christopher Plantyn, 1586), p. 188. For contemporary Puritan texts condemning the prelates' favouring of their children, see *The Works of Edmund Spenser*, VII, 73–102n, pp. 299–300.

[5] **wote**] although Ms has 'wot', the context favours the Q1 subjunctive form.

[6] **Fained similitudes […] good grace**] 'Ficta similitudo pare vim habet superioribus illis, sed praeciove haec explicata similitudine Aesopi apologi excellunt' (Ramus/Piscator, I.21, E2ʳ). LL adds: 'Menenius Agrippa, using the tale of the rebellion between the belly and other parts of the body, and comparing that with the rebellion between the common people and senators of Rome, persuaded those that were fled to the Holy Hill quickly to return home to Rome and become comfortable citizens' (T4ᵛ–U1ʳ). On the Aesopic tradition of this fable, see 'Appendix', 130, in *Babrius and Phaedrus*, Loeb, pp. 446–47. On Menenius Agrippa's speech, see Livy, *Ab urbe condita*, II.32.9–12, Loeb I: pp. 322–25. Fraunce also employed this instance in 'Of the Nature and Use of Logic' (see 17n to that essay). On fables, with reference to the example of Menenius Agrippa, see Thomas Wilson, *The Arte of Rhetorique* (London: Richard Grafton, 1553), Dd1ᵛ: 'The feigned fables, such as are attributed vnto brute beastes, would not be forgotten at any hand. For not onely they delite the rude & ignoraunt, but also they helpe muche for perswasion […] The Romaine Menenius Agrippa allegyng vpon a tyme a fable of the conflicte made betwixt the partes of a mans bodie, and his belie: quieted a marueilouse stirre that was lyke to ensewe & pacified the vprore of Single sediciouse rebelles, whiche els thought for euer to destroy their countrie'.

CHAPTER 18

∾

Of the Unlike

Unlike is that whose quality is unlike or not the same, the notes whereof are: 'unlike', 'differing', 'otherwise', etc; and the denial of the like.[1]

Palinode, in 'May', showeth the unlike behaviour of others and themselves:

> Is not thilk° the merry month of May,
> When love lads masken in fresh array?
> How falls it then, we no merrier bene.
> Ylike° as others, girt in gaudy green?
> [...]
> Yougthes folk° now flocken in everywhere
> 10   To gather May buskets and smelling briar,
> [...]
> But we here sitten as drowned in a dream. (1–4, 9–10, 16; SC 33ₐ)

Thomalin, in 'July:'

> But nothing such thilk° shepherd was
>   Whom Ida hill did bear,
> That left his flock to fetch a lass,
>   Whose love he bought too dear. (145–48; SC 66ₐ)

[The notes be oftentimes omitted, and the dissimilitude more fully enlarged. Colin, in 'June':

> O happy Hobbinol, I bless thy state,
> 20   That Paradise hast found which Adam lost.
> Here wander may thy flock early or late
> Withouten dread of wolves to bene ytossed:°
> Thy lovely lays here may'st thou freely boast.
> But I, unhappy man, whom cruel fate
> And angry Gods pursue from coast to coast,
> Can nowhere find to shroud° my luckless pate. (9–16; SC 51)][2]

Unlike] The difference between arguments unlike and arguments diverse is that in *diversis* the simple and the absolute disagreeing of two things is considered; but in unlike arguments, the unlike comparison of four terms, that is, of two things and the two qualities of the same.[3]

---

[1] **Unlike [...] the like**] Translated from Ramus/Piscator, I.22, E2ʳ–E3ᵛ.

[2] **The notes [...] luckless pate**] Added in LL, U3ʳ.

[3] *Unlike [...] the same*] '*Dissimilia*] Hic locus quandam cum diversis affinitatem habet: et P. Ramum diutius exercuit: attamen si simplex illic et absoluta duorum dissensio spectetur, hic dissmilis quattuor terminorum comparatio discrimine percipietur' (This argument has some affinity with diverse arguments, and it kept Ramus

30 In *diversis*, we affirm the one and deny the other after a certain manner; in unlikes, we deny neither, but only distinguish the one from the other by the difference in quality. So that all disagreeable arguments may be handled as unlike, if the diverse quality be respected.

---

busy for a long time. Nevertheless, if there the simple and the absolute is considered as the disagreement of two things, the unlike is understood as the comparison of four terms by division), Ramus, *Dialectica, Audomari Talaei praelectionibus illustrata*, I3ʳ; **diversis**] Fraunce uses the ablative plural form in the Latin original as the plural form of 'diverse'.

CHAPTER 19

Of Distribution[1]

Thus much for the first argument. Now followeth that which is made of the first.

The argument made of the first is that which is made of the joining together of the first arguments, and it is either distribution or definition. And in either of them there is a certain affection° of reciprocation: in the distribution, of all the parts with the whole; in the definition, of the thing defined with the definition itself.

A distribution is when the whole is distributed into his parts.

The whole is that which containeth parts.

A part is that which is contained in the whole.

And, as the distinguishing of the whole into his parts is called distribution, so the collecting of all the parts to make up the whole is named induction.

Distribution is made of arguments which are agreeable to the whole, but disagreeable among themselves. So that it is so much the more perfit° by how much the parts do more agree with the whole, and contrarily more disagree among themselves.[2]

Here will some man seek for two other kinds of arguments made of the first, I mean, *coniugata* and *notationem*: offsprings or conjugates, and notation.[3] I have purposely omitted them, and that, although contrary to the mind of most men, yet according to the judgement of Master Chaderton, whom, as I have followed in this point and in some others, so I here name him for the reverence I owe to his life and learning, and set down his judgement in this behalf, as a reason of this mine attempt. His words be these:[4] 'As for those arguments which are called *coniugata*, that is, offsprings or conjugates, because they have none other power to argue or declare a thing

---

[1] **distribution**] Fraunce differs substantially from Ramus in this chapter. He reduces Ramus's classification of 'arguments made of the first' (i.e., *orta de primis*) from four to two kinds by eliminating conjugates and notation, and keeping distribution and definition only. Accordingly, he skips I.23 and I.24 (except for the last paragraph of this chapter) and proceeds to I.25, 'De distributione'.

[2] **A distribution [...] among themselves**] Translated from Ramus's 'De distributione', in Ramus/Piscator, I.25, E5ᵛ–E6ʳ.

[3] **offsprings or conjagates, and notation**] Ramus's clearest account of his taxonomy is found in *Dialectique*, F3ᵛ: 'Iusques icy les lieux des premiers argumentz sont exposez, s'ensuiuent les issus des premiers, Raison du nom, Distribution, Définition: Raison du nom, quand quelque raison est tirée du nom, comme, Notation, Coniugation'.

[4] **Master Chaderton [...] his words be these**] Fraunce might be quoting his teacher's only extant words from his lectures on logic. His enthusiasm accords with Dr. William Dillingham's biographical account: '[Chaderton] himself was encyclopaedic in his reading. No doubt he wrote much more than has come into our hands. His lectures on logic, and those on Cicero's *Topica* and *Pro Marcello*, though they were received with great admiration, his modesty would never suffer to be published, being content it seems to having inflamed the minds of his hearers to extend the same studies further' (Schuckburgh, *Laurence Chaderton*, p. 25).

but that only which they have of the cause, effect, subject, or adjunct, of which only they are made, therefore they may be very well referred unto them, and here be omitted, namely for that there are no other diverse kinds of arguments belonging to invention. Also for etymology, or notation, because it respecteth the names of things rather than any conception in reason, and also for that it is drawn from other arguments by whose force only it doth argue or declare the thing for which it is brought, it may be altogether omitted, as making no diverse kind of argument from those that are the first'.

[17ʳ]   Hitherto I have repeated his words. Yet, lest any man should think I mangle Logic and | injure the reader, I have here briefly put them down among these notes, and not so largely set them
30   forth in the text.⁵ Thus then should of distribution be continued out of Ramus.⁶

Arguments made of the first be either offspring and notation, or distribution and definition.
Offspring, or conjugates, be words diversely derived from one head as 'justice', 'just', 'justly'.
Notation, or etymology, is the interpretation of the word: as Lady Flora, because she is the goddess of flowers, is called Flora.

Now, again to our purpose.

---

⁵ **notes […] text**] Although Fraunce seems to consider the three paragraphs/sentences dealing with conjugates and notation notes rather than main text, Ms does not clearly mark such difference.
⁶ **continued out of Ramus**] that is, continued in the next chapter. However, the definitions of conjugates and notation also follow Ramus. For conjugates, Fraunce translates Ramus/Piscator I.23, E3ᵛ. For notation, I.24, E4ʳ.

CHAPTER 20

~

Of the Distribution Made of Causes

Distribution is made either of arguments absolutely agreeable, or after a certain manner.

Absolutely, as first of the cause.

The distribution made of the cause is when the parts are yet causes of the whole, and then they are properly called members. For a member is a part which giveth essence or being to the whole, which whole, in respect of the members, is called the integral, which hath his essence or being of the members.[1]

Hobbinol confuteth Diggon Davy in 'September', proving, by a distribution of England into her parts, no wolves to be in England:

> Fie on thee, Diggon, and all thy foul leasing:°
> Well is known that, sith° the Saxon king,
> Never was wolf seen — many nor some —
> Nor in all Kent, nor in Christendom. (150–53; SC 90)

10

For most part of England being Christian in Ethelbert's time, Kent only continued in paganism.[2] By this example we see that this kind of distribution, which is properly called partition, as the other also of the general unto his specials, which is called division,[3] may be used both in a distinct propounding of parts, where any long matter is to be handled of poets, orators, preachers, etc.; and also syllogistically, in arguing either the parts by the whole, or the whole by the parts.

---

[1] **Distribution is […] members**] Adapted from Ramus/Piscator, I.26, E6ᵛ. See also Beurhaus, *Inv*₂₂. In spite of terminological differences, Fraunce adapts Fenner's translation: 'A Diuision made of the cause, is when the partes be cause of the whole, and then they are properly called members: for a member is that parte which giueth being to the whole, and the whole being of such members, is called integrall', *The Artes*, B4ʳ.

[2] **For most […] in paganism**] On the proverbial paganism of Kent see Tilley, K₁₆. E.K. calls this proverb 'strange and unreasonable' (Brooks-Davies, p. 155). Ethelbert of Kent is reported to have been the first Anglo-Saxon king to convert to Christianity in 597, although his subjects remained in paganism. But the proverb may refer to the times of King Ethelbert of Wessex, who was King of Kent between 855 and 860.

[3] **By this […] division**] Adapted from Piscator, I.26, E7ʳ: '*Distributio integri*] Haec peculiari vocabulo appelatur partitio, sicut distributio generis in species nominatur divisio: teste Cicerone in *Topicis*. Sic decalogi distributio in duas tabulas, partitio: distributio legum Mosaicarum in morales, ceremoniales et forenses, divisio est' (*The distribution of the whole*] This is called with the specific name partition, just as the distribution of the general into its specials is named division, as witnessed by Cicero in the *Topics*. Thus the distribution of the Ten Commandments in two tables is a partition; the distribution of the Mosaic laws into moral, ceremonial and forensic is a division). See Cicero, *Topica*, 5.28, Loeb II: p. 400.

CHAPTER 21

~

Of the Distribution of the Effect

The distribution of the thing caused, or of the effect, is whose parts are effects of the whole, as when the general or universal is divided into his specials.

The general is a whole which giveth the essence or being to his parts, or specials.

A special is a part of the general.

The general is either most general or subalternal.°

The special is either most special or subalternal,° that is, put under.

The chief, or most general, is that which hath no general above it.

The general and special subalternal,° or under another, are those which may be in diverse respects° both generals and | specials: generals in respect of their inferiors, specials in respect of their superiors.

The most special is that which cannot be divided into specials.

And, as all generals are notes and signs of causes in them comprehended, so all specials are notes and signs of effects. Therefore, of divisions made into effects this division when the general is divided into his specials is most chief and principal. Neither is the general and special only thus handled in form of distribution, but also in arguing either this by that, or that by this.[1]

So in 'July', Morrel, having first praised hills in general, afterward rehearseth particulars, as St Michael's Mount, St Bridget's Bower, Mount Olivet, Parnassus, the Hill Ida, Sinai, Our Lady's Bower,[2] by the repeating of which particulars he concludeth the general praise of hills, which he in the beginning had put down thus:

What ho, thou jolly shepherd's swain,°
    come up the hill to me:
Better is than the lowly plain
    als° for thy flock and thee. (5–8; SC 56)

Against whom Thomalin, in the same place, with the like argument[3] bringing forth a number of particular examples of lowly and mild shepherds, inferreth the general commendation of

[17ᵛ] (margin, line 10)

---

[1] **The distribution [...] by this**] Ramus/Piscator, I.27, G7ʳ–G8ᵛ.

[2] **St Michael's Mount**] A tidal island situated on the South coast of Cornwall; **St Bridget's Bower**] Unidentified; **Mount Olivet**] The mount adjacent to Jerusalem, associated with several moments of the life of Jesus and his accession to heaven (*Acts*, 1.9–12); **Parnassus**] A mountain in central Greece associated with the oracular god Apollo and with poetic inspiration; **Hill Ida**] E.K. refers the story in Diodorus Siculus (90–21 BC) of the fire burning the sky that rises in the morning in the form of the sun; **Sinai**] The hill in Egypt where God appeared to Moses (*Exodus*, 9, 24); **Our Lady's Bower**] The shrine of Our Lady of Loretto, mentioned in one of Mantuan's *Eclogues* (Brooks-Davies, p. 124). See 'July', 33–90.

[3] **in the same place**] in the same eclogue; **with the like argument**] using the same sort of logical argument, that is, a distribution of the general into its particulars.

valleys and those that keep below. The particulars be: Abel, the twelve Patriarchs, Moses, Aaron, etc.,[4] by whose examples he urgeth that which in the beginning he had generally answered unto Morrel in these words:

> Ah, God shield, man, that I should climb,
30 >   and learn to look aloft:
> This rede° is rife,° that oftentime
>   great climbers fall unsoft. ('July', 9–12; SC 57ₐ)

So that particular and special examples referred to their general belong to this place.

Examples of illustration be in the song of Hobbinol in 'April', where he nameth many particular flowers which he would have to be strewed on the ground where Elisa was to tread, as pinks, gillyflowers, columbines, coronations, sops-in-wine, daffadillies, cowslips, kingcups, lilies, paunce,° chevisaunce,° delice.° The verses I have put down elsewhere for another purpose (136–44, SC 32_c). When Cuddy, in 'February', had exclaimed against the winter's rage, Thenot rebuketh him with the opposing of his own special example:

40 > Self have I worn out thrice threttie° years,
> Some in much joy, many in many tears,
> Yet never complained of cold nor heat,
> Of Summer's flame, nor of Winter's threat. (17–20; SC 11_b)

---

[4] **Abel […] etc.]** See 'July', 125–64, for Spenser's use of these well-known Old Testament examples.

CHAPTER 22

Of the Distribution Made of the Subject

The second kind of distribution is made of arguments agreeable after a certain manner, as of subjects and adjuncts.

The distribution made of the subject is when the parts are subjects to the whole.[1]

Hobbinol, in his song of Elisa, divideth her beauty, being the adjunct, into her several subjects, as face, eye, cheek, etc.:

> Tell me: have ye seen her angelic face,
>   Like Phoebe fair?
> Her heavenly haviour,° her princely grace,
>   Can you well compare?
> 10 The red rose meddled with the white yfere,°
> In either cheek depeincten° lively cheer:
>   Her modest eye,
>   Her majesty,
> Where have you seen the like but there? ('April', 64–72; SC 30)

---

[1] **The second [...] whole]** See Ramus/Piscator, I.28, F2ᵛ.

CHAPTER 23

Of the Distribution Made of the Adjuncts

The distribution made of the adjunct is when the parts be adjuncts unto the whole.[1]

Thomalin, in 'July', divideth the countryman into goatherds and shepherds — they, keeping hills; these, loving valleys:

> Alsoon° may shepherd climb to sky
>   that leads in lowly dales
> As goatherd proud that, sitting high,
>   upon the mountain sails. (101–04; SC 63ᵦ)

Diggon, in 'September':

> For either the shepherds bene idle and still,
> And led of their sheep what way they will;
> Or they bene false and full of covetise,°
> And casten° to compass many wrong emprise.°
> But the more bene freight with fraud and spite,
> Ne in God[2] nor goodness taken delight. (80–85; SC 83)

Piers, in 'May', divideth them into hirelings and idle bellies:

> I muse what account both these will make —
> The one for the hire which he doth take.
> And th' other for leaving his lords' task
> When great Pan account of shepherds shall ask. (51–54; SC 37)

Piscator addeth hereunto the distinction of words that have many significations, which rather belongeth to a dictionary-maker than a teacher of Logic, as diverse have answered.[3]

---

[1] **The distribution […] the whole**] This definition draws on Ramus/Piscator, I.29, F3ᵛ.

[2] **God**] Both Ms and LL have 'god' instead of 'good', the reading in Spenser's Q1 and in modern editions. The variant seems intentional in the context of the chapter, which derives all its instances from the so-called theological eclogues: 'May', 'July' and 'September'.

[3] **Piscator addeth**] Piscator provides instances of the distribution of words by polysemy: 'Divisionis nominis exempla a quovis observari possunt. Quales sunt illae Theologorum: Libertas alia civilis, alia spiritualis est. Sic, Mors alia corporalis, alia spiritualis est: item alia temporalis, alia aeterna. Sic, cibus alius corporalis alius spiritualis est' (Examples of divisions of names can be observed everywhere, such as are these from the theologians: freedon is either civil or spiritual; thus death is either bodily or spiritual, also temporal or eternal. Thus food is either bodily or spiritual.). See his 'Appendix ad locum distributionis' (Appendix to the argument of distribution), in I.29, F3ᵛ–F4ʳ.

CHAPTER 24

❧

Of a Definition

A definition is that which declareth what a thing is.

A definition is either perfit° or unperfit,° otherwise called a description.

The perfit° definition is that which is made only of the material and formal causes, which give unto everything his peculiar essence and being.[1]

[18ᵛ] Diggon, in 'September', defineth a shepherd by his end and duty, where that standeth for the formal cause:

> For-thy° with shepherds sits not play,
> Or sleep (as some doen) all the long day,
> But ever liggen° in watch and ward
> 10 From sudden force their flocks for to guard. (232–35; SC 92)

And, by an argument set from this definition, Piers, in 'May', proveth hirelings to be no shepherds, because the true definition of a shepherd agreeth not to them:

> Thilk° same bene shepherds for the devil's stead
> That playen while their flocks be unfed. (43–44; SC 35ᵦ)

Whereafter followeth a definition of a hireling, by the application of the which unto them he proveth them to be hirelings:

> Well is it seen their sheep bene not their own
> That letten them run at random alone;
> But they bene hired for little pay
> 20 Of others that caren as little as they
> What fallen the flock, so they han° the fleece
> And get all the gain, paying but a piece. ('May', 45–50; SC 36ₐ)

A definition is called of the Grecians ὅρος, ὁρισμος, ὁριστικος λόγος,[2] which is a translated word from bounds and limits of ground. And for as they hedge in and include the ground, so doth a definition limit and circumscribe, or, as it were, bind in the natural of that which is defined.[3]

---

[1] **A definition [...] being]** Adapted from Ramus/Piscator, I.30, F4ʳ.

[2] **ὅρος, ὁρισμος, ὁριστικος λόγος]** As used in Aristotle, *Topics*, VI, Loeb II: pp. 560–647.

[3] **that which is defined]** Later Fraunce added the Latin etymology: 'And that also is the natural signification of this word which the Latinists use, *finire* or *definire*, from whence *finitio* and *definitio*, which we now use as an English word. *Finis* is an end; *finire* and *definire* signify to limit or end, or circumscribe one from another, that so it may be known from other', LL, R2ᵛ.

The chief use then of a definition is to show and make plain. Yet an argument proving may be fet° both from the definition to that thing defined, and from this to that, negatively and affirmatively. And so it is in descriptions.

30   *And formal causes*] And this formal cause is sometimes fet° from the very internal form and essential cause of the thing defined, which is best but hard to be found, and therefore instead thereof, sometimes the end is used, sometimes the proper adjunct, sometimes many adjuncts together, sometimes the subject.[4]

One relative doth define and explicate another.[5]

---

[4] **And this [...] the subject]** Adapted from Piscator's Aristotelian discussion of *differentia* as the complement of *genus* in a perfect definition: 'Interdum a forma: quae ut omnium praestantissima, sic rarissima est inventum difficilissima est: ut, Homo est animal rationale. Interdum a fine: ut Musica est ars canendi, Arithmetica est ars numerandi [...] Interdum a subjecto: ut Febris est calor praeter naturam, accensus in corde. Interdum ab adiuncto: ut magnes est lapis trahens ferrum ...' (Sometimes from the formal cause, which, as it is the most excellent of all, it is thus the rarest and the most difficult to be invented, as in 'Man is a rational animal'. Sometimes from the end, as in 'Music is the art of singing', 'Arithmetic the art of numbering' [...] Sometimes from the subject, as in 'Fever is heat in excess of nature aroused in the heart'. Sometimes from the adjunct, as in 'A magnet is a stone that attracts iron'), Piscator, I.30, F4^v. See Aristotle, *Topics*, VI, 143b.1–10, Loeb II: pp. 588–91.

[5] **One relative [...] another]** 'Relationes definiuntur per utrumque relatum: ut coniugium est mariti et uxoris mutua obligatio ad procreandum liberos et adiuvandum' (Relations are defined by both relatives, as in 'Marriage is the mutual obligation of husband and wife for the procreation and raising of children') Piscator, I.30, F4^v.

CHAPTER 25

∾

Of a Description

Description is a definition which is made not only of the material and formal causes, but also of other arguments, and it is sometimes brief, sometimes more largely amplified.[1]

Thenot, in 'February', describeth an oak thus:

> There grew an aged tree on the green.
> A goodly Oak sometime had it been.
> With arms full strong and largely displayed,
> But of their leaves they were disarrayed;
> The body big and mightily pight.°
> Thoroughly rooted and of wondrous height:
> Whilom° had been the king of the field
> And mochel° mast° to the husband° did yield,
> And with his nuts larded many swine.
> But now the grey moss marred his rine.°
> His bared boughs were beaten with storms,
> His top was bald and wasted with worms,
> His honour decayed, his branches sere,° etc. (102–14; SC 18)

In 'May', Piers describeth the Kid:

> She set her youngling before her knee
> That was both fresh and lovely to see,
> And full of favour, as kid mought° be:
> His vellet° head began to shoot out,
> And his wreathed horns gan newly sprout;
> The blossoms of lust to bud did begin
> And spring forth rankly under his chin. (182–88; SC 44)

Whereafterward° followeth the description of the counterfeit Pedlar the Fox by adjuncts, effects, etc.:

> It was not long after she was gone,
> But the false Fox came to the door anon:
> Not as a fox, for then he had be kenned,°
> But all as a poor pedlar he did wend,°
> Bearing a truss° of trifles at his back,
> As bells, and babes, and glasses in his pack.
> A biggin° he has got about his brain,
> For in his headpiece° he felt a sore pain.

[19ʳ]

10

20

30

---

[1] **Description […] amplified]** Fraunce abbreviates Ramus/Piscator, I.31, F5ʳ⁻ᵛ.

His hinder heel was wrapped in a clout,°
For which great cold so had got the gout.
There at the door he cast me down his pack
And laid him down and groaned: 'Alack! Alack!
Ah, dear Lord, and sweet St Charity,²
40   That some good body would once pity me!' ('May', 235–48; SC 48)

² **sweet St Charity**] Notice E.K.'s gloss: 'the Catholics' common oath […] to have charity always in their mouth […] but never inwardly in faith and godly zeal', Brooks-Davies, p. 100.

CHAPTER 26

⁓

Of Inartificial Arguments

Having spoken sufficiently of the artificial argument, now it followeth by order to speak of the inartificial. Inartificial is that which argueth not of itself, but by the help and force of some artificial argument. It is properly called a testimony or witness.

A witness is either divine, that is, of God himself, or human, that is, of man.

A divine witness is a witness of God, as Holy Scriptures.

Human witness is the witness of man.[1]

In 'May', the Fox would prove himself kind to the Kid, because his grandsire told him so:

> And if that my grandsire me said be true,
> Siker° I am very sib° to you. (268–69; SC 49ₐ)

10   Morrel, in 'July':

> Beside, as holy fathers sayen,
>   there is a hilly place
> Where Titan riseth from the main
>   to ren° his daily race. (57–60; SC 60)

[And Thomalin, in 'July', useth a proverb to confute Morrel, the commender of hills:

> Ah, God shield, man, that I should climb,
>   and learn to look aloft:
> This rede° is rife,° that oftentime
>   great climbers fall unsoft. ('July', 9–12; SC 57ᵦ)][2]

[19ᵛ]   20   And again:

> *To kirk the narre, from god more farre*[3]
>   has been an old said saw;
> And he that strives to touch the star
>   oft stumbleth at a straw. ('July', 97–100; SC 62ᵦ)

[Man's testimony is either of one man, or of many. That of one, is either obligation or confession. To obligation be referred pledges or sureties. So, in 'August', the two shepherds

---

[1] **Having spoken […] of man**] Adapted from 'De testimonio divino' and 'De testimonio humano', in Ramus/Piscator, I.31–32, F6ʳ–G4ʳ. LL, R4ʳ prefers the term 'borrowed' to 'inartificial'. Fraunce's expansions in LL are given in square brackets.

[2] **And Thomalin […] unsoft**] Added in LL, S1ᵛ. **great climbers fall unsoft**] On this proverbial expression see Tilley, C₄₁₄.

[3] *to kirk […] more farre*] See SL, I.14, 3n.

Perigot and Willy, for want of better arguments to prove their skill in singing, lay down wagers, the one a cup, the other a spotted lamb. This is commonly called 'the fools' argument' (25–42; SC 73):[4]

30   I remember Diggon, in 'September', sweareth by his soul to give credit to his assertion, which I should have put before:

> They say they come to heaven the nigher way,
> But by my soul I dare undersay,°
> They never set foot in that same trod,°
> But balk° the right way and strayen abroad. ('September', 90–93; SC 84)][5]

As for other definitions, as testimonies with oath, without oath, free or constrained,[6] common or peculiar,[7] of dead men or alive, and so forth, if they have any art in them,[8] they may be had in Ramus, and such others in Piscator.[9]

---

[4] **the fools' argument**] 'The fool hath said in his heart, "There is no God"' (*Psalms* 14.1). The fool's denial of God's existence is based on the absence of empirical evidence that proves such existence. This is the argument refuted by St Anselm (1033–1109) in his *Proslogium*. See Anselm, *Basic Writings*, trans. by N. S. Deane, 2nd edn (Peru, Ill.: Open Court, 1962), p. 53.

[5] **Man's testimony […] strayen abroad**] Added in LL, S2ʳ.

[6] **free or constrained**] 'Confessio est libera vel expressa tormentis', Ramus/Piscator, I.32, F8ʳ.

[7] **common or peculiar**] 'Testimonium humanum est commune aut proprium', Ramus/Piscator, I.32, F7ʳ.

[8] **if they have any art in them**] if they can claim to be admitted into the art of Logic.

[9] **such others in Piscator**] 'Porro testimonium quattuor modis dividi potest: minimum a forma, ab efficiente, a subiectis, et ab adjunctis' [Testimony can be further divided into four modes: at least from the form, from the efficient, from the subjects and from the adjuncts), Piscator, I.32, F8ᵛ. This classification is developed extensively in I.32, F8ᵛ–G4ʳ.

BOOK II: OF JUDGEMENT

CHAPTER 1

~

[What Judgement Is]

Thus much of invention, the first part of Logic. Now followeth the second part, of judgement.

Judgement is the second part of Logic, containing the disposing of arguments, thereby to judge well of them, and therefore this second part is called both judgement and disposition.[1]

Τάξις among the Grecians is *dispositio* with the Latinists. So then the second part of Logic is called *dispositio*, of the form of the same second part. For that, as in Grammar *syntaxis*, being the second part, ordereth and disposeth simple words handled in the first, so *dispositio*, *τάξις*, or *iudicium* in Logic doth artificially place, settle, and dispose single arguments one with another, and that axiomatically, then proceeding forward to syllogism and method, as occasion shall serve. For example sake, this sentence, '*homo est animal*', is true Latin, because the nominative case and the verb be placed grammatically, according to the prescriptions of *syntaxis*. So the same sentence is a true logical axiom, because the general is affirmed of the special in a simple axiom according to art in judgement.

Now, the second part of Logic is also called *κρίσις*, *iudicium*,[2] of the use and commodity and end thereof. For that, by a certain direction, rule and prescription of disposition ariseth true judgement of the truth, untruth, consequence, inconsequence, perspicuity, or obscurity and confusion, and therefore also a great help to confirm memory and amend it.

---

[1] **Thus much [...] disposition**] Ramus/Piscator, II.1, G4ᵛ.
[2] ***iudicium***] Fraunce prefers to keep both terms, in spite of Piscator, II.1, G4ᵛ: 'Dispositio proprie: iudicium per metomymiam effecti: quia iudicium ex dispositione nascitur' (It is properly disposition. Judgement is by metonymy of the effect, since judgement is born out of disposition).

CHAPTER 2

~

Of an Axiom Affirmative or Negative

Judgement is the disposition either of one axiom or moe.°

An axiom or proposition is a disposition of one argument with another, whereby we judge to be or not to be.

An axiom or proposition is either affirmative or negative: affirmative, when the band° of the axiom is affirmed; negative, when it is denied.

From this affirmation or negation of the selfsame axiom or proposition arise all contradictions,[1] as:

> Dido my dear, alas, is dead. ('November', 58; SC 96$_a$)

> Dido nis° dead, but into heaven hent.° ('November', 169; SC 99$_b$)

[20^r]   10   *One argument*] That is, one word, one simple reason with another.

To be or not to be] That is, to be that which it is affirmed to be, or not to be that.

The band°] The band° is the middle part of the axiom, which joineth both the other parts together, as in this axiom or simple proposition: 'Bad is the best'.[2] But here observe, as Master Chaderton noteth,[3] that whereas in Latin and Greek the negation commeth before the band,° in our English tongue usually it doth follow. Nevertheless, it denieth the same thing in reason as if it should come before, which must necessarily be noted in all the parts of judgement, and therefore I do here put it down once for all.

---

[1] **Judgement [...] contradictions**] Ramus/Piscator, II.2, G4^v–G5^r. LL adds: 'Disposition is either of one sentence, called *axiomatical*, or more than one, called *dianoetical*' (Aa3^v).

[2] **The band**] '*Vinculum*] Quod in enunciato quidem simplici est verbum substantivum: in composito vero coniunctio Grammatica', Piscator, II.2, sig. G5^v. LL is more specific about the definition and structure of an axiom. On the definition: 'An axiome] The Greek word, ἄξιομα, signifieth dignity, authority. The Logicians, as it should seem, took it for anything spoken, pronounced, told, as it were, with authority. It here signifieth any sentence or proposition whatsoever, wherein one argument, reason, conceit, thing, is so conjoined with, or severed from, another, as that thereby we judge the one either to be or not to be, the cause, effect, whole, part, general, special; subject, adjunct, diverse, disparate, relative, repugnant, distribution, definition, testimony, like, unlike, equal, more or less to the other', LL, Aa4^r. On the structure: 'An axiom hath two parts: the band and the parts bound. The band is that which bindeth the other parts together. The parts bound be either the former or the latter. The former is that which goeth before, and is called antecedent. The latter, that which followeth, called the consequent, as: "Ah God, that love should breed both joy and pain!" ['January', 54; SC 7$_b$]. Where "love", being the cause and first part, is coupled by the band, "should breed", with his effects, both "joy" and "pain", the latter part', LL, Aa3^v.

[3] **as Master Chaderton noteth**] See SL, I.19, 4n.

CHAPTER 3

Of a True and False Axiom

Secondarily, an axiom is either true or false: true, when the thing is even so as it is said to be; false, when contrarily.

True is either contingent or necessary.

Contingent, or variable,° is whenas° it is true in such sort that it may be false.[1] So Hobbinol, in 'September':

> Ah fon,° now by thy loss art taught
> That seldom change the better brought:
> Content who lives with tried state,
> Need fear no change of frowning fate. (68–71; SC 82)

10   Thenot, in 'February':

> Thou art a fon° of thy love to boast:
> All that is lent to love will be lost. (69–70; SC 15ₐ)

The judgement therefore which we have of this variable° or contingent axiom is called opinion, which in things already past or present may be most certain to man. But in things to come it is altogether uncertain, although unto God there is no such difference of things in respect of time, to whom all things be present.

A necessary proposition or axiom is that which is always true, neither can be false which, being affirmed, is aptly called the rule of truth.°

And, contrarily, impossible is that which can never be true, but is always false.[2]

20   All precepts of arts are, or ought to be, rules of truth, righteousness, and wisdom.°[3]

A rule of truth° is a proposition which is always true without exception.

A rule of righteousness° is a proposition which giveth unto everything his own, wherein usually are disposed together the formal cause and the thing formed, the general and his special, the subject and his proper adjunct, all which are linked with most near affinity.

The rule of wisdom° is an axiom or proposition wherein the arguments disposed may be naturally affirmed one of another.[4] So that, as the latter is verified of the former, so the former

[20ᵛ] | may be of the latter, as that of Thomalin, in 'July':

---

[1] **Secondarily [...] false**] Ramus/Piscator, II.3, G5ᵛ; **Secondarily**] Secondly, after the first division of axioms into affirmative and negative.

[2] **The judgement [...] false**] Adapted from Ramus/Piscator, II.3, G5ᵛ. The first two sentences match Beurhaus, *Jud*₂.

[3] **All precepts [...] wisdom**] Beurhaus II, *Jud*₅.

[4] **All precepts [...] another**] The three rules or axioms of arts are derived from Ramus/ Piscator, II.3, G5ᵛ. On the three rules, see Glossary under 'Rules of truth, righteousness and wisdom'. See also Introduction, pp. 5–6; **righteousness**] 'justice' in LL, Bb1ʳ.

O blessed sheep, O shepherd great,
    that bought his flock so dear,
30   And them did save with bloody sweat
      from wolves that would them tear! (53–56; SC 59ᵇ)

For Christ saved his sheep with bloody tears, and whoso saveth his sheep with bloody tears is Christ. The judgement of this is sure and most certain knowledge.

True is either] And so by this we may perceive that false is also either contingent or necessary, that is, impossible. For the necessary false hath a proper and distinct name, to wit, impossible. But the necessary true hath no several° name, but is called necessary, by that general word.[5]

---

[5] *True is* […] **general word**] 'Contingens verum, est quod sic verum est, ut aliquando verum esse possit. Contingens falsum, quod sic falsum est, ut aliquando verum esse possit. Necessarium verum, est quod semper verum, nunquam falsum est: necessarium falsum, quod semper falsum est, nunquam verum. Hoc postremum speciali vocabulo nominatur impossibile: eius vero oppositum, apellatur vocabulo generalis necessarium', Piscator, I.3, G6ʳ.

CHAPTER 4

≈

Of a Simple Axiom

Thus much of the common proprieties of axioms. Now follow the specials of the same.

An axiom is either simple or compound.

Simple is that whose parts are coupled together with a verb.

The simple, then, hath two parts: the former and the latter. The former is the argument which commeth before the verb. The latter, which followeth, so that the verb affirmed or denied maketh the proposition affirmative or negative.

Affirmative, in 'January':

Ah God, that love should breed both joy and pain! (54; SC 7$_b$)

In 'July':

10 They bene yclad° in purple and pall.° (173; SC 68$_b$)

Negative, in 'November':

Dido nis° dead. (169; SC 99$_c$)

In the first example, the former part is 'love', the cause and author. The latter is 'joy and pain', the effect. The verb 'breed' is the band° coupling both these together, which here, being affirmed, maketh the proposition affirmative.

In the second example, the former part is the subject; the latter, the adjunct. The verb affirmed maketh this also affirmative.

In the third, 'Dido', the former part, is opposite unto 'dead', which is the latter part, and this to it. But here the verb denied maketh the proposition negative, as all other made of the same
20 sort.

And, as we see in these examples, the disposition of agreeable arguments, as of the cause and effect in the first, of the subject and the adjunct in the second, and of the disagreeable, as of the apposite with the opposite in the last, so we may dispose after the same manner all arguments agreeable and disagreeable, except distributions and full comparisons, such as have three or four *termini*, or parts, and therefore cannot be disposed in the simple axiom, but in the compound.

[21^r] The simple axiom is either general or special. General is that whose parts are general, generally disposed one with another. And in the general axioms, or propositions, one of them contradictory to the other is not always true or always false, for, if they be both variable° and not necessary,
30 they may be both false, as:

All that is lent to love will be lost. ('February', 70; SC 15$_b$)
Naught that is lent to love will be lost.

The special axiom is when the consequent or latter part is especially attributed unto the antecedent, or former part; not generally, whereof one being contradictory to the other, is always true or always false.

The special is either particular or proper. Particular, when the latter part general is attributed particularly unto the former. And to this the general is contradictory.

In 'May', Piers of shepherds saith:

> Some gan° to gape for greedy governance. (121; SC 41ᵦ)

40   The general contradictory whereof is:

> *None gan° to gape for greedy governance.*

The proper axiom is when the latter part is attributed unto the former, being a proper singular, or one thing.[1]

Diggon Davy, in 'September':

> Indeed thy Ball[2] is a bold big cur. (164; SC 91)

Whose negative and contradictory is:

> *Indeed thy Ball° is not a bold big cur.*

The general contradictory] As for those which others call subcontrary,° they make no true contradiction, for they may be both true. Nay, they rather make an argument of partition. For

50   these,

> *Some man is learned,*
> *Some man is not learned,*

be nothing but a partition, as if a man should distribute men into learned and unlearned, and may be both true.

Now for those which they call *subalternae*:° they be both affirmative or both negative, the one general and the other special, so that they make an argument of the general to his special, as,

> *Every hireling careth nought for his flock,*
> *Some hireling careth nought for his flock.*

As for *aequipollentia*,° conversion,° *modales*,° and such like trumperies,° I will hereafter speak

60   somewhat, if occasion serve, or else send the reader to the second part of Beurhusius, where he shall have a full comparison of those superfluous additions with Ramus his Logic.[3]

---

[1] **Thus much [...] one thing**] Translated, with the exception of the examples, from Ramus/Piscator, II.4, G6ʳ⁻ᵛ. This section also enunciates Beurhaus II, *Jud*₁₀₋₁₄.

[2] **Ball**] Fraunce, like some modern editors of Spenser, seems to take 'Ball' as the dog's name. See *Edmund Spenser: The Shorter Poems*, ed. by Richard A. McCabe (Harmondsworth: Penguin, 1999), p. 556, 164n.

[3] **The general contradictory [...] his Logic**] Fraunce postpones his exposition and critique of the different modes of relation between propositions mentioned here to the essay 'A Brief and General Comparison' (see below); **trumperies**] This term seems Fraunce's equivalent of *commentitia*, as attributed by Freigius to Ramus in his biography: '*Quaecumque ab Aristotele dicta essent, commentitia esse*'. On this issue, see Introduction, 19n; **the second part of Beurhusius**] Fraunce's source for his Ramist critique of contraries and subcontraries, subalterns, equipollence and conversion is Beurhaus II, Oo4ʳ⁻ᵛ.

CHAPTER 5

~

Of the Congregative Axioms

Thus much of the simple axiom. Now followeth the compound.

[21ᵛ] The compound axiom is that whose parts be coupled together | with a conjunction, the which, being affirmed or denied, maketh the axiom affirmative or negative. So the contradictory parts are always one of them true and the other false.

The compound axiom, according to the nature of his conjunction, is either congregative or segregative. Congregative is that which gathereth or coupleth together the agreeable or disagreeable arguments, affirming the one and denying the other. The congregative is either copulative or connexive. Copulative is that whose conjunction is copulative, as Thomalin, in 'July':

> But shepherd mought° be meek and mild,
> 10   well-eyed, as Argus[1] was,
> With fleshly follies undefiled,
>   and stout as steed of brass. (153–56; SC 67)

The negative and contradiction is: 'but shepherd mought° not, etc.'

The true judgement of this copulative axiom dependeth of the truth of every part, for, if all the parts be true, that is a true axiom; false, if any be false.

Hereunto must be referred full comparisons and similitudes, wherein the conjunction is the very relation itself, as Colin, in 'January':

> And from mine eyes the drizzling tears descend
> As on your boughs the icicles depend.° (41–42; SC 6ᵦ)

20 Here the judgement is compound, as if he had said: 'the icicles depend on your boughs, and the tears fall from mine eyes'.

The contradictions of those are the denials to every part.[2]

Compound] The word hypothetical, which is here commonly used, is not proper, for in *copulatis absolutis*, as we call them, and *discretis*, there is no ὑπόθεσις, no condition at all. It is a world to see the infinite rabble° that some have invented of compound axioms, so that they have risen to the number of ten thousand several° kinds.[3]

---

[1] **well-eyed [...] Argus**] Argus (or Argos) Panoptes (i.e., the all-seeing) was the 100-eyed monster whom Hera employed as a guardian of her priestess Io, with whom Zeus had fallen in love, after she transformed her into a cow.

[2] **Thus much [...] every part**] Translated, with the exception of the examples, from Ramus/Piscator, II.5, G8ʳ–G8ᵛ. **Congregative is [...] the other**] Beurhaus II, *Jud*₁₅. **The true [...] be false**] Beurhaus II, *Jud*₁₆.

[3] **Compound**] The division of compound axioms is dealt with in Beurhaus II, sigs Oo1ᵛ–Oo2ʳ. Contrary to Fraunce, Beurhaus reflects the division of hypothetical axioms into copulative, disjunctive and conditional. **It is [...] several kinds**] suppressed in LL, Cc2ʳ.

CHAPTER 6

⌇

Of a Connexive Axiom[1]

A connexive axiom is that whose conjunction is connexive, as Hobbinol, in 'June':

> Then if by me thou list advised be,
> Forsake the soil that so doth thee bewitch. (17–18; SC 52)

Whose contradiction is: 'though thou be advised by me, yet thou need not forsake the soil, etc.' For the affirmation signifieth, if the former part be true, then the latter must needs follow. Wherefore the negative contradiction must be thus: if, or though, the antecedent be granted, yet the consequent doth not necessarily follow.[2]

Wherefore, when we judge the connexive axiom to be absolutely true, we judge it also to be necessary, albeit the necessary ariseth only of, or dependeth upon, the necessary coupling together of the parts, which may be whenas° notwithstanding[3] both the parts severally° | disposed are false, as in the former example, for neither did he leave the soil, nor follow Hobbinol his counsel, [which counsel if he had followed, then must he necessarily have left that country. For this was his counsel].[4]

The judgment of this axiom is certain knowledge when the parts be necessary. But if the parts be variable° and the sequel but only probable, then our judgement thereof is only an opinion.[5]

In 'May', the mother to the Kid:

> Thy father, had he lived this day
> To see the branch of his body display,
> How would he have joyed at this sweet sight! (195–97; SC 45)

Hitherto must be referred that consequent or relation which is expressed by an adverb of time.[6]

In 'December':

> Whilom° in youth, when flowered my joyful spring,
> Like swallow swift I wandered here and there. (19–20; SC 103_b)

[22ʳ]

---

[1] **A connexive axiom]** With the exception of the examples, this chapter translates or adapts Ramus/Piscator, II.6, H1ʳ⁻ᵛ.

[2] **For the affirmation [...] follow]** Beurhaus II, *Jud*19.

[3] **whenas notwithstanding]** when nevertheless.

[4] **which counsel [...] his counsel]** Added in LL, Cc3r.

[5] **The judgement [...] opinion]** Beurhaus II, *Jud*20.

[6] **Hitherto [...] time]** Beurhaus II, *Jud*21.

CHAPTER 7

Of the Segregative Axiom

The segregative axiom is that whose conjunction is segregative, and therefore is fittest to dispose disagreeable arguments, which must be severed.

The segregative is either discretive or disjunctive.

Discretive is that whose conjunction is discretive. Wherefore of disagreeable arguments it is most apt to dispose those that are diverse only in respect° or in reason,[1] as in 'December':

> But ah, unwise and witless Colin Clout,
> That kiddest° the hidden kind of many a weed,
> Yet kiddest° not ene° to cure the sore heart root
> Whose rankling wound as yet doth rifely° bleed. (91–94; SC 108)

10   Whose contradiction is the denial of the principal conjunction.

This axiom is judged to be true when the parts be not only true, but diverse also the one from the other. Contrarily, it is judged false when the parts be neither true nor diverse.

---

[1] **The segregative [...] reason**] Translated or adapted from Ramus/Piscator, II.7, H1^v–H2^r; **fittest to dispose disagreeable arguments**] Beurhaus II, *Jud*$_{22}$.

CHAPTER 8

~

Of the Disjunctive Axiom[1]

The disjunctive axiom is that whose conjunction is disjunctive, [whereunto is referred the distributive. These are fittest to dispose repugnant arguments, and divisions of two parts],[2] as in 'September':

> Diggon Davy, I bid her god day:
> Or Diggon her° is, or I missay. (1–2; SC 78ₐ)

Here the contradiction doth not make the parts necessarily[3] true or false, for if the disjunction or separation be true absolutely, and also necessarily, without any mean, then the whole axiom is true and necessary, notwithstanding the special parts by themselves considered may be variable:°[4] 'or Diggon her° is, or I missay'. This disjunction is necessary, and yet 'Diggon her° is' is a variable° axiom. Also 'I missay' is a variable° axiom, but the necessity of the disjunction dependeth upon the necessary opposition and disjunction of parts, not upon the necessary truth thereof. If therefore the disjunction be but contingent, it is not absolutely true, as when Leander said he would either | die or have his desire.[5] Otherwise the judgement of this axiom, when the disjunction is necessary, is a certain knowledge.

[22ᵛ]

---

[1] **Of the Disjunctive Axiom**] This chapter is adapted from Ramus/Piscator, II.9, H2ʳ⁻ᵛ.

[2] **whose conjunction is disjunctive**] Added in LL, Cc4ᵛ.

[3] **necessarily**] although Ms has 'specially', the reading in LL is preferred, since it renders Ramus's 'necessario' (H2ᵛ).

[4] **if the disjunction [...] variable**] Beurhaus II, *Jud*₂₆.

[5] **as when Leander [...] his desire**] 'Ovid, in Epistola Leandri, *Aut mihi continget felix audacia salvo, / Aut mors solliciti finis amoris erit*', Ramus/Piscator, II.8, H2ʳ. Fraunce reproduces these lines in LL, Dd1ʳ. See Ovid, *Heroides*, XVIII.195–96, Loeb, pp. 256–57: 'either happy daring shall leave me safe, or death shall be the end of my anxious love!'.

CHAPTER 9

⁓

Of a Syllogism and his Parts

Thus much touching the judgement and disposition of one axiom. Now followeth the disposition of moe° axioms.

The disposition of moe° axioms is when one axiom by reason is inferred of another, or drawn out of another, and then is called either syllogism or method.

A syllogism is a disposition of three axioms, whereby or wherein a doubtful question disposed with an argument invented, and the antecedent or former part being put and granted, is necessarily concluded and determined. For, where an axiom is doubtful, it maketh a question. Therefore, for the proof of the truth we must invent a third argument and dispose it with the parts of the question severally, once with one and once with the other.

10   There be two parts of a syllogism: the antecedent and the conclusion.

The antecedent proveth the conclusion and hath two parts: to wit, the proposition and the assumption.

The proposition is the first part, wherein the whole proposition, or at the least the latter part of the question, is disposed with the argument invented.

The assumption is the second part, which is taken out of the proposition.

The conclusion is the last part, proved by the antecedent and concluding the question which was in doubt.

If any part of a syllogism be wanting, it is called then an imperfect syllogism, or enthymeme.

If anything be added more and above these three axioms appertaining° thereunto, that addition
20   is called a prosyllogism.

The parts also of the syllogism are oftentimes disorderedly and confusedly disposed or placed. Notwithstanding, if any doubt shall arise hereof, the axiom which is wanting must be supplied, the superfluous prosyllogisms or additions must be cut off, and every part methodically or orderly reduced to his own place.[1]

He is greatly deceived that thinketh there is no part of judgement but only in syllogisms, for, to speak nothing now of method, the first and almost the chief kind of judgement is in axioms and propositions, yea, and the very foundation of all other judgement. For hereby the proper affection° of arguments is judged, all principles of arts, all plain and manifest propositions are perceived, yea, all such questions to the which we cannot answer 'yea' or 'nay' (as 'what is it?',

---

[1] **Thus much […] own place**] Adapted from Ramus's 'De syllogismo et eius partibus', Ramus/Piscator, II.9, H3^{r-v}, in varying degrees of faithfulness to the original's letter. Fraunce's most significant change is the translation of the concept *iudicium dianoeticum* as 'disposition of moe axioms', and *dianoia* as merely 'disposition'. Later he adopted the adjective 'dianoetical' (LL, Dd2^r). This passage is also indebted to Fenner, *The Artes*, C3^r; **inferred […] another**] 'inferred' is Fraunce's later correction of Ms 'referred', which makes little sense. See LL, Dd2^r. Ramus's original reads 'deducitur'; **where an axiom […] the other**] Beurhaus II, *Jud*$_{30}$.

30   'what parts hath it?', 'where is it?', 'what qualities hath it?', 'when will it come?') are answered by
this kind of judgement. For, if ye answer to that which was demanded, the hearer is satisfied.

[23ʳ]   But if these axioms be not plain | enough of themselves, they must be sent to syllogism, there
to be discussed, and so to method, there to be ordered. So that whatsoever is either by syllogism
or method judged, it is all judged by the help of this first and axiomatical judgement.²

A syllogism] Or Συλλογισμός, is, as it were, συλλογή καὶ ἐπαριθμῆσις, an arithmetical deduction
of sums in accounts, and so here metaphorically of axioms and arguments.³

The necessity of the consequence in a syllogism dependeth of that old ground that such things
as agree in any third thing must also agree among themselves. As, then, in things that be to be
measured with line or by weight, we judge of them as they agree both either in line or weight, so
40   is it also when an axiom doth affirm or deny anything of another, whereof we doubt. For, if the
line or measure, I mean the third argument, agree with both the parts of the proposition, it
showeth that then the affirmation is true. But if it agree but with one of them, it declareth the
negation to be true. So that this *medium*° is, as it were, an *honorarius arbiter*⁴ to determine of
those things which in the questions are obscure.

There is but one kind of argumentation, and that is a syllogism, for an enthymeme is nothing but
a contracted syllogism. The word 'enthymeme' signifieth a cogitation or tossing of a man's mind,
for the mind never rests when an imperfit° syllogism is put down, before it have supplied that which
wanteth, the better to conceive of the whole perfect syllogism.⁵ Whereupon the satirical poet saith:

                    aut curvum sermone rotato
50   *torqueat Enthymema.*⁶

The proposition] In an hypothetical syllogism, as they call it, the *maior*, as they term it, contains
the whole question; but in a categorical, only the *praedicatum*.

The latter part] Which they call the predicate, or attribute.

The assumption, etc. taken out of] As from a thing put down, and granted, and now applied
more nearly to the purpose.

An imperfect syllogism] As I said before, so that those four kinds of argumentations come all
to one. For an induction is the name of an argument concluded by a syllogism from the
enumeration of the parts. A dilemma is an argument from the contraries. A *sorites* is nothing
but an enthymematical progression by certain degrees. Neither is there in all those or any others
60   any new collocation of axioms whereof any new form of necessary consequence should arise.⁷

---

² **axiomatical judgement**] LL, Dd3ʳ. adds: 'For, if the premises in a syllogism be not sometimes certain and so
judged by axiomatical judgement, and granted, there will be no end of making syllogisms, when still we call
the grounds thereof into controversy, for want of axiomatical judgement'.
³ *A syllogism*] the annotation is very loosely adapted from Piscator, II.9, H3ᵛ; συλλογή καὶ ἐπαριθμῆσις] literally,
'assembly and addition'. See also *Dialectique*, M1ʳ: 'tout ces deux motz [i.e. logisme, syllogisme] signifient
proprement compte et denombrement'.
⁴ *honorarius arbiter*] an arbitrator appointed by the two parties in a litigation (*Oxford Latin Dictionary*,
honorarius, adj.).
⁵ **The word 'enthymeme'** [...] **perfect syllogism**] Adpated from Piscator, II.9, H4ʳ: 'Quum enim enthymema
sit syllogimus imperfectus, nempe una sui parte truncatus ac mutilus: sit ut partem illam omissam audienti
cogitandam et in animo supplendam relinquat. Non enim acquiescit mens, donec perfectum syllogismum
complexa sit. Itaque syllogismus imperfectus apellatus est ἐνθύμημα, id est, cogitatio'.
⁶ **nec curvum** [...] **enthymema**] 'let her not hurl at you in whirling speech the crooked enthymeme!', Juvenal,
6.449–50, in *Juvenal and Persius*, Loeb, pp. 120–21.
⁷ *An imperfect syllogism* [...] **should arise**] This matter is tackled more at large in LL, Dd4ʳ–Ee1ᵛ, adapting
Piscator, I.9, H3ᵛ–H6ᵛ; **four kinds of argumentations**] Fraunce later listed 'syllogism, enthymeme, induction,
[and] example' as the four kinds 'to the which some add *sorites* and *dilemma*', LL, Dd4ʳ. On Ramus's reduction
of all these kinds of reasoning, see Introduction, p. 7.

CHAPTER 10

≈

Of a Simple Syllogism

A syllogism is either simple or compound.

The simple is that wherein the latter part of the question is disposed in the proposition, the former part in the assumption; and is affirmative when all the parts be affirmed; negative, when the conclusion with the proposition or the assumption | is denied; general, when the proposition and assumption be general; special, when one of them only is general; proper, when both of them are proper or singular.[1]

---

[1] **A syllogism […] singular**] Abridged from Ramus/Piscator, II.10, H7ᵛ–H8ʳ.

CHAPTER 11

Of the Contracted Syllogism

The simple syllogism is either contracted or fully expressed.

Contracted is that wherein the argument invented to a particular question is put for an example, as:

> *Some shepherd's hap was ill, but will be better in time, as Algrin's.*

After this manner only, the contracted syllogisms are disposed in all authors. Notwithstanding, if it shall be thought good unto any man fully to express it in all his parts, the argument invented must come before both the parts of the question and be affirmed in the assumption, as followeth:

> *Algrin's hap was ill, but will be better in time;*
> *Algrin was a shepherd;*
> *Therefore, some shepherd's hap that was ill will be better in time.*

> [Ah, good Algrin', his hap was ill,
>   but shall be bett' in time ('July', 229–30, SC 70)]

But the clearness of reason and judgement requireth no such disposition.[1]
This is Aristotle's third figure.°[2]

---

[1] **The simple […] such disposition]** This chapter continues adapting Ramus's 'De syllogismo simplici contracto', Ramus/Piscator II.10, H7ᵛ–H8ʳ. Fraunce enlarged this issue in LL, Ff1ʳ–Ff1ᵛ, adapting Piscator, II.10, H8ᵛ–I1ᵛ. **Ah, Algin' […] in time]** Algrin (or Algrind) is an anagram of Edmund Grindal (1519–83), Archbishop of Cantebury since 1575, whose radical Protestantism caused his fall from Queen Elizabeth's grace between 1577 and 1582. The lines, not in Ms, have been added here; **the clearness […] such disposition]** 'Sic usus disserendi, magister syllogistici iudicii, contrahitur, nec aliter explicatur' (Thus the use of reason, the master of all syllogistic judgement, is shortened, not badly explained), Ramus/Piscator, II.10, H8ʳ. See also Beurhaus II, *Jud*₃₂.
[2] **third figure]** In the third figure, the middle term is the subject in both premises — i.e., 'Algrin' in this chapter's instance. See Aristotle, *Prior Analytics*, I.6, Loeb I: pp. 224–33.

CHAPTER 12

~

Of the Explicate Syllogism

In the syllogism fully expressed, the proposition must always be general or proper; the conclusion, negative, if either the proposition or assumption be negative.

There be two kinds of syllogisms fully expressed.

The first, when the argument invented doth follow both in the proposition and assumption, and must be denied in one of them.[1]

The first general, Piers, in 'May':

> *He that playeth while his flock is unfed can give no account to great god Pan;*
> *A good shepherd can give account to great god Pan;*
> *Therefore, he that playeth while his flock is unfed is no good shepherd.* (43–44; SC 35$_c$)

10　The second general, in the same place:

> *The hireling letteth his sheep run at random;*
> *The good shepherd letteth not his sheep run at random;*
> *Therefore, the good shepherd is not a hireling.* (May, 45–50; SC 36$_b$)

The first special, in 'July':

> *A shepherd is not idle;*
> *Paris is idle;*
> *Therefore Paris is no good shepherd.* ('July', 145–48; SC 66$_b$)

The second special:[2]

> *He that sitteth below, sitteth safely;*
20 > *Algrin did not sit safely;*
> *Therefore Algrin sat not below.*

Or thus:

> *He that sitteth safely sitteth below;*
> *Algrin did not sit below;*
> *Therefore Algrin sat not safely.*

> [He is a shepherd great in gree°
> 　　but hath bene long ypent.°

---

[1] **In the syllogism [...] them]** Fraunce's source for the definition and classification into kinds is Ramus/Piscator, II.11, I1^v–I3^r.

[2] **The first general, The second general, The first special, The second special]** Fraunce omits here the scholastic mnemonic names of these four modes of the second figure (*Cesare, Camestres, Festino, Baroco*). These are provided in LL, Ff2^v–Ff3^r, following Ramus/Piscator, II.11, I1^v–I2^v.

One day he sat upon a hill
    as now thou woldest me
30   (But I am taught by Algrin's ill
    to love the low degree);
For, sitting so with bared scalp,
    an eagle soared high
That, weening° his white head was chalk,
    a shellfish down let fly:
She weened° the shellfish to have broke,
    but therewith bruised his brain.
So now astonied° with the stroke
    he lies in lingering pain. ('July', 215–28; SC 69$_a$)][3]

[24^r]   40   The first proper:

> *Morrel's brain was not bruised by an eagle;*
> *Algrin's brain was bruised by an eagle;*
> *Therefore Algrin is not Morrel.* ('July', 215–28; SC 69$_b$)

The second proper:

> *Paris was proud;*
> *Moses was not proud;*
> *Therefore Moses was not Paris.* (July, 145–60; SC 66$_c$)

Other logicians leave out these two last,[4] but injuriously, for they be as artificial as the rest, and oftentimes used to discern particulars that seem the same.

50   As before, the contracted syllogism was according to the third sign put down by Aristotle, where the *medium*° is *subiectum* in either of the premises. So this first kind of the explicate syllogism is the same that Aristotle putteth down in his second figure,° where the argument is the attribute in either premise.[5] In like manner also the second kind of explicate syllogisms, which followeth next, is contained in that first Aristotelical figure,° wherein the *medium*° is the subject in the *maior*, and the predicate in the *minor*.[6]

---

[3] **He is […] lingering pain]** These lines are not originally in Ms.

[4] **Other logicians leave out these two last]** These modes are explained by Ramus, but not by the scholastics. See Ramus/Piscator, II.11, I3^r.

[5] **second figure […] either premise]** 'In qua medium est praedicatum in utraque praemissa' (in which the middle term is the predicate in either premise), Piscator, II.11, I3^r; **the argument]** the middle term; **the attribute)** the predicate. On Aristotle's second figure, see *Prior Analytics*, I.5, Loeb I: pp. 216–24.

[6] **first Aristotelical figure […] the *minor*]** 'Prima figura est in qua medium in maiore praemissa est subiectum, in minore praedicatum', Piscator, sig. I5^r. This definition therefore applies to the syllogisms explained in the next chapter. On the first figure, see Aristotle, *Prior Analytics*, I.4, Loeb I: pp. 208–16.

CHAPTER 13

~

Of the Second Kind of
Syllogisms Fully Expressed

Now, in this second kind the argument goeth before the proposition, and followeth affirmatively in the assumption.[1]
The general affirmative:

> *That which bringeth to good is good;*
> *Death bringeth to good;*
> *Therefore death is good.*

So reasoneth Colin in 'November':

> Unwise and wretched men to weet° what's good or ill:
> We deem of death as doom of ill desert;
> But knew we fools what it us brings until,
> Die would we daily, once it to expert.°
> Not danger there the shepherds can astert:°
>   Fair fields and pleasant layes° there bene,
>   The fields aye° fresh, the grass aye° green:
>   Oh happy hearse;
>   Make haste, ye shepherds, thither to revert:°
>   Of joyful verse. (183–92; SC 101)

The general negative:

> *They that be men must not be bound to more misery than men can bear;*
> *Shepherds be men;*
> *Therefore shepherds must not be bound to more misery than men can bear.*

Hobbinol, in 'September':

> Ah, Diggon, thilk° same rule were too strait
> All the cold season to watch and wait.
> We bene of flesh — men as other be:
> Why should we be bound to such misery?
> Whatever thing lacketh changeable rest
> Mought° needs decay when it is at best. (236–41; SC 93)

---

[1] **Now […] assumption]** Fraunce follows Ramus in the definition and classification into kinds. See Ramus/Piscator, II.12, I3ᵛ–I5ʳ.

The special affirmative:

30   *He that hath loved ought to pity lovers;*
        But Pan hath loved;
        Pan therefore ought to pity lovers.

So Colin, in 'January':

        And Pan, thou shepherds' god, that once didst love,
        Pity the pains that those thyself didst prove. (17–18; SC 4)

The special negative:[2]

        The pipe which pleaseth where it should not please is not to be kept;
        Colin's pipe pleaseth where it should not please;
        Therefore Colin's pipe is not to be kept.

40   Wherefore, my pipe, albe° rude Pan thou please
        (Yet for thou pleasest not where most I would),
        And thou, unlucky Muse, that wontst° to ease
        My musing mind (yet canst not when thou should),
        Both pipe and Muse shall sore the while abye:°
        So broke his oaten pipe and down did lie. ('January', 67–72; SC 9)

It may be also affirmatively framed.
The proper affirmative, in 'July':

        The great god Pan saved his sheep with bloody sweat;
        Christ is the great god Pan;
50   *Therefore Christ saved his sheep with bloody sweat.* ('July', 53–56; SC 59c)

The proper negative, in 'April':

        Elisa cannot be blemished with any mortal blot;.
        She that sits upon the grassy green is Elisa;
        Therefore she that sits upon the grassy green cannot be blemished with any mortal blot.
            ('April', 91–94; SC 31b)

As for that kind of demonstration of syllogisms which is done by reduction,° it is unnecessary. For syllogisms, if they be once artificially put down, need no further demonstration, as being of themselves sufficiently confirmed by their several° definitions, divisions, examples, and explications. Read the second part of Beurhusius.[3]

---

[2] The general affirmative, The general negative, The special affirmative, The special negative] LL, Ff4ʳ–Gg2ᵛ, following Piscator, also provides the mnemonic names (*Barbara, Celarent, Darii, Ferio*) for these four modes of the first figure.

[3] **the second part of Berhusius**] Beurhaus II, Qq7ᵛ–Rr1ᵛ, which considers the mnemonic words and the operations of reduction and conversion unnecessary.

CHAPTER 14

~

Of the First Kind of a Connexive Syllogism

Thus much for the simple syllogism. The compound syllogism is that wherein the whole question maketh the one part of the proposition affirmed and compounded. And the argument invented maketh other parts of the proposition.

To remove any part in the compound syllogism is to set down the special contradiction thereof. The compound syllogism is either connexive or disjunctive.

The connexive is that whose proposition is connexive, and is made after two sorts.

First, when the former part of the proposition maketh the assumption, the latter part the conclusion.[1]

If ye gods of love pity lovers' pain, then pity me;
But ye gods of love do pity lovers' pain;
Therefore pity me.

Colin Clout, in 'January':

Ye gods of love that pity lovers' pain
(If any gods the pain of lovers pity),
Look from above, where you in joys remain,
And bow your cares unto my doleful ditty. (13–16; SC 3)[2]

Here oftentimes the former part of the proposition maketh not the assumption, but that which is greater and of more force to conclude than it is:[3]

If there were none but other beasts thine enemies, yet oughtest thou to take heed;
But now the Fox, also the master of collusion, is thine enemy;
Therefore much more oughtest thou to take heed.

Piers useth this in 'May', in the mother's speech to her young one:

'Kiddy', quoth she, 'thou kennest° the great care
I have of thy health and thy welfare,
Which many wild beasts liggen° in wait
For to entrap in thy tender state;
But most the Fox, master of collusion,

---

[1] **Thus much [...]conclusion]** Ramus/Piscator, II.13, I5ᵛ. **To remove [...] thereof]** Beurhaus II, *Jud*₃₅.

[2] **Ye gods [...] doleful ditty]** LL, Gg2ʳ provides a different instance from Spenser: 'And if that my grandsire me said be true, / Siker I am very sib to you' ('May', 268–69; SC 49ᵦ). The syllogism is developed thus: 'If my grandsire told me truth, I am sib to you; / But my grandsire told me truth; / Therefore I am sib to you'.

[3] **Here oftentimes [...] it is]** 'Frequenter hic non assumitur idem, sed Maius', Ramus/Piscator, II.13, I6ʳ. Also Beurhaus II, *Jud*₃₆. This passage is derived verbatim from Fenner, C4ᵛ, quoted in the Introduction, p. 22.

For he has vowed thy last confusion.
For-thy,° my Kiddy, be ruled by me
30   And never give trust to his treachery.
And if he chance come when I am abroad
Sperre° the yate° fast for fear of fraud:
Ne for all his worst, nor for his best
Open the door of his request.' (215–26; SC 46)

The same kind of syllogism or reasoning is framed by a conjunction of time⁴, with the same force which this connexive hath, as:

When night draws on, it is time to go homeward;
But now night draws on;
Therefore now it is time to go homeward.

40   Thus reasoneth Willy, in 'March':

But see the welkin thicks apace.
And stooping Phoebus steeps his face:
          It's time to haste us homeward. (115–17; SC 25)

To remove any part] This doth plainly appear by the examples before put down.
To set down the special contradiction] When that which was affirmed in general is denied in special, or, contrarily, affirmed when it was denied. And when the same thing in special is both affirmed before and denied after.

[25ᵛ]   A compound axiom or proposition may be affirmative, although it | consist of two simple axioms both denied, for it is not the denying of the parts that maketh it a negative, but the denying
50   of the consecution° and coherence of the one with the other. The which consecution,° if it be affirmed, maketh the proposition also affirmative, albeit the parts be both negative. For otherwise there might be a good syllogism only of negatives, as this:

If he be not in Europe, he is not in England;
But he is not in Europe;
Therefore he is not in England.

Where indeed the first axiom is affirmative, for the consecution° of the one upon the other is affirmed.⁵

⁴ **The same […] of time**] 'Concludendi modus hic idem est, quando propositio est relata temporis', Ramus/Piscator, II.13, I6ʳ. See also Beurhaus II, *Jud₃₇*.
⁵ **To set down […] affirmed**] Based on Piscator's annotation *'Tollere autem'*, II.13, I6ᵛ. LL, Gg3ᵛ–Gg4ʳ, adds a final example of a spurious sort of connexive syllogism, not admitted by his authoritative sources. His instance from *The Shepherds' Calendar* is 'June', 93–112; SC 54.

CHAPTER 15

Of the Second Kind of Connexive Syllogism

The second connexive is wherein the consequence or latter part of the proposition is removed in the affirmation, that the former also may be removed in the conclusion, as:

> *If May games were decent for us, then we should be young;*
> *But we be not young;*
> *Therefore they do not become us.*

Piers, in 'May':

> For younkers,° Palinode, such follies fit;
> But we tway° bene[iii] men of older wit. (17–18; SC 34ᵦ)

Of all kinds of syllogisms these two last be most used.[1]

10   There be some connexive syllogisms in which the former part is removed that the latter may be removed also, as:

> *If a tree have sense, then a tree is a sensible, or feeling creature;*
> *But a tree hath no sense;*
> *Therefore a tree is not such creature.*

But these syllogisms have then only force° when the parts be mutually reciprocal. Otherwise they be false and inconsequent, as:

> *If a man be an ass, he must be a feeling creature;*
> *But a man is no ass;*
> *Therefore he is no feeling creature.*

20   This followeth not. But in the former, where the parts were reciprocal, there was a true consequence, and yet not for the disposition sake, but only because the parts may be turned mutually, which, if they so may, then all the force of consequence commeth from the second kind of connexive syllogisms, not from any new disposition, as thus:

> *If a tree be a sensible creature, then it hath sense;*
> *But it hath no sense;*
> *Therefore it is no such creature.*

And this is the reason why sometimes in simple syllogisms the conclusion is good in the second kind, that is, in Aristotle's first figure,° when the *minor* is negative, because the parts be reciprocal.[2]

---

[1] **The second [...] most used**] Adapted from Ramus/Piscator, II.14, I6ʳ. Compare with Fenner: 'The second kinde of a knotting or connexiue Sillogisme is, when the consequence or latter parte of the proposition is denyed in the assumption, that the former also may be denided in the conclusion', *The Artes*, C4ᵛ; **consequence**] Although Ms has 'sequence' (which makes no sense as synonymous with 'the latter part'), Fraunce is translating Ramus's 'consequens'.

[2] **But these [...] reciprocal**] This discussion of different sorts of connexive syllogisms is an abridged translation from Piscator's lengthy 'ɴᴏᴛᴀ', in I.14, I7ᵛ–I8ʳ. The examples are also taken from Piscator.

CHAPTER 16

❧

Of a Disjunctive Syllogism

The disjunctive syllogism is that whose proposition is disjunctive, and is framed also after two sorts. | The first doth remove one part of the proposition in the assumption, and concludeth the other in the conclusion:[1]

> *Or Diggon her° is or I missay;*
> *But her° is not Diggon;*
> *Therefore I missay.*

Or thus:

> *Or Diggon her° is or I missay;*
> *But I do not missay;*
> *Therefore her° is Diggon.* ('September', 1–2; SC 78$_b$)

10

---

[1] **The disjunctive [...] conclusion**] Ramus/Piscator, II.15, 18^r.

CHAPTER 17

Of the Second Disjunctive Syllogism

The second is that which maketh the assumption of one part of the proposition being affirmed, and removeth the other in the conclusion, as:

> *Or Diggon her° is or I missay;*
> *But her° is Diggon;*
> *Therefore I do not missay.* ('September', 1–2; SC 78$_c$)

This same syllogism is also made of a copulative proposition being denied, because it hath the same force° with a proposition disjunctive being affirmed, as:[1]

> *Shepherds cannot live in pleasure and pain at once;*
> *But they must live in pleasure;*
> *Therefore not in pain.* ('January', 54; SC 7$_c$)

10

---

[1] **The second [...] affirmed**] Translated, with the exception of the examples, from Ramus/Piscator II.16, K1^r. In spite of terminological differences, Fraunce's second sentence follows Fenner: 'The same Sillogisme is also made of a coupled or copulatiue axiome being denied, because it hath the same force with a disioyned axiome', *The Artes*, C4^v. **This same [...] being denied**] Beurhaus II, Jud$_{40}$.

CHAPTER 18

~

Of Method[1]

Thus much as touching one and three axioms in a syllogism. Now followeth method. Method is a disposition of many and diverse axioms, having natural affinity among themselves, being placed orderly one before another according as everyone is more plain and easy than another to be conceived and known, so that thereby all of them may be judged easily to agree among themselves, as also be continually retained in memory.

And, as we consider in one axiom only truth and falsehood, in a syllogism consequence and inconsequence, so in method we respect order and confusion.

Order, whenas° that which is best known is placed in the first room, and those which be less known of themselves do follow in order, as everyone is better known than another. Therefore, method descendeth always from the general to the specials, even to the most singular thing, which can be divided into no more parts.[2]

The most general definition is first to be placed; distribution next, which, if it be manifold, partition into the integral parts must be set down first; then, division into the specials must follow. And these parts and specials are in the same order to be handled and defined as they were divided.

If the discourse be long, it must be knit together with transitions, [telling briefly what is done, and what is to be done, for confirmation of memory and recreation of the reader].

[26ᵛ]   Also the peculiar and natural properties must in order be declared, and familiar examples used. This method only and none other is to be observed so often as we teach any art or science, or take upon us to entreat perfitly° of any general matter.[3]

Confusion is where this order is not observed either in part or in whole, albeit historiographers, poets, orators, and such other writers or speakers are not bound so strictly to observe the perfection of this order, but may, according to their matter, meaning, purpose, time, place, persons, wisely observe the best for their intent, altering, hiding, and changing it when and how they list. So poets seek to please, and therefore Homer, as Horatius reporteth:

---

[1] **Of Method]** Fraunce's discussion abridges the longer exposition in Ramus/Piscator, II.17–20, K2ᵛ–K6ʳ. Fraunce advocates the idea of a single method, an ambiguous point in the source. Although Ramus believes in one single method ('solam methodum Aristoteles docuit', II.17, K2v), he then proceeds by illustrating three uses: the first, by examples of the arts (II.18: 'De prima methodi illustratione per exempla artium'); the second, by the poets, orators and historians (II.19: 'De secunda methodi illustratione per exempla poetarum, oratorum, historicorum'); the third consists in several inversions of order practised mainly by poets (II.20: 'De crypticis methodi').

[2] **Method is [...] parts]** Abridged from Ramus/Piscator, II.17, L2ᵛ. **And [...]confusion]** Beurhaus II, *Jud*₄₁. **Therefore [...] no more parts]** Beurhaus II, *Jud*₄₃.

[3] **The most [...] general matter]** These paragraphs adapt Ramus/Piscator, II.18, L2ᵛ–L3ᵛ; **telling [...] the reader]** Added in LL, Hh2ᵛ.

> *nec gemino bellum Troianum orditur ab ovo;*
> *semper ad eventum festinat et in medias res*
> *son secus ac notas auditorem rapit, et quae*
> *desperat tractata nitescere posse, relinquit,*
> *atque ita mentitur, sic veris falsa remiscet,*
> 30 *primo ne medium, medio ne discrepet imum.*

And Virgil beginneth the narration of Aeneas from Sicilia, making him declare the rest at supper in Carthage. So also orators, for that they refer all to persuasion and victory, place the best first and last, leaving the worst arguments together in the middle of their speech. Notwithstanding, because this method put down is so agreeable unto reason and so easy to be practised, both these and all other writers or speakers have done, and must generally, as occasion serveth, follow and express this method and order in all their writings and speakings. Therefore, when men alter and hide or change it, it is called the concealed or hidden method, because it wanteth sometimes plain and easy definitions, or divisions, or proprieties orderly placed.[4] Examples of the perfit° and exact method appear in the artificial putting down of sciences, as in 40 those especially which Ramus hath put down.[5]

For our *Calendar*, although shepherds are not wont° to bind themselves to any over-strict method in speaking, yet that song of Colin Clout rehearsed by Hobbinol, in 'April', may be a pretty president° of others to follow, where he, after a poetical invocation and general proposition of that which he hath in hand, I mean the praises of Elisa, commeth nearer the matter and first putteth down the causes, then the subject and adjuncts of Elisa orderly.[6] The verses I have partly put down in invention for other considerations, but are there most particularly to be examined where his song is, I mean, in 'April' (136–44; SC 32_d).

[27ʳ] Μέθοδος, or μετά, which signifieth 'with', and ὁδός, which is 'a way': for this is the right and compendious way in writing or speaking to be observed. The word therefore is metaphorically 50 applied to any orderly proceeding. And therefore, lest speaking of method we should seem to break order in confounding sophistical fallations° with true Logic, we have in a word or two satisfied the expectation of some, reserving the peculiar discourse of fallations° to these short notes, rather than thrusting them in among the precepts of Art. Some use, I confess, there may be had of them (although I know that whoso thoroughly perceiveth the truth of this art will

---

[4] **Confusion is […] placed]** These paragraphs fuse Ramus/Piscator II.19 and II.20, K3ᵛ–K6ʳ; **as Horatius reporteth]** Horace, *Ars Poetica*, 147–52, Loeb: p. 462, also quoted by Ramus. Instead of the Latin text, LL provides an English paraphrase: 'Therefore Homer maketh not a historical narration of the Trojan War from the beginning to the ending thereof, but so mingleth truth with tales, and tempereth them both with a probable show and delightsome continuation, that neither the middle do seem discrepant from the beginning, nor the ending from the middle' (Hh2ᵛ); *ab ovo*] from the beginning or, literally, 'from the egg' out of which Helen of Troy was alleged to be born; *in medias res*] in the middle of the narrative. **And Virgil […] Carthage]** 'immo age et a prima dic, hospes, origine nobis insidias […] Danaum' ('Nay, come […] and tell us, my guest, from the first beginning the treachery of the Greeks'), *Aeneid*, I.752–753, Loeb I: pp. 292–93. Dido's request justifies Aeneas's narrative in Book II. The example is also in Ramus. At this point LL, Hh2ᵛ adds: 'Comical poets also, albeit very exactly divide their comedies into acts and scenes, yet for the pleasure of the people bring in everything in such order as though it were by chance, hap or hazard come to pass'.
[5] **which Ramus hath put down]** Ramus's instance is the divisions of Dialectic and Grammar. See Ramus/Piscator, II.18, L3ʳ⁻ᵛ.
[6] **For our *Calendar* […] orderly]** Compare with LL, Ii3ʳ⁻ᵛ: 'For our *Calendar*, although shepherds be not wont to bind themselves to any over-strict method in speaking, yet that song of Colin Clout rehearsed by Hobbinol in 'May' may make vs believe that even shepherds, by the light of nature, did, as much as in them lay, express this method in their speeches. For there he, after a poetical invocation and general proposition of that which he hath in hand, I mean the praises of Elisa, commeth nearer the matter, and first putteth down the causes, then adjuncts and other arguments incident to Elisa'.

never seek other means to avoid these deceits). But if we shall put down everything in Logic, which hath any little show of profit thereunto, Grammar will be good Logic, because it maketh us utter that which we have logically conceived. Well, if anything be in them, here they be as I had them.[7]

---

[7] **as I had them**] as they were taught to me.

[CHAPTER 19]

Of the Elenchs[1]

Sophistical fallations° be either in words, or in the things themselves.

In the words be six several° fallations,° whereof the first is that which proceedeth from one word signifying diverse things,[2] as:

Euery dog can bark;
The dogfish is a dog;
Therefore the dogfish can bark.

The second commeth by reason of the ambiguity or doubtfulness which ariseth of the disposition and intricate placing of diverse words in one sentence,[3] whereupon grow diverse senses, as that old sophister° the devil deluded Croesus by giving him such an intricate answer:

10   Κροῖσος Ἅλυν διαβὰς μεγάλην ἀρχὴν καταλύσει
Croesus Halym penetrans magnam pervertet opum vim.[4]

Where he, thinking to destroy his enemies, undid himself.

The third, when we join such things together as ought severally° to be considered,[5] as:

Homer was blind;
Homer was a poet;
Therefore Homer was a blind poet.

For here the accidental form of the body is coupled with the internal habit of the mind, blindness with poetry.

The fourth, when we sever those things that are to be joined,[6] as:

---

[1] **Of the Elenchs**] This chapter division is added in the present edition. Ms places this section, somehow incoherently, as a continuation of the discussion of method. Fraunce might have derived this directly from Aristotle, *On Sophistical Refutations*, IV–V (see Loeb III: pp. 16–35 for references below), or via Sturm, *Partitionum Dialecticarum Libri IIII*, IV, Ii4ʳ–Ll6ʳ), or Freigius, *Rhetorica, Poëtica, Logica*, M1ʳ–M4ʳ. The latter, like Fraunce, appends the discussion of the fallacies to that of method.

[2] **one word signifying diverse things**] Aristotle's ὁμωνυμία — i.e., homonymy.

[3] **ambiguity or doubtfulness**] Aristotle's ἀμφιβολία.

[4] *Κροῖσος* [...] *καταλύψας / Croesus* [...] *vim*] 'Croesus, by crossing the Halys, shall ruin a mighty dominion', Aristotle, *Art of Rhetoric*, III.5, 1407a, Loeb XXII: pp. 372–73. The story of Croesus's own destruction when deciding to attack the Persians by believing the oracle of Delphos is recounted in Herodotus, I.53, Loeb I. pp. 58–61. The Latin version is found in Cicero, *De divinatione*, II.61.115–16, Loeb XX: pp. 500–01.

[5] **when we [...] considered**] Aristotle's σύνθεσις —i.e., synthesis.

[6] **when we [..] joined**] Aristotle's διαίρεσις — i.e., diaeresis.

20   *Two and three be even and odd;*
        Five is two and three;
        Therefore five is even and odd.

The fifth is from the accent,[7] as:

        Every altar is consecrated;
        The rope that hangeth a thief is a halter;
        Therefore the rope is consecrate.

[27ᵛ]   The sixth is of the order and form of speech,[8] when the same thing is not expounded after the
same manner, as:

        God is everywhere;
30   *Everywhere is an adverb;*
        Therefore God is an adverb.

Or thus,

        A house keepeth out rain;
        A house is a syllable;
        Therefore a syllable keepeth out rain.

Those that consist in the things be seven. The first is that which commeth from the accident
or adjunct, as when the same thing is attributed to substance and accident:

        Snow is white;
        Hail is white;
40   *Therefore hail is snow.*

The second, when we apply that absolutely and generally which was spoken, but in part and
in respect,° as:

        Apelles was a good painter;
        Therefore Apelles was good.

The third is of the want of knowledge of a contradiction,[9] and is four ways practised:
First, when one thing is referred not to the same but to diverse things, for then there is no true
contradiction, as:

        Two is double to one, and not double to three;
        Therefore true is double and not double.

50   Secondly, when it is not considered in the same respect° as:

        An Ethiopian hath white teeth;
        Therefore an Ethiopian is white.

Thirdly, when not simply and after the same manner as:

        He is learned in Music and not learned in Logic;
        Therefore he is learned and not learned.

---

[7] **the accent**] Aristotle's προσῳδία — i.e., prosody.

[8] **order and form of speech**] Aristotle's σχῆμα λέξεως.

[9] **want of knowledge of a contradiction**] 'Other fallacies arise because no definition has been given of what a
syllogism is and what a refutation, and there is some defect in their definition', Aristotle, *On Sophistical
Refutations*, V, 167a, Loeb III: p. 29. This fallacy is commonly known as *ignoratio elenchi*.

Fourthly, when not in the same time, as:

> *I saw Cambridge yesterday;*
> *I see not Cambridge today;*
> *Therefore I see it and I see it not.*

50   And unto this fallation° may all the rest be referred, saith Aristotle.[10]

The fourth fallation° in the thing is of the consequent, when in the sequel there is no necessity, as:

> *Here is wine;*
> *Therefore here is claret wine.*

The fifth is when either the same thing is proved by itself, as:

> *The soul is immortal, because it never dieth.*

Or when a doubtful thing is confirmed by that which is as doubtful, as:

> *The earth moveth, because the heaven standeth still.*

[28ʳ]   This is called *petitio principii*, when to prove one thing | we seek to have either the same in
60   effect granted us, or some other thing as doubtful.[11]

The sixth, when that is put for a cause which is no cause in deed, as:

> *Wine is naught;*
> *Because drunkenness is naught.*

The seventh and last when two or more questions be propounded as one, as:

> *Is honey and gall sweet?*

Here we must distinguish of the questions, and then apply several° answers thereunto.

Finis

---

[10] **And unto […] saith Aristotle**] 'We must either divide apparent reasonings and refutations in the manner just described or else refer them all to a false conception of refutation, making this our basis; for it is possible to resolve all kinds of fallacy which we have mentioned into violations of the definition of refutation', *On Sophistical Refutations*, VI, 168a, Loeb III: p. 35.

[11] *petitio principii*] 'to beg the point at issue [*petitio principii* or ἀρχῇ' αἰτεῖσθαι] is to prove by means of itself that which is not self-evident', Aristotle, *Prior Analytics*, II.16, 65a, Loeb I: p. 489. See also *On Sophistical Refutations*, VI, 168b, Loeb III: p. 39.

~

Of the Nature and Use of Logic

Julius Florus, by continual meditation for three days' space, could not frame a beginning for his oration. And I, when I think on that which I have to speak, may rather wish an ending than want a beginning in so large a discourse and plentiful disputation. Caius Plinius, in his panegyrical speech of the Emperor Trajan, first prayeth, before he praiseth, that his words might be worthy of Trajan His Majesty. And what then I, seeing that all that I can say is not enough, and to say enough is most than I can say? It is a shame to be always silent whenever to speak is scarce sufficient. And it is to small purpose to use a small speech when the greatest cannot be over-great. So that I perceive myself brought to a very near strait, when that I can neither be silent without shame nor speak to my contentation. If I say as others say, I shall be but simple; if I gainsay° them, I must be plain
10 impudent. But be it as it may, seeing he desireth to hear, which deserveth to have, and willeth me now, who may command me ever, I had rather be thought over-rash by writing than not so thankful by concealing. And, as I am not so well pleased with myself as to contemn the authority or correct the judgement of my betters (for I write not this to teach others, which have always desired to learn myself), so would I have neither myself to seem so sheepish as to speak for fashion and hang on other men's sleeves, nor them so injurious as to bind my wit to their will and rule my fancy by their affection. I love Plato, I like Aristotle, and Ramus always I cannot reprehend. If there be anything either good in Plato, or profitable in Aristotle, I take it by their leave. I thank them for that I take. But if Ramus and the rest amend that which they began, I am not either so unthankful toward these as not to accept their pains well employed, or so injurious to nature as
20 to think her so beneficial or rather prodigal in over-liberally lashing out her gift upon Aristotle only, as that she should leave nothing to bestow upon others.¹

This by the way, now to my purpose, and that in a word, rather pointing with the finger than painting with pen the true use and nature of this art, and hewing rather what might be said than saying that I ought to show in this behalf. For, having in Latin largely put down my mind,² I will

---

¹ **Julius Florus […] upon others]** This paragraph is an almost literal translation from Fraunce's earlier Latin essay: 'Junius Florus […] aliis largiatur', Rawlinson, fol. 5ʳ. **Julius Florus […] oration]** Quintilian refers the story of Julius Secundus as told by his uncle, the Gallic orator Julius Florus. Secundus had worked on an exordium for three days unsuccessfully. See *Institutio Oratoria*, 10.3.12–15, Loeb IV: pp. 96–99. **Caius Plinius […] majesty]** Pliny the Younger delivered in 100 AD a panegyric to Emperor Trajan for having appointed him Consul: 'Quo magis aptum piumque est te, Iupiter optime, antea conditorem, nunc conservatorem imperii nostri precari, ut mihi digna consule digna senatu digna principe contingat oratio' (Wherefore, mighty Jupiter, once the founder and now the preserver of our realm, it is my right and proper duty to address my prayers to you: grant, I pray, that my speech prove worthy of consul, Senate, and prince), *Panegyricus*, 1.6, Loeb II: pp. 322–25; **he desireth […] me ever]** Philip Sidney. On this dedication see Introduction, pp. 45–46; **hang on other men's sleeves]** depend on others' ideas (Tilley, S₅₃₃).

² **having […] my mind]** having written a longer treatise on the art of logic in Latin.

now but repeat some part of the same, briefly contracting and abridging that my former speech. First, therefore, generally of the whole nature and use of Logic; thenafter,° particularly of some special operations in the parts of the same; and so an end of a confused meditation, patched up, I fear me, in more haste than good speed.

[29ᵛ]   30   It is an old axiom, and as true as old, that art ought to imitate nature,³ in so much that nothing should be put down | in artificial Logic which hath not some resemblance or similitude of the pattern and foundation of all true Logic,⁴ which either God hath drawn or nature laid down in man's mind. I mean the reasonable capacity, wit, or intelligence of man, and those that excel the rest among men. For nature beginneth the work which art must finish. Nature, I say, declareth her goodness in several° particulars; and art, by experience, sense, observation, and induction, maketh of diverse particulars a general collection, whereof ensueth the absolute constitution of every art.

That therefore is true Logic, which is agreeable to reason imprinted in man, and apparent in the writings, arguments, and disputations of the most excellent in every kind, as Plato, Aristotle, Demosthenes, Cicero, Homer, Virgil and such like, whose particular examples collected by
40   observation have brought this art to her perfection, and so in others. For what first taught astronomers the number and course of the planets? Sense. What first told the natural philosopher that a lion feareth a cock, an elephant hateth a rhinoceros?⁵ Experience. What made the physicians believe that rhubarb was good to purge, that eupatorium cured the infected liver?⁶ Daily observation in diverse particulars. Now, if either a physician should bring in some herb not formed by nature, but forged by his own device, who would not deride him? Or, if an astronomer should make a discourse of such stars whose examples are not extant in the heavens, who would not laugh him to scorn? Or, if a natural philosopher would contend that fire were cold or water hot, which nature hath forbidden, who could abide him? Then, if in Physic, etc., we cannot suffer this, why should it be winked at in Logic? Or why should that be
50   taken for a rule in Logic which neither can be found in reason, the mother of Logic, nor in Demosthenes, Plato, and the rest, the authors of the same? For what author did ever use, what fruit can be perceived, nay, what Logic is there in these men's Logic, that wrangle of quiddities° and perseities,° substantialities° and formalities,° albedinities° and such like trumperies?° By whose dunsicality° it came to pass that Logic, being an art of arts, a science of sciences, an instrument of instruments, the hand of Philosophy, in power mighty, in authority great, in profit excellent, was so oppressed with sophistical brabbling,⁷ and overshadowed with dunsical°

---

³ **art ought to imitate nature**] On different forms of art as mimetic representations of life or nature see Aristotle, *Poetics* I–II, 1447a–b, Loeb XXIII: pp. 28–33.

⁴ **true Logic**] natural Logic.

⁵ **a lion feareth a cock**] see Pliny, *Natural History*, VIII.19.52, Loeb III: pp. 40–41; **an elephant hateth a rhinoceros**] 'The *Rhinoceros in Aethiopia*, a perpetuall enimie to the Elephant', trans. by Stephen Batman, *Uppon Bartholome his Booke De proprietatibus rerum* (London: Thomas East, 1582), fol. 378ᵛ.

⁶ **rhubarb**] 'In Rhubarb the purging vertue riseth of the subtle substance', Timothy Brighte, *A Treatise of Melancholie* (London: Thomas Vautrollier, 1586), D5ᵛ; **eupatorium**] 'Agrimonia […] is the ryght Eupatorium, as it appereth as well by the description of Dioscorides […] and other mooste excellent phisitions of this tyme. The decoction of this herbe […] is an excellent remedy agaynste oppylations of the lyuer by reason of fleume. It is hot in the fyrste degree, and drye in the second', Sir Thomas Elyot, *Bibliotheca Eliotiae* (London: Thomas Berthelet, 1542), B6ʳ.

⁷ **sophistical brabbling**] 'All the Fathers haue with one harte accursed, and with one mouth pronounced it abhominable, that the holy woorde of God should be entangled with the suttleties of Sophisters, and brawlynges of Logitians. Doo they holde themselues within these boundes, when they goe about nothyng ells in their whole lyfe, but with endlesse striues and more then Sophisticall brablynges to wrappe and encombre the simplicitie of the Scripture […]?', Jean Calvin, *Institution of Christian Religion*, trans. by Thomas Norton (London: Reynold Wolfe and Richard Harrison, 1561), A5ᵛ. Norton's translation seems to have impregnated Fraunce's anti-Catholic and anti-scholastic lexicon.

inventions,[8] that neither physicians knew it nor philosophers had it, nor astronomers cared for it, being never indeed brought into light, but always kept in enclosed among those intricate labyrinths of barbarous and idle-headed sophisters,° who, if they had either read the ancient
60 learned writers, or considered the simple country-labouring men, they might have seen Logic in those, and Logic in these, far different from their own Logic. For, to let pass the learned poets and orators, whom they never saw, much less perused, send for a poor and silly husbandman,° ask him what hope he hath of his harvest to come. He will roundly make answer, and that not

[30ʳ]   instructed | by learning, but taught by nature, that there is no hope at all of any fertility this year to ensue, because the weather hath been so unseasonable.

Lo, here is Logic not found by man, but framed of nature. Lo, here the two parts of Logic, the one in invention of the proof, the other in disposition of the proof invented. This is nature's work, and art must follow nature, or else no cause why we should follow art. The causes of plenty, saith the countryman, be taken away; therefore the effect must needs be removed. Here is no
70 mention made, no ground,° no oration whereby to bring in any of those monkish devices. But this is not all. For, as they have thus pestered this noble art with such unnecessary and unprofitable sophistry, so have they on the other side taken as much away from her of her own virtue, and greatly detracted from her dignity. For, whereas Logic is of herself so general, as that she can in no wise suffer her liberty to be restrained, yet these unhappy loiterers have so injuriously[vi] dealt with her, and handled her so hardly, by pinning her up in their loathsome cloisters, that nothing at the time was hight° to be Logic which bare° not some note and token of their sophistry. How subtle they were in this, let them judge themselves; but how injurious to Logic, and prejudicial to the lovers of the same, let others confess.

Logic hath her name of the Greek word Λόγος, which signifieth either *ratio* or *oratio*, reason
80 or speech. So that the virtue of this art doth so far extend itself, as either man's reason can reach unto, or speech discourse upon. Whereas these fellows never saw or never would seem to have seen any such thing, measuring the most excellent worthiness of such a science by the little capacity of their own confused brains, wherein they follow the unhonest example of Philoxenus and Eudoxus Gnidius,[9] two famous, or rather infamous, gluttons and bellygods,° who were not ashamed most impudently to convey the excrements of their noses into the dishes of meat, to the intent that others, abstaining by the reason of their beastliness, they might have the full and only fruition of the same themselves. Better it were for a scholar never to learn than to be taught of such masters, whose learning they must unlearn if ever they purpose themselves to be learned.

90   But what, do I renew the grievous remembrance of that time so miserable? Seeing it is past, let it be passed with silence, or rather overpassed with forgetfulness. Learning was abused then, the time was unhappy, those men unlucky, but Logic most unfortunate, which of herself is so gentle, familiar, tractable, and amiable that she excludeth no man, is nowhere excluded, is always at hand, ever in readiness, and suffereth no part of our life to be deficient of her good help. With lovers, she loveth to speak like a wanton; with kings, she counselleth in a prince's palace; with men of the country, she sits in the sheepcotes;° with senators, she gravely decideth controversies; in school, she directeth subtle philosophers; at home, she admitteth the simple artificer. As high

---

[8] **inventions**] fancies (not in the logical sense used throughout this volume).

[9] **Philoxenus**] Many anecdotes (though not the one mentioned here) are told about the proverbial gluttony of Philoxenus (435–380 BC). Besides being the alleged author of a poem called *The Banquet*, he is reported to have 'wished he had a necke like a Crane, that the sweet meate which he eate might bee long in going downe', Robert Albbott, *Wits Theater of the Little World* (London: James Roberts, 1599), Ll3ʳ⁻ᵛ. This same anecdote in referred by Aristotle in reference to 'a certain gourmand', *Nicomachean Ethics*, III.10, Loeb XIX: pp. 176–79. **Eudoxus Gnidius**] No mention of the astronomer and mathematician Eudoxus of Gnidus (408–355 BC) as a glutton has been tracked down.

as the highest, as low as the lowest, and mean with those of middle meaning.¹⁰ A preacher
commeth to persuade the people, to exhort the congregation; but who can away with his
100 persuasion, or who careth for his exhortation, unless he bring a sermon rather fraught and
furnished with store of arguments than flowing and flourishing with show of ornaments — the
one being the effort of Logic, of all men commended, the other but a trick of Rhetoric, of many
condemned?¹¹

[30ᵛ]   Let primers° read the orations of Cyrus put down in Xenophon,¹² but counsellors peruse, as I
have elsewhere spoken, Sir John Cheke his exhortation to our English rebels.¹³ Let philosophers
harken to Socrates disputing, as in Plato. Lastly, let politic men and governors give ear to Scipio.¹⁴
Then shall they see, both primers° and the rest, the necessity of Logic in them all. As for lawyers,
I let them pass, for I think there is no man so ignorant or unthankful that neither can see nor
will confess the help of Logic in law-like disputations.¹⁵ Again I speak nothing of primers, legates,
110 and ambassadors, when I know and they acknowledge to have what they have by the having of
Logic. Whoso readeth Homer shall well perceive that neither the strong Ajax nor fierce Achilles
did so much prevail in battering down the walls of Troy, as the wise Nestor and prudent Ulysses.
The speech of Nestor was sweeter than honey, the talk of Ulysses sharper than the winter snow.
But what made either that of Nestor so sweet or this so piercing of Ulysses, but that Nestor was
wise and Ulysses prudent? Well therefore did Agamemnon, the chieftain of the Grecians, wish
not ten like to Ajax but ten such as Nestor to conquer the Trojan town.¹⁶ For little can war abroad
unless wit be at home; and less can wit at home unless we rule heady wit with heedy wisdom, the
only gift of *Dialectica*.

        That place of Livius is very notable, wherein the oration of Menenius Aprippa is rehearsed.
120 For, whenas° the Roman rascal people had forsaken Rome, and fled by rebellion to the Holy Hill
— that which others neither by force nor favour, promise nor prowess, could perform —
Menenius Agrippa brought to pass by one only argument framed by Logic in comparing together
the members of a human body and parts of a commonwealth.¹⁷ As for all other arts, it is well
known that they can neither be well taught, truly learned, nor orderly put down but by the help
of Logic.

        Now, if any man should be desirous to peruse the monuments° of ancient writers, historical,
poetical, or philosophical, and be not first instructed with this faculty, I shall not so much envy
his good hap as pity his little discretion, who seeketh to meddle with sacred mysteries with

---

¹⁰ **As high [...] meaning**] Logic is equally valid for speeches in any of the three rhetorical styles.
¹¹ **Rhetoric, of many condemned**] On the Ramist reduction of Rhetoric to mere ornament see Introduction,
pp. 6, 9, 30–35.
¹² **the orations [...] Xenophon**] the speeches of Cyrus, Emperor of Persia, composed by Xenophon of Athens
in his fictional biography *Cyropedia* (4th c. BC).
¹³ **Sir John Cheke [...] rebels**] Sir John Cheke wrote *The Hurt of Sedition* (1549) on the occasion of the Norfolk
peasants' revolts.
¹⁴ **Scipio**] Scipio Africanus the Younger (185–129 BC) is prominent for his political ideas in Cicero's *De
republica*.
¹⁵ **the help [...] disputations**] As Fraunce's own *The Lawyers' Logic* (1588), in the tradition of Freige's *Partitiones
Iuris* (1571) or *Logica Iureconsultorum Libri Duo* (1582).
¹⁶ **Whoso readeth Homer [...] Trojan town**] Agamemnon's praise of Nestor's eloquence and Ulysses's
prudence and cunning is frequent in Homer's *Iliad*; **speech of Nestor sweeter than honey**] 'Then among them
uprose Nestor, sweet of speech, the clear-voiced orator of the men of Pylos, he from whose tongue flowed
speech sweeter than honey', *Iliad*, I.247–49, Loeb I: pp. 20–21.
¹⁷ **The place of Livius [...] commonwealth**] Livy registers Agrippa's oration to appease the plebeians' anger
agaisnt the City Fathers (494 BC). According to Livy, the speech was made 'in the quaint and uncouth style of
that age' ('prisco illo dicendi et horrido modo'), *Ab urbe condita*, II.32.9, Loeb I: pp. 322–23, see also SL, I.17, 6n.;
one only argument] comparison, or 'the like'.

polluted hands, to read good authors without any Logic. In reading of Cicero, Plato, Aristotle, I
130 love their eloquence, I praise their wit, I admire their copious and ample style. But why either
Tully his wise eloquence is to be loved, or Aristotle's wit to be praised, or Plato his divine
philosophy to be admired, I know not at all, but do what I do by haphazard. Neither can their
art and style any more delight me, which cannot perceive it, than the precious stone could please
Aesop's cock, whereof he knew no use.[18]

So then Logic is general and appliable° to every disputation, yet the matter to be disputed of is
not of Logic, but the manner how to dispute. And although in common meetings and assemblies
the words and terms of Logic be not named, yet the force° and operation is always used and
apparent. For as in Grammar we name neither noun, pronoun, and verb, nor any other part of
speech, and as in Rhetoric we make mention neither of *metonymia*,° *agnominatio*,° nor any other
[31ʳ] 140 rhetorical figure or trope, yet use in our | speech the help of the one in speaking orderly, and the
aid of the other in talking eloquently, so, although in common conference we never name
syllogisms, majors, minors and other words of art, yet do we secretly practise them in our talk, the
virtue whereof is to make our orator seem true to the simple, and probable to the wise.

And thus much generally of the nature and use of Logic. Now, in a word, of the particular
consideration of the same in every several° part. As Logic therefore itself is divided into two parts, the
first whereof is conversant in searching and finding out of arguments, the second in framing and
partly[19] disposing the same, so is then in either part a double practice, and the least of them both of
wonderful excellency. The one is called genesis, when we seek by our proper labour and meditation
to make some piece of work (for so the Greek word signifieth). The other analysis, whenas° we
150 mind to undo that which others have done, and to resolve and dissolve the same into his particular
parts, the better to perceive the art of the author in making, and his conveyance in handling.[20]

The use and commodity of genesis in invention will then be perceived and perfitly° known,
when for our own exercise in this behalf we take some argument and draw the same throughout
all the places of invention, showing what be the causes, effects, subjects, adjuncts, etc., of the
same. As for example sake, in Latin I propounded this word, 'Nobility', out of Sturmius, and so
deduced the same.[21] In like manner for analysis in invention, I take that piece of Cicero, which
is entitled *Laelius*, wherein I examined the causes, effects, etc., of *amicitia*, the better to
understand what art Tully had used in that disputation.[22]

For the second part of Logic in disposition either axiomatical, syllogistical, or methodical, as
160 Apelles was wont° to say, *nulla dies sine linea*, so would I wish him that would be a logician to
let no day pass without some practice in this part.[23] Wherein yet I will not be so severe a censor
as to exact every syllogism to the straight forms and rigorous rules of some dunses° prescribed.
Let sophisters° beat their brains about these in schools: it shall be sufficient for a political man to

---

[18] **Aesop's cock**] The cock in the fable attributed to Aesop preferred a barleycorn to a precious jewel that he
found on a dunghill. See 'Appendix', 562a, in *Babrius and Phaedrus*, Loeb, pp. 525–26. McCormick (p. 185)
notes the proverbial uses of the fable by reference to Tilley, B₈₈.

[19] **partly**] here, by division into parts.

[20] **The one [...] handling**] Fraunce's best summary of the uses of genesis and analysis appears in tabular form
in LL, Ee4ʳ. See Appendix I.3; **making, handling**] the procedures of invention and disposition.

[21] **'Nobility', out of Sturmius**] Johann Sturm, *Ad Weteros Fratres, Nobilitas literata: liber unus* (Strasbourg:
Rihel, 1549), translated by Thomas Browne as *A Ritch Storehouse or Treasurie for Nobility and Gentlemen*
(London: Henry Denham, 1570). Fraunce developed his deduction in Rawlinson, fols 8ᵛ–10ʳ.

[22] **Cicero [...] disputation**] Fraunce analyses Cicero's *De amicitia* (*Laelius*), in Rawlinson, fols 10ʳ–12ʳ.

[23] *nulla dies sine linea*] 'not a single day without [drawing] a line'. Pliny the Elder reports that the painter
Apelles's custom of not letting a day pass without practising his art grew into the well-known proverb (*Natural
History*, XXXV.36.84–85, Loeb IX: pp. 322–23). Erasmus popularized a negative version, '*Nullam hodie lineam
duxi*', in *Adagiorum Chiliades Tres* (Tübingen: Ludwig Anshelm, 1514), H2ᵛ.

follow a more easy and elegant kind of disputation, joining Rhetoric with Logic, as Plato in Greek, and Cicero in Latin used to do. For example sake in this behalf, I took for my theme the praise of Logic, and thereon disputed logically, after my manner, in Latin.[24]

This for genesis; now for analysis. In this second part of Logic, and namely in axioms and syllogisms, that is most necessary for the avoiding of the captious and sophistical circumventions of our adversaries. For otherwise, as a good tale may be marred in the telling, so a false surmised
170   fable will be taken for a truth, for want of judgement in this part to sever good from bad, truth from falsehood, show from substance. An example for this part we take out of Tully his *Paradoxes*, where he hath these words, *quod solum honestum est, id bonum est*. Wherein I laid down in a table the orders, proofs, examples, confirmations, confutations, axioms, syllogisms,
[31ᵛ]   enthymemes | secretly contained in this disputation, and, as in this example I have done, so must every logician take pains to do better, if ever he purpose to have use of his Logic.[25]

The last part of judgement remaineth yet, but not the least, and that is method, which, if you take away, all other things in a logician, although they be most excellent, are of small force° and little estimation. For what availeth it to search and find our arguments to frame and conclude them, if there be no order kept in propounding them, no method observed for conservation and help of
180   memory? It is like a confused heap of stones and timber in respect of a well-ordered house. For this part I refer the lovers of Logic to the last chapter of Ramus his Logic, where he shall have examples to make this plain, and counsel when to use an exact method, and when to admit of an inverted order, as occasion of place, time, and other circumstances shall seem to require. And this inventing of method is called of some *methodus prudentiae*, because it requireth the wisdom and discretion of the speaker or writer, in judging the time when such a perturbation of order may be used.[26] For, as it is a point of art to cover art,[27] so sometimes to proceed methodically, defining, dividing, etc., is very prejudicial to the speaker, because the circumstances may be such that better it were to convey the matter straightly than to put down it simply. But this by the way, for my meaning is not to give precepts of Logic, but to show the use of those that be given.
190   Now, as the use of this art is strange and wonderful, so the abusing of the same hath been intolerable, partly in supplanting thereby and circumventing the simple, but especially by overcharging it with rude and barbarous quiddities,° as also by detracting from it the most necessary ornaments of the same. Somewhat I have already spoken of this abuse. More I might, and more I could, if either time were favourable to my will, or other affairs not prejudicial to my natural inclination, which ever hath been and always will be, as a lover of Logic, so a proposed enemy to those lazy and confused monkish heads, the only defacers of this so noble a science, which have brought in whole cartloads of unusual superfluities, better never named than ever known.

---

[24] **elegant kind of disputation**] Fraunce's recommendations for logical disputations were tabulated in LL, sigs Ee2ʳ–Ee4ʳ. **the praise [...] in Latin**] See Rawlinson, fols 13ʳ–14ʳ.

[25] **Tully his paradoxes [...] Logic**] Fraunce's tabular analysis of this paradox can be consulted in Rawlinson, fols 15ʳ⁻ᵛ. Cicero's paradox reads 'Quod honestum sit, id solum bonum esse' ('That only what is morally noble is good'), *Paradoxa Stoicorum*, I.1, Loeb IV: pp. 258–67.

[26] **For this [...] be used**] The last chapter, or chapters, on method and its kinds vary in content and name in different editions of Ramus (four chapters after 1569, like Ramus/Piscator II.18–21). The distinction between *methodus doctrinae* and *methodus prudentiae* was first formulated by Ramus in 1546 under the name of Omer Talon (and thus perhaps Fraunce's 'called of some'). There prudence is recommended in inversions of natural disposition (i.e., from the universal to the particular) by considering several circumstances: 'pro conditione personarum, rerum, temporum, locorum', *Dialectici Commetarii tres* (Paris: Grandini, 1546), L4ʳ⁻ᵛ. The theory was developed later in the *Dialectique*, Q4ᵛ–R4ʳ). On *methodus prudentiae* in the evolution of Ramus's thought, see Ong, *Ramus, Method*, pp. 246–47.

[27] **it is a point of art to cover art**] art must hide its own artifice (Tilley, A₃₃₅). Compare with: 'O, quoth Antigone, I loue the terribly, but it is a chiefe point of art to dissemble art', Brian Melbancke, *Philotimus* (London: Roger warde, 1583), G1ᵛ.

~

A Brief and General Comparison of Ramus his Logic with That of Aristotle, to the Right Worshipful his Very Good Master and Patron, Master Philip Sidney

Phormio, by report, Right Worshipful, was scoffed, although he spake well, because he spake to Hannibal.¹ And might not I be scorned for writing ill, and writing to Philippus?² For, as I am sure of the one, that Phormio was as well renowned for a philosopher as I am rejected for a philosophaster,° so am I certain of the other, that Hannibal had as much need to hear precepts of war as hath Philippus to read rules of Logic. But herein is the difference: that Hannibal, as he was hardy in field to revenge him of his foes, so was he too hasty at whom to reject his friend the well-meaning Phormio; whereas Philippus, as in Logic he goeth before many, so for gentleness and courtesy more may come behind him. And yet, because it were an odious thing for me to sit as judge and censor of Aristotle and Ramus, who, as I never name Ramus without some
10   reverence, so I always speak of Aristotle with admiration, I have laid aside the person of a determiner, and supplied the place of a plain interpreter, exhibiting that, in writing to Your Worship briefly, which two Cambridge sophisters° did speak more diffusedly. The one is, as they say, a methodical° Ramist; the other, an obstinate Aristotelian.³ The speech was theirs; the judgement shall be yours; the report must hang upon my credit. Only this for myself I must desire Your Worship: to read this not as my mind, but as their meaning. And if they seem either over-bold, or scarce well-mannered before such a judge so to behave themselves, attribute it rather to the rudeness of wailing and wrangling sophisters° that spake it than the disposition of him that put it down. The Aristotelian, being almost besides° himself, partly with anger and partly with admiration, burst forth into these exclamations:
20   'Good God, what a world is this? What an age do we now live in? I think on it daily, yet can I never conceive in thought. I wonder always, yet can I never marvel enough, and still I speak, yet as good I were still, as still to speak to no purpose. A sophister° in times past was a title of credit and a word of commendation. Now, what more odious? Aristotle then the father of Philosophy,

---

¹ **Phormio [...] Hannibal]** During his banishment in Ephesus (195–90 BC), the Carthaginian general Hannibal pronounced the peripatetic philosopher Phormio the greatest of fools after listening to the for several hours. See Cicero, *De oratore*, II.18.75–76, Loeb III: pp. 254–55.
² **Philippus]** Philip Sidney, compared to Alexander's father, Philippus of Macedon (382–336 BC).
³ **methodical Ramist [...] obstinate Aristotelian]** On the likely identification of these characters with William Temple and Everard Digby, see Introduction, pp. 3, 46.

now who less favoured? The good St Thomas of Aquine (that angelical and seraphical doctor), the subtle Scot, the learned Bricot, the profound Holkot,[4] with the rest which then did flourish — where are they now? Ramus rules abroad, Ramus at home, and who but Ramus? Antiquity is nothing but dunsicality,° and sophistry nothing but unfruitful quiddities.° Newfangled,° young-headed,° hare-brain° boys will needs be masters which never were scholars, prate° of method which never knew order, rail against Aristotle as soon as they creep out of the school, profess to

30   know that in one year which Antiquity confessed to require seven.[5] True substance is not apparent; superficial appearance beareth away the bell.[6] A face is all, and only a face; a grace is all, albeit past grace.[7]

[32ᵛ]   'Logic is now but six leaves long, and eight days' labour, which before was seven years' study, and filled the world with volumes almost infinite. Hereby it comes to pass that every cobbler° can cog° a syllogism,[8] every carter crack° of propositions. Hereby is Logic profaned, and lieth prostitute, removed out of her sanctuary, robbed of her honour, left of her disciples, ravished of strangers, and made common to all, which before was proper to schools, and only consecrated to philosophers. We fly with wings of wax, we rule the chariot of the sun without discretion. So must we fall with Icarus, and perish with falling. So must we burn with Phaeton, and die with

40   burning.[9] A sound scholar is called a dunse,° and dunse° is taken for a fool. A logician of eight years' standing is controlled of a boy of six weeks' continuance. And — that which most tormenteth the heart of well-settled Aristotelians — Aristotle himself is quite defaced, his *Organon* called a confused chaos,[10] his Logic a hump of matter without order, more fit to confound the memory than apt to instruct the mind, more worthy to serve in a silkwoman's shop than furnish a scholar's library.[11] What a blaspheme° is this? What a madness to put it up with silence? What a meritorious deed to revenge it with contradiction?° I gainsay° therefore that which they say, and yet say no more than I mind to prove, that his *Organon*, as it was always called, so it shall ever be, Ὄργανον ὀργάνων ἢ ἡ τῆς φιλοσοφίας χείρ.[12] For proof whereof, and

---

[4] **good St Thomas of Aquine**] Thomas Aquinas (1225–74) is the chief philosopher and theologian of the High Middle Ages. His work is crucial for the reinterpretation of Aristotle in Western philosophy; **subtle Scot**] John Duns Scotus (1266–1308), nicknamed 'Doctor Subtilis' and one of the key figures of medieval scholasticism, is well-known for using logical argumentation in his proofs of God's existence; **learned Bricot**] Thomas Bricot (d. 1516), one of the leading 'Sorbonnists', abridged Aristotle's *Organon* and wrote a treatise on paradox, the *Tractatus insolubilium* (Paris, 1494); **profound Holkot**] The Oxford philosopher Robert Holkot (d. 1439) is reputed for his notion of *logica fidei*, i.e., the prior logical conditions constraining theological formulations.
[5] **one year [...] seven**] The training in logic at Cambridge in the late sixteenth century occupied the second year of a Bachelor's degree. See Costello, *The Scholastic Curriculum*, p. 41, and Jardine, 'The Place of Dialectic'.
[6] **beareth away the bell**] carries off the prize. See *OED*, *bell*, n.,¹ and Tilley, B₂₇₅.
[7] **A face [...] past grace**] appearance is more valued than substance. For variants see Tilley, F₁₃ and G₃₉₅.
[8] **cog a syllogism**] metaphorically, to connect the parts of a syllogism as a shipbuilder cogs or joins timbers (*OED*, *cog* 7 v.²).
[9] **Icarus [...] falling**] In Greek mythology, Icarus fell when trying to escape from the labyrinth in Crete by flying with the wings of wax and feathers made by his father Daedalus; **Phaeton [...] burning**] In order to prove his divine descendance from the sun, Phaeton drove the sun chariot but was unable to control its horses, and Zeus killed him with a thunderbolt. In the mouth of the Aristotelian, these two examples stress Ramist pride.
[10] **his *Organon* called a confused chaos**] the corpus of Aristotle's six works on dialectic, namely *Categories, On Interpretation, Prior Analytics, Posterior Analytics, Topics* and *Sophistical Refutations*. In Marlowe's *The Massacre at Paris* Ramus affirms: 'I knew the Organon to be confused', *The Complete Plays*, 9.45. See also Ong, *Ramus, Method*, pp. 41–44. On Ramus's opinions about Aristotle's confusing arrangement, see 40n to this same essay.
[11] **to furnish a silkwoman's shop**] because of the variety of items made by silkwomen. See Anne F. Sutton, 'Two Dozen and More Silkwomen of Fifteenth-Century London', *The Ricardian*, 16 (2006), 1–8 (p. 1).
[12] Ὄργανον ὀργάνων ἢ ἡ τῆς φιλοσοφίας χείρ] literally, 'the instrument of instruments and the hand of philosophy'. This is the title of the edition (Basel, 1536) of Porphyry's *Isagoge* and Aristotle's *Organon* by the

first for method, I say that a syllogysm, as it is the work and scope of Logic, so it is the matter
50 subject whereabout this *Organon* is conversant and altogether occupied. And may be considered
either as it is a whole integral, or an universal whole. As it is *totum universale*, it hath his specials,
to wit a demonstrative,° a topical, and a sophistical syllogism. Of the first he teacheth in his
Demonstrations,[13] of the second in his *Topics*, of the third in his *Elenchs*.[14] Whereof arise these
several° arts: the one eternal, necessary, and infallible, as *apodictiké*; the other probable, as
dialectiké; the third, false in deed yet bearing a show of truth, as *sophistiké*.[15] But, as it is *totum
integrum*,° it consisteh of his essential parts, I mean form and matter. The form is put down in
his *Analyticis prioribus*. The matter is double: either that which is new and jointly connexed with
it, as be propositions in his book Περί ἑρμενείας,[16] or somewhat removed and further off, as *voces
et termini*,° whereof at large in his *Categories*, and in the *Predicables* of Porphyry.[17] What is
60 order, if this be not method? Or what is method, if this be out of order? This hath Aristotle
observed in his *Organon*, and this have his scholars observed by imitation, beginning at the least
and so by little and little ascending to the greatest.[18]

'Now for the matter, I would fain learn of these precise logicians and methodical° masters of
Dialectica what is there either in the Captain Aristotle that is not fruitful, or in his fellow soldiers
that is not necessary. First they[19] begin with single words, which they call *voces* and *termini*,°
[33ʳ]　　whereof some be proper, | some common, some *ad placitum*, some *a natura*, and some of others
sorts,[20] which, being by diligence noted and carefully observed, we shall better perceive the nature
of propositions made hereof. After these follow *praedicabilia*,° five general words,[21] everyone
affording four several° commodities. The first is for the better understanding of the predicaments°
70 that ensue, which be nothing else but a methodical ordering and placing of *praedicabilia*,° as of
genus, *species*, *differentia*, and the rest. The second profit is for definitions, which, if they be perfit,°
consist of *genus* and *differentia*; if unperfit,° of properties and accidents. The third is for divisions,
which are, or ought to be, distinct severings of the general into his special by lawful differences.
The last is for demonstration, which is a conclusion of the proper quality in his own subject by
a true proper and immediate cause. All which things, as they cannot be performed without these
praedicabilia,° so do they necessarily presuppose the knowledge of the same. The predicaments°
in order follow, for the better conceiving of the which they handle some other things called

---

German philologist Simon Grynaeus (1493–1541). Despite this proper use, Fraunce appropriates the phrase
in translation twice as a general praise of Logic, not of Aristotle's work (see SL I.1, 92–93 [fols 4ʳ⁻ᵛ] and 'Of the
Nature and Use of Logic', 53–55 [fol. 29ᵛ]). In this second function it also appears (in Greek) in his untitled
Latin essay's praise of the art (see Rawlinson, fol. 13ᵛ).

[13] **Demonstrations**] Aristotle's books on demonstrative logic (the *Prior* and *Posterior Analytics*).

[14] **Elenchs**] Aristotle's *Sophistical Refutations*.

[15] **apodictiké** [...] **dialectiké** [...] **sophistiké**] These adjectives, in transliterated Greek in Ms, designate the arts
of demonstrative, topical and fallacious reasoning.

[16] Περί ἑρμενείας] Aristotle's *On Interpretation*.

[17] **Predicables of Porphyry**] The Neoplatonic philosopher Porphyry (234?–305? AD) wrote the *Isagoge*, a
commentary on Aristotle's *Categories*. His remarks on Aristotle's κατηγορούμενα (*praedicabilia* or *quinque
voces*) were adopted later through Boethius's translation (early 6th century). *Predicables* is understood here as
a title, in accordance with sixteenth-century editions of Porphyry/Boethius. See *Quinque vocum, quae
praedicabilia Porphirii liber [...] Boetio Severino interprete* (Paris: Guillaume le Bet, 1538).

[18] **beginning** [...] **greatest**] inductively, from the particular to the general, as opposed to Ramist method, which
proceeds from the general to the particular.

[19] **they**] Aristotle's followers.

[20] *ad placitum* [...] *a natura*] According to terminist logicians, like Jean Buridan (1300–58), a *vox* or 'utterance'
can signify naturally (*a natura*), like the barking of dogs, or by convention (*ad placitum*), like the noun 'man'.
See Buridan, *Summulae de dialectica*, trans. by Gyula Klima (New Haven: Yale University Press, 2002),
pp. 7–10.

[21] *praedicabilia*, **five general words**] the predicables, or *quinque voces*. See 17n to this essay.

antepredicaments,° as the distinction of words to know which be doubtful, ambiguous, *aequivoca*, and which of one simple and plain signification; which be primitives, which
80 derivatives.²² For in disputation he that taketh away distinction confoundeth art and bringeth in confusion. Other divisions and rules I omit, which are usually put down in these antepredicaments° — the use of them is so apparent.²³

'As for the ten predicaments° themselves, who seeth not what a help it is either to define curiously, or divide exactly, or dispute artificially, or to have all words, all things, all properties and natures of things so orderly put down, so plainly set forth, so easy to be used when occasion is offered, all bodies, spirits, substances, accidents, qualities, quantities, relations, actions, passions, circumstances, laid up, as it were, in their several° storehouses, so that a man shall easily find, although he differ to seek, till he have need to use?

'Next these predicaments° succeedeth the explication of some certain words, which, because
90 those be generally dispersed through all the predicaments,° and not severally° bound to any one of them, are therefore put after them all, as contraries, privatives, relatives, contradictions, *prius*, *simul*, and the other, very profitable for the more absolute explication of the predicaments.°²⁴

'Hitherto hath been spoken of the removed° matter of syllogisms. Now the matter which is more near is a proposition, which, because it consisteth of a noun and a verb, good reason the nature of them both should be put down, and because in a proposition the noun may be diversely taken, and in sundry senses. Supposition° followeth, showing the force and diverse acception° of every terming: when it is to be understood generally, when particularly, when distinctly, when confusedly.²⁵ Again, some propositions be contrary to some others, some like and equal, and therefore, as the one assertion is taught in the tractate° of opposition,° so the other is declared in
100 the discourse of *aequipollentia*.°²⁶ Some propositions also be pure,° some modificate,° which,
[33ᵛ] as they be diverse from the other and more different than they be, they have | a several° discourse and somewhat intricate, *nec iniuria: Nam de modalibus non gustabit assinus*.²⁷ Lastly, because the nature of propositions is such that, by changing the *termini*,° a certain inversion, or rather conversion,° is commonly made, there is a special place appointed for this purpose, and rules put down to avoid errors in this behalf.

'And thus much for the matter of syllogisms. Now, for the form which consisteth in a diverse disposition of *medium*.° There be three figures,° and a certain number of modes° adjoined to every figure.° But because the first is only perfit° and absolute, there be ordained letters as need to reduce the unperfit° to the perfit,° and this is called reduction.°²⁸ Now, if we leave this
110 consideration of a syllogism as it is *totum integrum*,° consisting of its natural and essential parts, and so speak of it as if an universal whole containing certain specials, so shall we find three

²² *aequivoca* [...] derivatives] on this classification see Glossary ('antepredicaments').
²³ **Other divisions [...] apparent**] i.e., Aristotle's division of expressions into complex and 'incomplex', or his discussion of presence. See *Categories*, II, Loeb I: pp. 14–17.
²⁴ **Next [...] the predicaments**] On this classification see Glossary ('postpredicaments').
²⁵ **generally [...] particularly [...] distinctly [...] confusedly**] These four adverbs vaguely correspond with scholastic classifications of supposition. See Peter of Spain, *Language in Dispute: An English Translation of [...] Summulae Logicales*, trans. by Francis D. Dinneen (Amsterdam: John Benjamins, 1990), pp. 70–71.
²⁶ **tractate of opposition**] Aristotle, *Categories*, X, Loeb I: pp. 80–95; **discourse of *aequipollentia***] Theories of equipollence were developed after Aristotle by scholastic logicians, like William of Ockham (1280–1349), and especially by Jean Buridan.
²⁷ *nec* [...] *assinus*] 'not without reason: the ass will not taste of the modals'. On this medieval saying of unknown origin see I. M., Bochénski, *A History of Formal Logic*, trans. by Ivo Thomas (Notre Dame, Ind.: University of Notre Dame Press, 1961), p. 86.
²⁸ **But because [...] reduction**] The reduction and conversion of imperfect to perfect syllogisms were explained by the presence of certain consonants in the mnemonic terms expressing the syllogistic modes.

several° syllogisms: the first apodictical, as I said in the *Demonstrations*; the second logical, in the *Topics*; the third sophistical, in the *Elenchs* — not to the intent any man should use them to abuse the simplicity of others, but that, knowing the vice, he might eschew it, and, detecting the fraud, avoid the same.

'This is the sum of that which is put down in Aristotle, and this is almost all that can be found in Aristotelians. If there be anything in them expressed which is not in him contained, it is added, either for the more ample declaration of that which is exactly put down of him, or for the more easy access and entrance to the hidden mysteries comprehended in that *Organon*.
120   And therefore he that liketh not this, I know not what he loveth, unless he love himself so well that he can like no Logic but his own, and so, by affectation of some vain singularity in opinion, will in any case undo that in one day wilfully which wise men have done in long time painfully. But here an end: for, if I persuade them, I have said enough; if I prevail not, I have spoken too much'.

Thus ended his melancholical° meditation the earnest Aristotelian, whose words the Ramist, perceiving most bitter than well he could digest, thought rather to put them back with little pain in the beginning than to surfeit thereby with less pleasure in the ending, and thus began:

'If you had been as diligent in meditation of the cause as you have been over-earnest in admiration of the effect, the knowledge of the one would have removed the strangeness of the
130   other.[29] For, if the wisdom of the ancient σοφοί be now degenerate in the wiliness of newfound *sophistae*, what mervail° is it, if, when the thing is not answering to the name, the name become odious? Such a world this is, and such an age we live in now, that neither the barbarous schoolmen can further deceive us nor rude dunsicalities° blind our eyes. And therefore indeed
[34ʳ]   as good be still at once, as still to prate° to no good purpose. | More cause had I to mervail° if men were now so mad as to take acorns with swine when bread is invented, to return with the dog to his vomit,[30] with dunses° to their animalities.[31] As for Aristotle: he was a father then, he is in favour now. They gave him too much in giving others nothing; we give him enough in leaving others something. And for Aquinas, I will never honour him for a saint,[32] yet I always reverence him as a philosopher, but so that by reason of the blindness of the time I think he saw
140   not everything, and, seeing it not, could never teach it. Bricot, Burley, and Bonaventure, Duns, Durand, and Dorbella are as men now take them to be.[33] Ramus doth not so rule but that he can suffer reason to overrule him. Antiquity joined with Philosophy never more loved, but sophistry linked with false antiquity never less liked. Old doting greybeards talk much of Baralipton,° whiles young-headed° boys bear away Logic. They think it much that a boy should conceive that in a week which they could scarce perceive in a year, but more that their old learning should be

---

[29] If [...] the other] If you had paid more attention to Aristotle (cause) and less to its scholastic degeneration (effect), then your speech would have been clearer.

[30] take acorns [...] bread is invented] Tilley, A₂₁; dog to his vomit] Tilley, D₄₅₈.

[31] dunses to their animalities] Fraunce listed *animalitas* as an example of the useless 'quiddities' or 'perseities' of scholastic philosophy, that is, the inherent nature of something — in this case, the quality of being an animal. See Rawlinson, fol. 16ʳ. On the use of this concept by Duns Scotus and his followers, see Cross, 'Medieval Theories of Haecceity'.

[32] Aquinas [...] saint] In accordance with the Ramist's Protestantism.

[33] Burley] Walter Burley (*c.* 1275–1344) was an Oxford philosopher who expressed his realist theories of meaning in his commentaries of the *Organon* and in *De puritate artis logicae* (*c.* 1328). Bonaventure] Giovanni di Fidanza (St Bonaventure, 1217–74) is one of the most prominent theological voices of medieval Christianity. Durand] Durandus of Saint-Pourçain (*c.* 1275–*c.* 1334), a French Dominican philosopher and theologian, wrote a commentary of Aristotle's *Categories*. Dorbella] Nicholas D'Orbellis (*c.* 1400–1472) was a French Franciscan philosopher, well-known as an expounder of the philosophy of Duns Scotus. The Ramist's mention of Dorbella and Scotus (and later Aquinas) may echo William Temple's invective against Everard Digby. See *Pro Mildapetti de unica methodo* [...] (London: Henry Middleton, 1581), B2ᵛ.

converted by new teaching, and their labour lost with so little profiting: *hinc illae lachrimae.*³⁴ A superficial show is little worth, and an outworn headpiece° is less esteemed. A mean is in the middle. A face is commended but with his grace. Seven years too much, eight days too little: a mean is had between them both. Cobblers be men — why therefore not logicians? And carters
150 have reason — why then not Logic? *Bonum quo communius, eo melius.*³⁵ The best thing in Logic you make to be worst in thinking it less commendable because it is more common. A spiteful speech, if I durst so say. A malicious meaning, if you give me leave, to lock up Logic in secret corners, never suffering her to see the height, who of herself, as she is generally good to all, so will she particularly be bound to none. The wings of wax be made by friars, the feathers fet from monkish trumperies.° Phaeton is the schoolmen's invention. But as fire of true Logic consumed the one, so the water of wisdom overwhelmed the other in this our flourishing age.

'Touching the grief you conceive for the contempt of Aristotle, I have not much to utter. Only this I say: that there be no greater enemies indeed to Aristotle than they that in word be Aristotelians, no better friends indeed than they that least profess in word. For whereas there
160 can be nothing invented and perfited° by the same man, if Aristotle did invent Logic, as he persuadeth you, then did he not perfit° it. If he did not finish it, there is some imperfection. If there be any want, why then allow you all? When Aristotle deserveth praise, who more commendeth him than Ramus?³⁶ Where he hath too much, Ramus cutteth off. Where too little, addeth. Where anything is inverted, he bringeth it to his own place. And all this according to
[34ᵛ] those three rules put down by | Aristotle: κατὰ παντός,° καθ'αὑτο,° καθόλου πρῶτον.°³⁷ To answer therefore to your general contradiction by particular confutation: it were an infinite thing, I say, to discuss every quirk. It shall suffice to touch some, and refer the further examination of the rest to the second part of Beurhusius.³⁸

'First Ramus maketh but one general art of Logic, which he divideth into his integral and
170 essential parts: invention and judgement. The Aristotelians, who untruly make a syllogism the matter subject of Logic, according to the placing of Aristotle's volumes, have made three several° arts: apodictical, topical and elenchical. But how absurdly, who seeth not? For what is sophistic Logic? Or is Logic sophistry? If not, why is it numbered as a special? Nay, why is it taught at all? For seeing that *rectum est index sui et obliqui,*³⁹ if Logic be truly taught, the false and captious fallations° may easily be discerned. For demostration: there is no such thing in nature, neither any one example among thirty, which proveth that which they pretend. Logic is general, her parts be general, neither is there one invention apodictical, another dialectical, but the same

---

³⁴ *hinc illae lachrimae*] 'hence those tears', Horace, *Epistles*, I,19.41, Loeb: p. 384.
³⁵ *Bonum quo comunius, eo melius*] 'the more common a good thing is, the better'. See Tilley, T₁₄₂.
³⁶ **who commendeth him more than Ramus?**] 'Aristoteli ipsi maximas gratias habui et egi, cum ex analyticis posterioribus logica illa velut oracula de materia artis deque forma artis deprompsissem' [It is to Aristotle himself that I am most thankful, because from the *Posterior Analytics* I discovered the matter and form of the art], Ramus, 'Scholae Dialecticae', in *Scholae in liberales artes* (Basel: Nikolaus Episcopius, 1569), IV, col. 155.
³⁷ **three rules**] On the three Aristotelian rules, or laws, see Glossary, under 'Rules of truth, righteousness and wisdom'.
³⁸ **the second part of Beurhusius**] See SL, I.2, 14n.
³⁹ *rectum est index sui et obliqui*] 'by menas of the straigh line we know both itself and the curved' ('γὰρ τῷ καὶ αὐτὸ καὶ τὸ καμπύλον γινώσκομεν'), Aristotle, *On the Soul*, I.5, 411a, Loeb VIII: pp. 460–61. The translation as such is not found in Renaissance Latin versions of the work. In his commentary of William Scott's use of the same tag, Gavin Alexander has pointed that Aquinas must be the source (*Summa theologiae*, 2.2.9.4), with *iudex* 'judge' as a more correct reading than *index*, 'sign', *The Model of Poesy*, p. 147, 30.40–1n. See, however, Roger Bacon, who wrongly attributed this dictum to Aristotle's *Of Animals* (*animalibus*) rather than to *On the Soul* (*anima*) in his treatise on optics: 'Aristoteles [...] in primo de Animalibus asserit quod rectum est *index* sui et ejus obliqui', *The 'Opus Majus' of Roger Bacon*, 2 vols, ed. by John Henry Bridges (London: Williams and Norgate, 1900), II: p. 23, emphasis added.

invention is in both. For as well might a grammarian say there is one *syntaxis* of civil speech, another of country talk. Indeed some axioms be necessary, some contingent, some false; but if
180 you therefore conclude the whole art to be either apodictical, topical, or elenchical, you may in like wise, because an axiom is affirmative or negative, say that one kind of Logic is affirmative, the other negative. If I should divide a man's body into his head, belly, and clothes, were it not a ridiculous distribution? So is this, for sophistry is nothing but, as it were, the cloak or garment covering with an outward show the inward deformity.

'But to come nearer, and to follow this confused *Organon* — confused I say, for what is error if this be not blindness? Or what is blindness, if this be not confusion? First to begin with a piece of invention in predicables° and predicaments,° then intermeddle a patch of judgement in Περί ἐρμενείας, after this to jumble both to gather in *Prioribus* and *Posterioribus analyticis*, and then to begin again with *Topics* and end with *Elenchs*?⁴⁰ But let us follow, I say, not for imitation, but
190 for confutation sake, this unorderly proceeding of theirs. There may be some use, I confess, of *voces et termini*,° for without words a disputation conceived cannot be uttered. But therefore in Logic to talk of words is no good Logic.

'But of this elsewhere. Let us come to the predicables,° where first those idle questions propounded by Porphyry, as whether genus, and species with the rest be indeed or not, have bodies or not. What Logic have they? What use in Logic? What help to Logic? *Praedicabilia*° be five. For genus and species, their proper place is in distribution, a place of invention. There are they generally taught of Ramus. For *differentia*, it is nothing but a form, and so it is put down in the first place of invention among the causes. For this word, *proprium*, there is no special use in
[35ʳ] Logic of it rather than of this word, *commune*. But of | *commune* nothing, nothing therefore of
200 *proprium*. We, marry, go throughout all the causes, and say causes be proper or common; and so through effects and the rest. But the thing comprehended under this word must be referred to the adjunct in invention.

'This word 'accident' is ambiguous, signifying, by Aristotle's own confusion, 'effects', 'adjuncts', and 'comparisons', which, being three several° and distinct things, must severally° be taught as Ramus hath done, making thereof three several° topical places: of effects, adjuncts, and comparates.⁴¹

'Thus much of predicables, which rules they be referred to invention. What use is in them, to prate° and wrangle of genus and species in schools without all sense? I omit the false definitions, imperfit° divisions, the palpable tautologies, a thousand times apparent in the whole *Organon*,
210 for it were an infinite thing to run over all. Only a word of the use of every several° book, and so an end.

'The predicaments° be next in order, but first we have certain forerunning antepredicaments,° to prepare the way for such honourable guests. And those be *æquivoca, univoca, denominativa*: rules and divisions. For *æquivoca* and his fellows, seeing they concern words, they belong to Grammar, not to Logic, which only respecteth reason.⁴² But if reason be uttered by word, then is Logic holpen by Grammar, and doth it not of herself, no more than an orator can be *ethicus*, *physicus*, or *astronomus* of himself, but by the help of Astronomy, of moral, and of natural

⁴⁰ **this confused *Organon* […] end with *Elenchs*?**] Ramus's remarks on the chaotic arrangement of the *Organon* were developed in his *Aristotelicae animadversiones*, B6ᵛ: 'Itaque, ad inventionis chaos, categoriae, septemque libri topici distrahantur: ad iudicii autem confusionem, Hermeneia, analitica'.
⁴¹ **Let us […] comparates**] Fraunce's critique abridges Beurhaus's 'Comparatio de praedicabilius', which redistributes the predicables in light of Ramist principles. See Beurhaus II, Q8ᵛ–T3ʳ.
⁴² **forerunning antepredicaments […] reason**] On Ramus's understanding of the antepredicaments as grammatical and not logical categories, see *Aristotelicae Animadversiones*, C5ʳ. See also Ong, *Ramus, Method*, p. 174. On the classification, see Glossary ('antepredicaments').

Philosophy. The rule *Quando alterum de altero, etc.*[43] is altogether superfluous, for he that knoweth what genus is may soon perceive that genus containeth his own parts, and the parts of
220 his own parts. The division which is *entium, etc.* is frivolous, for Logic is *entium et non entium.*[44]

'Now for the predicaments° themselves: in a word, it doth no more belong to Logic to settle and place those things in such order than unto any other art. For *substantia*, the Greek word οὐσία is common and general, signifying the causes of any thing, sayeth Aristotle in his *Metaphysics*. So he calleth the form the essence of the thing, and this only is the true logical acception° of this word, according to the which, not only a bodily substance but quality, quantity, with all the rest, yea *non entia*, shall have their cause of being, although they have no being in deed. The natures of heavens, earth, trees, plants, fishes, fouls, etc., belong not to Logic, but unto natural philosophy. But here will the dunses° distinguish: they belong to Logic in this respect, say they, that thereof be made axioms and syllogisms. So might they prove all arts to belong to
230 Logic, for of everyone be axioms framed. In quantity (to omit untruths, as *oratio, locus, tempus* belong to quantity, as: that *corpus* is an accident, in respect of a natural body), there is nothing logical, but only the general comparison of the like, unlike, more, less, or equal. For this
[35ᵛ] comparison is evident to everything, and therefore hath his peculiar | places in invention assigned by Ramus. *Relata* must be referred to disagreeable arguments, that is, their seat. In quality, whatsoever is logical is reduced either to the adjuncts, or like and unlike things. *Actio* is an effect. The rest be adjuncts.

'Now come in the postpredicaments° posting in haste, as though their lords the predicaments° had left somewhat unsaid that should have been declared. Whereof the four first — *adversa, relata, privantia, contradicentia* — be topical, and thereof to be taught in invention. As for those
240 trifles of *prius, simul,* and *habere*, they be rather foolish grammatical toys than logical considerations.[45]

'The book Περί ἑρμενείας in the beginnings is overcharged with grammatical controversies of nouns and verbs; the rest is consumed in an obscure, false, and intricate disputation *de futuris contingentibus*, and *de modalibus*, which being indeed no different in kind from the other, deserve no diverse doctrine.[46] For *suppositio*, the little use thereof may be perceived by that little which I have already spoken. An *aequipollentia*° reporteth words only, and for that respect° nothing logical.

'For his books called *Priora analytica*, we will take a taste of one or two, and by those judge of the rest of such inconveniences. For conversion° therefore, I would gladly see any use or example
250 thereof in probable authors. Nay, what man is so absurd as to attempt it? For the very same thing is both the conversion° and the argument of the conversion,° so that if you distinctly consider the two extremes of the question, you shall find no third thing as *medium*° to confirm them. For example, let this be the thing to be concluded:

> *No stone is a man.*

---

[43] **Quando alterum de altero, etc.**] 'When you predicate this thing or that of another thing as of a subject, the predicates then of the predicate will also hold good of the subject. We predicate "man" of *a* man; so of "man" do we predicate "animal". Therefore, of this or that man we can predicate "animal" too. For a man is both "animal" and "man"', Aristotle, *Categories*, III, 1b, Loeb I: p. 17. The Latin translation of Aristotle is by Boethius (Porphyry, *Quinque vocum*, B7ʳ). Fraunce derives his critique from Ramus, *Aristotelicae Animadversiones*, C5ᵛ, in which this sort of rule is called foolish and absurd ['rei stultae, et inutilis'].

[44] **Logic [...] non *entium*, etc.**] literally, Logic is about being and not being. See SL, II.2, 1–2 (fol. 19ᵛ).

[45] **Now come [...] considerations**] For this classification, see Glossary ('postpredicaments').

[46] **The book [...] nouns and verbs**] Aristotle's discusses nouns and verbs in *On Interpretation*, II–III, in Loeb I: pp. 116–21; **de *futuris* [...] doctrine**] The problem of affirmative or negative propositions of future contingencies being neither true nor false is discussed in *On Interpretation*, IX, in Loeb II: pp. 130–41. Fraunce affirms that, as this is a form of modality, it does not deserve separate discussion from the modals.

'The two extremes be 'stone' and 'man'. Neither is there anything else put down in this conversion.° So, instead of the proof of the question, you bring in back the question itself in this conversion:°

No man is a stone;
Therefore no stone is a man.

260 But how grossly and absurdly, we shall better perceive if of this enthymeme we make a full syllogism thus:

No man is a stone;
Every stone is a stone;
Therefore no stone is a man.

'Like this is that art of reduction° in syllogisms. For, seeing a syllogism of itself is clean and manifest, what needeth it the help of reduction° to confirm it?[47] Neither be all kinds of syllogisms contained in those his three figures,° as he supposeth.[48]

'His *Demonstrations* follow, whereof, as I said, there is no example in nature to be found. Some topical places and judicial precepts be thrown and then dispersed, which Ramus hath collected
270 and set in order. His *Topics* be almost nothing else but a mass of confusion, vain iterations,
[36ʳ] tedious repetitions, and sophistical tautologies.[49] His *Elenchs*, a perversion of Logic and | no true Logic. This for Aristotle, for if I should but only and barely name and rehearse the infinite rabble° of friars' inventions, more fit, as you say, to serve a silkwoman's shop than trouble a philosopher's library, *ante diem clauso componat Vesper Olympo*'.[50]

And thus did the Ramist cut off his discourse. I have made a simple narration and bare report. Nothing is determined. *Sub iudice lis est. Vestrum iudicium, Vestra existimatio valebit.*[51] Only pardon, I pray you, the stammering messenger, for the time was short, the place unquiet, my body crazed,° my mind molested, my books in Cambridge, my business in the country,[52] the reader famous, the writer obscure, the matter ill, seemed not worth the perusing, the thing well
280 put down, subject to sclandering.°

---

[47] **what needeth [...] confirm it**] For the Ramist critique of reduction, see *Aristotelicae animadversiones*, F6ʳ. See also SL, II.13 above.
[48] **Neither be all [...] supposeth**] A fourth figure, whose invention is attributed to Aristotle's disciple Theophrastus (c. 371–287 BC), was added to the classical three: See, Bochénski, *A History of Formal Logic*, p. 141. See also Glossary ('figure').
[49] **His *Topics* [...] tautologies**] On the confusion of Aristotle's *Topics*, see Ramus, *Aristotelicae animadversiones*, D3ʳ–D4ᵛ.
[50] ***ante diem clauso componat Vesper Olympo***] 'sooner would Vesper enclose the day in Olympus', Virgil, *Aeneid* I.374, Loeb I: pp. 266–67. These are Aeneas's words to Venus in order to spare her the long story of his sufferings.
[51] ***Sub iudice lis est***] 'the case is still before the court'; ***Vestrum iudicium, Vestra existimatio valebit***] Fraunce mixes the following lines 'Vostrum iudicium fecit; me actorem dedit' ['He made the judgement yours; he gave me the advocate's part'], and 'Arbitrium vostrum, vostra existimatio / Valebit' ['Your judgement, your opinion will suffice'], Terence, *Heautontimoroumenos* (*The Self-Tormentor*), Prologue.12, 25–26, Loeb I: pp. 118–19.
[52] **my books [...] in the country**] the first version of the essay must have been composed during a period of absence from Cambridge, perhaps at Shrewsbury in the summer of 1582. See Introduction, p. 46.

APPENDIX I

∾

Excerpts from *The Lawyers' Logic* (1588)

General Headnote

The following four excerpts offer passages from *The Lawyers' Logic* that illuminate certain aspects or expand certain passages of *The Shepherds' Logic* and its companion essays. They should be understood as additions, extensions, or revisions of Fraunce's earlier dialectical writings. I.1 prints the first paragraphs of the Preface, in which valuable information is found about the process of composition of Fraunce's logical works. This passage is also relevant in order to understand Fraunce's own conception of his scholarly and professional careers. I.2 is a revealing instance of Fraunce's methods of composition, particularly of the permanent revision of his texts. Whereas at this same point the manuscript exemplified the procedures of invention with an instance inspired by Cicero's *De lege agraria* (see SL, I.2, fols 5^v–6^r), here Fraunce replaces the former illustration with a syllogism derived from *The Shepherds' Calendar* ('July', 145–48; SC 66$_d$). I.3 is a section of the tabulation of 'Logical exercise', more specifically of its 'specials'. Fraunce defines exercise as 'that which expresseth that in particular practice which is generally put down in art. For as art followeth nature, so exercise followeth art' (Ee2^r). This table is evidence of the importance conceded by Fraunce to the practical dimension of logic, particularly in its application to writing — and by extension to poetry.

    I.4 includes Fraunce's translation of Virgil's Second Eclogue in hexameters, as well as a tabulated logical analysis of this poem. *The Lawyers' Logic* also printed the Latin text, which is not reproduced here. References to the Latin original in the footnotes follow the text of Loeb i: pp. 10–15. Fraunce's translation is an instance of his faithfulness to the cause of quantitative verse, in spite of this fashion having been abandoned by its early defenders (Sidney and Spenser, among others). Two years earlier, William Webbe had included another translation of this poem in hexameters in his *A Discourse of English Poetrie*, H4^r–I1^r. Fraunce's rules for quantitative verse are not discussed here. He devoted chapter 14 of the first book of *The Arcadian Rhetoric* to prosody, a commentary of which can be found in Victoria Pineda, 'Ramismo y retórica comparada (con unas notas sobre Boscán y Garcilaso en la *Arcadia retórica*)', *Anuario de estudios filológicos*, 20 (1997), 313–29 (pp. 321–23). On Fraunce's approach to quantitatve rules, see also Derek Attridge, *Well-Weighted Syllables: Elizabethan Poetry in Classical Metres* (Cambridge: Cambridge University Press, 1974), pp. 192–94, and 198–208. Fraunce published a revised version of this translation in *The Countesse of Pembrokes Yvychurch* (1591). Variant readings of this new version are given in the textual notes. The logical analysis can be taken as a remarkable instance of a Ramist reading of a whole poem, in stark contrast with the examination of fragments in *The Shepherds' Logic*. Fraunce claims to base his commentary on 'Freigius', i.e., Ramus's disciple Johann Thomas Freige. Although this fact has been noted by previous commentators of this table, most remarkably Sister Miriam Joseph in *Shakespeare's Use of the Arts of Language*, pp. 344–48, no specific text by Freige has been adduced as a source. I have not been able to trace such a source either. One year earlier Freige had published a full logical commentary of Virgil's *Aeneid* in tabulated form: *In XII. P. Virgilii Aeneid. libros, tabulae* (Basel, Sebastian Henricpetri, 1587). But this did not include anything on the *Eclogues*. Fraunce might have been inspired by Freige's formal procedure, although the letter of his commentary has its most direct source in Ramus's own analysis of the *Eclogues* (not in tabular form): *Bucolica, praelectionibus exposita* (Paris: André Wechel, 1555, 1st edn). Fraunce extracts the specific dialectical remarks from Ramus's more integral commentary combining logical, rhetorical and philological issues (B4^r–C1^r). Three samples of Fraunce's indebtedness to Ramus are provided here. First, 'the propounding of the argument, which is of the incontinency of a lover lamenting his love in solitary places', translates Ramus's 'Proponitur initio argumentum eclogae, incontinentia amantis, de suis amoribus in solitudine conquerentis'. Second, the three arguments of the unlike accusing Alexis of cruelty ('Alexidis crudelitas tribus dissimilibus') are also derived from Ramus. Finally, the 'remedy of love by contraries' and its later dichotomies, 'business' and 'hope of some other lover', also render literally Ramus's 'proponitur amoris remedium ex contrariis negotio & spe alterius amoris'.

The editorial policy for this Appendix is the same as for the rest of the text of this edition.

I.1: From the Preface 'To the Learned Lawyers of England, Especially the Gentlemen of Gray's Inn' (¶1ʳ–¶3ʳ)

There be almost seven years now overgone me since first I began to be a meddler with these logical meditations.[1] And whilst I have said and unsaid, done and undone, and now done all anew, methinks these seven years have quickly overgone me. I first began, when I first came in presence of that right noble and most renomed° knight Sir Philip Sidney, with a general discourse concerning the right use of Logic, and a contracted comparison between this of Ramus and that of Aristotle.[2] These small and trifling beginnings drew both him to a greater liking of, and myself to a further travailing in, the easy explication of Ramus his Logic.[3]

Six times in these seven years have I perused the whole, and by a more diligent overseeing corrected some oversights — thrice at St John's College, in Cambridge; thrice at Gray's Inn, since
10   I came to London. This last alteration hath changed the name of the book, and this new name of the book proceeded from the change of my profession. For, having resolutely determined to
[¶1ᵛ] | acquaint myself with our English laws and constitutions, I thought good to make trial whether my eight years' labour at Cambridge would anything profit me at an Inn of Court, whether Law were without Logic, or Logic not able to help a lawyer. Which, when I proved, I then perceived the practice of Law to be the use of Logic, and the method of Logic to lighten the Law. So that, after application of Logic to Law and examination of Law by Logic, I made plain the precepts of the one by the practice of the other, and called my book *The Lawyers' Logic*, not as though Logic were tied only unto Law, but for that our Law is most fit to express the precepts of Logic. Yet, because many love Logic that never learn Law, I have retained those old examples of the new
20   *Shepherds' Calendar* which I first gathered,[4] and thereunto added these also out of our Law books, which I lately collected.

I doubt not but that some well-willers° and many maliciously-disposed cavillers° will as much reprehend this strange conjunction of Law and Logic as they did mervail° at my sodain° departure from Philosophy to Law. To those that mean well, and speak according to their meaning, I wish no worse use of Logic than may be had in Law. For the rest, which make proclamations without authority, and exclamations with greater indignation than discretion, I leave them to their standish,° and pray for their good success, that after the term of seven years fully complete and ended, they may be in their blue velvet nightcaps[5] solemnly called to the bar for their extraordinary skill in making of obligations.
[¶2ʳ]   30   Tully, at the earnest request of Trebatius, a towardly° | lawyer of Rome, hath eloquently put down the first part of Logic in his *Topics*, to the precepts whereof he applieth law-like examples for the better instruction of Trebatius and help of other lawyers. Servius Sulpitius, as the same Tully reporteth, became the most excellent lawyer in all Rome, and that only by the help and direction of Logic, insomuch that he only, by these means, was said to have the art and knowledge of the Law, whereas the rest had nothing but the practice of the same, by continual beating of their brain about endless controversies.[6] He knew what was Law, and what was the reason of

───────────────

[1] **seven years [...] meditations**] 1581.
[2] **a general [...] use of Logic**] 'Of the Nature and Use of Logic'; **a contracted comparison [...] of Aristotle**] 'A Brief and General Comparison'.
[3] **the easy [...] his Logic**] *The Shepherds' Logic*.
[4] **old examples[...] gathered**] Spenser's work had been first published in 1579.
[5] **blue velvet nightcaps**] skullcaps worn by lawyers.
[6] **Tully [...] Trebatius [...] other lawyers**] See Cicero, *Topica*, I.1–5, Loeb II: pp. 382–86. Cicero explains his plan as a way of introducing the lawyer Trebatius in the intricacies of the first part of Aristotle's whole logical system. **Servius Sulpitius [...] endless controversies**] Cicero praises the excellence of his friend Servius Sulpicius Rufus (106–46 BC) as a lawyer as the result of his mastery of logic in *Brutus*, XLI.150–55, Loeb V: pp. 130–33.

Law; they, like good Catholics and modest-minded men, believed as the Church believed, but why the Church believed so it never came within the compass of their cogitation.

'But all this notwithstanding, it cannot be', said one great tenurist,° 'that a good scholar should
40   ever prove good lawyer'. 'God forbid, good sir, you offer yourself too much injury: for we countrymen take Your Worship for a great, wise, learned man, and I doubt not but that yourself are well persuaded of your wondrous knowledge in the Law, and yet you say that Law and Logic can never stand together. 'Tis great pity, God wot, that these two excellent qualities can never be reconciled. Alas, what should ail them, if it like your good Mastership?'° 'Marry', quoth he, 'these fine university men have been trained up in such easy, elegant, conceited, nice and delicate learning that they can better make new-found verses of Amyntas' death and popular discourses of ensigns, armoury, emblems, hieroglyphics and Italian impreses⁷ than apply their heads to the

[¶2ᵛ]   study of the Law, which is | hard, harsh, unpleasant, unsavoury, rude and barbarous'. 'Well said, good John-a-stile:°⁸

50   *Dii te, Damasippe, deaeque*
           Verum ob iudicium donent tonsore; sed unde
           Tam bene nos nosti?⁹

For myself, I must needs confess I was a university man eight years together, and for every day of these eight years I do not repent that I was a university man. But for that delicacy of study whereof you dream, because it seemeth somewhat strange, a word or two before we go further'. 'Surely sir, by your patience be it spoken, it seemeth you came abruptly from a country school to an Inn of Court, or else, riding post towards London, you changed horse at the University, and coming thither late in the evening, and riding away early in the morning, saw nothing but by candle-light'.¹⁰ 'It was incident to my nature (as I think) to be carried away with as delicate
60   and pleasant a kind of learning as any of my time in Cambridge. Which (notwithstanding an inestimable delectation that drowned the pains of study) did yet so rack my ranging head and bring low my crazed° body, that I felt at last when it was too late the perpetual vexation of spirit and continual consumption of body incident to every scholar'.

And, if the most easy conceits in universities be so hard, the most delicate studies so full of toil, how troublesome then and painful the foundation of arts, the framing of an English tongue to unknown languages must in any case be, I leave to be judged of them who can discern between a superficial appearance and true substance, between the bravery of a Midsummer's
[¶3ʳ]   Commencement¹¹ | and the seven years' pains of a Master of Arts' …

---

⁷ **new-found verses of Amyntas' death**] Fraunce's *The Lamentation of Amyntas for the Death of Phillis* (1587) is a translation into English hexameters of a Latin work by Thomas Watson; **popular discourses […] impreses**] Fraunce's *Insignium, Armorum, Emblematorum, Hieroglyphicorum, et Symbolorum, quae ab Italis Imprese nominantur, explicatio* (1588).
⁸ **John-a-stile**] Compare with Sir Philip Sidney: 'And doth the lawyer lie then, when under the name of 'John of the Stile' and 'John of the Nokes' he puts the case?', Alexander, ed., *Defence of Poesy*, p. 35.
⁹ ***Dii te […] nos nosti***] 'May the gods and goddeses give you, Damasippus, for your true judgement, a barber. But whence have you known us so well?', Horace, *Satires*, II.3.16–18, Loeb: *Satires, Epistles, Ars Poetica*, pp. 152–55 (Latin text slightly altered by Fraunce).
¹⁰ **by candle-light**] by continuous study at night.
¹¹ **Midsummer's Commencement**] the graduation ceremony, held in June, at the end of the academic year.

I.2: From 'Of the Parts of Logic, and the Several Kinds of Arguments' (C2ᵛ–C3ʳ)

The doctrine of invention or exposition is general, and not restrained only to the finding out of a *medium*,° which they commonly take for the only argument, but absolutely and universally appliable° to the inventing of anything, either true or fained° whatsoever.

Again, the arguments in invention must be considered severally,° singly, and alone, thenafter° to be disposed and ordered by certain precepts, thereby to judge of the truth or falseness of the same, as for example:

> Paris   *A good shepherd.*

These two, singly put down as two arguments, to wit, the subject and the adjunct, are afterwards disposed in an axiom, to judge of the truth thereof, as thus:

10   *Paris is no good shepherd.*

But, because this proposition is contingent and doubtful (for the arguments be but in part agreeable), therefore it is confirmed by another argument, that is to say, by an effect and working of Paris, I mean, that which Thomalin putteth down in 'July', in these words:

> But nothing such thilk° shepherd was
>   Whom Ida hill did bear,
> That left his flock to fetch a lass,
>   Whose love he bought too dear. (145–48; SC 66_d)

So then, here be three several arguments, or two joined in the axiom before, and the third following in these verses of Thomalin; which third they call *medium*,° or third argument, thus:

[C3ʳ]   20   1. *Paris.*
2. *A good shepherd.*
3. *To leave his flock to fetch a lass.*

Whereof it is concluded in this wise syllogistically, by disjoining the two first arguments, the subject and adjunct, 'Paris' and 'the good shepherd':

> *He that leaveth his flock to fetch a lass is no good shepherd;*
> *But Paris did leave his flock to fetch a lass;*
> *Therefore Paris is no good shepherd.*

That which they call *medium*,° and third argument, is as it were an *arbiter honorarius*,° a determiner, a reconciler, a daysman.° Which, if it agree with both the other arguments, maketh
30 the conclusion affirmative; but negative, if with one only, as in the former example of Paris, the *medium*,° the arbiter, the determiner, is that effect of 'Paris': 'To leave his flock to fetch a lass'. Which, because it is agreeable with the nature of 'Paris', but is flatly repugnant° to the duty of a good shepherd, therefore is the conclusion negative: 'Paris is no good shepherd'.

I.3: Exercise Dichotomized: from 'Of a Syllogism and His Parts' (Ee4ʳ)

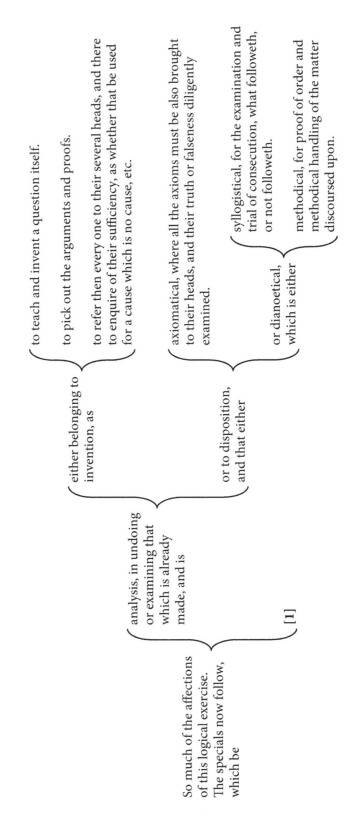

So much of the affections of this logical exercise. The specials now follow, which be [1] analysis, in undoing or examining that which is already made, and is either belonging to invention, as

to teach and invent a question itself.

to pick out the arguments and proofs.

to refer then every one to their several heads, and there to enquire of their sufficiency, as whether that be used for a cause which is no cause, etc.

or to disposition, and that either axiomatical, where all the axioms must be also brought to their heads, and their truth or falseness diligently examined.

or dianoetical, which is either syllogistical, for the examination and trial of consecution, what followeth, or not followeth.

methodical, for proof of order and methodical handling of the matter discoursed upon.

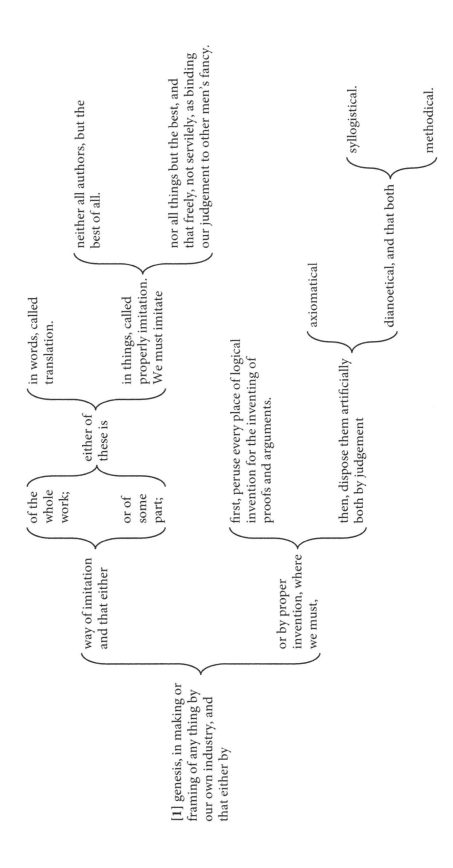

[1] genesis, in making or framing of any thing by our own industry, and that either by

way of imitation and that either

of the whole work;

or of some part;

either of these is

in words, called translation.

in things, called properly imitation. We must imitate

neither all authors, but the best of all.

nor all things but the best, and that freely, not servilely, as binding our judgement to other men's fancy.

or by proper invention, where we must,

first, peruse every place of logical invention for the inventing of proofs and arguments.

then, dispose them artificially both by judgement

axiomatical

dianoetical, and that both

syllogistical.

methodical.

I.4: Translation and Logical Analysis of Virgil's Second Eclogue (Kk2ᵛ–Ll1ʳ)

The same in English Hexameters, verse for verse.

Seely° shepherd Corydon loved heartily fair lad Alexis,
His master's dearling,° but saw no matter of hoping.
Only amid the forest thick set with broad-shadow beech-trees
Daily resort did he make — thus alone to the woods, to the mountains
With broken speeches, fond thoughts most vainly revealing:
   'O hard-hearted Alexis, I see my verse to be scorned,
Myself not pitied, my death by thee lastly procured.
Now do the beasts ev'n seek for cooling shade to refresh them,
Green lizards now too in bushes thorny be lurking,
10 And for faint reapers by the sun's rage, Thestylis, hast'ning,
Strong-smelling wild thyme and garlic beats in a mortar.
But, whilst I trace thee, with sunbeams all too bescorched,[1]
Groves by the hoarse-chirping grasshoppers yield a resounding.
   'Was't not far better t' have borne with surly Menalcas,
And sore displeased, disdainful, proud Amaryllis,
Although thou white were, although but swarty° Menalcas?
O thou fair white boy, trust not too much to thy whiteness:
Fair white flowers fall down, black fruits are only reserved.[2]
   'Thou car'st not for me, my state thou know'st not, Alexis:
20 What flocks of white sheep I do keep, of milk what abundance;
On Sicil high mountains my lambs feed more than a thousand;
New milk in summer, new milk in winter I want not.

[Kk3ʳ] My song's like Theban Amphion's song, when he called
His wand'ring bullocks on Greekish mount Aracynthus.[3]
Neither am I so foul: I saw myself by the seashore,
When seas all calm were; I doubt not, but[4] by thy censure,
Daphnis[5] I shall surpass, unless my face do deceive me.
   'O, let this be thy will, to frequent my rustical harbours,
And simple cottages, and stick in forks to uphold them,[6]
30 And drive on forward our flock of kids to the mallows:[7]
We will amid the forest contend Pan's song to resemble —
Pan was first that quills with wax tied jointly together.[8]

---

[1] **all too bescorched**] This phrase qualifies 'I' (Corydon), although Virgil's 'sole sub ardenti' suggests that it is the 'groves' ['arbusta'] that are burnt by the sun.
[2] **Fair white flowers fall down, black fruits are only reserved**] Lat. 'Alba ligustra cadunt, vaccinia nigra leguntur', literally 'white privet flowers fall down, blackberries are collected'.
[3] **Theban Amphion's song**] Lat. 'Amphion Dircaeus', from Dirce, a spring near Thebes. Amphion, the builder of the Theban walls, was taught to play the harp by Hermes. **Aracynthus**] Mount Aracynthus in Boeotia, near Thebes (a location much debated by scholars).
[4] **but**] unless.
[5] **Daphnis**] the Sicilian shepherd, son of Hermes, who invented pastoral poetry. He was loved by Pan, who taught him to play the pipe.
[6] **and stick in forks to uphold them**] Fraunce's translation of 'figere cervos' (to fix a forked stake). Alternatively, modern translators prefer 'to shoot at deer'.
[7] **mallows**] Lat. *hibiscus*, a purgative for cattle.
[8] **Pan […] together**] Pan is credited with the invention of the pipe or cross-flute by Bion, V.7, Loeb: *Greek Bucolic Poets*, pp. 406–07.

Pan is good to the sheep, and Pan is good to the sheepsman.
Neither think it a shame to thyself t' have played on a corn-pipe:
For, that he might do the same with skill, what did not Amyntas?
Damoetas long since did give me a pipe for a token,
Compact of se'en reeds, all placed in order, unequal,
And thus said, when he died: 'One used it only before thee'.
Thus said Damoetas; this grieved foolish Amyntas.

40 Also two pretty kids do I keep, late found in a valley
Dangerous, and their skins with milk-white spots be bedecked;
Of dam's milk not a drop they leave; and for thee I keep them.
Thestylis of long time hath these kids of me desired;
And they shall be her own, for that thou scorn'st what I give thee.
Come near, o fair boy, see the nymphs bring here to thee lilies
With full-stuffed baskets: fair Nais[9] now, to thy comfort
White violets gathering, and poppies daintily topping,
Daffodil adds to the same, and leaves late plucked fro the sweet dill.°
Then, mingling cassia° with diverse savoury sweet flowers,

50 With yellowish marigold, she the tender crow-toe° bedecketh.°
      'I'll pluck hoar° quinces, with soft down° all too besmeared,°
And chestnuts which were loved of my sweet Amaryllis.
Add will I wheat-plums° too — for this fruit will be regarded.
And you laurel leaves will I pluck, and thee, pretty myrtle
Next to the laurel leaves: for so placed yield ye the sweet scent.
      'Th' art but a fool, Corydon, for, first, gifts move not Alexis;
Then, though thou give much, yet much more give will Iollas.
But what alas did I mean, poor fool? I do let go the south wind
Into the flow'rs, and boars send forward into the clear springs.

[Kk3ᵛ] 60 Whom fliest thou, mad man? Many gods have also resorted,
And Paris of old Troy, to the woods.[10] Let towers by Minerva
Built, by Minerva be kept; and woods of us only regarded.
Grim lioness runneth to the wolf, and wolf to the young goat,
And wanton young goat to the flow'ring tetrifoil° hast'neth,
And Corydon to Alexis: a self-joy draweth on each man.°
But see, the plough comes home hanged fast by the yoke, to the bullocks,
And shadow, by Phoebus declining, double appeareth.
Yet do I burn with love: for what mean° can be to loving?
Ah Corydon, Corydon! What mad rage hath thee bewitched?

70 Thy vine's scarce half cut, pestered with leaves of her elm-tree.
Leave this churlish boy, and bend thyself to thy business.
With twigs and bulrush some needful thing be a-making:
Thou shalt find others, though th' art disdain'd of Alexis'.[11]

---

⁹ **Nais**] the Naiad, or river-nymph.
¹⁰ **and Paris of old Troy, to the woods**] Paris, the youngest son of Priamus, was foretold to be the cause of the
fall of Troy. He was sent out of the city and became a shepherd in Mount Ida.
¹¹ **Thou shalt find others, though th' art disdain'd of Alexis**] 'Invenies alium, si te hic fastidit Alexis'. Recent
editors prefer the variant 'Alexim' and thus interpret 'you shall find another Alexis, if this one disdains you'.

[Kk4ʳ]

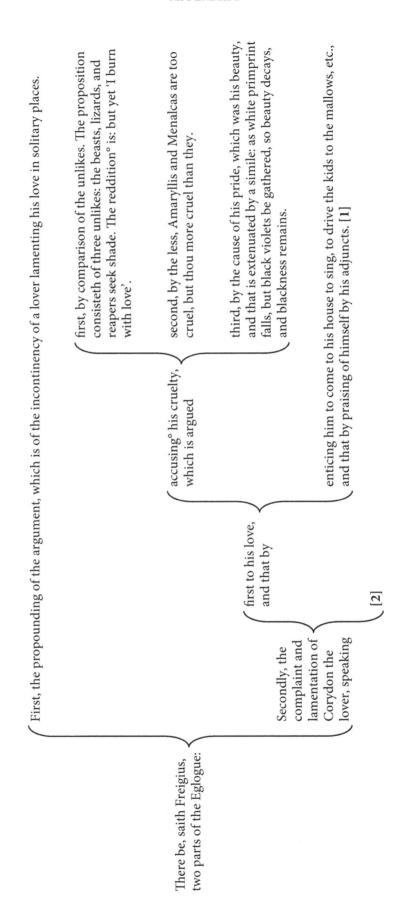

There be, saith Freigius, two parts of the Eglogue:

First, the propounding of the argument, which is of the incontinency of a lover lamenting his love in solitary places.

Secondly, the complaint and lamentation of Corydon the lover, speaking [2]

first to his love, and that by

accusing° his cruelty, which is argued

first, by comparison of the unlikes. The proposition consisteth of three unlikes: the beasts, lizards, and reapers seek shade. The reddition° is: but yet 'I burn with love'.

second, by the less, Amaryllis and Menalcas are too cruel, but thou more cruel than they.

third, by the cause of his pride, which was his beauty, and that is extenuated by a simile: as white primprint falls, but black violets be gathered, so beauty decays, and blackness remains.

enticing him to come to his house to sing, to drive the kids to the mallows, etc., and that by praising of himself by his adjuncts. [1]

[Kk4ᵛ]

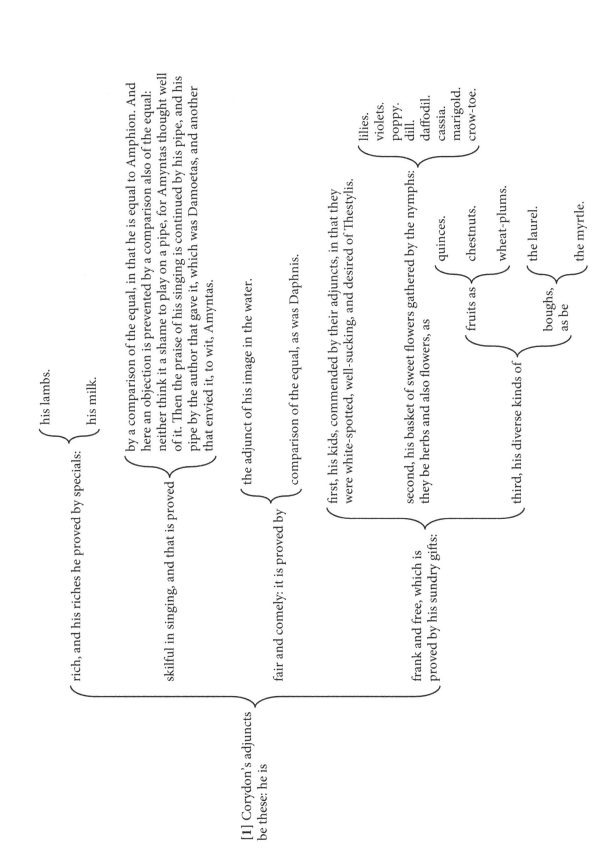

[1] Corydon's adjuncts be these: he is

- rich, and his riches he proved by specials:
  - his lambs.
  - his milk.
- skilful in singing, and that is proved by a comparison of the equal, in that he is equal to Amphion. And here an objection is prevented by a comparison also of the equal: neither think it a shame to play on a pipe, for Amyntas thought well of it. Then the praise of his singing is continued by his pipe, and his pipe by the author that gave it, which was Damoetas, and another that envied it, to wit, Amyntas.
- fair and comely: it is proved by
  - the adjunct of his image in the water.
  - comparison of the equal, as was Daphnis.
- frank and free, which is proved by his sundry gifts:
  - first, his kids, commended by their adjuncts, in that they were white-spotted, well-sucking, and desired of Thestylis.
  - second, his basket of sweet flowers gathered by the nymphs: they be herbs and also flowers, as
    - lilies.
    - violets.
    - poppy.
    - dill.
    - daffodil.
    - cassia.
    - marigold.
    - crow-toe.
  - third, his diverse kinds of
    - fruits as
      - quinces.
      - chestnuts.
      - wheat-plums.
    - boughs, as be
      - the laurel.
      - the myrtle.

[Ll1ʳ]

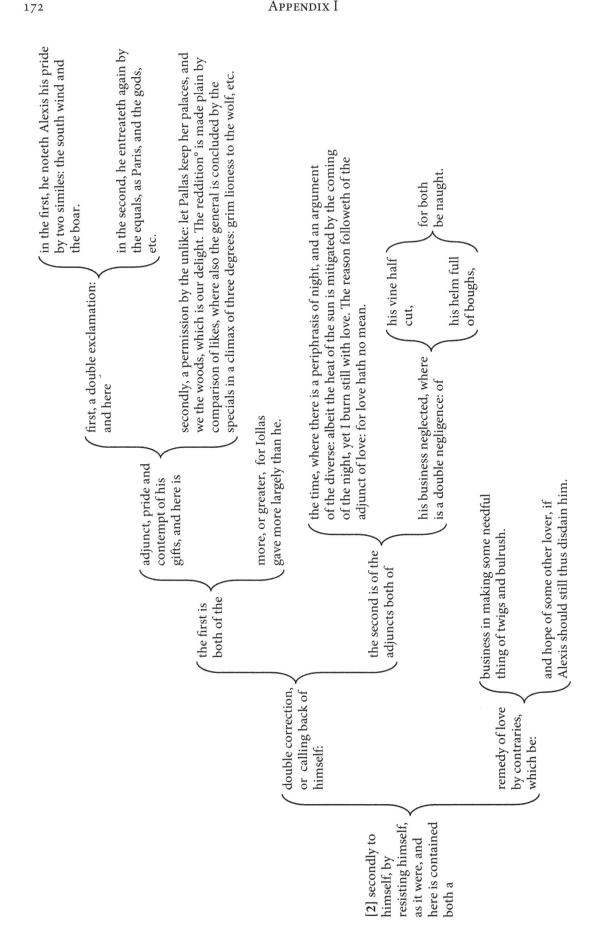

[2] secondly to himself, by resisting himself, as it were, and here is contained both a

- double correction, or calling back of himself:
  - the first is both of the
    - adjunct, pride and contempt of his gifts, and here is
      - first, a double exclamation: and here
        - in the first, he noteth Alexis his pride by two similes: the south wind and the boar.
        - in the second, he entreateth again by the equals, as Paris, and the gods, etc.
      - secondly, a permission by the unlike: let Pallas keep her palaces, and we the woods, which is our delight. The reddition° is made plain by comparison of likes, where also the general is concluded by the specials in a climax of three degrees: grim lioness to the wolf, etc.
    - more, or greater, for Iollas gave more largely than he.
  - the second is of the adjuncts both of
    - the time, where there is a periphrasis of night, and an argument of the diverse: albeit the heat of the sun is mitigated by the coming of the night, yet I burn still with love. The reason followeth of the adjunct of love: for love hath no mean.
    - his business neglected, where is a double negligence: of
      - his vine half cut,
      - his helm full of boughs,
      - for both be naught.
- remedy of love by contraries, which be:
  - business in making some needful thing of twigs and bulrush.
  - and hope of some other lover, if Alexis should still thus disdain him.

APPENDIX II

The Shepherds' Calendar in Fraunce's Logical Writings

'To His Book'

Number	SC lines	SL Location (Ms)	LL Location	Topic
1	13–15	I.7 (12^r)	—	argument: agreeable; adjunct

'January'

Number	SC lines	SL Location (Ms)	LL Location	Topic
2$_a$	7–8	I.7 (12^v)	I.8, M2^r	argument: agreeable; adjunct
2$_b$	7–9	I.7 (12^r)	I.8, M1^v	argument: agreeable; adjunct
3	13–16	II.14 (25^r)	—	syllogism: compound; connexive
4	17–18	II.13 (24^v)	II.13, Ff4^v	syllogism: simple; fully expressed; second kind
5	19–30	I.17 (15^v–16^r)	—	argument: compared in quality; the like; distinct or severed similitude (four terms)
6$_a$	31–42	I.17 (16^r)	I.20, T4^v	argument: compared in quality; the like; distinct or severed similitude (four terms)
6$_b$	41–42	II.5 (21^v)	II.5, Cc2^r	axiom: compound; congregative (comparisons)
7$_a$	49–54	I.3 (8^r)	I.3, D4^r	argument: cause; efficient
7$_b$	54	II.4 (20^v)	II.2, Aa3^v	axiom: affirmative
7$_c$	54	II.17 (26^r)	—	syllogism: compound; disjunctive; second kind
8	55–60	*I.8, 1n*	I.9, N2^r	argument: disagreeable; diverse
9	67–72	II.13 (24^v)	II.13, Gg1^r	syllogism: simple; fully expressed; second kind

'February'

Number	SC lines	SL Location (Ms)	LL Location	Topic
10	3–6	I.17 (15^v)	I.20, T4^v	argument: compared in quality; the like; continued similitude
11$_a$	17–18	I.7 (12^r)	I.8, M1^v	argument: agreeable; adjunct
11$_b$	17–20	I.21 (17^v)	—	argument: made of the first; distribution of the effect (specials)
12	29–30	I.17 (15^v)	—	argument: compared in quality; the like; continued similitude
13	41–44	I.6 (11^r)	I.7, L2^r	argument: agreeable; subject
14	65–66	I.4 (9^v)	I.4, G3^r	argument: cause; formal
15$_a$	69–70	II.3 (20^r)	—	axiom: contingent
15$_b$	70	II.4 (21^r)	II.4, Bb3^v–Bb4^r	axiom: simple; general
16	71–76	I.4 (9^v)	I.4, G3^r	argument: cause; formal (accidental and external)
17	87–90	I.14 (15^r)	I.20, T4^v	argument: compared in quantity; equal
18	102–14	I.25 (18^v–19^r)	I.18, R3^r	argument: made of the first; description
19	143–46	I.3 (8^r)	I.4, G3$^{r–v}$	argument: cause; final
20	163–68	I.3 (8^r)	—	argument: cause; final and efficient
21	169–86	I.5 (9^v–10^r)	I.5, I1$^{r–v}$	argument: effect (dispraise)

'March'

Number	SC lines	SL Location (Ms)	LL Location	Topic
22	10–12	I.7 (12^r)	I.8, M1^v	argument: agreeable; adjunct
23	25–27	I.5 (11^r)	—	argument: effect
24	61–102	I.5 (10^v–11^r)	I.5, I2$^{r–v}$	argument: effect
25	115–17	II.14 (25r)	II.14, Gg3^v	syllogism: compound; connexive

'April'

Number	SC lines	SL Location (Ms)	LL Location	Topic
26	9–11	I.8 (13^r)	—	argument: disagreeable; diverse
27	37–45	I.6 (11^r)	I.7, L2^r	argument: agreeable; subject (place)
28	50–54	I.10 (13^v)	—	argument: disagreeable; opposite; contrary (relative)
29$_a$	55–63	I.6 (11$^{r–v}$)	I.7, L2^v	argument: agreeable; subject
29$_b$	55–63	I.7 (12^r)	—	argument: agreeable; adjunct (colours)
30	64–72	I.22 (18^r)	I.16, Q3^r	argument: made of the first; distribution (adjunct into its subjects)
31$_a$	91–94	I.3 (8^r)	I.3, D4^r	argument: cause; efficient (procreant)

(Cont.)

'April'

Number	SC lines	SL Location (Ms)	LL Location	Topic
31$_b$	91–94	II.13(24^v)	II.13, Gg1^{r-v}	syllogism: simple; fully expressed; second kind or first figure; proper negative
32$_a$	136–44	I.9 (13^v)	I.10, N3^r	argument: disagreeable; opposite (disparate)
32$_b$	136–44	I.7 (12^r)	—	argument: agreeable; adjunct (colours)
32$_c$	136–44	I.21 (17^v)	—	argument: made of the first; distribution of the effect (general into specials)
32$_d$	136–44	II.18 (26^v)	II.17, Ii3^{r-v}	method (poetic)

'May'

Number	SC lines	SL Location (Ms)	LL Location	Topic
33$_a$	1–4, 9–10, 16	I.18 (16^r)	—	argument: compared in quality; the unlike
33$_b$	9–14	I.5 (10^r)	I.5, I1^v	argument: effect
34$_a$	17–18	I.7 (12^r)	—	argument: agreeable; adjunct (proper and common)
34$_b$	17–18	II.15 (25^v)	—	syllogism: compound; connexive; second kind
35$_a$	39–44	I.5 (10^r)	I.5, I1^v	argument: effect
35$_b$	43–44	I.24 (18^v)	I.17, Q4^v	argument: made of the first; definition
35$_c$	43–44	II.12 (23^v–24^r)	II.12, Ff2^v–Ff3^r	syllogism: simple; fully expressed; first general
36$_a$	45–50	I.24 (18^v)	I.17, Q4^v	argument: made of the first; definition
36$_b$	45–50	II.12 (23^v)	II.12, Ff2^v	syllogism: simple; fully expressed; second general
37	51–54	I.23 (18^r)	—	argument: made of the first; distribution (of adjuncts)
38	57–58	I.15 (15^r)	—	argument: compared in quantity; unequal; the more
39	71–72	I.3 (7^v)	I.4, G3^r	argument: cause; final
40	95–102	I.17 (16^r)	I.20, T4^{r-v}	argument: compared in quality; the like
41$_a$	117–23	I.3 (8r)	I.3, D4r	argument: cause; efficient (conservant)
41$_b$	121	II.4 (21^r)	II.4, Bb3^v	axiom: special; particular
42	164–67	I.11 (14^r)	I.11, N4^r	argument: disagreeable; opposite; contrary (repugnant)
43	168–69	I.13 (14^v)	I.11, N4^v	argument: disagreeable; opposite; contrary (privative)
44	182–88	I.25 (19^r)	I.18, R3^r	argument: made of the first; description
45	195–97	II.6 (22^r)	II.6, Cc3^r	axiom: connexive
46	215–26	II.14 (25^r)	II.14, Gg3^{r-v}	syllogism: compound; connexive; first kind
47	227–28	I.10 (13^v)	I.11, N4^r	argument: disagreeable; opposite; contrary
48	235–48	I.25 (19^r)	I.18, R3^{r-v}	argument: made of the first; description (by adjuncts and effects)
49$_a$	268–69	I.26 (19^r)	I.18, S1^r	argument: inartificial; testimony
49$_b$	268–69	*II.14, 2n*	II.14, Gg2^r	syllogism: compound; connexive; first kind

'June'

Number	SC lines	SL Location (Ms)	LL Location	Topic
50	1–8	I.3 (8ʳ)	I.3, D3ᵛ	argument: cause; efficient
51	9–16	I.18	I.21, U3ʳ	argument: compared in quality; the unlike
52	17–18	II.6 (21ᵛ)	II.6, Cc3ʳ	axiom: connexive
53	49–51	I.15 (15ʳ)	—	argument: compared in quantity; unequal; the more
54	93–112	II.14, 5n	II.14, Gg3ᵛ–Gg4ᵛ	syllogism: compound; connexive; first kind (spurious)
55	115–16	I.2 (7ᵛ)	I.2, D2ʳ	argument: cause

'July'

Number	SC lines	SL Location (Ms)	LL Location	Topic
56	5–8	I.21 (17ᵛ)	—	argument: made of the first; distribution of the effects (general into special)
57ₐ	9–12	I.21 (17ᵛ)	—	argument: made of the first; distribution of the effects (general into special)
57ᵦ	9–12	I.26	I.18, S1ʳ⁻ᵛ	argument: inartificial; testimony
58	17–24	I.3 (8ʳ)	I.3, D4ʳ	argument: cause; efficient
59ₐ	53–56	I.5 (10ʳ)	I.5, I1ᵛ	argument: effect
59ᵦ	53–56	II.3 (20ᵛ)	—	axioms: rule of wisdom
59꜀	53–56	II.13 (25ʳ)	—	syllogism: simple; fully expressed; second kind; proper negative
60	57–60	I.26 (19ʳ)	I.18, S1ʳ⁻ᵛ	argument: inartificial; testimony
61	93–96	I.8 (13ʳ)	—	argument: disagreeable; diverse
62ₐ	97	I.14 (15ʳ)	—	argument: compared in quantity; equal
62ᵦ	97–100	I.26 (20ʳ)	I.18, S1ᵛ	argument: inartificial; testimony
63ₐ	101–04	I.14 (14ᵛ)	I.22, U3ᵛ	argument: compared in quantity; equal
63ᵦ	101–04	I.23 (18ʳ)	—	argument: made of the first; distribution (of the adjunct)
64	113–16	I.7 (12ᵛ)	I.8, M2ʳ	argument; agreeable; adjuncts
65	129–32	I.7 (12ʳ)	I.8, M1ᵛ	argument; agreeable; adjuncts
66ₐ	145–48	I.18 (1ʳ⁻ᵛ)	I.21, U2ᵛ–U3ʳ	argument: compared in quality; the unlike
66ᵦ	145–48	II.12 (23ᵛ–24ʳ)	II.12, Ff2ᵛ–Ff3ʳ	syllogism: simple; fully expressed; first kind; first special
66꜀	145–60	II.12 (24ʳ)	—	syllogism: simple, fully expressed, first kind; second special
66ₔ	145–48	Appendix 2	I.2, C2ᵛ	invention
67	153–56	II.5 (21ᵛ)	II.5, Cc2ʳ	axiom; compound; congregative (copulative)
68ₐ	169–77	I.7 (12ʳ)	I.8, M1ᵛ	argument: agreeable; adjuncts
68ᵦ	173	II.4 (20ᵛ)	II.4, Bb3ʳ	axiom: simple
69ₐ	215–28	II.12 (23ᵛ)	—	syllogism: simple; fully expressed; first kind; second special
69ᵦ	215–28	II.12 (24ʳ)	—	syllogism: simple; fully expressed; first kind; first proper
70	229–30	II.11	II.11, N4ʳ	syllogism; simple; contracted

'August'

Number	SC lines	SL Location (Ms)	LL Location	Topic
71	5–6	*I.11*	I.11, N4^r	argument: compared in quantity; equal
72$_a$	25–26	I.4 (9^r)	I.3, E3^v	argument: cause; material
72$_b$	25–36	I.4 (9^v)	I.4, G3^r	argument: cause; formal (artificial form)
73	25–42	*I.26*	I.18, S1^v	argument: inartificial; testimony (the fool's argument)
74$_a$	61–72	I.7 (12^v)	I.8, M1^v–M2^r	argument: agreeable, adjunct
74$_b$	69–72	*I.16*	I.24, X4^r	argument: compared in quantity; unequal; the less
75	73–76	I.14 (15^r)	—	argument: compared
76$_a$	77–93	I.17 (15^v)	—	argument: compared in quantity; equal
76$_b$	80	I.14 (15^r)	—	argument: compared
77	137–38	I.14 (15^r)	I.22, U3^v–U4^r	argument: compared

'September'

Number	SC lines	SL Location (Ms)	LL Location	Topic
78$_a$	1–2	II.8 (22^r)	II.7, Cc4^v	axiom; compound; segregative; disjunctive
78$_b$	1–2	II.16 (26^r)	II.16, Hh1$^{r–v}$	syllogism: compound; disjunctive; first kind
78$_c$	1–2	II.17 (26^r)	—	syllogism: compound; disjunctive; second kind
79	3–4	I.12 (14^r)	—	argument: disagreeable; opposite; contrary (contradictory)
80	44–46	I.17 (15^v)	I.20, T4^r	argument: compared in quality; the like
81	58–61	I.17 (15^v)	I.20, T4^r	argument: compared in quality; the like
82	68–71	II.3 (20r)	—	axiom: true/false
83	80–85	I.23 (18^r)	I.16, Q3$^{r–v}$	argument: made of the first; distribution (of the adjuncts)
84	90–93	*I.26*	I.19, S2^r	argument: inartificial; testimony
85	106–07	I.2 (7^v)	I.2, D2^r	argument: cause/effect
86	120–21	I.17 (15^v)	I.20, T4^r	argument: compared in quality; the like
87	128–29	*I.15*	I.22, X1^v	argument: compared in quantity; unequal; the more
88	130–33	I.17 (15^v)	—	argument: compared in quality; the like
89	134–35	*I.15*	I.22, X1^v	argument: compared in quantity; unequal; the more
90	150–53	I.20 (17^r)	I.14, P2^r	argument: made of the first; distribution (of the adjuncts)
91	164	II.4 (21^r)	II.4, Bb4^r	axiom: simple; special; proper
92	232–35	I.24 (18^v)	—	argument: made of the first; definition
93	236–41	II.13 (24$^{r–v}$)	II.13, Ff4^v	syllogism: simple; fully expressed; second kind; general negative

'October'

Number	SC lines	SL Location (Ms)	LL Location	Topic
94	91–96	I.5 (10^r)	I.5, I1^v	argument: agreeable; effect

'November'

Number	SC lines	SL Location (Ms)	LL Location	Topic
95	53	I.6 (11^v)	—	argument: agreeable; subject
96$_a$	58	II.2 (19^v)	II.2, Aa2^v	axiom
96$_b$	58–62	I.12 (14^r)	—	argument: disagreeable; opposite; contrary (negative)
97	93–94	I.16 (15^r)	I.24, X4^r	argument: compared in quantity; unequal; the less
98	115, 116, 128	I.7 (12^v)	I.8, M2^r	argument: agreeable; adjuncts (proper)
99$_a$	167–72	I.12 (14^r)	—	argument: disagreeable; opposite; contrary (contradictory)
99$_b$	169	II.2 (19^v)	II.2, Aa2^v	axiom
99$_c$	169	II.4 (20^v)	II.4, Bb3^r	axiom: simple; negative
100	178–79	I.6 (11^v)	—	argument: agreeable; subject
101	183–192	II.13 (24^r)	II.13, Ff4$^{r–v}$	syllogism: simple; fully expressed; second kind; general affirmative
102	193–96	I.6 (11^v)	—	argument: agreeable; subject

'December'

Number	SC lines	SL Location (Ms)	LL Location	Topic
103$_a$	19–36	I.5 (10$^{r–v}$)	I.5, I2^r	argument: agreeable; effect
103$_b$	19–20	II.6 (22^r)	II.6, Cc3^v	axiom: connexive
104	53–54	I.11 (14^r)	I.11, N4^r	argument: disagreeable; opposite; contrary (repugnant)
105	67–70	I.4 (9^r)	I.3, E3^v–E4^r	argument: cause; material
106	77–78	I.4 (9^r)	I.3, E4^r	argument: cause; material
107	79–80	I.4. (9^v)	I.3, E4^r	argument: cause; material
108	91–94	II.7 (22^r)	II.8, Dd1^v	axiom; compound; segregative; discretive
109	137–38	I.13 (14^v)	—	argument: disagreeable; opposite; contrary (privative)

~

A Comparative Table of Contents of Ramus's *Dialecticae libri duo* (Ramus/Piscator), *The Shepherds' Logic*, and *The Lawyers' Logic*

Dialecticae libri duo (1581)	*The Shepherds' Logic* (c. 1585)	*The Lawyers' Logic* (1588)
Liber Primus: De Inventione	**Book I: Of Invention**	**Book I: Of Invention**
1. Quid Dialectica	1. What Logic Is	1. What Logic Is
2. De partibus Dialecticae, deque argumenti generibus	2. Of the Parts of Logic and Diverse Kinds of Arguments	2. Of the Parts of Logic, and the Several Kinds of Arguments
3. De efficiente, procreante & conservante	3. Of the Final and the Efficient Cause	3. Of the Efficient and the Material Cause
4. De efficiente sola, et cum aliis		
5. De efficiente per se, et per accidens		
6. De materia	4. Of the Matter and the Form	
7. De forma		4. Of the Formal and the Final Cause
8. De fine		
9. De effectis	5 Of the Thing Caused	5. Of the Thing Caused
		6. Of the Whole, Part, General and Special
10. De subiecto	6. Of the Subject	7. Of the Subject
11. De adiuncto	7. Of the Adjunct	8. Of the Adjunct
12. De diversis	8. Of Diverse Arguments	9. Of the Diverse or Different
13. De disparatis	9. Of the Opposite	10. Of Opposites
14. De relatis	10. Of Contraries	11. Of Contraries
15. De adversis	11. Of Repugning Arguments	
16. De contradicentibus	12. Of Contradictories	
17. De privantibus	13. Of Privatives	
	14. Of Comparison	20. Of Compared Arguments
18. De paribus		22. Of the Equal
19. De maioribus	15. Of the More	23. Of the Greater

(Cont.)

Dialecticae libri duo (1581)	*The Shepherds' Logic* (c. 1585)	*The Lawyers' Logic* (1588)
Liber Primus: De Inventione	**Book I: Of Invention**	**Book I: Of Invention**
20. De minoribus	16. Of the Less	24. Of the Less [with a Practical Appendix on Analysis and Genesis]
21. De similibus	17. Of the Like	
22. De dissimilibus	18. Of the Unlike	21. Of the Unlike
23. De coniugatis	—	
24. De notatione	—	
		12. Of Secondary Arguments
25. De distributione	19. Of Distribution	13. Of Distribution
26. De distributione ex caussis	20. Of the Distribution Made of Causes	14. Of Distribution of Causes
27. De distributione ex effectis, ubi de genere et specie	21. Of the Distribution of the Effect	15. Of Distribution of Effects
28. De distributione ex subiectis	22. Of the Distribution Made of the Subject	16. Of Distribution of Arguments After a Certain Manner Agreeable
29. De distributione ex adiunctis	23. Of the Distribution Made of the Adjuncts	
30. De definitione	24. Of a Definition	17. Of a Definition
31. De descriptione	25. Of a Description	18. Of a Description
32. De testimonio divino	26. Of Inartificial Arguments	19. Of the Argument Borrowed
33. De testimonio humano legis et sententiae		

Dialecticae libri duo (1581)	*The Shepherds' Logic* (c. 1585)	*The Lawyers' Logic* (1588)
Liber Secundus: De Iudicio	**Book II: Of Judgement**	**Book II: Of Disposition**
1. Quid Iudicium	1. [What Judgement Is]	1. [Of Disposition]
2. De axiomatis affirmatione ac negatione	2. Of an Axiom Affirmative or Negative	2. Of Axioms Affirmative and Negative
3. De vero et falso	3. Of a True and False Axiom	3. Of a True and False Axiom
4. De axiomate simplici	4. Of a Simple Axiom	4. Of a Simple Axiom
5. De axiomate copulato	5. Of the Congregative Axioms	5. Of a Congregative Axiom
6. De axiomate connexo	6. Of a Connexive Axiom	6. Of a Connexive Axiom
7. De axiomate discreto	7. Of the Segregative Axiom	8. Of the Discretive Axiom
8. De axiomate disiuncto	8. Of the Disjunctive Axiom	7. Of the Disjunctive Axiom
9. De syllogismo et eius partibus	9. Of a Syllogism and His Parts	9. Of the Syllogism and His Parts
10. De syllogismo simplici contracto	10. Of a Simple Syllogism	10. Of a Simple Syllogism
	11. Of the Contracted Syllogism	11. Of the Contracted Syllogism
11. De prima specie syllogismi simplicis explicati	12. Of the Explicate Syllogism	12. The Explicate Syllogism

(Cont.)

Dialecticae libri duo (1581)	*The Shepherds' Logic* (c. 1585)	*The Lawyers' Logic* (1588)
Liber Secundus: De Iudicio	**Book II: Of Judgement**	**Book II: Of Disposition**
12. De secunda specie syllogismi simplicis explicati	13. Of the Second Kind of Syllogisms Fully Expressed	13. Of the Second Kind
13. De syllogismo connexo primo	14. Of the First Kind of a Connexive Syllogism	14. Of the First Kind of a Connexive Syllogism
14. De syllogismo connexo secundo	15. Of the Second Kind of Connexive Syllogism	15. Of the Second Kind of a Connexive Syllogism
15. De syllogismo disiuncto primo	16. Of a Disjunctive Syllogism	16. Of a Disjunctive Syllogism
16. De syllogismo disiuncto secundo	17. Of the Second Disjunctive Syllogism	
17. De methodo secundum Aristotelem unica	18. Of Method	17. Of Method
18. De prima methodi illustratione per exempla artium		
19. De secunda methodi illustratione per exempla poetarum, oratorum, historicorum		
20. De crypticis methodi		
	[19. Of the Elenchs]	
		A General Table of the Whole Book; Conclusions; A Logical Analysis of 1) Virgil's Second Eclogue, 2) The Earl of Northumberland's Case in Plowden's Reports, and 3) William Stanford's Crown Pleas.

Square brackets represent added chapters and/or titles in this edition or in this catalogue.

TEXTUAL NOTES

Dedicatory Verse

12:     countryman] countrey man Ms.
14:     aught] ought Ms.
14:     naught] nought Ms.

I.1

9:      consisteth] consystethe McCormick; consytethe Ms.
14:     of some monkish brains] of some monkishe braynes McCormick; of some of monkyshe braynes Ms.
40:     off] McCormick; of Ms.
44:     countrymen] countreye men Ms.

I.2

9:      compared] McCormick; compounde Ms.
16:     Logic] Logike McCormick; Logikes Ms.
21:     or] i. Ms; i.e., McCormick.
55:     a *medium*] a *Medium* LL; medium Ms; media McCormick.
58:     thenafter] then after McCormick; ther after (?) Ms.
80:     consequence or inconsequence] McCormick; coherence or inconsequence Ms; coherence or consequence LL.
83:     maximae] maximaes Ms.
93:     maximae] maximaes Ms.
102:    maximae] maximaes Ms, LL.
118:    syllogistically] sullogisticallie Ms.
187:    there be] therbie Ms.
188:    Hobbinol] Hobbinal Ms.
190:    That] Q; thou Ms, LL.

I.3

Title: Of the Final and the Efficient Cause] of the final cause Ms.
6:      no] Ms, Q; not LL.
11:     surview] Brooks-Davies; seruewe Q; surueye Ms; surveye McCormick; suruey LL.
12:     in compass] in compasse Q, LL; incompasse Ms.
17:     longed] longd Q; lovd Ms; lou'de LL.
18:     ten] LL; tenne Q; x Ms.
22:     Briar] breare Ms.
32:     ever] euer Q, LL; it Ms, McCormick.

33:      bear] beare Q, haue Ms, LL; have McCormick.
35:      tract] Q, McCormick; detract Ms.
37:      security] securitye, etc. Ms (next four lines of verse added to this edition).
44:      here] Q, LL; heare Ms.
46:      work] worke Q; woork LL; make Ms.
48:      cool] coole Q, LL; coald Ms.
51:      plagues] Q, LL; plageas Ms.
63:      *causatum*] *Causatum* LL; causatam Ms.

I.4

8:       wexen] Wexen Q; waxen Ms, LL.
9:       mought] Q; might Ms, LL.
12:      cotes] Ms, Q; coats LL.
13:      fro] Q; from Ms; fro' LL; from McCormick.
26:      warre] Q, LL; ware Ms
28:      fierce] fyerce Ms; fyrce McCormick.
32:      renneth] Q; runnethe Ms; runneth LL.
32:      shepherd's swain] sheepheardes swayne Ms; shepheardes Swayne LL; shepheard Swayne
         Q1; shepheard swayne Q2.
38:      her] Q; thee Ms, LL.
46:      venteth] Q, LL; wenteth Ms.

I.5

5:       Briar] bryer Ms.
6:       Oak] oke Ms.
13:      sight] Q, LL; light Ms.
18:      cankerworms] cancker wormes Q; canckerd wormes Ms; cankred wormes LL.
19:      branches] braunches Q; braunche Ms, braunch LL.
21:      Wherewith] LL; Where with Ms, Q.
30:      lustihead] lustihede Q; lustyheade LL; lustie head Ms.
32:      playen] Q, LL; plaine Ms.
32:      while] whils Ms; whiles LL.
35:      Youghthes folk] Youghthes folke Q; Youthes folke Ms; Youths folke LL.
37:      home] whome Ms; home LL.
39:      hawthorn] Hawthorne Q, hawthorne LL; haythorn Ms.
46:      Tenth] tenth McCormick; eight Ms, LL.
52:      caitiff] caytiue Q; captyve Ms; captiue LL.
60:      wont] Q; went Ms; woont LL.
61:      gather] gathered LL.
64:      wreaked] Q, LL, McCormick; wriked Ms; recked Brooks-Davies.
94:      train] trayne Q, LL; twayne Ms.
103:     Tho] Q; the[n] Ms; the McCormick, LL.
103:     pumy] Ms, LL; pumie Q.
106:     leaped] lepped Q; stepped Ms, LL.
107:     pumies] Q; pumyes Ms, LL.
112:     Forthen] For-then Brooks-Davies; For then Ms, LL, Q.
116:     wote] Q; wott Ms; wot LL.

120:     assot] assot Ms; assott Q; a sott McCormick.
121:     Love] Q; love Ms.
126:     whenas] when as Ms, McCormick

I.6

3:       as] McCormick; not in Ms.
8:       eft] Q; oft Ms, LL.
14:      bathe] Q, LL; bath Ms.
26:      like a] Q; a Ms, LL.
29:      roses] rosses Ms.
31:      primroses] primerosses Ms.
36:      mourfulls't] mournefulst Q; mournefull Ms; mournfullest Brooks-Davies.

I.7

17:      For-thy] Q For thy; for thie Ms.
23:      threttie] Q; thritye LL; thirtye Ms.
28:      bene] Q; be Ms.
44:      pall] Q; pale Ms; Pale LL.
47:      they] Q; ther Ms; their LL.
48:      glitterand] Q1; glitter and Q2, Ms, LL.
53:      *Willy*] Second half-lines assigned to Willy neither in Ms nor LL.
70:      themself] themselfe Q; themselues Ms, LL; themselves McCormick.
71:      be] Q; bee LL; ben Ms.
74:      look] looke Ms; looks McCormick.
91:      frivolously] McCormick; frivoloustlie Ms.

I.8

4:       on] on[e] McCormick; one Ms.
7:       authors] auters Ms.
17:      Howbe] How be Ms, Q.
25:      effects] effect Ms.

I.9

1:       Opposites] LL; Opposite Ms.
2:       to] LL; unto Ms.
10:      hither] hether Q; here Ms.
18:      flower delice] flowre Delice Q; flowerdelyce Ms;

I.10

10:      Syrinx's] Syrinx Ms.
15:      For she […] her blot] (Not in Ms).

I.11

7:       he] Q; to Ms, LL.
12:      ill] Q; all LL.

I.12

8:      wight] Q; weighte Ms.
9:      November] McCormick; September Ms.
15:     Thenafter] Then after Ms.

I.13

9:      and] Q; an Ms.

I.14

17:     Alsoon] alsone Q; Al sone Ms; Al soone LL.
23:     Willy] Second half-lines assigned to Willy neither in Ms nor LL.
34:     Youngth] Youngth Q; youthe Ms; youth LL.

I.15

17:     leese] Q; leaue LL.

I.16

4:      wore] Q; bore LL

I.17

1:      Hitherto of the comparison in quantity] (This sentence closes I.16 in Ms).
12:     Wellaway] Wel-away Q; Wel awaye Ms; Well away LL.
19:     Wagmires overgrassed] wagmoires ouergrast Q; wagmeyres overcast Ms.
30:     Phoebus'] Q; Phaebus Ms.
30:     forthright] Q12; forthe right Ms.
47:     doen] Q; doone Ms, LL.
59:     reigneth] Q; ragethe Ms; rageth Brook-Davies.
61:     breed] Q; bread Ms.
62:     woxen] Q; waxen Ms.
69:     blossoms] bloosmes Q; blossmes Ms, blosmes LL, blooms Brooks-Davies.
69:     buds] Q, LL; birds Ms.
70:     rain] raine Q; rayne LL; raigne Ms.
72:     All so] Q; Also Ms, LL.
73:     timely] Q, LL; liuelye Ms.
83:     wote] Q; wot Ms, LL.
84:     strait] Brooks-Davies; straight Ms, Q.
86:     Whenas] when as Ms, LL.

I.18

4:      thilk] Q; this Ms.
6:      bene] Q; beene Ms.
7:      Ylike] Q; I like Ms.

7:      girt] Q; ygirt Ms.
26:     shroud] shrowd LL; shouder Q; shoulder Brooks-Davies.

I.20

9:      on] Q; one (?) Ms; one McCormick.

I.21

35:     strewed] Ms strawed.

I.22

11:     depeincten] Q depeincten; depaynten Ms, LL.

I.23

14:     God] god Ms, LL; good Q.

I.24

1:      definition] LL, difinition Ms.
14:     while] Q; whiles Ms; whilest LL.
17:     bene] Q; bee Ms; be LL.
19:     bene] ben Ms; bene LL.
22:     a piece] Q; a peece McCormick; apeece Ms.
29:     descriptions] discriptions Ms.

I.25

5:      Oak] Oake Q; oake Ms.
9:      thoroughly] Q; throughlie Ms.
11:     mochel] mochell Q; muche Ms.
14:     beaten] Q; beate Ms.
25:     Whereafterward] Wherafterward Ms; Wher afterward McCormick; Where afterwards
        LL.
28:     Fox] Foxe Q; fox Ms; foxe LL.
29:     be] Q; bee LL; beene Ms.
30:     all as] as Ms, LL.
32:     babes] Q, LL; babies Ms.

I.26

8:      me said] Q; said me Ms; tolde me LL.
11:     Beside] Besyde Q; Beside LL; Besides Ms.
14:     Ren] LL, Brooks-Davies; renne Q; ru[n]ne Ms.
20:     And again] LL; And Thomalin there Ms.
23:     star] LL; stars Q.

II.3

4:       whenas] McCormick; when as Ms.
26:     So that] LL; that Ms.
32:     bloody] McCormick; blooddy Ms.

II.4

25:     *termini*] Ms; tearmes LL.
27:     are] or Ms; ar McCormick
45:     Ball] Balle Ms; Ball LL; ball Q12.
59:     As for] For as for Ms.
59:     trumperies] Ms; trumperye McCormick.

II.5

9:      shepherd] shepheard Q, LL; shepheardes Ms.
11:     follies] follyes Q; follye Ms; folly LL.

II.6

9:      only of, or dependeth upon,] onely of, or dependeth vpon LL; onlie or dependethe vpon Ms.
10:     which may be whenas notwithstanding] which maie bee, when as not withstandinge, Ms; which maie bee, when as notwithstandinge, McCormick; which may bee when as, notwithstanding, LL.
12–13: which counsel [...] his counsel] LL (not in Ms).
16:     mother] Ms; gate LL.
20:     Hitherto] LL; Hither Ms.

II.7

4:      discretive. Wherefore] discretiue. Wherefore LL; discretiue, wherfore Ms.
8:      ene] en Ms; one LL.
8:      heart root] hart roote Q; heart roote LL; heart-root Brooks-Davies; hartes roote Ms.
11:     when] LL; when as Ms.
12:     when] LL; when as Ms.

II.8

4:      god] Q; good Ms.
6:      necessarily] LL; specially Ms.

II.9

3:      inferred] LL; referred Ms.
13:     the whole proposition, or] LL (not in Ms).
31:     satisficed] LL, McCormick; satisfacied Ms.
35:     ἐπαριθμῆσις] ἐπαριτμῆσις Ms.

42–43: But […] true] (This Ms line is skipped in McCormick).
49:     *aut*] LL, Loeb; nec Ms.
49:     *curvum*] Loeb; curtum Ms, LL.

II.12

48:     injuriously] iniurouslye Ms.
50:     contracted] LL; contract Ms.

II.13

10:     us brings] Q; bringes vs Ms, LL.
11:     it] Q, LL; that Ms.
13:     layes] Ms, LL, Q; leas Brooks-Davies.
14:     fields] LL; fyelde Ms.
23:     strait] Brooks-Davies; strayte Ms; straight Q.

II.14

24:     health] Q; wealthe Ms, LL.
36:     connexive hath] LL; connexiue Ms.
37:     homeward] whomwarde Ms.

II.15

1:      consequence] sequence Ms..
7:      younkers] Q; yonkers Ms.

II.17

7:      with] Ms; which McCormick.

II.18

42:     April] McCormick; Maye Ms.
47:     April] McCormick; Maye Ms.
50:     lest] least Ms.

II.19

9:      Croesus] Craesus Ms.
10:     καταλύσει] Aristotle, *Rhet.*, 1407a (Loeb); καταλύψας Ms.

'Of the Nature and Use of Logic'

1:      Julius] McCormick; Junius Ms.
10:     it] bee Ms.
26:     thenafter] Then after Ms.
52:     there] theyr Ms.

70: mention] McCormick; mancion Ms.
75: injuriously] McCormick; injurously Ms.
77: injurious] McCormick; injurous Ms.
83: of] McCormick (not in Ms).
85: dishes] McCormick; diches Ms.
98: home] whome Ms.
99: his] this Ms.
112: walls] walles McCormick; waylles Ms.
117: home] whome Ms.
162: dunses] Dunses Ms.
184: *methodus prudentiae*] metodus prudentiae Ms.

'A Brief and General Comparison'

51: *totum universale*] McCormick; to totum vniuersale Ms.
55: *apodictiké*] apodictice Ms.
56: *dialectiké*] dialectice Ms.
56: *sophistiké*] sophistice Ms.
59: in the] McCormick (not in Ms)
63: fain] fain Ms; gladly McCormick (based on a conjectural reading of the scribal correction above the blot).
79: *aequivoca*] McCormick; aequivioca Ms.
100: *aequipollentia*] aequipolentia Ms.
106: thus] Ms; this McCormick.
107: modes] moodes Ms.
144: it] McCormick (not in Ms)
172: sophistic] sophistica Ms.
244: different in] different Ms.
256: in] inne Ms (conj.); me McCormick.
270: Topics] Topikes Ms.
274: *Vesper*] vesper Ms.

Appendix I.1

40: too much] tootoomuch LL.
67: appearance] apparance LL.

Appendix I.2

4: singly] singlely LL.
29: daysman] dayes man LL.

Appendix I.4

1: Seely] Silly CPY.
3: thick set] thickset CPY.
5: most] there CPY.
8: them] CPY; the LL.
9: Green lizards now too in bushes] And now greene Lyzards in bushes CPY.

12:        too] to LL.

12:        But whilst I trace thee, with sun beams all too bescorched] But whil'st scorcht *Corydon*
           doth trace his louely *Alexis* CPY.

18:        only] duely CPY.

25:        Neither am I so foul: I saw myself by the seashore] Nor soe fowle be my lookes: for I saw
           myself by the sea-shore CPY.

26–27:   I doubt not, but by thy censure, / Daphnis I shall surpass, unless my face do deceive me]
           Ile orecome Daphnis, I doubt not, / Eu'n by thy owne iudgement, vnles my face doe
           deceaue mee CPY.

29:        and stick] sticking CPY.

31:        amid] amidst CPY.

36:        Damoetas] Damaetas LL.

45:        thee] CPY; the LL.

45:        see the nymphs bring here to thee lilies] loe, Nymphs here bring thee the Lillies CPY.

46:        now] loe CPY.

51:        with soft down all to be smeared] with soft downe daintily clothed CPY.

52:        chestnuts] Chessnuts LL.

53:        wheat-plums] wheateplumbs LL.

54–55:   and thee, pretty myrtle / Next to the laurel leaves] and next to the Lawrell / Leaues, Ile
           pluck Myrtle CPY.

58:        But what alas did I mean, poor fool? I do let go the south wind] But what alas did I
           meane? I do let goe madly the Southwinde CPY.

60:        mad man] fond boy CPY.

60:        also] gladly CPY.

66:        But see the plough] But loe, Plow CPY.

GLOSSARY

This Glossary contains obsolete, archaic, or uncommon words and meanings in Fraunce's text and the quotes from Spenser. It also considers terms from logic or related disciplines only when they are not explained sufficiently or at all by Fraunce. Most definitions are based on *OED*, from which part of speech, grammatical form or sense number are given if necessary. Abbreviations also follow *OED*. For words used in different grammatical forms, the uninflected form is listed. For definitions of words from *The Shepherds' Calendar*, references to E.K.'s glosses or to modern editors' notes are given parenthetically when necessary. This procedure also applies to specific sources used in definitions of logical terms.

A

abye: pay a penalty.

acception: meaning.

accusing: blaming.

aequipollentia: (Lat.) equipollence, the procedure by which two opposite propositions are rendered equivalent, i.e., by denying the predicate of one of them: '*All books are (not) boring / No book is boring*'.

affections: properties.

agnominatio: (Lat.) rhetorical figure bringing together words of similar sound although dissimilar in meaning.

albe: albeit.

albedinities: (pl., from Lat. *albedo*, *albus*) whiteness understood as essence.

als: also.

alsoon: as soon.

antepredicaments: the three modes of naming discussed by Aristotle before the predicaments (*Categories*, I), i.e., *equivocal* (as 'man' applied to a man and his portrait), *univocal* (as 'animal' applied to a man and a dog), and *derivative* or *denominative* (inflected words when differentiated from their primitive form).

apaid: satisfied.

appertain: belong, as a part to a whole.

appliable: suitable, pertinent.

arguitur quod sic: (Lat.) argued in the affirmative (a formulaic answer in disputations).

assayed: tried with afflictions (*assay*, v. 12).

assot: infatuated.

astert: happen (*astart*, v. 2).

astonied: benumbed, paralyzed.

attemper: bring into harmony.

aught: worth in anything.

aye: always.

B

balk: overlook (v. 2).

band: circle (in SL, I.1, 118); copula or middle part of an axiom (all other usages).

Baralipton: mnemonic word for the fifth **mode** of the first-**figure** syllogism, i.e., two universal affirmatives (A-A) concluding in a particular affirmative (I): '*Every animal is a substance. Every man is an animal. Therefore, some substance is man*'.

bare: bore (pa. t. *bear*).

bedecketh: adorns.

behote: named (pa. pple. *behight*, v. 6).

bellibone: fair lass (Fr. *belle et bonne*).

bellygods: gluttons.

beseem: suit, befit.

besides: beside, out of.

besmeared: anointed.

betokeneth: signifies.

biggin: night-cap.

blaspheme: blasphemy.

blissed: made happy (*bliss*, v. 2).

blub: bubble (not in *OED*; trans. of Lat. *bulla*, as in Beurhaus 1, C4ʳ).

bonnibel: fair lass (Fr. *bonne et belle*).

borrell: unlearned.

brabbling: cavilling, quibbling.

brag: haughtily (adv. 3).

breme: raging (adj. 6).

bugle: tubular glass bead.

C

caitiff: captive (adj.)

careful: mournful.

cassia: cinnamon-like flower.

casten: contrived (pa. pple. *cast*, v. 43).

catachrestically: by catachresis, or improper lexical use.

cavillers: quibbling disputants.

chamfered: furrowed.

chaplet: a wreath for the head.

chevisaunce: unidentified name of a flower, perhaps 'cherisance' (*The Works of Edmund Spenser: A Variorum Edition*, VII: p. 287).

clout: rag.

cobbler: mender, clumsy workman.

cog: join.

consecution: sequential arrangement of logical propositions.

consectaries: deductions.

contradiction: refutation.

conversion: logical procedure of inversion of subject and predicate without altering the truth of a proposition.

corollaries: conclusions.

coronal: garland.
covetise: inordinate lust, covetousness.
crag: neck (E.K.).
craggy: rough-barked, difficult to climb (Brooks-Davies, p. 190).
crack: boast (v. 6).
crank: lustily.
crazed: diseased, infirm (adj. 4).
cremosin: crimson.
crow-toe: wild hyacinth.

D

daysman: umpire.
dearling: darling.
delice: (see flower delice).
dempt: judged (pa. t. deem).
demonstrative: of argumentations, logically certain and self-evident (apodictic).
depeincten: depicted.
depend: hang (in Spenser only).
dianoetically: in Ramist logic, pertaining to the disposition of axioms through syllogisms or their
    proper arrangement through method.
dight: adorn.
dill: fennel-flower, used as a spice.
down: pubescent hair of a fruit or plant.
dunse (PDE dunce): scholastic philosopher, follower of Duns Scotus; derog., pseudo-philosopher,
    fool.
dunsical, dunsicality: derivatives of dunse.

E

earned: desired strongly (earn, v.³).
eft: afterwards.
embossed: carved in relief.
emprise: undertaking, enterprise.
enchased: engraved.
ene: even once.
entrailed: entwined.
ergo: (Lat.) therefore (formulaic in syllogistic conclusions).
excogitation: contrivance, invention.
expert: experience (v.).

F

fained: feigned, fictional.
faitours: impostors.
fallation: fallacy; deceptive or misleading argument that vitiates a syllogism.
fay: faith.
fet: fetched.

figures: the three dispositions of the *medium* in a syllogism. In the first, or perfect figure, the middle term is the subject in one premise and the predicate in another; in the second, the predicate in both premises; in the third, the subject in both (Aristotle, *Prior Analytics*, I.IV–VI).

flower delice: fleur-de-lis (false Lat. *flos deliciae*).

fon: fool.

force: power to persuade the reason or judgement.

forceable: persuasive.

forcibly: persuasively.

formalities: distinctive properties of things.

forthen: as a result of which (adv.).

for-thy: therefore.

G

gainsay: contradict.

galage: shoe (E.K.).

gan: began (contr.).

gars: causes (3rd sing., Northern dial.).

Gate: Goat (Northern dial.).

gelt: gilt (adj. Kentish dial.).

gins: begins (contr.).

girlonds: garlands.

glitterand: glittering (pres. pple. Northern dial.).

goodlihead: excellence (n. 3).

gree: degree (E.K.).

gross: the whole (E.K.).

ground: fundamental principle in a discipline.

H

han: have (3rd pl. ME *habben*).

hare-brain: reckless.

haviour: complexion.

headpiece: brain.

hent: seized, gone (v. 1, 6).

her: he, in literary representations of Gaelic.

hight: called.

hoar, hoary: grey.

howbe: howbeit, although (conj.).

husbandman (also **husband**): farmer.

I

igitur: thus (formulaic in logical inference).

imperfit: imperfect.

indued: endowed, invested.

injury: wrong (v. 1).

institutions: treatises.

ivy-tod: ivy branch.

J

John-a-stile: feigned name for one of the parties in a legal action; lawyer (*OED, John-a-nokes*).

K

κατὰ παντός, καθ'αύτο, καθόλου πρῶτον: see **rules of truth**, etc.
kennest, kenned: knowest, knew (pres. 2nd sing. and pa. *ken*).
kiddest: knewest (E.K., *kithe*, different sense from *OED*).
kirtle: skirt.

L

law of justice: see **rules of truth, etc.**
layes: pastures (*lea*, poet.).
leasing: lie, falsehood.
leese: lose.
lever: rather (comp. of *lief*).
levin: lightning.
liggen: lie (3rd pl.).
list: desire (v.).
lithe: soft, gentle (E.K.).
lope: leaped.
lording: sitting in lordly manner (E.K.).
lorel: rogue.
louring: dark, threatening (*lower*, v. 2).

M

mast: fruit of woodland trees used for fattening pigs.
Mastership (your good): the holder of a Master of Arts.
mazer: footless wooden cup.
mean: limit (n.).
medium: (Lat.) middle term or third argument of a syllogism, common to the major and minor premises, but absent in the conclusion, as *man* in: '*Socrates is a man. A man is mortal. Therefore Socrates is mortal*'.
melancholical: causing melancholy, depressing (adj. 4).
mervail: marvel (n. and v.).
methodical: meticulous; practitioner of Ramist method.
metonymia: (Lat.) metonymy, rhetorical trope by which a thing is given another thing's name by dint of some semantic relation.
missay: abuse (v.).
mochel: much (variant of *mickle*).
modes: the different dispositions of a syllogism by considering the quantity and quality of its propositions (A, universal affirmative; E, universal negative; I, special affirmative; O, special negative). Each **figure** has several valid modes. Scholastic logic assigned to each mode a mnemonic word in which the first three vowels tell the sort of proposition used by the major, the minor and the conclusion. See **Baralipton**.
moe: more.

modals (also **modificate**, adj., and Lat. *modales*): propositions in which the copula is modified so as to express relations of possibility, impossibility, necessity or contingency between subject and predicate.

monuments: exemplars of classical literature.

mought: must (*mote*, v.1, 2).

N

naught: worthless.

newfangled: gratuitously attracted to novelty.

nis: is not

O

opposition: see **postpredicaments**.

P

Palinode: ode of recantation; also the name of a shepherd in Spenser's.

pall: pallium; a wollen vestment conferred by the Pope on high church authorities as a sign of their participation in his power.

pampering: overindulgence, with insinuations of fondling.

paunce: pansie (Fr. *pensée*).

perfit: perfect (adj.); to make perfect (v.);

perfitly: perfectly.

perforcely: inevitably.

perseities: (pl.) independent existence or essential quality of a subject (Lat. *perseitas, per se*; Greek *καθ'αὑτό*).

philosophaster: pseudo-philosopher.

pight: fixed, set up (arch. pa. pple. *pitch*).

pine: affliction (n. 1).

plow: ploughland.

postpredicaments: modes of relation that follow the predicaments. These are the four kinds of opposition (*contraries, relatives, privatives* and *contradiction*), priority in time, necessity, order and affection (*prius*), the negation of priority or coincidence in time or nature (*simul*), change or motion (*motus*) and possession (*habere*) (Aristotle *Categories*, X–XV). The last two Fraunce simply mentions as 'the other'.

praedicabilia: see **predicables**.

prate: talk idly.

predicables: the five modes of relation (*genus, species, difference, property* and *accident*) between the subject and the predicate of a proposition.

predicaments: the ten categories under which all things can be discussed logically, namely substance, quantity, quality, relation, place, time, posture, habit, action and affection (Aristotle, *Categories*, IV–IX).

president: precedent.

primers: princes (n. 3).

probatur quod non: (Lat.) it is proved negatively (formulaic answer in disputations).

pure: of propositions, categorical or without any modification (as opposed to **modal**).

Q

quaffing: copious drinking of alcoholic beverages.
quidditaries: those who discuss **quiddities**; scholastic logicians.
quiddity: (from Lat. *quidditas*) inherent nature or essence; derog., unnecessary subtlety in an argument.
quodlibet: (Lat.) literally, 'whatever you please'; academic disputation on any subject.

R

rabble: endless nonsense, referring to the intricacies of scholastic thought.
reddition: second term of a comparison.
rede: proverb.
reduction: conversion of the imperfect syllogistic figures into perfect (first-figure) syllogisms.
removed: separate (adj.).
repugn: contradict, go against (v. 5).
ren: to expedite, run.
renomed: celebrated.
respect: reason, consideration (n.).
revert: return.
rife: widespread.
rifely: abundantly, amply.
rine: rind, bark of a tree.
rules of truth, righteousness and wisdom: the three Ramist laws by which an axiom is tested in order to become a necessary precept of an art. The **rule of truth** (Lat. *lex de omni, lex veritatis*, Greek κατὰ παντός) requires that axioms be always true and not a matter of mere opinion. The **rule of righteousness** (also law of justice, Lat. *lex per se, lex iustitiae*, Greek καθ'αὐτο) prescribes that judgements join things that are related by affinity in order to establish clear boundaries between the arts. The **rule of wisdom** (Lat. *lex sapientiae*, Greek καθόλου πρῶτον) dictates that the subject and the predicate of an axiom must remain at the same level of generality (Howell, *Logic and Rhetoric*, pp. 149–53; Webster, ed., *William Temple's 'Analysis'*, pp. 46–47).
runts: small oxen.

S

sam: together, mutually (adv.).
say: wool.
sclandering: slandering, offense.
seely: pitiable, innocent.
sheepcote: a cottage for sheep.
sere: withered
several(ly): specific(ally), different(ly).
shend: confound, disgrace (v. 2).
shroud: shelter (Spenser, *The Shorter Poems*, ed. by Richard A. McCabe, p. 541).
sib: kin.
sike: such.
siker: certainly.
sith: since (causal and temporal senses).

sithes: times (E.K.).

smirk: trimly, elegantly (adv.).

stoop-gallant: anything (i.e., age) that makes gallants decline.

stour: turmoil, turbulent time.

straightways: immediately.

sodain: sudden.

sophisters: scholars; derog., practitioners of **sophistry**.

sophistry: the making of fallacious arguments.

sops-in-wine: clove-pinks, gillyflowers.

sperre: shut (E.K.; *spar*, v.).

sprong: sprang (arch. pa. t. *spring*).

standish: a desk-stand for writing material.

subalternal (Lat. *subalternae*): mode of relation between universal and less universal arguments or propositions.

subcontrary: mode of opposition that affirms that two propositions, one special affirmative (I) and one special negative (O), can be true, but not false, at the same time.

substantiality: the capacity of a substantive to designate substance.

supposition: denotation, relation between a term and the object it designates.

surview: take a general view, survey.

swain: a shepherd's boy or attendant.

swarty: black.

swink: labour, toil.

T

team: set of harnessed animals.

termini: see *voces et termini*.

tenurist: a lawyer dealing with tenures.

tetrifoil: four-leaved clover.

thenafter: secondly.

thilk: this same.

tho: then.

threttie: thirty.

tooting: peeping.

totum integrum: an integral whole.

towardly: promising (adj.).

tractate: subject; discussion or treatise on a specific subject.

trod: footpath (dial.)

trumperies: fabrications, impostures.

truss: bundle.

tway: two.

U

uncouth: unknown.

undersay: reply.

unperfit: imperfect.

usucapio: (Lat.) acquisition of property by custom of possession.

untolerably: intolerably.

V

variable: of axioms, contingent.
vellet: velvet (arch.).
vent(eth): snuffs up the air (*v*.², 14).
voces et termini: (Lat.) utterances, or vocal expressions, and terms.

W

wagmires: quagmires
warre: tree knot.
weaned: deprived, as a child from his mother's milk.
well-willers: addicted to a particular study.
wend: depart (v. 10).
ween: think.
weet: know.
wellaway: alas (int.).
wexen: of wax (dial.).
wheat-plums: waxen-coloured plums (by mistranslation of Latin *cerea pruna* as 'cereal plums').
whenas: seeing that, inasmuch as, whereas (sometimes in adversative sense), as.
whereafterward: after which.
whilom: while (conj.); some time ago (adv.).
wight: creature.
wight: agile (adj. 3, dial.).
wimble: swift (dial.).
wood: mad.
wont: habit, accustomed, to accustom (n., adj., or v.).
wote: know (1st sing. pres ind. or subj.)
woxen: grown (pa. pple. *wax*).
wreaked: took notice (*reck*, v. 1, of which *wreak* is dial.).

Y

yate: gate.
yfere: together.
ylike: similar, alike (adj. or adv.).
yond: yonder (adj.).
young-headed: inexperienced.
youngth: youth.
younkers: young men.
yougthes folk: young people.
y-: arch. pref. in pa. pple. forms, as in *ywrought, yclad, ygirt, ytossed, ypent*.

BIBLIOGRAPHY

This list is divided into five sections: 1) Works by Abraham Fraunce (Manuscript, First Editions, and Modern Editions); 2) Pre-1660 Primary Sources; 3) Post-1660 Editions; 4) Secondary Sources; 5) Dictionaries.

Abbreviations of frequently quoted sources follow each reference in square brackets.

1) Works by Abraham Fraunce

Manuscripts

London, British Library, Add MS 34361: *The Sheapheardes Logike: Conteyning the Praecepts of that Art Put Downe by Ramus [...] Together with Twooe General Discourses, the One Touchinge the Prayse and Ryghte Vse of Logike, the Other Concernynge the Comparison of Ramus his Logike with that of Aristotle*: [Ms]

Oxford, Bodleian Library, Rawlinson MS 345.1: Untitled, containing a Latin essay in praise of Dialectic, followed by a collection of Latin emblems: [Rawlinson]

Kent Archives Office Ms, U1475/Z15 (Penshurst MS): Containing the Latin comedy *Victoria* and 'Symbolicae Philosophiae Liber Quartus et Vltimus, Abrahamo Franso Auctore'

First Editions

ALLOTT, ROBERT, *Englands Parnassus, or, The Choysest Flowers of our Moderne Poets [...]* (London: For N. L[ing,] C. B[urby] and T. H[ayes], 1600; STC 379). Fraunce's poetry is anthologized in sigs. E4^r (one line), G4^r (1), K2^v (4), N3^r (20), N5^v (3), O1^r (15), O8^r (1), R7^v (2), T6r (1), X5^r–X5^v (7), X6^r (3, attributed to A Fr.), Ii2^v (6)

Insignium, Armorum, Emblematum Hieroglyphicorum, et Symbolorum, quae ab Italis Imprese Nominantur, Explicatio: Quae Symbolicae Philosophiae Postrema Pars Est (London: Thomas Orwin, for Thomas Gubbin and Thomas Newman, 1588; STC 11342)

The Arcadian Rhetorike: or The Praecepts of Rhetorike Made Plaine by Examples Greeke, Latin, English, Italian, French, Spanish (London: Thomas Orwin, 1588; STC 11338)

The Countesse of Pembrokes Yuychurch. Conteining the Affectionate life, and Vnfortunate Death of Phillis and Amyntas (London: Thomas Orwin, for William Ponsonby, 1591; STC 11340): [CPY]

The Lawiers Logike, Exemplifying the Praecepts of Logike by the Practise of the Common Lawe (London: William How, for Thomas Gubin and Thomas Newman, 1588; STC 11344): [LL]

The Third Part of the Countesse of Pembrokes Yuychurch Entituled, Amintas Dale (London: Thomas Orwin, for Thomas Woodcock, 1592; STC 11341)

WATSON, THOMAS, *The Lamentations of Amyntas for the Death of Phillis, Paraphrastically Translated out of Latine into English Hexameters by Abraham Fraunce* (London: John Wolfe, for Thomas Newman and Thomas Gubin, 1587; STC 25118.4; later editions 1588 and 1596)

Facsimiles

The Lawyer's Logic, 1588 (Menston: Scolar Press, 1969)

The Lawiers Logike, Exemplifying the Praecepts of Logike by the Practice of the Common Lawe, intro. by Steve Sheppard (New Jersey: The Lawbook Exchange, 2013)

The Shepherd's Logic [ca? 1585] (Menston: Scolar Press, 1969)

Modern Editions

McCORMICK, SISTER MARY M., ed., *A Critical Edition of Abraham Fraunce's 'The Shepheardes Logike' and 'Twooe Generall Discourses'* (Unpb. PhD Dissertation: St Louis University, 1968): [McCormick]

MOORE SMITH, G. C., ed., *Victoria, A Latin Comedy by Abraham Fraunce, Edited from the Penshurst Manuscript* (Louvain: A. Uystpruyst, 1906)

SEATON, ETHEL, ed., *The Arcadian Rhetorike, Edited from the Edition of 1588* (Oxford: Basil Blackwell, for The Luttrell Society, 1950)

SNARE, GERALD, ed., *Abraham Fraunce: The Third Part of the Countess of Pembroke's Ivychurch* (Northridge, CA: University of California Press, 1975)

STATON, W. F. and F. M. DICKEY, eds, *Thomas Watson's 'Amyntas' / Abraham Fraunce's 'The Lamentations of Amyntas' [1587]* (Chicago: Publications of the Renaissance Text Society, 1967)

2) Primary Sources: Pre-1660 Editions

Academiae Cantabrigiensis Lachrymae tumulo nobilissimi equitis, D. Philippi Sidneii sacratae per Alexandrum Nevillum (London: John Windet, 1587; STC 4473)

ASCHAM, ROGER, *The Scholemaster, or Plaine and Perfite Way of Teachyng Children* (London: John Daye, 1570; STC 832)

——, *Disertissimi viri Rogeri Aschami, Angli, Regiae maiestati non ita pridem a Latinis epistolis, familiarium epistolarum libri tres* (London: Francis Coldock, 1576; STC 826)

BATMAN, STEPHEN, *Uppon Bartholome his Booke De proprietatibus rerum, Newly Corrected, Enlarged and Amended* (London: Thomas East, 1582; STC 1538)

BAXTER, NATHANIEL, *Quaestiones et responsiones in Petri Rami dialecticam* (Frankfurt: Johann Wechel, 1588; USTC 665281; 1st edn 1585)

BEURHAUS, FRIEDRICH (FRIDERICUS BEURHUSIUS), *In P. Rami Regii professoris Clariss. Dialecticae libros duos [...] Explicationum quaestiones: quae Paedagogiae logicae de docenda discendaque dialectica. Pars Prima* (London: Henry Bynneman 1581; STC 1982): [Beurhaus I]

——, *De P. Rami dialecticae praecipuis capitibus disputationes scholasticae, & cum iisdem variorum logicorum comparationes: quae Paedagogiae logicae pars secunda, qua artis veritas exquiritur* (London: Henry Bynneman, 1582; STC 1983): [Beurhaus II]

BRIGHTE, TIMOTHY, *A Treatise of Melancholie, Containing the Causes thereof, and Reasons of the Strange Effects It Worketh in our Minds and Bodies* (London: Thomas Vautrollier, 1586; STC 3747)

CALVIN, JEAN, *The Institution of Christian Religion*, trans. by Thomas Norton (London: Reinolde Wolfe and Richard Harison, 1561; STC 4415)

CHARPENTIER, JACQUES (IACOBUS CARPENTARIUS), *Animadversiones in Libros tres dialecticarum Institutionum Petri Rami* (Paris: Thomas Richard, 1554; USTC 196697)

CHEKE, JOHN, *The Hurt of Sedicion Howe Greveous It Is to a Commune Welth* (London: John Daye and William Seres, 1549; STC 5109)

DIGBY, EVERARD, *De duplici methodo libri duo unicam P. Rami methodum refutantes: in quibus, via plana, expedita, & exacta, secundum optimos autores, ad scientiarum cognitionem elucidator* (London; Henry Bynneman, 1580; STC 6841)

——, *Admonitioni F. Mildapetti navareni de unica P. Rami methodo retinenda, responsio* (London; Henry Bynneman, 1580; STC 6838)

ELYOT, THOMAS, *The Boke Named the Gouernour* (London: Thomas Berthelet, 1531; STC 7635)

——, *Bibliotheca Eliotae, Eliotis Librarie* (London: Thomas Berthelet, 1542; STC 7659.5)

ERASMUS, DESIDERIUS, *Adagiorum chiliades tres* (Tübingen: Ludwig Anshelm, 1514; USTC 653256)

FENNER, DUDLEY, *The Artes of Logike and Rethorike Plainelie Set foorth in the Englishe Tounge [...]* (Middelburg: R. Schilders, 1584; STC 10766)

FREIGE, JOHANNES THOMAS, *Partitiones Iuris* (Basel: Sebastian Henricpetri, 1571; USTC 667369)

——, *Rhetorica, Poëtica, Logica ad usum rudiorum in epitomen redactae* (Nuremberg: Catharina Gerlach, 1580; USTC 691143)

——, *De Logica Iureconsultorum libri duo* (Basel: Sebastian Henricpetri, 1582; USTC 667396)

——, *In XII. P. Virgilii Aeneid. libros, tabulae: omnibus poeticae artis studiosis utiles et necessariae* (Basel: Sebastian Henricpetri, 1587; USTC 667398)

——, *Petri Rami Vita per Joannem Thoman Freigium*, in Petrus Ramus, *Collectaneae*, pp. 580–625

GREENE, ROBERT, *Menaphon, Camillas Alarum to Slumbering Euphues, in his Melancholie Cell at Silexedra* (London: T[homas] O[rwin], 1589; STC 12272)

HARVEY, GABRIEL, *Rhetor, vel duorum dierum oratio, de natura, arte, & exercitatione rhetorica ad suos auditores* (London: Henry Bynneman, 1577; STC 12904.5)

LEVER, RALPH, *The Arte of Reason, Rightly Termed, Witcraft Teaching a Perfect Way to Argue and Dispute* (London: Henry Bynneman, 1573; STC 15541)

LODGE, THOMAS, *Phillis: Honoured with Pastorall Sonnets, Elegies, and Amorous Delights* (London: John Busbie, 1593; STC 16662)

MACILMAINE, ROLAND, *The Logike of the Moste Excellent Philosopher P. Ramus Martyr, Newly Translated, and in Diuers Places Corrected, after the Mynde of the Author* (London: Thomas Vautrollier, 1574; STC 15246)

MELANCHTON, PHILIPP, *Erotemata dialectices, continentia fere integram artem: Ita scripta, ut Iuuentuti utiliter proponi possint* (Leipzig: Valentin Bapst, 1549; USTC 653582; 1st edn 1547)

MELBANCKE, BRIAN, *Philotimus: The Warre betwixt Nature and Fortune* (London: Roger Warde, 1583; STC 17801)

MERES, FRANCIS, *Palladis Tamia* (London: P. Short, 1598; STC 17834)

NASHE, THOMAS, *The Anatomie of Absurditie* (London: J. Charlewood, 1589; STC 18364)

OPSOPOEUS, VINCENTIUS, *De arte bibendi libri tres* (Nuremberg: Johann Petreius, 1536; USTC 628364)

PEELE, GEORGE, *The Honour of the Garter Displaied in a Poeme Gratulatorie* (London: Charlewood, 1593; STC 19539)

PISCATOR, JOHANNES, *In P. Rami Dialecticam Animadversiones. Exemplis Sacr. literarum passim illustrata* (London: Henry Bynneman, 1581; STC 19961; 1st edn Frankfurt, 1580): [Piscator; Ramus/Piscator]

PORPHYRY [ARISTOTLE, BOETHIUS], *Quinque vocum, quae praedicabilia Porphirii liber [...] Boetio Severino interprete* (Paris: Guillaume le Bet, 1538; USTC 186083; 1st edn 1535)

RAMUS, PETRUS, *Aristotelicae Animadversiones* (Paris: Jacques Bogard, 1543; USTC 116824. Facsimile: *Dialecticae Institutiones / Aristotelicae Animadversiones*. Stuttgart: Friedrich Frommann, 1964)

——, *Bucolica, praelectionibus exposita: quibus poëtae vita praeposita est* (Paris: André Wechel, 1555; USTC 197910)

——, *Ciceronianus* (Basel: Peter Perna, 1573; USTC 683650; 1st edn 1557)

——, *Collectaneae praefationes, epistolae, orationes Petri Rami Professoris Regii* (Maburg: Paul Egenolff, 1599; USTC 683563)

——, *Dialecticae institutiones* (Paris: Jacques Bogard, 1543; USTC 140867. Facsimile: *Dialecticae Institutiones / Aristotelicae Animadversiones* (Stuttgart: Friedrich Frommann, 1964)

——, *Dialecticae libri duo, praelectionibus illustrati* (Paris: André Wechel, 1556; USTC 152027, 1st edn)

——, *Dialecticae libri duo, Audomari Talei praelectionibus illustrata* (Paris: André Wechel, 1566; USTC 158111)

——, *Dialectica, Audomari Talaei Praelectionibus Illustrata* (Cologne: Theodor Gras, 1573; USTC 681974)

——, Roland McIlmaine, *Dialecticae libri duo. Exemplis omnium artium et scientiarum illustrati, non solum divinis, sed etiam mysticis, mathematicis, physicis, medicis, juridicis, poëticis et oratoriis, per Rolandun Makilmenaeum Scotum* (Frankfurt: Andreas Wechel, 1579; USTC 682003)

——, *Dialecticae libri duo* (Frankfurt: Andreas Wechel, 1586)

——, *Dialectique* (Paris: André Wechel, 1555; USTC 37660)

——, *Pro Philosophica Parisiensis Academiae disciplina oratio* (Paris: André Wechel, 1557; USTC, 152328)

——, *Scholae in liberales artes* (Basel: Nikolaus Episcopius, 1569; USTC 681989)

SCALIGER, JULIUS CAESAR, *Poetices libri septem* (Geneva: Jean Crespin, 1561; USTC 450294)

SPENSER, EDMUND, *The Shepheardes Calender Conteyning Twelue Aeglogues Proportionable to the Twelue Monethes* (London: Hugh Singleton, 1579; 2nd edn London: Thomas East for John Harrison, 1581; STC 23089 and 23090): [Q₁ and Q₂]

STURM, JOHANN (IOANNES STURMIUS), *Ad Werteros Fratres, Nobilitas literata: liber unus* (Strasbourg: Wendelin Rihel, 1549; USTC 667642), trans. by Thomas Browne, *A Ritch Storehouse or Treasurie for Nobility and Gentlemen* (London: Henry Denham, 1570; STC 23408)

——, *Partitionum dialecticarum libri IIII. Emmendati et Aucti* (Strasbourg: Josias Rihel, 1566; 1st edn 1549; USTC 667894)

TALON, OMER (AUDOMARUS TALAEUS), *Dialectici commentarii tres* (Paris: Louis Grandin, 1546; USTC 199908)

——, *Rhetorica, e P. Rami regii professoris praelectionibus observata* (Frankfurt: Andreas Wéchel, 1577; USTC 613829)

TEMPLE, WILLIAM [PETRUS RAMUS], *Dialecticae libri duo, scholiis G. Tempelli Cantabrigiensis illustrati. Quibus accessit, eodem authore, de Porphyrianis praedicabilibus disputatio [...]* (Cambridge: Thomas Thomas, 1584; STC 15243)

——, *Francisci Mildapetti Nauerreni ad Euerardum Digbeium Anglum admonitio de unica P. Rami methodo reiectis Caeteris retinenda* (London: Henry Middleton for Thomas Man, 1580; STC 23872)

——, *Pro Mildapetti de unica methodo defensione contra diplodophilum, commentatio Gulielmi Tempelli, e regio Collegio Cantabrigiensis. Huc accessit nonnullarum e physicis et ethicis quaestionum explicatio, una cum epistola de Rami dialectica ad Joannem Piscatorem Argentinensem* (London: Henry Middleton for Thomas Man, 1581; STC 23874)

——, *Epistola de Dialectica P. Rami, ad Ioan. Piscatorem Argentinens una cum Joan. Piscatoris ad illam epist. responsione* (London; Henry Middleton for John Harrison and George Bishop, 1582; STC 23873)

WEBBE, WILLIAM, *A Discourse of English Poetrie* (London: John Charlewood, 1586; STC 25172)

WILSON, THOMAS, *The Rule of Reason, Conteinyng the Arte of Logique* (London: Richard Grafton, 1551; STC 25809)

WHITNEY, GEFFREY, *A Choice of Emblemes, and other Deuises, for the Moste Parte Gathered out of Sundrie Writers, Englished and Moralized. And Diuers Newly Deuised* (Leiden: Christopher Plantyn, 1586; STC 25438)

3) Primary Sources: Post-1660 Editions

ALEXANDER, GAVIN, ed., *Sir Philip Sidney's 'The Defence of Poesy' and Selected Renaissance Literary Criticism* (London: Penguin, 2004)

ANSELM (ST), *Basic Writings*, trans. by N. S. by Deane, 2nd edn (Peru, IL.: Open Court, 1962)

ARISTOTLE, *Categories, On Interpretation, Prior Analytics*, ed. by Harold P. Cooke and H. Tredennick, Loeb I (Cambridge, MA: Harvard University Press, 1938)

——, *Posterior Analytics, Topica*, ed. by H. Tredennick and E. S. Forster, Loeb II (Cambridge, MA: Harvard University Press, 1960)

——, *On Sophistical Refutations, On Coming-To-Be and Passing Away, On the Cosmos*, ed. by E. S. Forster and D. J. Furley, Loeb III (Cambridge, MA: Harvard University Press, 1955)

——, *On the Soul, Parva Naturalia, On Breath*, ed. by W. S. Hett, Loeb VIII (Cambridge, MA: Harvard University Press, 1936, revised 1957)

——, *Nicomachean Ethics*, ed. by H. Rackham, Loeb XIX (Cambridge, MA: Harvard University Press, 1926)

——, *The Art of Rhetoric*, ed. by J. H. Freese, Loeb XXII (Cambridge, MA: Harvard University Press, 1926)

——, LONGINUS and DEMETRIUS, *The Poetics, On the Sublime, On Style*, ed. by W. Hamilton Fyfe and W. Rhys Roberts, Loeb XXIII (Cambridge, MA: Harvard University Press, 1927)

Babrius and Phaedrus, ed. by Ben Edwin Perry, Loeb (Cambridge, MA: Harvard University Press, 1965)

BACON, ROGER, *The 'Opus Majus' of Roger Bacon*, ed. by John Henry Bridges, 2 vols (London: Williams and Norgate, 1900)

BURIDAN, JOHN, *Summulae de dialectica*, trans. by Gyula Klima (New Haven: Yale University Press, 2002)

CICERO, MARCUS TULLIUS, *De Inventione, De Optimo Genere Oratorum, Topica*, ed. by H. M. Hubbell, Loeb II (Cambridge, MA: Harvard University Press, 1949)

——, *De Oratore, Books I, II*, ed. by E. W. Sutton and H. Rackham, Loeb III (Cambridge, MA: Harvard University Press, 1942)

——, *De Oratore: Book III, De Fato, Paradoxa Stoicorum, De Partitione Oratoria*, ed. E. W. Sutton and H. Rackham, Loeb IV (Cambridge, MA: Harvard University Press, 1942)

——, *Brutus, Orator*, ed. by G. L. Hendrickson and H. M. Hubbell, Loeb V (Cambridge, MA: Harvard University Press, 1939)

——, *Pro Quinctio, Pro Roscio Amerino, Pro Roscio Comoedo, On the Agrarian Law*, ed. by J. H. Freese, Loeb VI (Cambridge, MA: Harvard University Press, 1930)

——, *De Senectute, De Amicitia, De Divinatione*, ed. by W. A. Falconer, Loeb XX (Cambridge, MA: Harvard University Press, 1923)

Greek Bucolic Poets, ed. by J. M. Edmonds, Loeb (London: William Heinemann, 1912)

HARVEY, GABRIEL, *Ciceronianus*, ed. by Harold S. Wilson, trans. by Clarence A. Forbes (Lincoln, NE: University of Nebraska Studies, 1945)

——, *Rhetor*, trans. by Mark Reynolds (2001) <http://comp.uark.edu/~mreynold/rhetengn.html>

——, *Marginalia*, ed. by Henry Moore Smith (Stratford-upon-Avon: Shakespeare Head Press, 1913)

——, *The Works of Gabriel Harvey*, ed. by Alexander B. Grosart, 3 vols (Printed for Private Circulation, 1884)

HOMER, *The Iliad: Books I–XII*, ed. by A. T. Murray, Loeb I (London: Heinemann, 1924)

HORACE, *Satires, Epistles, Ars Poetica*, ed. by H. R. Fairclough, Loeb (Cambridge: MA: Harvard University Press, 1926)

JONSON, BEN, *The Complete Poems*, ed. by George Parfitt (Harmondsworth: Penguin, 1984)

Juvenal and Persius, ed. by Susanna Morton Braund, Loeb (Cambridge, MA: Harvard University Press, 2004)

LIVY, *Ab urbe condita: Books I and II*, ed. by B. O. Foster, Loeb I (Cambridge, MA: Harvard University Press, 1919)

Lucian, 8 vols, Loeb (Cambridge, MA: Harvard University Press, 1913–67), III: ed. by A. M. Harmon (1921)

MACILMAINE, ROLAND, *The Logike of the Moste Excellent Philosopher P. Ramus Martyr (1584)*, ed. by Catherine M. Dunn, Renaissance Editions, 3 (San Fernando, Cal.: San Fernando Valley State College, 1969)

MACRAY, WILLIAM DUNN, ed., *The Pilgrimage to Parnassus, with the Two Parts of The Return from Parnassus* (Oxford: Clarendon Press, 1896)

MARLOWE, CHRISTOPHER, *The Complete Plays*, ed. by Mark Thornton Burnett (London: J. M. Dent, 1999)

OVID, *Heroides and Amores*, ed. by Grant Showerman, Loeb (London: William Heinemann, 1914)

PADELFORD, FREDERICK MORGAN, ed. and trans., *Select Translations from Scaliger's Poetics* (New York. Henry Holt, 1905)

PETER OF SPAIN (PETRUS HISPANUS), *Summulae logicales*, ed. by I. M. Bochenski (Turin: Marietti, 1947)

——, *Language in Dispute: An English Translation of [...] Summulae Logicales*, trans. by Francis D. Dinneen (Amsterdam: John Benjamins, 1990)

PLINY THE ELDER, *Natural History: Books XXXIII–XXXV*, ed. by H. Rackham, Loeb IX (Cambridge, MA: Harvard University Press, 1952)

PLINY THE YOUNGER, *Letters and Panegyricus*, ed. by Betty Radice, Loeb II (Cambridge, MA: Harvard University Press, 1969)

PUTTENHAM, GEORGE, *The Art of English Poesy*, ed. by Frank Whigham and Wayne E. Rebholz (Ithaca: Cornell University Press, 2007)

QUINTILIAN, *Institutio Oratoria: Books X–XII*, ed. by H. E. Butler, Loeb IV (London: William Heinemann, 1922)

SCOTT, WILLIAM, *The Model of Poesy*, ed. by Gavin Alexander (Cambridge: Cambridge University Press, 2013)

SHARRATT, PETER, 'Nicolaus Nancelius, *Petri Rami Vita*. Edited with an Introduction', *Humanistica Lovaniensia: Journal of Neo-Latin Studies*, 24 (1975), 161–277

SIDNEY, PHILIP, *Defence of Poesie, Political Discourses, Correspondence, Translations*, ed. by Albert Feuillerat (Cambridge: Cambridge University Press, 1923)

SPENSER, EDMUND, *Selected Shorter Poems*, ed. by Douglas Brooks-Davies (London: Longman, 1995): [Brooks-Davies]

——, *The Shorter Poems*, ed. by Richard A. McCabe (Harmondsworth: Penguin, 1999)

——, *The Yale Edition of the Shorter Poems*, ed. by William Oram and others (New Haven, CT: Yale University Press, 1989)

——, *The Works of Edmund Spenser: A Variorum Edition*, ed. by Edwin Greenlaw and others, 11 vols (Baltimore, MD: The Johns Hopkins University Press, 1932–49), VII: *The Minor Poems, Part One*, ed. by Charles Grosvenor Osgood and Henry Gibbons Lopsteich (1943)

——, *The Works of Edmund Spenser: A Variorum Edition*, X: *The Prose Works*, ed. by Rudolf Gottfried (1949)

TEMPLE, WILLIAM, *William Temple's Analysis of Sir Philip Sidney's 'Apology for Poetry'*, ed. and trans. by John Webster (Binghamton, NY: Center for Medieval and Early Renaissance Studies, 1984)

TERENCE, *The Lady of Andros, The Self-Tormentor, The Eunuch*, ed. by John Sargeaunt, Loeb I (London: William Heinemann, 1918)

VARRO, *Of the Latin Language*, ed. by Roland G. Kent, 2 vols, Loeb I–II (Cambridge, MA: Harvard University Press, 1938)

VIRGIL, *Eclogues, Georgics, The Aeneid (Books I–VI)*, ed. by H. R. Fairclough, Loeb I (Cambridge, MA: Harvard University Press, 1916, revised 1932)

VOS, ALVIN, ed., *Letters of Roger Ascham*, trans. by Maurice Hatch and Alvin Vos (New York: Peter Lang, 1989)

4) Secondary Sources

ADAMS, JOHN C., 'Ramus, Illustrations and the Puritan Movement', *Journal of Medieval and Renaissance Studies*, 17 (1987), 195–210

——, 'Gabriel Harvey's *Ciceronianus* and the Place of Peter Ramus' *Dialecticae libri duo* in the Curriculum', *Renaissance Quarterly*, 43.3 (1990), 551–69

ALEXANDER, GAVIN, *Writing After Sidney: The Literary Response to Sir Philip Sidney, 1586–1640* (Oxford: Oxford University Press, 2006)

ARMSTRONG, E., *A Ciceronian Sunburn: A Tudor Dialogue on Humanistic Rhetoric and Civic Poetics* (Columbia, SC: University of South Carolina Press, 2006)

ASHWORTH, E. JENNIFER, *Language and Logic in the Post-Medieval Period* (Dordrecht: D. Reidel, 1974)

——, 'Developments in the Fifteenth and Sixteenth Centuries', in *Handbook of the History of Logic*, 11 vols, ed. by Dov M. Gabbay and others (Amsterdam: Elsevier, 2004–), II: *Medieval and Renaissance Logic*, ed. by Dov M. Gabbay and John Woods (2008), pp. 609–43

ATTRIDGE, DEREK, *Well-Weighted Syllables: Elizabethan Poetry in Classical Metres* (Cambridge: Cambridge University Press, 1974)

Austin, Warren B., 'Gabriel Harvey's "Lost" Ode on Ramus', *Modern Language Notes*, 61.4 (1946), 242–47

BAKER SMITH, DOMINIC, 'Great Expectation: Sidney's Death and the Poets', in *Sir Philip Sidney: 1586 and the Creation of the Legend*, ed. by Jan Adrianus van Dorsten, Dominic Baker-Smith and Arthur F. Kinney, pp. 83–102

BARKER, WILLIAM, 'Fraunce, Abraham (1559?–1592/3?)', *ODNB* (2010) <http://www.oxforddnb.com/view/article/10133> [accessed 5 Aug. 2013]

BOCHÉNSKI, I. M., *A History of Formal Logic*, trans. by Ivo Thomas (Notre Dame, Ind.: University of Notre Dame Press, 1961)

BORAN, ELIZABETH, 'Temple, Sir William (1554/5–1627)', *ODNB* (2004) <http://www.oxforddnb.com/view/article/27121> [accessed 19 Aug. 2013]

BOS, SANDER, MARIANNE LANGE-MEYERS and JEANINE SIX, 'Sidney's Funeral Portrayed', in *Sir Philip*

Sidney: 1586 and the Creation of a Legend, ed. by Jan Adrianus van Dorsten, Dominic Baker-Smith and Arthur F. Kinney, pp. 38–61

BRENNAN, MICHAEL G., 'The Date of the Death of Abraham Fraunce', *Library*, 6.5 (1983), 391–92

BURROW, COLIN, 'Spenser's Genres', in *The Oxford Handbook of Edmund Spenser*, ed. by Richard McCabe, pp. 403–19

BUXTON, JOHN, 'The Mourning for Sidney', *Renaissance Studies*, 3 (1989), 46–56

CARROLL, D. ALLEN, 'The Meaning of E.K.', *Spenser Studies*, 20 (2005), 169–81

CHENEY, PATRICK, 'Spenser's Pastorals: *The Shepheardes Calender* and *Colin Clouts Come Home Againe*', in *The Cambridge Companion to Spenser*, ed. by Andrew Hadfield, pp. 79–105

COLLINSON, PATRICK, 'Fenner, Dudley (*c.* 1558-1587)', *ODNB* (2008) <http://www.oxforddnb.com/view/article/9287> [accessed 5 Aug. 2013]

COOPER, HENRY and THOMSON COOPER, *Athenae Cantabrigienses*, 2 vols (Cambridge: Deighton, Bell, and Co., 1858-61), II: *1589-1609* (1861)

COSTELLO, WILLIAM T., *The Scholastic Curriculum at Seventeenth-Century Cambridge* (Cambridge, MS: Harvard University Press, 1958)

CRAIG, HARDIN, *The Enchanted Glass: The Elizabethan Mind in Literature* (New York: Oxford University Press, 1936)

CROSS, RICHARD, 'Medieval Theories of Haecceity', *The Stanford Encyclopedia of Philosophy*, ed. by Edward N. Zalta (2014) <http://plato.stanford.edu/archives/sum2014/entries/medieval-haecceity> [accessed 10 Dec. 2014]

CUMMINGS, PHILIP W., 'A Note on the Transmission of the Title of Ramus's Master's Thesis', *Journal of the History of Ideas*, 39.3 (1978), 481

DORSTEN, JAN ADRIANUS VAN, DOMINIC BAKER-SMITH and ARTHUR F. KINNEY, *Sir Philip Sidney: 1586 and the Creation of a Legend* (Leiden: Brill, 1986)

DUHAMEL, PIERRE ALBERT, 'The Logic and Rhetoric of Peter Ramus', *Modern Philology*, 46.3 (1949), 163–71

DUNCAN-JONES, KATHERINE, *Sir Philip Sidney: Courtier Poet* (London: Hamish Hamilton, 1991)

EADE, J. C., 'Constellations', in *The Spenser Encyclopedia*, ed. by A. C. Hamilton, pp. 189–91

ERICKSON, WAYNE, 'Spenser's Patrons and Publishers', in *The Oxford Handbook of Edmund Spenser*, ed. by Richard A. McCabe, pp. 106–24

FALCON, ANDREA, 'Aristotle on Causality', *The Stanford Encyclopedia of Philosophy*, ed. by Edward N. Zalta (2014) <http://plato.stanford.edu/archives/spr2014/entries/aristotle-causality> [accessed 12 Jul. 2014]

FARRINGTON, BENJAMIN, *The Philosophy of Francis Bacon* (Chicago: The University of Chicago Press, 1966)

FEINGOLD, MORDECHAI, JOSEPH S. FREEDMAN and WOLFGANG ROTHER, eds, *The Influence of Petrus Ramus: Studies in Sixteenth and Seventeenth Century Philosophy and Sciences* (Basel: Schwabe, 2001)

——, 'English Ramism: A Reinterpretation', in *The Influence of Petrus Ramus*, ed. by Mordechai Feingold, Joseph S. Freedman and Wolfgang Rother, pp. 127–76

FREEDMAN, JOSEPH S., 'Melanchton's Opinion of Ramus and the Utilization of Their Writings in Central Europe', in *The Influence of Petrus Ramus*, ed. by Mordechai Feingold, Joseph S. Freedman and Wolfgang Rother, pp. 68–91

GILBERT, NEAL W., *Renaissance Concepts of Method* (New York: Columbia University Press, 1960)

GOEGLEIN, TAMARA E., '"Wherein hath Ramus been so offensious?" Poetic Examples in the English Ramist Logic Manuals (1574-1672)', *Rhetorica*, 14 (1996), 73–101

——, 'Reading English Ramist Logic Books as Early Modern Emblem Books: The Case of Abraham Fraunce', *Spenser Studies*, 20 (2005), 225–52

GRAFTON, ANTHONY and LISA JARDINE, *From Humanism to the Humanities: Education and the Liberal Arts in Fifteenth- and Sixteenth-Century Europe* (Cambridge, MS: Harvard University Press, 1986)

GURNEY, EVAN, 'Spenser's "May" Eclogue and Puritan Admonition', *Spenser Studies*, 27 (2012), 193–219

HADFIELD, ANDREW, 'Baxter, Nathaniel (*fl.* 1569-1611)', *ODNB* (2004) <http://www.oxforddnb.com/view/article/1733> [accessed 19 Aug. 2013]

——, *Edmund Spenser: A Life* (Oxford: Oxford University Press, 2012)

——, ed., *The Cambridge Companion to Spenser* (Cambridge: Cambridge University Press, 2001)

HALLAM, GEORGE H., 'Sidney's Supposed Ramism', *Renaissance Papers* (1963), 11–20

HAMILTON, A. C., ed., *The Spenser Encyclopedia*, ed. by Toronto: University of Toronto Press, 1990)

HARTMANN, ANNA-MARIA, 'Abraham Fraunce's Use of Giovanni Andrea dell'Anguillara's *Metamorfosi*', *Translation and Literature*, 22 (2013), 103–10

HOTSON, WILLIAM, *Commonplace Learning: Ramism and its German Ramifications, 1543–1630* (Oxford: Oxford University Press, 2007)

HOWELL, WILBUR SAMUEL, *Logic and Rhetoric in England: 1500–1700* (New York: Russell & Russell, 1961)

HUME, ANTHEA, *Edmund Spenser: Protestant Poet* (Cambridge: Cambridge University Press, 1984)

JARDINE, LISA, *Francis Bacon: Discovery and the Art of Discourse* (Cambridge: Cambridge University Press, 1974)

——, 'The Place of Dialectic Teaching in Sixteenth-Century Cambridge', *Studies in the Renaissance*, 21 (1974), 31–62

JOSEPH, SISTER MIRIAM, *Shakespeare's Use of the Arts of Language* (New York: Columbia University Press, 1947)

KEARNEY, HUGH F., *Scholars and Gentlemen: Universities and Society in Pre-Industrial Britain* (London: Faber & Faber, 1970)

KEARNEY, JAMES, 'Reformed Ventriloquism: *The Shepheardes Calender* and the Craft of Commentary', *Spenser Studies*, 26 (2011), 111–51

KING, JOHN N., *Spenser's Poetry and the Reformation Tradition* (Princeton: Princeton University Press, 1990)

——, 'Spenser's Religion', in *The Cambridge Companion to Spenser*, ed. by Andrew Hadfield, pp. 200–16

KNAPP, JEFFREY, 'Spenser the Priest', *Representations*, 81.1 (2003), 61–78

KNIGHT, SARAH M., 'Flat Dichotomists and Learned Men: Ramism in Elizabethan Drama and Satire', in *Ramus, Pedagogy and the Liberal Arts*, ed. by Steven J. Reid and Emma Annette Wilson, pp. 47–67

KOLLER, KATHRINE, 'Fraunce and Edmund Spenser', *English Literary History*, 7.2 (1940), 108–20

KUIN, ROGER, *Chamber Music: Elizabethan Sonnet Sequences and the Pleasures of Criticism* (Toronto: University of Toronto Press, 1988)

MACK, PETER, *Renaissance Argument: Valla and Agricola in the Traditions of Rhetoric and Dialectic* (Leiden: Brill, 1993)

——, 'Spenser and Rhetoric', in *The Oxford Handbook of Edmund Spenser*, ed. by Richard A. McCabe, pp. 420–36

——, *Elizabethan Rhetoric: Theory and Practice* (Cambridge: Cambridge University Press, 2002)

——, 'Ramus and Ramism: Rhetoric and Dialectic', in *Ramus, Pedagogy and the Liberal Arts*, ed. by Steven J. Reid, and Emma Annette Wilson, pp. 7–23

——, 'Agricola and the Early Versions of Ramus's Dialectic', in *Autour de Ramus*, ed. by Kees Meerfoff and Jean Claude Moissan, pp. 17–35

——, 'Ramus Reading: The Commentaries on Cicero's *Consular Orations* and Virgil's *Eclogues* and *Georgics*', *Journal of the Warburg and Courtland Institutes*, 61 (1998), 111–41

MALONE, EDMOND, *The Plays and Poems of William Shakespeare Comprehending a Life of the Poet and an Enlarged History of the Stage*, 10 vols (London, 1821), II: pp. 239–45

MARENGO VAGLIO, CARLA, 'Words for the English Nation: Toquarto Tasso in Abraham Fraunce's *The Arcadian Rhetorike* (1588)', *Revue de Littérature Comparée*, 62.4 (1988), 529–32

MAY, STEVEN W., 'Marlowe, Spenser, Sidney and — Abraham Fraunce?', *The Review of English Studies, New Series*, 62 (2010), 30–63

McCABE, RICHARD A., ed., *The Oxford Handbook of Edmund Spenser* (Oxford: Oxford University Press, 2010)

McCONICA, JAMES, 'Humanism and Aristotle in Tudor Oxford', *The English Historical Review*, 94 (1979), 291–317

McEACHERN, 'Spenser and Religion', in *The Oxford Handbook of Edmund Spenser*, ed. by Richard A. McCabe, pp. 30–47

MEERHOFF, KEES and JEAN CLAUDE MOISSAN, eds, *Autour de Ramus: Texte, théorie, commentaire* (Cap-Saint-Ignace, Quebec: Nuit Blanche, 1997)

——, '"Beauty and the Beast": Nature, Logic and Literature in Ramus', in *The Influence of Petrus Ramus*, ed. by Mordehaci Feingold, Joseph S. Freedman and Wolfgand Rother, pp. 200–14

NELSON, NORMAN E., 'Peter Ramus and the Confusion of Logic, Rhetoric and Poetry', *The University of Michigan Contributions in Modern Philology*, 2 (1947), 1–22

OLDRINI, GUIDO, 'The influence of Ramus' Method on Historiography and Jurisprudence', in *The Influence of Petrus Ramus*, ed. by Mordechai Feingold, Joseph S. Freedman and Wolfgang Rother, pp. 215–27

ONG, WALTER J., 'Johannes Piscator: One Man or a Ramist Dichotomy?', *Harvard Library Bulletin*, 8 (1954), 151–62

——, *Ramus, Method, and the Decay of Dialogue: From the Art of Discourse to the Art of Reason*, 2nd edn, intro. by Adrian Johns (Chicago: The University of Chicago Press, 2004, 1st edn 1958)

——, *Ramus and Talon Inventory: A Short-Title Inventory of the Published Works of Peter Ramus (1515–1572) and of Omer Talon (ca. 1510–1562) in Their Original and in Their Variously Altered Forms* (Cambridge, MS: Harvard University Press, 1958)

PETRINA, ALESSANDRA, 'Polyglottia and the Vindication of English Poetry: Abraham Fraunce's Arcadian Rhetorike', *Neophilologus*, 83 (1999), 317–29

PHILLIPPY, PATRICIA BERRAHOU, *Love's Remedies: Recantation and Renaissance Lyric Poetry* (Cranbury, NJ: Associated University Presses, 1995)

PINEDA, VICTORIA, 'Ramismo y retórica comparada (con unas notas sobre Boscán y Garcilaso en la *Arcadia Retórica*', *Anuario de Estudios Filológicos*, 20 (1997), 313–29

POMEROY, RALPH S., 'The Ramist as Fallacy-Hunter: Abraham Fraunce and *The Lawiers Logike*', *Renaissance Quarterly*, 40.2 (1987), 224–46

REID, STEVEN J. and EMMA ANNETE WILSON, eds, *Ramus, Pedagogy and the Liberal Arts: Ramism in Britain and the Wider World* (Farnham: Ashgate, 2013)

RYAN, LAURENCE V., *Roger Ascham* (Stanford: Stanford University Press, 1963)

SARGENT, RALPH M., *At the Court of Queen Elizabeth: The Life and Poems of Sir Edward Dyer* (Oxford: Oxford University Press, 1935)

SCHLEINER, LOUISE C., 'Spenser's "E.K." as Edmund Kent (Kenned/of Kent): Kyth (Couth), Kissed, and Kunning-Conning', *English Literary Renaissance*, 20 (1990), 374–407

SCHUCKBURG, EVELYN SHIRLEY, *Laurence Chaderton, First Master Of Emmanuel; Richard Farmer, Master Of Emmanuel, An Essay (1884)* (Cambridge: Macmillan and Bowes, 1884)

SCOTT WILSON-OKANAMURA, DAVID, *Spenser's International Style* (Cambridge: Cambridge University Press, 2013)

SGARBI, MARCO, *The Aristotelian Tradition and the Rise of British Empiricism: Logic and Epistemology in the British Isles, 1570–1689* (Dordrecht: Springer, 2013)

SKALNIK, JAMES VEAZIE, *Ramus and Reform: University and Church at the End of the Renaissance* (Kirksville, MT: Truman State University Press, 2002)

SKRETKOWICZ, VICTOR, 'Abraham Fraunce and Abraham Darcie', *Library*, 5.31 (1976), 239–42

SMITH, A. J., 'An Examination of Some Claims for Ramism', *The Review of English Studies, New Series*, 28 (1956), 348–59

SUBBIONDO, JOSEPH S., 'Ralph Lever's *Witctaft*: 16th-Century Rhetoric and 17th-Century Philosophical Language', in *Historical Linguistics 1993: Papers from the Sixth International Conference on the History of the Language Sciences*, ed. by Kurt R. Jankowsky (Amsterdam: John Benjamins, 1993), pp. 179–86

SUMNER, G. V., 'Cicero, Pompeius and Rullus', *Transactions and Proceedings of the American Philological Association*, 97 (1966), 569–82

SUTTON, ANNE F., 'Two Dozen and More Silkwomen of Fifteenth-Century London', *The Ricardian*, 16 (2006), 1–8

THORNE, J. P., 'A Ramistical Commentary on Sidney's *An Apologie for Poetrie*', *Modern Philology*, 54.3 (1957), 158–64

TUVE, ROSEMOND, *Elizabethan and Metaphysical Imagery: Renaissance Poetic and Twentieth-Century Critics* (Chicago: The University of Chicago Press, 1947)

WADDINGTON, CHARLES, *Ramus: sa vie, ses écrits et ses opinions* (Paris: Ch. Meyrueys, 1855)

WALTON, CRAIG, 'Ramus and Bacon on Method', *Journal of the History of Philosophy*, 9.3 (1971), 289–302

WATSON, GEORGE, 'Ramus, Miss Tuve, and the New Petromachia', *Modern Philology*, 55.4 (1958), 259–62

WIGGINS, MARTIN and CATHERINE RICHARDSON, *British Drama 1533–1642: A Catalogue*, 10 vols (Oxford: Oxford University Press, 2011–), II: *1567–1589* (2012)

WILSON, EMMA ANNETTE, 'Method in Marlowe's *Massacre at Paris*', *Renaissance Papers 2011*, ed. by Andrew Shifflett and Edward Gieskes (Rochester, NY: Camden House, 2012), pp 41–52

WOUDHUYSEN, H. R., 'Leicester, Robert Dudley, Earl of', in *The Spenser Encyclopedia*, ed. by A. C. Hamilton, p. 432

ZUNINO GARRIDO, MARÍA DE LA CINTA, 'Boscán and Garcilaso as Rhetorical Models in the English Renaissance: The Case of Abraham Fraunce's *The Arcadian Rhetorike*', *Atlantis*, 27.2 (2005), 119–34

5) Dictionaries

Greek-English Lexicon, comp. by Henry George Liddell and Robert Scott (New York: Harper & Brothers, 1883, 7th edn)

Oxford Dictionary of National Biography, ed. by David Cannadine (2004, online edn) <http://global.oup.com/oxforddnb/info/>, [*ODNB*]

Oxford English Dictionary (2013, 3rd online edn) <http://www.oed.com>, [*OED*]

Oxford Latin Dictionary (Oxford: Clarendon Press, 1968)

TILLEY, MORRIS PALMER, *A Dictionary of Proverbs in England in the Sixteenth and Seventeenth Centuries* (Ann Arbor: University of Michigan Press, 1950): [Tilley]

INDEX

MHRA Critical Texts

This series aims to provide affordable critical editions of lesser-known literary texts that are not in print or are difficult to obtain. The texts will be taken from the following languages: English, French, German, Italian, Portuguese, Russian, and Spanish. Titles will be selected by members of the distinguished Editorial Board and edited by leading academics. The aim is to produce scholarly editions rather than teaching texts, but the potential for crossover to undergraduate reading lists is recognized. The books will appeal both to academic libraries and individual scholars.

Malcolm Cook
Chairman, Editorial Board

Editorial Board

Professor Malcolm Cook (French) (Chairman)
Professor Guido Bonsaver (Italian)
Dr Tyler Fisher (Spanish)
Professor David Gillespie (Slavonic)
Professor Justin D. Edwards (English)
Dr Stephen Parkinson (Portuguese)
Professor Ritchie Robertson (Germanic)

www.criticaltexts.mhra.org.uk

Lightning Source UK Ltd.
Milton Keynes UK
UKOW05f0311210516

274698UK00001B/7/P

9 781781 881248